RED HOT AND BLUE

FIFTY YEARS of WRITING about MUSIC, MEMPHIS, and MOTHERFUCKERS

STANLEY BOOTH

CHICAGO
REVIEW
PRESS

An A Cappella Book

Copyright © 2019 by Stanley Booth
All rights reserved
Published by Chicago Review Press Incorporated
814 North Franklin Street
Chicago, Illinois 60610
ISBN 978-1-64160-106-1

Library of Congress Cataloging-in-Publication Data
Names: Booth, Stanley, 1942- author.
Title: Red hot and blue : fifty years of writing about music, Memphis, and
    motherfuckers / Stanley Booth.
Description: Chicago, Illinois : Chicago Review Press, [2019] | Includes
    bibliographical references and index.
Identifiers: LCCN 2019005126 (print) | LCCN 2019005515 (ebook) | ISBN
    9781641601078 (Pdf) | ISBN 9781641601085 (Kindle) | ISBN 9781641601092
    (Epub) | ISBN 9781641601061 (trade paper : alk. paper)
Subjects: LCSH: Popular music—Southern States—History and criticism. |
    Musicians—Southern States.
Classification: LCC ML3477 (ebook) | LCC ML3477 .B65 2019 (print) | DDC
    781.6430975—dc23
LC record available at https://lccn.loc.gov/2019005126

Cover design: Preston Pisellini
Cover photo: Calvin Newborn at the Flamingo Club of Beale Street,
    photo by George Hardin
Author photo: Self-portrait by Stanley Booth
Interior design: Nord Compo

Printed in the United States of America
5 4 3 2 1

For Dewey

CONTENTS

BLUES DUES

"Underpaid and overprivileged," is how one reporter described his liveli-
hood. That's how it's been with me. While barely surviving, I've hung
out with the most amazing characters. A few years ago, I received in the
mail, with increasing urgency, a series of postings that consisted of at
least two galley proofs and three letters from a New York literary agent
whose client (a regular, probably salaried, contributor to one of the oldest
American periodicals, one named after an ocean) had written a history of
the blues. My collection of blues- and jazz-related pieces, *Rythm Oil*, had
appeared about four years earlier and, according to the agent, her client
liked it a bunch. He wanted my endorsement, desperately, it seemed.

So, finally, I picked up one of the proofs to look it over. I hadn't
read far before I came upon these words: "The weekend I was in Memphis . . ." Unlike many before him, who'd simply bought a lot of blues
records, listened to them, and written a book, this writer had made the
extra effort of going to the blues museum in Clarksdale, Mississippi,
passing through Memphis on his way there, thus becoming an authority.
I, who lived in Memphis twenty-five years, going in the course of my
research to the city and county jails as a guest more times than I cared
to remember, found it hard to restrain myself from hurling the galley
all the way back to New York.

They have in Memphis an expression, "blues pukes" (BP). The blues
book author (call him BP1) was just one of many who've crossed my
path. They come from everywhere, though California, the American

1

Northeast, Europe, and Japan seem to have more than their share. All BPs seem to suffer from the same delusion. They think they can vicariously absorb some essence that will permit them to interpret the mysteries of the blues. The shallowest BP thinks that he is somehow, by divine right, an arbiter of the authentic. Never happen. But still people persist in such delusions.

Of course, being jealous of the blues is like being jealous of heartburn. The truth is, knowing nothing about the blues is preferable to knowing anything about the blues. Here, however, we run into semantics. There's the blues, an emotional state, and there's the blues, an art form, or a group of art forms. Believe me, when you're in the Memphis jail, city or county, you got the blues. When you're in your cozy room, listening to Robert Johnson's plaintive tunes, you're hearing the blues. Two different worlds. But some people, people from Berkeley, or Boston, or wherever, are so highly imaginative that they make a leap of funk and become Spokesmen of the Blues. No, really, they make a living this way. People in Dublin, London, Kyoto, Amsterdam, and Lower Slobbovia read them and feel somehow enhanced, enlightened, end manned by the blues.

I never intended to have anything to do with the blues. They came into my life through my bedroom window when I was a child. It wasn't a matter of choice. What I learned, I paid for in experience at the school where they arrest you first and tell you why later.

———————

Here's an attempt to communicate with the genus BP, species television producer (BP2, let's say). It combines a modest amount of truth with an admixture of insincerity, self-promotional hyperbole (I never really knew Annie Mae McDowell all that well), and justifiable distrust.

September 6, 1996

Dear BP2,

Thanks for calling. I enjoyed our chat, and I appreciate your asking for my thoughts on a video series based on the blues. As you can imagine, this idea has come up a number of times in the past. The problem to a man in my position, which is nearly unique (others, among them men like Sam Charters and Paul Oliver and such esteemed friends of mine as Peter Guralnick and Greil Marcus, have written about the blues, but they, superb fellows and decent writers though they surely are, have all seen the blues in at best a secondhand fashion, at a certain remove), is to talk about my knowledge and experience without giving away all I have: my decades-long personal observation of the human reality, the tragic pain and transcendent joy, of the blues and all that word connotes in human life and passion.

Unlike any other writer about the blues, I grew up in a turpentine camp on the edge of the Okefinokee Swamp. A little later, I (and I alone among writers) kept Furry Lewis company as he swept the streets of Memphis. I (alone again) watched Otis Redding write and record "Dock of the Bay" and other soul classics. Dewey Phillips, the first man to play an Elvis Presley record on the radio, took me, no other writer, to Graceland and Elvis's ranch. As a veteran of many Southern campaigns, I have seen fiery crosses and whole black neighborhoods burning. I stood behind Keith Richards and watched Meredith Hunter stabbed to death at Altamont. I am the only living person, writer, or what you will who has been friends with Brian Jones, Sam Phillips, Dewey Phillips, Bukka White, Gram Parsons, Alexis Korner, Ian Stewart, Huey Meaux, Sam the Sham, Alex Chilton, Anita Pallenberg, Keith Richards, Johnny and Eva Woods, Fred and Annie Mae McDowell, Shelby Foote the Civil War historian and his daughter Maggie the stripper, Jerry Wexler, Ahmet Ertegun, James Carr, Al Green, Rufus Thomas's whole family, Steve Cropper, Jimi Hendrix, Mike Bloomfield, Phineas and Calvin and Mama Rose Newborn, Chris and Rich Robinson of the Black Crowes, Mississippi John Hurt, B. B. and Albert King. And Charlie Rich and Charlie Freeman and Waylon Jennings. And Little Richard and Duane Allman and Tinsley Ellis. And on and on. Jim Keltner and Charlie Watts. And Joe Venuti and Slim Gaillard and Lash LaRue. This might argue nothing more than an unseemly gregariousness, but you have read my book *Rythm Oil*, which gives rather more than an inkling of the stories I know and the way I tell them, that is, in effective dramatic scenes.

There are many great, thrilling, exciting stories arising from the blues. Any time someone can manage to pay me to tell one or a few, I am pleased. They all have something to do with slavery and freedom and betrayal and hatred and love and loss and death. "Some people say the worried blues ain't tough," Furry used to sing. "I declare if they don't kill you, they'll handle you mighty rough." The stories are many, waiting to be told. But if I tell them in letters, not only will the letters be perhaps rather long, then everybody will know my stories, and I will have to go to work for a living, a fate I am determined to avoid, cost what it may.

Yours bluely,

The letter worked, in the sense that the people who read it decided to pay me for a "treatment," an outline of a blues TV series, an enormous hype:

The Blues, featuring the incomparable bluesman B. B. King as host of eight one-hour programs, celebrates as television never has the present flourishing and the fascinating history of this essential musical form. Incorporating classic archival material as well as exclusive original performances and interviews, *The Blues* follows the music from its beginnings in slavery and oppression to its contemporary global prominence.

I gave them—two Europeans with a production company—pages and pages of such drivel, a description of a TV series that didn't exist. Luckily, I got half the money up front. That was in the fall. By the end of the following Lent, having delivered all material owed them according to our contract, I was still waiting for the second half.

Fax Transmission April 11, 1997

BP2—

If you'd had a check sent to me by Federal Express as you said you were going to do, I'd have it now. Your failure to do what you say

you will is deeply disturbing and extremely inconveniencing. I assure
you that I have been treated with greater rudeness and insensitivity,
but this amount of rudeness and insensitivity will suffice—'tis not
so deep as a well, nor so wide as a church door, but 'tis enough,
'twill serve.

The last line comes, as you know, from *Hamlet*. Ham, as I call him,
is describing the wound that will soon usher him off this mortal coil. I
don't think BP2 recognized the line's provenance. He sent me a return
fax accusing me of attacking him with "bile" and saying he couldn't pay
me without his partner's approval. BP2 had come to my house, stayed
as a guest by right of imposition, and now was telling me that he wasn't
in charge, at least when it came to disbursing funds.

My reply:

Well, of co'se, Massa, I's mighty grateful you notice me at all,
Cap'm—'scuse de hat. Please don't whup po' ole me, I don't mean
no ha'm—I been wo'kin' out here in you Europeans' fields so long,
under dis broilin' sun, dat my brains get a lil fried, you know, and I
start to think I's yo' equal. Crazy ole man, please forgive me, Massa.

On the other hand, where she wore a glove, to hide that unsightly
wart: Bile? Bill Shakespeare is bile? Deeply disturbing and greatly inconveniencing is bile? Well, let me put it this way. It's going to be deeply
disturbing and greatly inconveniencing to the Glynn County High Sheriff if he has to come out here and repossess the car for the bank. It's going
to be d.d. and g.i. to the people at Georgia Power when they have to
send somebody out here to cut off my lights. Ditto the phone company.
It's going to be d.d. and g.i. to Father Germain when I can't make it
to serve as lector at mass because I no longer have a car. A number of
other people will find it d.d. and g.i. also, and only because you haven't
done what you said you'd do weeks ago and pay me. You come to me
and buy my small portion of the wisdom of the ages for pennies—you'd
have bought it for a thousand bucks if you'd been a bit smoother—and
are indignant when I simply ask that you do what you've said repeatedly
that you would do? Who and what do you think you are?

One of the best things I ever overheard was a man seated at a table near mine in a Mexican restaurant in Mt Dora, Florida, saying, "She never would've testified against me if she hadn't been caressed into it."

"Coerced," said the bottle-redhead eating with him.

"Whatever."

So you have to caress [your partner], whom everyone to my delight keeps calling Boze, perfect name for a field boss, into paying me? Wow, you such a standup guy. Me mighty grateful. I really hadn't the slightest concept how dignified and righteous you could be when asked to part with money in an expedient fashion. 'SCUUUUUUUUUUUUUUUUSSSE lil ole me. But you know what? The first time it was the agent's fault. This time it's my fault. Next time it'll be B. B.'s fault. You want me to introduce you to Sam Phillips? And Fred Ford? Are you sure? Search your heart, lil red rooster. You ain't in a barnyard full of rockoids now.

I was discussing this sort of behavior with [another producer] a few days ago, and he said something I found interesting, about how dismissive it is, how it involves denial, the fundamental denial of the value of a unique vision in the first place.

> I wash my teef wif di'mon' dus'
> I don' care if de bank go bus'
> Done got to de place
> Where my money don' never run out

I see now that to disport myself among such international gents as you & [Boze] I should have attained such status. The people who robbed Furry would have made little profit with your attitude. You can pay me quick and rob me and my friends much better. See, Furry never met anybody who was responsible for his economic status, either.

But Furry, God bless him, had the courtesy to die. If I were dead, you could talk to BP1, who spent in his life one weekend in Memphis, and be much more certain of your goal and so on.

Months later, they paid me. Naturally, the series didn't get made. Why am I telling you all this? Because this is part of the blues. No bluesman was born rich and I've never known one who died rich. Insofar as I've learned about the blues, I've suffered from the basic blues conditions. I used to wonder why Furry sang so much about poverty, loneliness, and death. I don't wonder anymore.

––––––––––––

Nobody told me it would be like this, all those years ago when I started out with the blues. The first book about the blues I ever read, or heard of, was Sam Charters's *The Country Blues*. Published in 1959, the year I came to Memphis, Charters's book introduced me to Furry Lewis, Gus Cannon, Bukka White, and Sleepy John Estes, each of whom turned out to be a character in my life.

In those days, there were no blues records. A few existed, of course, but there were, as they say, none to speak of. The odd rhythm and blues hit—"Good Golly, Miss Molly," "Corrine, Corrina," "Good Rockin' Tonight"—had been cast in twelve-bar blues form, but that was incidental. Today, there are a zillion blues recordings to choose from. Then, to give an example, Columbia had the four-LP Bessie Smith set. That was it until the appearance of a series of long-playing vinyl records marketed as "Adventures in Sound." Included in the series were two Italian albums recorded in Sicily (by San Domenico Barbers of Taormina) and Naples, respectively; three French albums—one, called *Delirium in Hi-Fi*, "Recorded Somewhere in France," by Elsa Popping and her Pixieland Band—two in Spanish, and one instrumental album of folk songs from the Russian steppes. Another single album, consisting of music approximately as esoteric as folk songs from the Russian steppes, was recorded in Denmark on acoustic guitar by the bluesman Bill Broonzy. Though the bulk of Broonzy's work had featured his electric guitar and other amplified instruments, at this time European intellectuals hadn't accepted instrumental electricity—in order to be "authentic," Broonzy had to assume a primitivism he didn't possess. He still cut a great album, with classic versions of "Troubled in Mind," "See See Rider," and "Ananias."

I'd heard of an album on I think United Artists called *Blues in the Night*, featuring Broonzy, Memphis Slim, and the original Sonny Boy Williamson. Jim Dickinson and Johnny Cash had it, I later learned, but I never saw it until it came out on CD. Real blues was rare, precious. Then the first great rhythm and blues albums appeared: Fats Domino on Imperial; Jimmy Reed on VeeJay; Ray Charles, Joe Turner, and Champion Jack Dupree on Atlantic; Muddy Waters, Howlin' Wolf, Bo Diddley, and Chuck Berry on Chess and Checker. I obtained *Leadbelly's Last Sessions* on Folkways from the Readers' Subscription Book Club and memorized every one of its four sides. "We in the same boat, brother, we in the same boat, brother—and if you shake one end you gonna rock the other—in the same boat, brother. Well, it taken some time for the people to learn, what's bad for the bow ain't good for the stern—"

Genius. The message rang loud and clear in those days of civil rights struggle. In 1959, I came to Memphis and, though it took me a few years to find what I was looking for, by the mid-sixties was sitting at the foot of Furry Lewis's bed, happy as a dead pig in the sunshine.

Furry and other friends gave me more stories than I have breath to tell. After Furry's death, I returned to my Georgia roots without leaving the blues. The blues is, for better or worse, where I stay. In recent years I've written about a number of different aspects of the blues, and many of those essays, along with some vintage pieces, censored by previous editors, are contained herein.

"CHIMES BLUES,"
BY JOE "KING" OLIVER

For a few years Bill Forman, one of the finest editors I've ever known—let's see, that makes, what, three good ones?—worked at *Grammy* magazine. Through him I got cool assignments like the following, which is a minor definition of the blues, though it's ostensibly about a jazz giant.

Fred Ford asked me, late in his life, "Why didn't Louis Armstrong send Joe Oliver some money?" He was asking a larger question, one I couldn't, and still can't, answer. Dana Fradon said, "If God hadn't intended there to be poor people, he'd have made rich people more generous."

Joseph "King" Oliver, the New Orleans cornetist who led the Creole Jazz Band, which made what have been called "the first genuine masterpieces in jazz recording," among them "Chimes Blues," lies in an unmarked grave in New York City's Woodlawn Cemetery. Born May 11, 1885, Oliver, while also working as a butler, was perhaps the leading Crescent City cornetist of the period between Buddy Bolden and Louis Armstrong. Armstrong's idol, Oliver had played with the Henry Allen, Sr., Brass Band, the Magnolia, Olympia, Melrose, and Eagle Bands, and the Original Superior Orchestra.

"He was a riot in those days," a contemporary of Oliver's observed, "his band from 1915 or '16 to 1918 being the best in New Orleans."

"The great King Joe Oliver," Armstrong called him, "(my my whatta man) . . . How he used to blow that cornet of his down in Storyville for Pete Lala . . . I was just a youngster who loved that horn of King

9

Oliver's . . . I would delight delivering an order of stone coal to the prostitute who used to hustle in her crib right next to Pete Lala's cabaret . . . Just so's I could hear King Oliver play . . . Oh that music sounded so good . . ."

In 1918, the year after New Orleans's famous red-light district closed, Oliver joined the exodus of blacks from the South to Chicago, where he was featured simultaneously in Bill Johnson's Original Creole Orchestra at the Royal Garden Cafe and Lawrence Dewey's New Orleans Jazz Band at the Dreamland Cafe. After two years, the Dreamland offered Oliver the chance to form his own group to play there exclusively.

Oliver took his role as leader seriously: "This is a matter of business," he once wrote, "I mean I wants you to be a band man, and a band man only, and do all you can for the welfair of the band in the line of playing your best at all times." Oliver and his seven-piece Creole Jazz Band toured California in 1921, returning to Chicago the next year, when Oliver, perhaps thinking that two hot cornets would afford the band absolute supremacy, sent to New Orleans for Louis Armstrong, who had replaced him in Kid Ory's Brownskin Band.

Oliver was a master of special cornet effects, apparently the first, using pop bottles, water glasses, cups, buckets, and other devices to make his horn bark like a dog, crow like a chicken, or cry like a baby. Armstrong was by 1922 simply a master. Oliver's band recorded for the Paramount label in Chicago in March of 1923, but their first released records, the first real jazz recordings by an authentic black jazz group, were made on April 5 and 6 at the Gennett Studios in Richmond, Indiana. Legend has it that because Armstrong was so much louder than the other musicians, he had to stand far behind them as they played into the acoustic recorder's horn.

"Chimes Blues," the fifth tune recorded that first day, is honored principally because it contains Louis Armstrong's first recorded solo, but even without Armstrong, it would be worth remembering, as are the other personnel: Oliver's old boss, Bill Johnson, on inaudible string bass; Honoré Dutrey on tailgate trombone; one of the earliest great N.O. brother teams, Johnny and Baby Dodds, virtuosi on clarinet and percussion, respectively; and Miss Lillian Hardin, the Memphis belle, on Thelonious Monk–like piano. Lil's chiming chords place the listener of

1923 or 2023 in a new world of strange intervals, a world of musical novelty where master musicians have serious fun, where Baby Dodds makes his woodblocks talk, where Johnny is eloquent, Lil magisterial. Louis's solo, which closely follows as written the piece's four twelve-bar strains, is rendered with strength, clarity, rhythmic sureness, and perfect control. And bringing it all together is the old master, the King, Joe Oliver. If he had never played a note, but simply had written such compositions as "Chimes Blues," "Snake Rag," "Snag It," "Sugar Foot Stomp," "Doctor Jazz," and "West End Blues," he would be a jazz immortal.

Keeping it together was another story. By February of the next year, Louis and Lil were married, and in June Louis left the Creole Jazz Band to play with the Chicago singer Ollie Powers. "He'll find out, he'll have to come back," Oliver said, but it never happened. While Armstrong became an international superstar, Oliver had other bands, with such great musicians as Henry Allen Jr. and Lester Young, but bad luck dogged his steps: a nightclub where he would have had steady work burned down; he made a serious error in judgment by turning down a residency at New York's Cotton Club (Duke Ellington took it, and never looked back); reduced to working in and around Huntington, West Virginia, he was stymied by having his band bus's motor freeze and burst. He got it fixed only to have the bus wrecked in an accident a month later.

By this time, it was 1935. He started having trouble with his teeth, and before he could afford to visit a dentist, he contracted pyorrhea and lost them all, death to a brass player. By the end of 1937, he was in Savannah, Georgia, with no teeth, no bus, no band. "I got teeth waiting for me at the dentist now," he wrote to his sister, who lived in New York City. "I've started a little dime bank saving. Got $1.60 in it and won't touch it. I am going to try and save myself a ticket to New York. The Lord is sure good to me here without an overcoat."

Unable to play, Oliver sold fruit on the street and worked as a janitor in a billiard parlor. "I open the pool rooms at 9 A.M. and close at 12 midnite," he wrote in another letter to his sister. "If the money was only ¼ as much as the hours I'd be all set. But at that I can thank God for what I am getting. Which I do night after night. . . .

"I've got high blood pressure and I am unable to take treatments because it cost $3.00 to take treatments and I don't make enough money to continue my treatments. I can not asking you for any money or anything. Should anything happen to me will you want my body?"

Oliver died two months later, on April 10, 1938. His sister used her rent money to bring his body north and gave up her plot in Woodlawn for him. But there is still no headstone on the grave of one of the true founding fathers of jazz.

MA RAINEY: THE MOTHER OF THE BLUES

Not too long ago I started writing a series of essays on Georgia's musical artists for the Georgia Music Hall of Fame. They appeared in the Allman Brothers' Macon-based house organ, *Hittin' the Note*. It paid some bills, and I'm grateful to my friend Lisa Love, director of programs and publicity at the hall of fame, for the gig. In a consideration of seminal Georgia artists, Ma Rainey's name was bound to come up early. I fell in love with her when, one Sunday afternoon, I chanced to come upon a plaque commemorating her by the Chattahoochee River in Columbus. I knew her by reputation, but after that I came to know her powerful, epochal voice and the unique path of her life.

Toward the end of her career, Ma Rainey met two young Fisk University professors, John Wesley Work and Sterling Brown, when they attended one of her performances. They were interested in the history of the blues and what W. C. Handy called "art, in the high-brown sense." Rainey was interested in what the young men had in their trousers, and I don't mean in their pockets.

She was a poet and a great entertainer, but she was also, in a way few artists can ever be, an authentic expression of her origins. She was a black woman from the working class in Georgia. Her immense influence on the history of music came in a way that seems in retrospect natural and inevitable. In fact, it was neither. Rainey had tremendous courage as a person and as an artist. Her songs contain references to male and female homosexuality, domestic violence, moonshine, floods, jails, hoodoos, serial murder, prostitution, and her own black bottom. With her gold teeth, gaudy jewelry, and primitive stagecraft, she presented an image that could be appreciated by the most unlettered of her fans. But there was a validity about her that even intellectuals could not deny.

Brown, who was a bit put off by her directness when they met, nonetheless composed "Ma Rainey," an ode that testifies to her lasting power as an artist:

> O Ma Rainey,
> Li'l and low,
> Sing us 'bout de hard luck
> Round our do'.
> Sing us 'bout the lonesome road
> We must go . . .
>
> I talked to a fellow, and the fellow say,
> "She jes' catch hold of us, some kinda way."

The woman known to history as the Mother of the Blues was born Gertrude Pridgett, poor and black, on April 26, 1886, in Columbus, Georgia. Her parents came from Alabama, and no one knows what her father, Thomas, did for a living. After his death in 1896, her mother, Ella Allan Pridgett, worked for the Central of Georgia railroad. Doing what, I wonder? What would a middle-aged black woman do for the C. of Ga. at the end of the nineteenth century? Maybe she cleaned railroad cars or waiting rooms, or both. She sure as hell wasn't an officer of the company.

By 1886, Reconstruction was a faded, though still bitter, memory; segregation—white supremacy—was the rule on both sides of the Mason-Dixon Line. We alive today find it hard to envision what society was like so long ago. The only media were writing, drawing, painting, sculpting, photography (incipient), dance, musical instruments, and the voice, and the only places where these, with the exception of photography, could be approached were libraries, museums, and the stage, the last category including everything from churches to bordellos.

The first musical production in the New World, a one-act distillation of the English ballad opera *Flora, or the Hob in the Well*, was presented on February 8, 1735, at Charleston, South Carolina, in a courtroom—draw your own comparisons—without scenery or costumes. On December 30, 1790, an actor named Graupner appeared in blackface at the Old Federal Street theater in Boston, singing a "Negro" song in the play *Oroonoko; or, the Royal Slave*. In 1815 "Pot-Pie" Herbert sang, in blackface, "The Siege of Pittsburgh" at the Albany (New York) Theatre, receiving so many calls for encores that he became too exhausted to continue. In 1843 four white performers played the Chatham Theatre in New York City, billed as the Virginia Minstrels. Soon thereafter other minstrel companies emerged, among them the Kentucky Minstrels and the Original Christy Minstrels.

Minstrel shows celebrating a caricature of plantation life became a staple of American (and English) popular theater. Years before Harriet Beecher Stowe provided the world with the stereotypically noble black man Uncle Tom, the minstrel stage introduced many white audiences to that theatrical staple, the comic darky, lazy, superstitious, hyper-romantic, dishonest, ignorant, overindulgent, um, am I leaving anything out? Anglo-American theater has always depended on racial, ethnic, and social stereotypes: The stingy Jew or Scotsman, the drunken Irishman, the wise butler, the fat-headed politician, the unfaithful wife, the dim-witted cuckold/husband, and so on. Theater works in broad strokes, always has and probably always will, for practical reasons of stagecraft. But there are worlds within worlds, and the minstrel stage presented a broad array of characters. Still, none of them was more than a type.

Ma Rainey, who created a powerful and highly varied type—the hard-drinking, free-loving, trash-talking blues mama, to whom all subsequent blues mamas remain in debt—was the recipient of a popular music tradition whose roots went back to the broadsides, poems on topics of the day, sold for a penny on the streets of England's colony. One was "Yankee Doodle." Collections of sacred and secular songs were also popular; as a boy Abraham Lincoln sang from *The Missouri Songster*, first published in 1808. Hymnbooks such as William Walker's *Southern Harmony and Musical Companion* (which, over a hundred and fifty years after its publication in 1835, would give the Black Crowes an album title), and the *Carmina Sacra* (pub. 1841) of Lowell Mason, composer of "Nearer My God to Thee" and "Blest Be the Tie That Binds," sold hundreds of thousands of copies.

The "darky songs" that formed a substantial part of the minstrel shows were not written by black composers but derived largely from European sources. (A salient exception is Thomas Dartmouth Rice's "Jim Crow." Rice, a white man, is said to have lifted the piece's central rhymed couplet from a black, crippled stable groom in Baltimore or Louisville.) Another white man, George Washington Dixon, claimed authorship of "Zip Coon," published in 1834. Its tune, still familiar today as "Turkey in the Straw," probably comes from an old Irish folk song. (The suggestion has been made that the same "jig" was earlier known as "Natchez under the Hill," summoning up associations of the demimonde antecedents of the Killer, Jerry Lee Lewis, and his cousins Mickey Gilley and Jimmy Swaggart, who all grew up in Ferriday, Louisiana, across the river from that infamous Mississippi port.)

Ohioan Daniel Decatur Emmett's compositions, including "Old Dan Tucker," "Blue Tail Fly," and "Dixie," were the product of his own genius, as were the songs of Stephen Foster of Pennsylvania. Foster, the most popular American songwriter of all time (with the possible exception of Irving Berlin), died at thirty-seven with three pennies and thirty-five cents in scrip in his pockets. No more fortunate was the first significant black composer of popular songs, James Bland, born the son of free black parents in Flushing, New York, in 1854. Bland wrote such durable songs as "Carry Me Back to Old Virginny," "In the Evening by the Moonlight," "Oh Dem Golden Slippers," "Hand Me Down My Walkin' Cane," and "They Gotta Quit Kickin' My Dog Around." When he died of tuberculosis in 1911 he, too, was alone and in poverty.

This period, from just before the (so-called) Civil War to the early years of the twentieth century, saw the establishment of genuine black music as a commercial entity. In 1865 in Macon, Georgia, Charles B. Hicks, a black man who was light enough to, but did not, pass for white, organized the Original Georgia Minstrels, the first all-black minstrel troupe, the first blacks in American show business. An 1872 review from New York City found the O. Ga. Minstrels "eighteen saddle colored darkies . . . brim full of melody." One piece they performed was titled "Happy Colored Children from the South":

Keep your eyes on the children from the south.
We're as merry as the little birds a-singing in the trees.
Our hair's so tight that we cannot shut our mouth,
We're always just as happy as can be.

Repellent as it might seem today, singing such songs beat the hell out of hoeing corn. Soon there were many blacks in show business, in minstrel and other types of shows. In 1871 the Fisk Jubilee Singers, hoping to rescue the five-year-old Nashville university from its financial troubles, launched a concert series in the Northeast. By 1878, after touring the United States and Europe, they had endowed the school with $150,000, the equivalent of as many millions today. The term, or label, Spiritual would replace Jubilee in the record market, but the music had become a permanent part of the modern repertoire and would influence scores of composers, "classical" and otherwise.

Two other musical genres of lasting importance emerged during this era, ragtime and blues. Between the two, a technological revolution occurred as music consumers left sheet music for records.

Invented in 1877, when its creator, Thomas Alva Edison, was thirty, the phonograph began to adumbrate its commercial potential about 1890. The recording medium, a wax cylinder, each one, since no method of duplication existed, a unique *objet*, caught at most two minutes of a dim echo. If Edison (who, W. C. Handy tells us, "did not approve of blues") needed a hundred copies of something by Johannes Brahms (whom he did record in 1889), Brahms had to play it a hundred times. In 1887, a German immigrant, Emile Berliner, applied to patent a reproduceable disc.

By the end of 1901, a process for mass-producing cylinders was developed, but cylinders were still limited to a two-minute playing time, while flat twelve-inch discs lasted up to twice as long. Later Edison developed the four-minute Amberol Record, a sturdier cylinder whose grooves were closer together. It went on sale in 1908, but in mid-1912, the Columbia Phonograph Company announced "The Finish of the Cylinder Record"; henceforward they would produce only discs. Edison continued to manufacture cylinders for a few more years before conceding that they were indeed finished.

Early recorded fare included the marches of John Philip Sousa, popular songs like Charles K. Harris's "After the Ball," and comic stage-ethnic recitations including "Darky Specialties," "German Comedy," "Hebrew Comic," and "Irish Songs and Specialties." These, along with American Indian music, bird calls, arias from operas—early catalogs reveal an amazing, albeit sometimes spurious, variety of sound recordings. Among the vocal offerings (baritone) in Victor's initial catalog of 1902 were Italian arias by Signor Carlos Francisco, English songs by Herbert Goddard, and French arias by someone named M. Fernand. The catalog did not include the information that all three of these names were pseudonyms of a young man from Brooklyn named Emilio de Gogorza.

William Krell's "Mississippi Rag" became the first copyrighted piano rag in January 1897. St. Louis brothel owner Tom Turpin's "Harlem Rag," the first published (as sheet music) piano rag, appeared that December. In the next year, Scott Joplin, composer of "The Entertainer," "Nonpareil," and "Euphonic Sounds," began publishing his rag masterpieces. His "Maple Leaf Rag" (1899), the first big ragtime hit, sold over seventy-five thousand copies in sheet music its first year.

That was also the year of Ernest Hemingway's birth. Maybe there's no connection, but Hemingway's was the first generation I know of to be given an appellation; they were the Lost Generation. For Americans as well as Europeans the First World War, 1914—1918, brought new attitudes and approaches to life. The machine age, threatened by Edison, had arrived.

For one thing, though enormously influential (affecting even Sousa's marches), those ragtime pieces were hard, way beyond the abilities of the young ladies who'd rendered on the parlor pianoforte such simple tunes as Carrie Jacobs-Bond's "I Love You Truly" and "A Perfect Day." But anyone could play ragtime on the phonograph. Record players would even play jazz, after the Original Dixieland Jazz Band traveled from New Orleans to New York (via Chicago) for the first jazz recording sessions in 1917.

The popular success of the phonograph paralleled the reemergence of Manifest Destiny and American involvement in such areas as the Caribbean, Panama, the Philippines, and Hawaii. Spanish and Portuguese sailors had introduced the guitar to the Hawaiians, who laid it down flat and, retaining the Spanish manner of tuning the instrument to an open chord, played barre chords with a piece of bone, bottleneck, or metal tubing. Many American country musicians, black and white, played in similar ways. For the first two decades of the twentieth century, Hawaiian music was the US rage. Ragtime had started as a primarily guitar-based music; the stage was set for the blues.

Among the few facts we possess about Ma Rainey's early life are that she was a member of Columbus's First African Baptist Church and gave her first stage performance at the (still-extant) Springer Opera House. She was fourteen, appearing in a revue featuring local talent called the "Bunch of Blackberries." She soon found steady work in traveling tent shows. At one of these, in a small Missouri town, she heard a local girl sing "about the 'man' who had left her," a song "strange and poignant." According to what Fisk University professor John Wesley Work says she told him in the late thirties, Gertrude (she was not yet, at the time of which she was speaking, Ma Rainey) "became so interested that she learned the song from the visitor, and used it soon afterwards in her 'act' as an encore." This happened, Rainey told Work, in 1902. She also told him that, often asked what kind of song it was, "one day she replied, in a moment of inspiration, 'Why, it's the *Blues*.'"

That ain't likely—the term *blues*, short for "blue devils" (boredom and, later, depression), has been around since the late eighteenth century—but it's credible that she heard some form of blues in 1902. W. C. Handy spoke of hearing protoblues in St. Louis in 1892 and in Mississippi in 1903, when in his words "life suddenly took me by the shoulder and wakened me with a start."

On February 2, 1904, when Gertrude was eighteen, she married a comedian, singer, and dancer named William Rainey, whose stage name was "Pa." Together they worked with such minstrel units as the Rabbit Foot, Silas Green, C. W. Parks, and Al Gaines, as well as Tolliver's Circus, sometimes billed as "Rainey and Rainey—Assassinators of the Blues."

While other black women from Birmingham worked at washing, ironing, cooking, mopping, or doing field work, Gertrude Rainey, who was a bit taller but no wider than an oak barrel, sang, danced, and cracked jokes onstage. Like the woman in the Willie McTell song, she had "a mouth chock full of good gold" and was famous for wearing necklaces of twenty and fifty dollar gold pieces. She had large, expressive eyes and an endearing, if metallic, smile, but she was no beauty. "Yes, she was ugly," Clyde Bernhardt, a trombonist and contemporary of Rainey's, said. "But I'll tell you one thing about it: she had such a lovely disposition, you know, and personality, you forget all about it. She commence to lookin' good to you."

Bernhardt saw Ma Rainey and Her Georgia Smart Set at the little ALCOA company town—five thousand employees—of Badin, North Carolina, in 1917. Her troupe then traveled by private train car (maybe one like her mother had cleaned—in any case, the car was made necessary because of segregation laws) and played under a large tent to audiences split down the middle, whites seated on the right. The female members of the chorus were darker than usual in such groups, it's said because Rainey was dark herself and didn't want lighter-colored females in the act. For two hours, accompanied by piano, violin, guitar, bass viol, and drums (or some similar instrumentation), the Smart Set performed dances, songs, and edifying comic bits involving such Ethiopian Delineations as chicken-stealing sketches, with live, possibly trained, chickens.

By the last century's late teens, when the Raineys went their separate ways, Ma had developed a stage persona that would not change. Warm, direct, plainspoken but poetic, she was the mature mistress, fully in charge of her younger, handpicked lovers, whom she referred to as "pig meat" (young) and "bird liver" (younger).

The first blues sheet music appeared in 1912: March saw Hart Wand's "Dallas Blues," August, Arthur Seals's "Baby Seals' Blues," and September, W. C. Handy's 1909 composition, "Mr. Crump," now titled "Memphis Blues." Songs with the word *blues* in the title, used as slang, had appeared before, but these 1912 numbers were serious efforts at capturing the folk idiom on paper. Songs like them have been called "vaudeville blues" to distinguish them from their origins. Those distinctions meant little to most people. In 1914 Handy published "The St. Louis Blues," which became, eventually, the most popular blues composition of all time.

Records by such black groups as the Unique Quartette and single black men as Bert Williams had been around for years, and in 1914 the Victor Military Band made "The Memphis Blues," the earliest known record containing an authentic blues strain. But not until 1920 did Mamie Smith become, in Handy's words, "the first colored girl to make a record." Her second release, "Crazy Blues," the first vocal blues record, sold seventy-five thousand copies, mostly to black buyers, in its first month of release, ushering in the blues era.

Yet Mamie Smith, a native of Cincinnati, Ohio, has never been called the mother of the blues. In the early 1960s, Norman Mason, who played trumpet with the Rabbit Foot Minstrels, said of the blues singers who worked with the show, "I guess Ma Rainey was the most famous. Because Ma Rainey was quite a character or legend in America here, in that she had such an outstanding voice for the blues, and she sang songs like the 'Florida Blues' and the 'Kansas City Blues' and the 'Jelly Roll Blues.' She sang songs then that would sound as up-to-date as if it were played right now." Billie Pierce, who played piano with her cornetist husband De De Pierce after working as a chorus girl with Ma Rainey, said, "Only thing I can tell you about Ma Rainey was—she had a real good voice; a heavy gross voice for the blues and everybody liked her singing."

Sometime between 1912 and 1916, Rainey met her younger counterpart, Bessie Smith, and probably worked with her in traveling shows, among them Tolliver's Circus and Moses Stokes's company. Rainey, eleven days less than twelve years Smith's senior, must have seemed a "Ma." However, when they met, Ma Rainey had not been called the blues' mother, and Bessie Smith was not yet its empress.

They both started recording in 1923; Ma Rainey would record over a hundred sides, but Bessie Smith, whose recording career lasted five years longer, recorded more than twice as many. Starting around 1921 Rainey may have retired for a couple of years, during which she is supposed to have been in Mexico. But by December 1923 she was in Chicago, making records for Paramount, one of the first companies to do significant black recording. (Other such companies were OKeh with Mamie Smith,

Columbia with Bessie Smith, and Black Swan with Trixie Smith and Ethel Waters. So many blues-singing Smiths—Clara and Ivy, too—and none of them any kin.)

As befitted an established star, from her first session Rainey recorded with excellent musicians. Lovie Austin and her Blues Serenaders (clarinetist Jimmy O'Bryant and cornetist Tommy Ladnier, both great, though little-remembered, jazzmen) accompanied Rainey on many of her earliest recordings.

Pianist Austin, who wrote "Downhearted Blues" with the Paramount artist Alberta Hunter, was prevented from touring by her regular employment at the Monogram Theater. Paramount talent scout J. Mayo "Ink" Williams introduced Rainey to Thomas Andrew Dorsey, who as a boy had seen Rainey in her minstrel days at the 81 Theater in Atlanta. Dorsey, later known as the father of gospel music—he went on to write "Take My Hand, Precious Lord" and "Peace in the Valley," among other songs—arrived in Chicago around 1916 and made his living playing piano in wine rooms, rent parties, and buffet flats.

Dorsey and Rainey got along from the start. Dorsey said, "She was grand, gracious, and easy to talk with. I played some songs for her and then rehearsed her on a couple of the blues tunes that she was to use on the road. She was impressed with my playing and hired me as her accompanist and director of her 'Wild Cats Jazz Band,' which I was to assemble and organize." The unpublished autobiography *The Thomas A. Dorsey Story* (ca. 1961) presents a vividly detailed portrait of Rainey in action:

> The room is filled with a haze of smoke, she walks into the spotlight, face decorated with Stein's Reddish Make-up Powder. She's not a young symmetrical streamed-lined type; her face seems to have discarded no less than fifty some years. She stands out high in front with a glorious bust, squeezed tightly in the middle. Her torso, extending in the distance behind, goes on about its business from there on down. She opens her mouth and starts singing:
> "It's storming on the ocean, it's storming on the sea.
> My man left me this morning, and it's storming down on me."

When she started singing, the gold in her teeth would sparkle. She was in the spotlight. She possessed her listeners; they swayed, they rocked, they moaned and groaned, as they felt the blues with her. A woman swooned who had lost her man. Men groaned who had given their week's pay to some woman who promised to be nice, but slipped away and couldn't be found at the appointed time. By this time she was just about at the end of her song. She was "in her sins" as she bellowed out. The bass drum rolled like thunders and the stage lights flickered like forked lightning:

"I see the lightning flashing, I see the waves a dashing
I got to spread the news; I feel this boat a crashing
I got to spread the news; my man is gone and left me
Now I got the stormy sea blues."

As the song ends, she feels an understanding with her audience. Their applause is a rich reward. She is in her glory. The house is hot. Then she lets go again:

"Lawdy, Lawdy I hear somebody calling me,
If it ain't my regular, it must be my used-to-be.
If I had wings and could fly like Noah's dove,
I'd heist my wings and fly to the man I love."

By this time everybody is excited and enthusiastic. The applause thunders for one more number. Some woman screams out a shrill cry of agony as the blues recalls sorrow because some man trifled on her and wounded her to the bone. [Ma Rainey] is ready now to take the encore on her closing song. Here she is tired, sweaty, swaying from side to side, fatigued but happy. Then she sings:

"Honey, Honey, Honey, look what you done done,
You done made me love you, and now your woman done come.
If anybody ask you who wrote this lonesome song,
Tell 'em you don't know the writer, but a lonesome woman put it on."

Trombonist Al Wynn, who at seventeen toured the Theater Owners and Bookers Association circuit in the South and Midwest as a member of the Wild Cats, recalled,

Ma was a wonderful person to work with—very loveable disposition. She was always doing nice things and taking everyone as if they were her own kids because at that time we were very young. And contrary to what most people believe—Mother—Ma Rainey wasn't old at that time although she was well known and well established because she started so young, she was a child prodigy in her time. . . . She had started as a young girl and I had the pleasure of meeting her mother and her grandmother who were still living at the time, and going to her home in Columbus, Georgia. They were very active and remarkable people. Ma Rainey was rather heavy—she wasn't attractive at all, but what she lacked in looks she made up in personality and sweetness—her heart was so big it made her beautiful in the eyesight of everyone that got to know her. . . . But when she would come out to sing she would prove herself to be the real star of the whole evening. Her entrance was—she would come out of a large victrola—it was made just like an old-style phonograph and she would walk out of that singing the 'Moonshine Blues' which was her big hit at the time.

I been drinkin' all night, babe, and the night before,
But when I get sober, I ain't gonna drink no more,
'Cause my friend left me, standing in my door.

"Moonshine Blues," Rainey's first release (though not her first recording) was a hit, increasing her fame among northern blacks—southerners black and white already knew about her. Paramount advertised her work extensively in the *Chicago Defender*, billing her as "the Mother of the Blues," "the Songbird of the South," and "the Paramount Wildcat."

In 1924 the company launched a contest to name "Ma Rainey's Mystery Record," saying, "This record is so good—so unusual—that we couldn't think of a name good enough for it." Fourteen thousand dollars worth of prizes were awarded, including phonograph consoles, Paramount-Black Swan records, and pictures of Rainey. (The winning title was, simply and unimaginatively, the song's first line, "Lawd, I'm Down with the Blues.") That year she recorded eighteen sides for Paramount, including two New York sessions with a group led by Fletcher Henderson. On three tracks from these sessions the band included Louis Armstrong. One of the tunes Rainey and Armstrong cut together was "See See Rider," a traditional blues that had never before been recorded but would be hundreds of times, by a wide variety of artists including Jelly Roll Morton, George Lewis, Bill Broonzy, Ray Charles, Lightnin' Hopkins, Eric Burdon, B. B. King, Peggy Lee, and Elvis Presley.

Nineteen twenty-four saw the formation of Rainey's Georgia Jazz Band, also known as the Georgia Band, the Georgia Boys, and the Tub Jug Washboard Band. Personnel had, it seems, nothing to do with the names. At first the Jazz Band was identical to the Blues Serenaders, with the addition of Charles Harris (not the songwriter) on alto saxophone. Later the Jazz or Georgia Band included at times not only such jazz immortals as Henderson and Armstrong but also Don Redman, Charlie Green, Joe Smith, Coleman Hawkins, Buster Bailey, Doc Cheatham, Kid Ory, and Claude Hopkins.

Though a certain prejudice against blues had obtained among northern urbanites, music had not yet been categorized as it would come to be. In any case, Rainey's audience was primarily rural and southern. She also recorded with such blues players as guitarist Blind Blake and the Pruitt Twins, Miles and Milas, on banjo and guitar, respectively. Her recording career lasted only five years, from December 1923 to December 1928. Paramount seems to have made an effort, in Rainey's last year of recording, to get away from the jazz influence of her early sides. In 1928 she recorded nineteen tracks with Dorsey, nine with the Tub Jug Washboard Band, and ten with Dorsey and guitarist Tampa Red (born Hudson Whitaker in Smithville, Georgia).

Her final recordings were accompanied only by the ragtime banjoist Papa Charlie Jackson, who's been called the first black folk singer to record. Jackson began recording in 1924; such country blues artists as Blind Lemon Jefferson, Jim Jackson, Peg Leg Howell, Texas Alexander,

Henry Thomas, and Gus Cannon, among others, came soon after. "'Ma' Rainey's Black Bottom," recorded in 1927, was released the following February to considerable success. Her traveling band, now billed as the Paramount Flappers, continued on the T.O.B.A. and tent show circuit, but radio, records, and talking pictures were luring the audience away from the old-time vaudeville shows.

———————

Dorsey, who had suffered a nervous breakdown in 1920, had another in 1926 and stopped traveling with Rainey. Though he regained his health, he never rejoined her road show, which in 1929 fell on hard times. Unable to sustain themselves on their own, the Flappers joined first the C. A. Worthham circus, then in turn the Sugarfoot Green tent show, William Jordan's minstrel musical comedy "The Arkansas Swift Foot," and Boisey De Legge's Bandanna Babies. In 1930 the T.O.B.A. theaters closed, never to reopen. As Dorsey recalled, "The blues ran out. It collapsed, seemingly, or the blues singers, they had nothing to do. I don't know what happened to the blues, they seemed to drop it all at once, it just went *down* and Mayo Williams and . . . all the big wigs there . . . couldn't see what was happening, and all the artists were falling out because they couldn't get work. Well, there was just a slump on the record business after two or three years. And I just did get out before it happened. It just seemed like the whole thing changed around, and wasn't no work for anybody and they began to lose contact with each other. The record companies, they started publicizing some other types of music."

Paramount, having recorded over a hundred blues and gospel records in 1930, recorded about three dozen in 1931 and recorded its last black music session in 1932.

By the early thirties, Rainey and her troupe were with the Donald MacGregor Carnival, working in East Texas oilfield towns. MacGregor, who had appeared as the Scottish Giant in Ringling Brothers' Circus, was a barker with his own show, wearing a kilt, announcing Rainey as "the Black Nightingale." Her necklace of gold pieces was gone, replaced by one of imitation pearls. The touring bus that had replaced her private railroad had vanished too, and she traveled in a homemade house trailer built on an old car chassis, with a floor and sides of rough timber and a canvas roof. She cooked her own meals on a gas camp stove.

In 1935, her sister Malissa died in Columbus. Rainey retired and came back to the house she had bought there for her family. Her mother died that same year. Rainey managed to purchase two theaters in Rome, Georgia, the Lyric and the Airdrome, and operated them, though she no longer performed. She joined the Friendship Baptist Church, where her brother Thomas was a deacon. On December 22, 1939, Rainey died of heart disease and was buried in Porterdale Cemetery in Columbus. Her gravestone bears her dates and the inscription, "Gertrude 'Ma' Rainey, Mother of the Blues."

BLIND WILLIE McTELL

When I was asked to do the series on Georgia musical giants, Willie McTell was my first choice. His star in the firmament of Blues Heaven will never diminish.

In his book, *Father of the Blues*, W. C. Handy tells of playing at a dance in Cleveland, Mississippi, with his band of reading musicians, when he was asked to let a hometown trio play a few numbers. Handy's men stepped aside, and the unschooled local boys commenced to strum their instruments: a ragged guitar, mandolin, and bass. "A rain of silver dollars began to fall," Handy wrote. "There before the boys lay more money than my nine musicians were being paid for the entire engagement. Then I saw the beauty of primitive music."

That was in the early twentieth century, around 1903. The Cleveland band played a kind of music that, partly through Handy's efforts (he was not so much the father of a new musical form as one of its midwives), in a few years would evolve into the blues. On August 10, 1920, a vaudeville singer named Mamie Smith (no relation to Empress of the Blues Bessie Smith) recorded a song written by the composer, pianist, singer, and song plugger Perry Bradford called "Crazy Blues." It sold a million copies in the first six months after its release and created a blues craze that lasted into the Depression.

Hoping to capitalize on the blues, early record companies like Victor and Columbia sent agents into the South to make field recordings. They visited such places as Memphis, New Orleans, the Carolinas, and

Georgia. In October of 1927 in Atlanta, Victor's Ralph Peer, who produced "Crazy Blues," made the first recordings of Willie McTell, one of the most talented singers and guitarists who would ever perform blues. Between 1927 and 1956, McTell recorded over a hundred blues and gospel performances under the names Blind Willie, Blind Sammie, Georgia Bill, Hot Shot Willie, Red Hot Willie Glaze, Barrel House Sammie, and Pig and Whistle Red.

He was born William Samuel McTier (or McTear), on May 5, 1901, near Thomson, Georgia, in the eastern part of the state, as he said, "between the two creeks, they call it—Little Briar and Big Briar." No one knows for sure how he came to be called McTell; some say the change came from a misunderstanding when he registered at a school for the blind, others that his father's people were notorious bootleggers who took McTell as an alias. His mother, a teenager named Minnie Watkins, came from Wadley, thirty-five miles to the south of Thomson. According to McTell, when he was nine, his parents separated, his mother taking him south to Bulloch County. "I stayed there till I run away," he said. "I run away and went everywhere. Everywhere I could go—without any money."

Though blind from birth, McTell came from a musical family—his mother, father, and an uncle played guitar—and he became a guitar virtuoso, starting with six-string and changing to twelve-string probably sometime in the early twenties. Unlike most twelve-string guitarists, who exploited the resonance of the instrument in a rhythmic mode, McTell played single-note lines, surprising grace notes, and unusual effects, reproducing the sounds of trains, bells, whistles, knocking on doors, footsteps, such instruments as mandolin, string bass, cornet, and other noises. He had total command of the guitar whether fingerpicking or playing with a bottleneck.

From the beginning of his recording career, McTell was a finished artist as player, singer, composer, and lyricist. His first release, "Writin' Paper Blues," begs, "Mm-mm, hear me weep and moan. Honey, hear my pleading, hear my grief and groans." That record's B side presents the vivid image, remarkable for a sightless person, "Big star fallin', Mama, 'taint long fo' day." A later stanza tells us, "The woman I love got a mouth chock full of good gold—every time she hug and kiss me it makes my blood run cold."

There were similar figures—Arthur Blake, Fulton Allen (Blind Boy Fuller), Arvella Gray, Lemon Jefferson, Joe Taggart, John Estes, Sonny Terry, Gary Davis, Willie Johnson, among other blues and gospel artists, were sightless and itinerant to varying degrees. Blind musicians have been around forever. But many, if not most, had a lead-man, someone to help. McTell traveled all over the country, coast to coast, alone. He carried maps of various towns, cities, and the New York Subway System in his head.

In 1922 McTell entered the Georgia state school for the blind in Macon. He stayed there three years, learning broom making, leatherwork, carpentry, sewing, and Braille. He also attended blind schools in New York, Michigan, and North Carolina, learning music theory. He could thread a needle, count paper money, and once shot a mad dog with a pistol. Like many other blues artists, he worked on carnivals and medicine shows, but for much of his life he stayed in or near Atlanta, playing on Ponce de Leon Avenue for the white patrons' tips at drive-in cafés such as the Pig & Whistle and more upscale restaurants like the Blue Lantern.

In October of 1929 he made a second series of recordings for Victor. Later that month, as Blind Sammie, he recorded for Columbia. This was standard practice among blues artists, who never saw any record royalties. They would sign whatever contract the companies put before them no matter how restrictive, and sign another "exclusive" contract the next week or the next day.

In 1933, playing the graduation ceremony of Paine College High School in Augusta, Georgia, he encountered Ruthie Kate Williams, whose family had known his years before. In fact, their mothers had been friends, and Williams's mother had promised her to McTell when she was four years old and he was a teenager. "Mama Sarah, give me that baby," McTell had said, and Williams recalled her mother telling him, "All right, when you get grown, and she get [to be] a big girl, you come back and get her."

In 1934 Williams and McTell were married. He put her through school to become a nurse, a profession she followed for over thirty years. She also recorded with McTell for Decca in Chicago during April of 1934 and traveled extensively with him, making live appearances on medicine shows and tobacco auctions in the early years of their marriage.

McTell's 1940 Library of Congress sessions with folklorist John Lomax came about after Lomax's wife, Ruby, spotted McTell playing for the barbecue eaters at the P & W. As Lomax later recalled, neither he nor Ruby remembered the way back to their hotel. "I'll show you," McTell said.

"Between us and the hotel," Lomax said, "there were six or eight right-angled cross streets and two places where six streets crossed. Chatting all the while with me, Willie called every turn, even mentioning the location of the stoplights. He gave the names of the buildings as we passed them."

The next day—it was November 5—McTell spent two hours with the Lomaxes in their hotel room, singing and playing guitar, recording about forty minutes' worth of material: blues, gospel, and reminiscence. At one point Lomax repeatedly questions McTell: "I wonder if you know any songs about colored people having hard times here in the South."

"Well, that's all songs that have reference to our old people here, and it hasn't very much [to do with] the people nowadays."

"Or any complaining songs, complaining about the hard times, and sometimes mistreatment of the whites. Have you got any songs that talk about that?"

"No sir, we haven't; not at the present time, because the white people's mighty good to the southern people, as far as I know."

"You don't know any complainin' songs at all? 'Ain't It Hard to be a Nigger, Nigger?' Do you know that one?"

"That's not in our time. Now there's a spiritual down here, 'It's Mean World to Live In,' but that still don't have reference to the hard time [whites give blacks]."

"Why is it a mean world to live in?"

"Well, no, it's not altogether; it has reference to everybody."

"It's as mean for the whites as it is for the blacks, is that it?"

"That's the idea."

Though the session produced the earliest recordings of the McTell classics "Delia" and "Dying Crapshooter's Blues," none of it was released until many years later. One account has it that Lomax paid McTell, in total, ten dollars. (At the time Lomax already had, in the Texas bluesman Leadbelly, a formidable and commercially successful twelve-string guitarist and may have felt that McTell's work was too similar.)

Nine years would pass before McTell recorded again. In 1949, Herb Abramson and Ahmet Ertegun of the fledgling record company Atlantic came to Atlanta and recorded McTell performing eight blues and seven gospel tunes. The following year, Fred Mendelsohn of New Jersey–based Regal Records cut twenty tracks in Atlanta by McTell with Curley Weaver, his picking partner from back in the thirties. Both sessions found McTell in, if anything, greater command than ever of his astonishing talent. By now McTell had performed his signature tunes, among them "Kill It Kid," "The Razor Ball," "Little Delia," "Broke Down Engine Blues," and "Dying Crapshooter's Blues," thousands of times for audiences whose main interest was in barbecue. He had honed each of his musical pieces into three-minute dramas of surpassing vividness.

> Little Jesse was a gambler, night and day
> He used crooked cards and dice
> Sinful guy, good-hearted but had no soul
> Heart was hard and cold like ice
>
> . . .
>
> Police walked up and shot my friend Jesse down
> "Boys, I got to die today."
> He had a gang of gamblers and crapshooters at his bedside
> Here are the words he had to say:
>
> "I guess I ort to know
> Exactly how I want to go."
> (How you wanta go, Jesse?)
>
> "Eight crapshooters to be my pallbearers
> Let 'em be veiled down in black

I want nine men goin' to the graveyard, buddy,
And eight men comin' back

I want a gang of gamblers gathered 'round my coffinside
Crooked card printed on my hearse
Don't say that crapshooters'll never grieve over me
My life's been a doggoned curse

Send poker players to the graveyard
Dig my grave with the ace of spades
I want twelve polices in my funeral march
High sheriff playin' blackjack, leadin' the parade

I want the judge and solicitor who jailed me fo'teen times
Put a pair of dice in my shoes."
(And then what?)
"Let a deck of cards be my tombstone, buddy,
I got the dyin' crapshooter's blues."

"The Dying Crapshooter's Blues"
W. S. McTell

Classic blues is filled with examples of powerful poetic imagery, but McTell takes a backseat to no blues lyricist. His guitar work on the 1949–50 Atlanta sessions is superlative. He plays blues, rags, gospel songs, even the Gene Autry hit "Pal of Mine," right at home with them all. Living much of his life on the street, recording over a hundred performances without ever having a hit, McTell nevertheless made for himself a home in his music. It's still there, warm and waiting for anyone who will listen.

———————

Following the Japanese attack on Pearl Harbor, Kate McTell, who had been graduated from nursing school in 1936, found a job as a nurse at Fort Gordon near Augusta and stayed there thirty years. Until McTell's death they continued to see each other on occasion. His last recording session took place in 1956, once again in Atlanta, at a music shop owned by a man named Ed Rhodes. By this time McTell was disillusioned and wary of recording. But he liked Rhodes, took to hanging around his shop, and when Rhodes began to record him, McTell said, "Now I ain't in no hurry—not if you ain't."

Though McTell recorded no gospel material on that last session, Kate McTell said later that in 1957 or 1958 he had given up blues and become a preacher. In the spring of 1959 McTell suffered a stroke that caused some paralysis. He went to live with relatives in Thomson. There his health seemed to improve, but after a family barbecue in August he suffered another stroke. He was admitted to the state hospital in Milledgeville on August 12 and died there a week later from the effects of cerebral hemorrhages.

McTell's cousin, Eddie McTier, ordered a gravestone for the burial site at Jones Grove Church in Thomson, but there was a misunderstanding, and so McTell's grave originally bore the legend

> Eddie McTier
> 1898 [sic]
> AUG 19 1959
> AT REST

The error has since been corrected, and McTell now has, at least, his own name on his grave.

FURRY'S BLUES

In one of those downtown Memphis alleys, or just off it, I found Furry Lewis, and we adopted each other. "Me and him just like brothers," Furry would say, pointing at me, and it was true, though he never allowed me to forget which brother was the older and wiser.

In the fall of 1963, I had gone to New Orleans to do graduate work in art history at Sophie Newcombe College, part of Tulane University. I attended school for about six weeks and stayed in New Orleans nearly a year. When I came back to Memphis, I went to work for the Tennessee Department of Public Welfare, leaving it in 1966 to write a novel about poor people that ended with mass demonstrations and tanks on Main Street. A day or two after I finished (I'd written a chapter a day for eighteen days) I ran into Charlie Brown and asked him to take me to see Furry Lewis. We stopped by Charlie's flat, he picked up a .38, and we went to Fourth and Beale.

When we came into the alley, the children stopped playing. They stood poised, watching us. There were two-story brick buildings on both sides, with wooden stairways that shut out all but a thin blue strip of sky. Filthy rags and broken bottles lay on the concrete pavement. There were women sitting on the doorsteps, some of them together, talking, but most of them alone, sitting still, ignoring the heat and the buzzing flies.

"How are you?" Charlie Brown spoke to one of them.

"I ain't doin' no good," she said.

She did not look up. The children's gaze followed us as we walked on. The women talking would stop as we came near and then, as we went past, would start again.

Close by, a fat woman was holding a small brown-and-white dog to her bosom.

"What you got there?" Charlie asked her.

"Little spitz," she said. "Look how dirty he is. He pretty when he clean."

"Nice dog," he said. "Is Furry home?"

"De up deah. De ain't been long gone up."

We climbed the back stairs of the building on our left and went down a bare, dusty hall to a door with a metal number 3 over the cloth-patched screen. Charlie started to knock, and then we heard the music and he waited. "Got a new way of spellin'," a quiet musing voice sang. "Memphis, Tennessee." A run of guitar chords followed, skeptical, brief: "Double M, double E, great God, A Y Z." Then two closing chords, like a low shout of laughter, and Charlie knocked.

The door swung open. There, sitting next to a double bed, holding a guitar, was Furry Lewis.

During the heyday of Beale Street, when the great Negro blues artists played and sang in the crowded, evil blocks between Fourth and Main, Furry, a protégé of W. C. Handy, was one of the most highly respected musicians. He was also one of the most popular, not only in the saloons and gambling dives of Memphis but in the medicine shows and on the riverboats all along the Mississippi. In Chicago, at the old Vocalion studios on Wabash Avenue, he made the first of many recordings he was to do, both for Vocalion and for RCA Victor's Bluebird label. But Beale Street's great era, and the young Furry Lewis's recording career, ended at the close of the 1920s; Furry would not record again until 1959. Nor, since the Depression, has he performed regularly, even in his hometown. He makes his living as a street-sweeper. When he does play, it is usually at the Bitter Lemon, a coffeehouse that caters mainly to the affluent East Memphis teenage set, but whose manager, Charlie Brown, is a blues enthusiast and occasionally hires Furry between rock and roll groups.

Charlie, a tall, blond young man, bent to shake hands with Furry. Furry did not stand. One leg of his green pajamas hung limp, empty below the knee.

The boy wearing gold-rimmed spectacles who had got up from a chair to let us in said, "I'm Jerry Finberg. Furry's been giving me a little guitar lesson." We shook his hand, then Charlie introduced me to Furry and we all sat down. The room held a sizable amount of old, worn furniture: the bed, a studio couch, three stuffed chairs, a chifforobe, and a dresser. Beside the bed, there was a table made from a small wooden crate.

"It's good to see you, Furry," Charlie said.

"You too," said Furry. "You hadn't been here in so long. I thought you had just about throwed me down."

Charlie said that he could never do that and asked Furry if he could come out to the coffeehouse for a couple of nights in the coming week. Furry picked up a pair of glasses from the bedside table, put them on, then took them off again. He would like to, he said, but his guitar was at Nathan's. "This here belongs to this boy, Jerry." He put the glasses back on the table. It held aspirin, Sal Hepatica, cigarette papers, and a Mason jar full of tobacco. Charlie said not to worry, he'd get the guitar.

"Will you, sure 'nough?" Furry asked, looking at Charlie with serious, businesslike, gray eyes.

"I'll get it tomorrow. What's the ticket on it?"

"Sixteen dollars."

"I'll get it tomorrow."

"All right," Furry said, "and I'll come play for you." He reached out and shook hands solemnly with Charlie.

"Could you play something now, or don't you feel like it?" Charlie asked.

Furry smiled. "I may be weak, but I'm willing," he said. He took a small metal cylinder from his pajama pocket and picked up the guitar. "I believe I'll take you to Brownsville." He slipped the cylinder over the little finger of his left hand and started to play, his short leg crossed over the longer one, his bare narrow foot softly patting the plain brown boards as he sang. "Well, I'm goin' to Brownsville, I'm goin' take that right-hand road"; the cylinder slid, whining, over the treble strings.

"I was in Brownsville, Tennessee," Furry said, "working on a doctor show, and I met a little girl I liked; but her parents wouldn't let me come around to see her, 'cause I was showfolks, and they was respectable. So I wrote this: 'And the woman I love's got great long curly hair.'" The guitar repeated the line, added a delicate, punctuating bass figure, and then, as if it were another voice, sang the next line with Furry, staying just behind or slightly ahead of the beat: "But her mother and father do not allow me there."

As he played, I looked around the room. The brown-spotted wallpaper was covered with decorations: over the bed were a few sprigs of artificial holly, an American flag hanging with the stripes vertical and the stars at the bottom left, three brightly colored picture postcards, and an ink sketch of Furry. On the wall behind the couch, there was a child's crayon drawing in which Jesus, dressed in handsome red-and-blue robes, held out his arms to an enormous white rabbit.

Furry's right hand swooped and glided over the guitar, striking notes and chords in what looked, but did not sound, like complete random. At times, he slapped the guitar-box with two fingers or the heel of his hand as, in the same motion, he brushed the strings. "Call that spank the baby," he said. The guitar was both an echo of his voice and a source of complex and subtle accents. He sang, "Don't you wish your woman was long and tall like mine?" then repeated the line, leaving out, or letting the guitar speak, half the words. "Well, she ain't good-lookin', but I 'clare, she takes her time." The bass figure followed, then one amused, final chord. Furry laid the guitar down.

"You play beautiful guitar," Charlie said.

"Yes, it is," Furry said, holding up the instrument. "Believe I'll be buried in this one."

"Was that Spanish tuning?" asked Jerry, who had been leaning forward, elbows on his knees, listening intently.

"They some beer in the icebox," Furry said.

Jerry sighed and stood up. "Come on," he said to me. "Help bring the glasses." We went into the kitchen. It was almost as large as the front room, with a stove, a refrigerator, a good-sized table, and, in one corner, another double bed. A cabinet held gallon jars of flour, sugar, lima beans, and an assortment of canned goods: Pride of Illinois white sweet corn, School Days June peas, Showboat pork and beans, Lyke's beef tripe, Pride of Virginia herring, Bush's Best black-eyed peas and turnip greens.

Jerry took a quart of Pfeiffer's beer out of the refrigerator. I found four glasses on a newspaper-lined shelf, rinsed them in the square metal sink ("They clean," Furry called, "but no tellin' what's been runnin' over 'em"), and we went back into the other room. We had just finished pouring when there was a knock at the door.

"That's my wife," Furry said, sliding the latch open. "Come in, Versie."

She came in, a compact, handsome woman. I introduced myself and the others said hello. Versie, in a pleasantly hoarse voice, told us that only that morning, she had been asking Furry what he had done to make his boyfriends stay away so long.

"They all threw me down," Furry said, then laughed and told Versie he was going out to play at the Bitter Lemon. She smiled and asked if she could get us anything to eat. We all said no, thank you, and she sat down.

"My wife loves to see after folks," Furry said. "Do anything in the world for people. Feed 'em, give 'em something to drink; if they get too drunk to go home, got a bed in there to put you to sleep on. And I'm the same way. But you know, there's one old boy, I see him every day at work, and every time I see him, he bum a cigarette from me. Now, it ain't much, but it come so regular. So the other day, I told him, 'Boy, ain't but one difference 'tween you and a blind man.' And he said, 'What's that?' And I told him, 'Blind man beg from everybody he hear, you beg from everybody you see.'"

"Well," Versie said, from her chair on the other side of the room, "it's a pleasure to do things for people who are so nice to us. We tried and tried to find out Furry's age, so he could get this Medicare, and Jerry went out to Furry's old school and made them look through the records and find out when he was born. He spent several days, just to help us."

"Found out I was born 1893," Furry said. "March the sixth, in Greenwood, Mississippi. But I moved to Memphis, with my mother and two sisters, when I was six. My mother and father were sharecroppers and they separated before I was born. I never saw my father, never even knew what he looked like." He took a drink of beer.

"Where did you live when you came here?" I asked.

"My mother had a sister lived on Brinkley Avenue," he said. "Call it Decatur now. We stayed with her. They a housing project there now, but I could still show you the spot." He took another drink, looked at the glass, then emptied it. "I was raised right there and walked a few blocks to the Carnes Avenue School. Went to the fifth, and that's as far as I got.

Started going about, place to place, catching the freights. That's how I lost my leg. Goin' down a grade outside Du Quoin, Illinois, I caught my foot in a coupling. They took me to a hospital in Carbondale. I could look right out my window and see the ice-cream factory."

He took a cigarette from a pack of Pall Malls on the bedside table. "That was 1916," he said. "I had two or three hundred dollars in my pocket when that happened, too; I had just caught a freight 'cause I didn't feel like spending the money for a ticket." He struck a match, but the breeze from the window-fan blew it out. Charlie took the cigarette, lit it, and handed it back. "Love you," Furry said. "Goin' put you in the Bible."

He stuck the cigarette in the corner of his mouth, picked up the guitar, and played a succession of slow, blues-drenched chords that seemed to fill the room. "I'm doing all right," he said. "What you want to hear?"

"Do you remember 'Stagolee?'" I asked.

"What song?"

"One you recorded a long time ago, called 'Stagolee.'"

"Long time ago—I wasn't born then, was I?" He quickly changed tunings and started to sing the song. He did one chorus, but it went off after the second, which began, "When you lose your money, learn to lose . . ."

"What was that last?" Charlie asked.

Furry repeated the line. "That means, don't be no *hard* loser. That's what this song is about." He began again, but after a few bars, he lost the tune. He was tired.

Charlie stood up. "We've got to go, Furry."

"No," Furry said. "You just got here."

"Got to go to work. I'll pick you up Tuesday night."

"I'm so glad you came by," Versie told Charlie, in the hall. "Sometimes Furry thinks everybody has forgotten him."

It had rained while we were inside, and the air in the alley smelled almost fresh. The women were gone now and only a few of the children were still out. It was nearly dark. We walked back to the car and drove down Beale Street, past the faded blocks of pawn shops, liquor stores, and poolrooms. The lights were coming on for the evening.

———————

After the Civil War, many former slaves came in from the country, trying to find their families. There were only about four thousand Negroes in Memphis in 1860, but by 1870 there were fifteen thousand. Beale Street drew them, it has been said, "like a lodestone."

The music the country Negroes brought, with its thumping rhythms, unorthodox harmonies, and earthy lyrics, combined with the city musicians' more polished techniques and regular forms to produce, as all the world knows, the Beale Street blues. Furry cannot remember when he first heard the blues, nor is he certain when he started trying to play them.

"I was eight or nine, I believe," he said, "when I got the idea I wanted to have me a guitar." We were at the Bitter Lemon now, Furry, Versie, Charlie, and I, waiting for the crowd to arrive. The waitresses, pretty girls with long straight hair, were lighting candles on the small round tables. We sat in the shadows, drinking bourbon brought from the liquor store on the corner, listening to Furry talk about the old days.

He was coatless, wearing a white shirt with a dark blue tie, and he was smoking a wood-tipped cigar. "I taken a cigar box, cut a hole in the top and nailed a piece of two-by-four on there for a neck. Then I got some screen wire for the strings and I tacked them to the box and twisted them around some bent nails on the end of the two-by-four. I could turn the nails and tune the strings like that, you see. I fooled around with it, got so I could make notes, but just on the one string. Couldn't make no chords. The first real guitar I had, Mr. Cham Fields—who owned a roadhouse, gambling house—and W. C. Handy gave it to me. They brought it out to my mother's and I was so proud to get it, I cried for a week. Them days, children wasn't like they are now." His cigar had gone out; he relit it from the candle on our table, puffing great gray clouds of smoke. "It was a Martin and I kept it twenty years."

"What happened to it?" Charlie asked.

"It died."

Furry put the candle down and leaned back in his chair. "When I was eighteen, nineteen years old," he said, "I was good. And when I was twenty, I had my own band, and we could all play. Had a boy named Ham, played jug. Willie Polk played the fiddle and another boy, call him Shoefus, played the guitar, like I did. All of us North Memphis boys.

We'd meet at my house and walk down Brinkley to Poplar and go up Poplar to Dunlap or maybe all the way down to Main. People would stop us on the street and say, 'Do you know so-and-so?' And we'd play it and they'd give us a little something. Sometimes we'd pick up fifteen or twenty dollars before we got to Beale. Wouldn't take no streetcar. Long as you walked, you's making money; but if you took the streetcar, you didn't make nothing and you'd be out the nickel for the ride."

"That was Furry's wild days," Versie said. "Drinking, staying out all night. He'd still do that way, if l let him."

Furry smiled. "We used to leave maybe noon Saturday and not get back home till Monday night. All the places we played—Pee Wee's, Big Grundy's, Cham Field's, B. B. Anderson's—when they opened up, they took the keys and tied them to a rabbit's neck, told him to run off to the woods, 'cause they never meant to close."

I asked Furry whether he had done much traveling.

"A right smart," he said. "But that was later on, when I was working with Gus Cannon, the banjo player, and Will Shade. Beale Street was commencing to change then. Had to go looking for work." He rolled his cigar ash off against the side of an ashtray. "In the good times, though, you could find anything you could name on Beale. Gambling, girls; you could buy a pint of moonshine for a dime, store-bought whiskey for a quarter. We'd go from place to place, making music, and everywhere we'd go, they'd be glad to see us. We'd play awhile and then somebody would pass the hat. We didn't make too much, but we didn't need much back then. In them days, you could get two loaves of bread for a nickel. And some nights, when the people from down on the river came up, we'd make a batch of money. The roustabouts from the steamboats, and *Kate Adams*, the *Idlewild*, the *Viney Swing*—I've taken trips on all them boats, played up the river to St. Louis, down to New Orleans—white and colored, they'd all come to Beale. Got along fine, too, just like we doing now. Course, folks had they squabbles, like they will, you know. I saw two or three get killed."

There were enough squabbles to make Memphis the murder capital of the country. In the first decade of the century, 556 homicides occurred, most of them involving Negroes. Appeals for reform were taken seriously only by those who made them. When E. H. Crump ran for mayor on a reform ticket, W. C. Handy recorded the Beale Streeters' reaction: "We don't care what Mr. Crump don't allow, we goin' barrelhouse anyhow."

But as the self-righteous Crump machine gained power, the street slowly began to change. Each year the red-light district grew smaller; each year, there were fewer gambling houses, fewer saloons, fewer places for musicians to play.

Then came the Depression. Local newspapers carried accounts of starving Negroes swarming over garbage dumps, even eating the clay from the river bluffs. Many people left town, but Furry stayed. "Nothing else to do," he said. "The Depression wasn't just in Memphis, it was all over the country. A lot of my friends left, didn't know what they was goin' to. The boy we called Ham, from our band, he left, and nobody ever knew what became of him. I did have a little job with the city and I stuck with that. I had been working with them off and on, when there wasn't anyplace to play. They didn't even have no trucks at that time. Just had mules to pull the garbage carts. Didn't have no incinerator; used to take the garbage down to the end of High Street, across the railroad tracks, and burn it."

Before Beale Street could recover from the Depression, World War Two brought hundreds of boys in uniform to Memphis; and, for their protection, Boss Crump closed the last of the saloons and whorehouses. It was the final blow.

Furry sat staring at the end of his cigar. "Beale Street really went down," he said after a moment. "You know, old folks say, it's a long lane don't have no end and a bad wind don't never change. But one day, back when Hoover was president, I was driving my cart down Beale Street and I seen a rat, sitting on top of a garbage can, eating a onion, crying."

Furry has been working for the City of Memphis Sanitation Department since 1923. Shortly after two o'clock each weekday morning, he gets out of bed, straps on his artificial leg, dresses, and makes a fresh pot of coffee, which he drinks while reading the Memphis *Press-Scimitar*. The newspaper arrives in the afternoon, but Furry does not open it until morning. Versie is still asleep and the paper is company for him as he sits in the kitchen under the harsh light of the ceiling bulb, drinking the hot, sweet coffee. He does not eat breakfast; when the coffee is gone, he leaves for work.

The sky is black. The alley is quiet, the apartments dark. A morning-glory vine hanging from a guy-wire stirs like a heavy curtain in the cool morning breeze. Cars in the cross alley are covered with a silver glaze of dew. A cat flashes between shadows.

Linden Avenue is bright and empty in the blue glare of the street lamps. Down the street, St. Patrick's looms, a sign, 100 YEARS WITH CHRIST, over its wide red doors. Furry, turning right, walks past the faded, green-glowing bay windows of an apartment house to the corner. A moving van rolls past. There is no other traffic. When the light changes, Furry crosses, heading down Hernando. The clock at Carodine's Fruit Stand and Auto Service reads, as it always does, 2:49.

The cafés, taverns, laundries, shoe-repair shops, and liquor stores are all closed. The houses, under shading trees, seem drawn into themselves. At the Clayborn Temple A.M.E. Church, the stained-glass windows gleam, jewellike against the mass of blackened stone. A woman wearing a maid's uniform passes on the other side of the street. Furry says good morning and she says good morning, their voices patiently weary. Beside the Scola Brothers' Grocery is a sycamore, its branches silhouetted against the white wall. Furry walks slowly, hunched forward, as if sleep were a weight on his shoulders. Hand-painted posters at the Vance Avenue Market: CHICKEN BACKS 12 1/2c LB.; HOG MAWS, 15c; RUMPS, 19c.

Behind Bertha's Beauty Nook, under a large, pale-leafed elm, there are twelve garbage cans and two carts. Furry lifts one of the cans on to a cart, rolls the cart out into the street and, taking the wide broom from its slot, begins to sweep the gutter. A large woman with her head tied in a kerchief, wearing a purple wrapper and gold house slippers, passes by on the sidewalk. Furry tells her good morning and she nods hello.

When he has swept back to Vance, Furry leaves the trash in a pile at the corner and pushes the cart, with its empty can, to Beale Street. The sky is gray. The stiff brass figure of W. C. Handy stands, one foot slightly forward, the bell of his horn pointing down, under the manicured trees of his deserted park. The gutter is thick with debris: empty wine bottles, torn racing forms from the West Memphis dog track, flattened cigarette packs, scraps of paper, and one small die, white with black spots, which Furry puts into his pocket. An old bus, on the back of which is written, in yellow paint, LET NOT YOUR HEART BE TROUBLE, rumbles past; it is full of cotton choppers: their dark, solemn faces peer out the grimy windows. The bottles clink at the end of Furry's broom. In a room above the Club Handy, two men are standing at an open window looking down at the street. One of them is smoking, the glowing end of his cigarette can be seen in the darkness. On the door to the club, there is a handbill: BLUES SPECTACULAR, CITY AUDITORIUM: JIMMY REED, JOHN LEE HOOKER, HOWLIN' WOLF.

Furry pushes the garbage onto a flat scoop at the front of the cart, then goes to the rear and pulls a jointed metal handle, causing the scoop to rise and dump its contents into the can. The scoop is heavy; when he lets it down, it sends a shock from his right arm through his body, raising his left leg, the artificial one, off the ground. Across the street, in a chinaberry tree, a gang of sparrows are making a racket. Furry sweeps past two night clubs and then a restaurant, where, through the front window, large brown rats can be seen scurrying across the kitchen floor. A dirty red dog stands at the corner of Beale and Hernando, sniffing the air. A black soldier in a khaki uniform runs past, heading toward Main. The street lamps go off.

When Furry has cleaned the rest of the block, the garbage can is full and he goes back to Bertha's for another. The other cart is gone and there is a black Buick parked at the curb. Furry wheels to the corner and picks up the mound of trash he left there. A city bus rolls past; the driver gives a greeting honk and Furry waves. He crosses the street and begins sweeping in front of the Sanitary Bedding Company. A woman's high-heeled shoe is lying in the sidewalk. Furry throws it into the can. "First one-legged woman I see, I'll give her that," he says and, for the first time that day, he smiles.

At Butler, the next cross street, there is a row of large, old-fashioned houses set behind picket fences and broad, thickly leafed trees. The sky is pale blue now, with pink-edged clouds, and old men and women have come out to sit on the porches. Some speak to Furry, some do not. Cars are becoming more frequent along the street. Furry reaches out quickly with his broom to catch a windblown scrap of paper. When he gets to Calhoun, he swaps cans again and walks a block—past Tina's Beauty Shop, a tavern called the Section Playhouse and another named Soul Heaven—to Fourth Street. He places his cart at the corner and starts pushing the trash toward it.

From a second-story window of a rooming-house covered with red brick-patterned tarpaper comes the sound of a blues harmonica. Two old men are sitting on the steps in front of the open door. Furry tells them good morning. "When you goin' make another record?" one of them asks. "Record?" the other man, in a straw hat, says. "That's right," says the first one. "He makes them big-time records. Used to."

Furry dumps a load into the cart, then leans against it, wiping his face and the back of his neck with a blue bandanna handkerchief.

Down the stairs and through the door (the old men on the steps leaning out of his way, for he does not slow down) comes the harmonica player. He stands in the middle of the sidewalk, eyes closed, head tilted to one side, the harmonica cupped in his hands. A man wearing dark glasses and carrying a white cane before him like a divining rod turns the corner, aims at the music, says cheerfully, "Get out the way! Get off the sidewalk!" and bumps into the harmonica player, who spins away, like a good quarterback, and goes on playing.

Furry puts the bandanna in his pocket and moves on, walking behind the cart. Past Mrs. Kelly's Homemade Hot Tamales stand, the air is filled with a strong odor. Over a shop door, a sign reads: FRESH FISH DAILY.

Now the sky is a hot, empty blue, and cars line the curb from Butler to Vance. Furry sweeps around them. Across the street, at the housing project, children are playing outside the great blocks of apartments. One little girl is lying face down on the grass, quite still. Furry watches her. She has not moved. Two dogs are barking nearby. One of them, a small black cocker spaniel, trots up to the little girl and sniffs at her head; she grabs its forelegs and together they roll over and over. Furry starts sweeping and does not stop or look up again until he has reached the corner. He piles the trash into the can and stands in the gutter, waiting for the light to change.

For the morning, his work is done. He rolls the cart down Fourth, across Pontotoc and Linden, to his own block, where he parks it at the curb, between two cars. Then he heads across the street toward Rothschild's grocery, to try to get some beer on credit.

While we were talking, people were coming in, and now the tables were nearly filled. Charlie looked at his watch, then at Furry. "Feel like playing?" he asked. "I always feel like playing," he said. He drank the last of the bourbon in his glass. "Yes, sir. *Always* feel like that."

"I'll announce you," Charlie said. He carried a chair onto the stage, sat down, and repeated the lecture he uses whenever he hires an old-time musician. It begins, "Without the tradition of American Negro music, there would be no rock music." The lecture's purpose is to inspire the rock generation with love and respect for the blues. However, the audience, none of whom looks older than twenty, seem more interested in each other than anything else.

When the speech ended, with "I am proud to present . . ." Furry, carrying his battered Epiphone guitar, limped onto the stage. The applause was polite. Furry smiled and waved. "Ladies and gentlemen," he began, "I'm very pleased to be here tonight to play for you all. I've been around Memphis, playing and singing, for many years. My wife is with me tonight; we've been married many years. When we got married, I only had fifteen cents and she had a quarter." I looked at Charlie. He avoided my eyes.

"And then one day," Furry went on, his tone altering slightly, "she upped and quit me, said I had married her for her money."

Furry laughed, Versie laughed, the crowd laughed, and Charlie and I looked at each other and laughed and laughed, shaking our heads. "I love him, the old bastard," Charlie said. "Sorry, Versie."

But Versie, watching Furry proudly, had not heard.

He had begun to play a slow, sad blues, one that none of us had ever heard, a song without a name: "My mother's dead," he sang, the guitar softly following, "my father just as well's to be. Ain't got nobody to say one kind word for me."

The room, which had been filled with noise, was now quiet. "People holler mercy," Furry sang, "don't know what mercy mean. People . . ."— and the guitar finished the line. "Well, if it mean any good, Lord, have mercy on me."

When, after nearly an hour, Furry left the stage, the applause was considerably more than polite. But I knew that it was only the third time Furry had heard public applause during the year and that in this year, as in most of the years of his life, his music would probably bring him less than $100. Soon, we would take him home and he would change clothes and go out to sweep the streets. I wondered, as Charlie and Versie were congratulating him and pouring fresh drinks, how he had managed to last, to retain his skill.

Furry was sitting back in his chair, holding a drink in one hand and a new cigar in the other, smiling slightly, his eyes nearly closed. I asked him if he had ever been tempted to give up, to stop playing. "Give out but don't give up," he said. He tasted his drink and sat straighter in the chair. "No," he said, "all these years, I kept working for the city, thinking things might change, Beale Street might go back like it was. But it never did."

"But you went on playing."

"Oh, yes, I played at home. Sometimes, nothing to do, no place to play, I'd hock the guitar and get me something to drink. And then I'd wish I had it, so I could play, even just for myself. I never quit playing, but I didn't play out enough for people to know who I was. Sometimes I'd see a man, a beggar, you know, playing guitar on the sidewalk, and I'd drop something in his cup, and he wouldn't even know who I was. He'd think I was just a street-sweeper."

FURRY'S BLUES AGAIN

The time I spent with my friend—my brother, as he said—Walter "Furry" Lewis was many things. Instructive above all. He was a true shaman, a wise man for our tribe. In the long-ago days a few of us recognized Furry for what he was and became his disciples. My good fortune was to help him a bit at times. My greater fortune was to have him as a guide through life.

One night, over thirty years ago, I went to a blues concert at the Overton Park Shell in Memphis. Furry Lewis, among others, was performing. With me were my lady friend Christopher and a male friend named David Mays. My elegant older friend George Campbell came by for the show. Afterward, he invited David, Christopher, Furry, and me to a party he was attending in East Memphis. George's wife and mistress were both there, along with several Crumps and other Memphis swells. They thought Furry was an old drunk nigger and the rest of George's friends were beatniks, and they threw us out, including George, who, by way of formal protest, pitched one of the host's Princeton glasses against the chimney as we departed. We went to George's house on Morningside Park, being harassed by white racist punks who yelled at us as we drove down Poplar. "I got a knife," Furry told me. "I'll stick right wit' you."

At George's big Tudor-style house, David announced that he was hungry. I went into the kitchen with George and David, leaving Christopher with Furry, who immediately began to improve the time and, he hoped, his chances. "I got forty dollars," he said. "Don't nobody know where it's at but me." Furry liked Christopher a lot. Once, outside Sid

49

and Shirley Selvidge's house on Autumn, as I scraped ice off the windshield of my Cadillac Coupe de Ville, Furry explained to Christopher (they were inside the car where it was nice and warm), "I don't want to put nothin' *in* it—I just want to *kiss* it."

"Settle down, Furry," she said. She knew how to talk to him. At George's, she said, "Let's see what they're doing in the kitchen." George was scrambling eggs. David and I were at the wooden table. Furry, sitting down, said, "I want to pick—guitar. I want to play, 'Lay My Burden Down.' My guitar's in the car. Bring—bring me my burden."

One night, at the Holiday Inn in Nashville, after everyone else had gone home or passed out, Furry and I found ourselves alone with the Parthenon. Again. We were there to meet people from Hollywood who were thinking of casting Furry as himself in a Burt Reynolds movie called *W. W. and the Dixie Dancekings*, and part of Furry's approach to auditioning was to outlast everybody every night. It was 1973, and Furry was a very vigorous eighty years of age.

Older by nearly half a century, Furry would still point at me, white and crazy, and say, "Me and him just like brothers." The boys and girls from California in the denim and turquoise would sit around, drinking and listening to him play, until they all gave up and went to their rooms, and finally even the hardier souls, like Knox Phillips and Jerry Reed, would vanish to their revels or whatever revelations, and Furry and I would be left.

On this particular evening, a warm one, I sat, thoroughly transfixed through chemical and aesthetic processes, looking at and listening to Furry, sitting on the bed across the room from me.

Whenever possible, Furry before going to work would get a rather severe haircut, clipped to the skin all over except for a quiff, a tuft above the widow's peak at the center of his forehead. He had done that before coming to Nashville, and now as he played and sang he told me that how you know you are really doing it is when your guitar answers you:

"'Just one, kind, favor I ask of you, just see—' What is it, guitar? And the guitar says, 'Is my grave kept clean.' . . ."

And at that moment I flashed on the voice booming from the hole in the guitar belly, held over Furry's belly, his voice emerging from his—the karate term is ki—and with his heavy earlobes and shaven peppercorn head and voice speaking from the center of his being I see the simple eternal truth, that Furry is the Buddha—and at that precise instant, raising the hair on the back of my head, Furry says, "Stanley—I'm gon' play it in Japanese one time—" And he plays *My heart stopped beating my hands got cold* three times in some bizarre Oriental scale, then sings, "Next thing, I's in that shady grove." As if he had read my mind. As if . . .

I knew people who had been seduced by Furry into believing—seeing him strike the guitar strings, stand it on end, twirl it like a top, and watch arms folded as it continued to play—that he was some kind of magician. Yes, he was that kind of magician; he used, every so often, to say that he was going to teach me "to pick—pockets." He was also a much greater kind of magician.

Indeed, it would not be entirely untrue to say that Furry was not so much a man as a set of techniques, the central and most reliable of which was, "Give out but don't give up."

———————

Born in Greenwood, Mississippi, in 1893, Furry came to Memphis at the age of six and died there in his ninetieth year. He was there in 1909, when Edward Hull Crump ran for mayor and W. C. Handy wrote a song about it called "The Memphis Blues."

"I'm gon' pick 'St. Louis Blues,'" Furry used to say, "the way I and Handy used to play it." My favorite among his recordings of the song begins with the lines, "Bang away my Lula/ Don't bang away so strong/ Whatcha gon' do for bangin'/ When Lula dead and gone" and then, "Baby/ I hate to see that evenin sun go down." I don't remember anything about Lula in Handy's version of his song, but maybe she slipped his mind.

In 1967, Furry and I were teaching in a War on Poverty program at a Methodist church whose pastor, James Lawson, helped start the Student Nonviolent Coordinating Committee. Furry lived in a small apartment near the corner of Fourth and Beale, the place where the songs on this

CD were recorded. There wasn't a level floor in that whole apartment building—it's gone now—the hallway had a wavy pitch like the swell of the sea. The place smelled like the blues, like sweat and poverty and last night's turnip greens. Many nights I sat up with Furry, drinking, singing, listening, learning. It was the best way to hear him, with his wooden leg off, sitting comfortably in bed, his Pall Malls, glass of beer, revolver, and shotgun (the latter two items out of sight, but only just) within reach.

Less than a year before this recording, a few blocks away, Martin Luther King Jr. had been killed. Furry and I were both caught up in the turmoil that ensued, because he lived in the middle of it and I was already in the middle of it anyway. Or, in a way. Because one of the remarks that stands out from those difficult times, when Memphis was in flames, is something a black friend of mine said to a mutual white friend: "This don't have anything to do with us."

That was true. It didn't have anything to do with Furry, either, though he and I were both for social change and I marched and he was a strong supporter of civil rights. What had to do with Furry was inventive genius and encyclopedic memory of lines and images: "Sal went up the new-cut road, I went up behind her/ Sal bent down to tie her shoe, and I saw her sausage grinder." Furry transformed traditional elements, making them magical or more magical; among his constructions are Nero My God to Thee, Only Forgotten Son, and Will the Circus Be Unbroken. "I want to be a rangel," Furry sang, "And join that rangel band, with a crown upon my fore-head, and a harp-oh, in my hands."

"I don't mean no harm," Furry said every so often. "We just carryin' on fun." It was fun, but it was more than that. Furry sang about a strange traveler who would "eat my supper in the Gulf of Mexico, wake up one thousand miles below." He had songs as old as the plantations: "My ole miss, she promise me/ When she die, she set me free/ She lived so long till her head got bald, and God had to kill her with a white oak maul."

The night Furry died, I saw that fat yellow moon and knew it would carry him off. The funeral was crowded, lots of TV and speeches by people who never knew him, who couldn't have found his house with a police escort. Never mind. He didn't get the three white horses in a line, he didn't get lowered down with a silver chain. I'm sorry to say I haven't visited his grave since his burial, so I don't know if it is being, as he incessantly requested, kept clean.

To tell you the truth, I can hardly believe he's dead. I know a number of people like that, who are simply too talented to be dead. "I ain't got nothin', ain't never had nothin', don't 'spect to never get nothin'," he used to say, "but I'll tell you this: I'm jus' as smart as any man in this house." He always was, too.

SITUATION REPORT:
ELVIS IN MEMPHIS, 1967

My Memphis friend John Fergus Ryan, who once said, "Room service? Would you send up a jar of molasses and an anthill?" told me the name of an editor he knew at *Esquire*, to whom, late in 1966, I sent "Furry's Blues." In December I entered a form of marriage with my mentor, Christopher. We went on our honeymoon to New York City, where we stayed out all night listening to people like Miles Davis and slept until late the next afternoon. Daily I'd call the *Esquire* editor, Robert Sherrill, but never heard from him. The day before we left New York I phoned one last time and told Sherrill's secretary that I was leaving town so if he wanted me he'd better get in touch. Then I took a shower, in the midst of which Sherrill called. Having heard that *Esquire* wanted an Elvis Presley profile, I reminded him of "Furry's Blues" and suggested that I could provide the Presley piece.

"Why don't you come over," Sherrill said. "I ain't got anything to do this afternoon. We can go to the Chock Full and talk about it."

"Where you from?" I asked.

"North Carolina."

Sherrill turned out to be a fine editor and one of the smartest men I've ever met. (He predicted in 1967 that the era of peace and love would end in violence and bloodshed, as I recalled at Altamont.) I told him stories about Elvis I'd heard from my mother, who saw Priscilla at the beauty parlor, and Charles Clarke, my family's physician, who'd been Gladys Presley's doctor. Sherrill laughed at the stories and told me to go ahead with the piece. That's how hard it was to do business with *Esquire* in 1967.

Doing business with Elvis Presley was another matter. John Ryan, attempting to do a Presley story after four or five other writers had failed, drafted a request to Colonel Parker, Presley's manager, saying in essence, "Presley is loved by everyone except the intellectuals.

Let me write a piece about him and make the intellectuals love him." Colonel Parker, aware that there are at most three or four dozen intellectuals on Earth, declined the honor. I didn't approach the Colonel; I started looking for Dewey Phillips. He had been, a dozen or so years before, maybe the most famous and influential character in the Mid-South. By 1967 he had vanished.

Milton Pond, who worked at Poplar Tunes record store, located a number for Dewey at a business in Millington, Tennessee, a suburb of Memphis. The man who answered said he might not see Dewey for a week. Ten minutes later my phone rang. "Hello! Elvis?" Dewey would always call me Elvis or Birdbrain.

In Millington I found Dewey alone in a furniture store that contained nothing but a desk, a folding chair, and a phone. God knows what went on there. Dewey and I had been talking for a while about some of our favorite singers, such as Wynonie Harris and Percy Mayfield, recalling the designs of certain record labels, when he looked out the plate-glass window, made a characteristic palm-against-chest neck-stretching gesture, and gave me the lead of a lifetime. I knew that anyone who saw the first four words would finish reading the piece, hoping that it contained more of the same. I also knew *Esquire* wouldn't print it, so I double-spaced after the first paragraph and started over.

". . . Talkin' about eatin' pussy, me and Sam Phillips used to make old Elvis sick with that stuff. We'd sit around the studio, down at Sun Records, and talk about how good it was, and he'd get so sick he'd go out back and puke. Then he went to Hollywood, made all them movies and come back, and one night we're all down at the studio, Elvis and Sam and me, and Jerry Lee Lewis, whole bunch of us there, and Elvis says, 'Mister Sam, you remember when yawl used to make me sick talkin' about eatin' pussy?' Sam says, 'What about it?' 'Well,' Elvis says, 'I eat me some the other night. But man, now I'm in trouble.' So Sam asks him, 'Who was it you eat?' because we thought right off that Elvis had eat somebody's wife and got caught. But he says, 'Natalie Wood,' and Sam says, 'Well, hellfire, boy, what's your trouble?' and Elvis said, 'Damn if I didn't fall in love with it.'"

Between Memphis and Walls (you turn right a bit past a big sign saying Church of God, Pastor C. B. Brantley, drink dr. pepper), there is a small ranch, 160 green and gently rolling acres, a prettier spread than you'd expect to see in the poor, bleak land of north Mississippi. The owner, at thirty-three, has been a millionaire for more than ten years. He has other, more elegant homesteads, but these days he prefers the ranch. Behind the formidable chain-link fence and the eight-foot picket walls that hide his neat red-brick house, he finds a degree of privacy to share with his pretty new wife. The privacy is also shared by twenty-two pure-bred horses, counting colts, and nine hired hands, counting guards. (There were twelve hands, but the number was reduced recently, so the story goes around the ranch, at the request of the owner's wife.) Then, too, there are the continual visitors—the ones who are allowed inside (some driving Cadillacs given them by the owner as Christmas or birthday presents) and the ones who must stay outside, peering over or through the fences. At times, such as when the owner is out riding, the roadside is solidly lined with sightseeing cars. Privacy—the privacy in which to enjoy his leisure time—is extremely valuable to the ranch's young owner, especially since he works less than half the year. Taxes would make more work pointless; his annual income is about $5 million.

And yet, not too many years ago, he was living in a federal low-rent housing project, working as a truck driver, movie usher, sometimes forced to sell his blood at ten dollars a pint. Elvis Presley, a Great American Success Story.

By the ranch's main gate, in an air-conditioned hut, sits Elvis's Uncle Travis, a small, grinning man, with hair as black and skin as dark as an Indian's. A straw cowboy hat rests on his knee. He wears black Western pants and a white shirt with E. P. monogrammed in black Gothic script across the front. Travis likes to reminisce about the girls he has captured and ejected from his nephew's premises. "I dragged one out from under the old pink Cadillac. She must have heard me comin' and hid under there, and all I saw was her feet stickin' out. I said, 'Come on out of there,' and she didn't move, so I reached down, took ahold of her feet, and pulled. She had a coat of motor oil a inch thick." Travis belches.

"Slip in. Jump a fence like a billygoat. If they can't climb over, they'll crawl under. If the gate ain't locked they'll drive right through. I had a carload slip past me up at Graceland. Hell, I didn't even go after them, I just locked the damn gate. They made the circle in front of the house, come back down the drive, and when they seen they couldn't get out, the one drivin' says, 'Please op'n the gate.' I told her, 'Yes, ma'am, soon's the sheriff's got there.' Made out I was real hot, you know. She says, 'Please don't call the sheriff, my mama will kill me.' I said, 'Not till you get out of jail, I don't reckon.' She like to died. Then I started laughin', and they seen it was all right, and asked me if they could come back after a while and talk. So I told them yeah, but while they was gone I got to thinkin', Why'd they have to leave, why couldn't they just stay and talk? But one of they mamas came back with them, and she told on them. I'd scared her daughter so bad she'd peed her pants."

Travis pitches his head back and laughs, displaying a strong white set of uppers. Parked in the drive is a shiny red Ford Ranchero with his name, T. J. Smith, on one door under the ranch's Circle G brand, actually a flying Circle G. I asked what the G stands for.

"Could be Graceland," Travis says, "or it could be his mother's name. He meant it to stand for her name." Travis's expression becomes serious when he speaks of Elvis's dead mother, his own sister. "He still keeps that old pink Cadillac he bought for her. Don't never drive it, just keeps it as a keepsake. He's got all the cars he needs. Had a Rolls-Royce up on blocks four or five years. Bought a hundred thousand dollars' worth of trucks and trailers right after he got this place. Money ain't nothing to him. Ole boy from Hernando was down there the other evenin' workin' on the fence, and Elvis drove down in one of his new pickups to take a look. Feller says, 'Shore do like that truck. Always wanted me one of them.' So Elvis says, 'You got a dollar?' Feller says, 'Yeah, I got one,' and gives it to Elvis. 'It's your truck,' Elvis says."

Next Travis tells how Priscilla, the new wife, likes Elvis to take her for rides in one of his souped-up go-karts (top speed, more than 100 mph) around the driveway at Graceland, tantalizing the squealing girls outside the fence.

Then he spits. "I sit down here, keepin' people out, seven in the mornin' till six in the evenin', five days a week, and I'm about wore out. I think I'll go in the hospital for two or three weeks, take me a rest."

"Maybe you could get a television set to watch while you're working," I suggest.

"Yeah, I believe I will get me one. Either that, or some funny books."

Just outside the gate, in a rented green Impala, are two girls who have come, so they tell me, all the way from New Zealand. "Is he home?" they ask.

"Who?"

One sneers, one ignores. "Did you talk to him? What did he say?"

I look away, trying to select a representative quote. On the roof of the house across the road a man is kneeling behind a camera, snapping pictures of the Circle G. "Let's ride up to Rosemark tomorrow and look at that mare," I tell the girls.

"Pardon?"

"That's what he said."

"What, is that all?"

"You should have been here yesterday. He said, 'Would somebody please bring me a Pepsi?'" Pepsi-Cola, I would have explained to the girls, is Elvis's favorite drink, just as his favorite snack is peanut-butter-and-mashed-banana sandwiches; but the Impala roars away, leaving a cloud of dust to settle on my shoes.

Some time ago, before I saw for myself what Elvis is like, I asked a mutual acquaintance about him. "He's all right," I was told. "Pretty interesting guy to talk to."

"Really? What's the most interesting thing he's ever said to you?" My friend sat and thought, pulling the hair on his chin. Finally he said, "Well, once he told me, 'Like your beard. How long'd it take you to grow it?' I said it took about three months, and he said, 'I'd like to grow me one sometime, but I don't think I could get away with it. Y'know?' And he sort of winked."

Another friend, whose relation to the Presley household was for a time unique, told me that Elvis is a very straight guy, who uses neither grass nor acid. In Hollywood, Elvis never goes to nightclubs or premieres. Except for work, he hardly leaves his Bel-Air mansion. "He's afraid he wouldn't know how to act," says one of his oldest friends. "And he wouldn't."

Even in Memphis, his recreational activities have been, for a millionaire, unpretentious. In the early days at Graceland (the large, white-columned estate, rather like an antebellum funeral parlor, which Elvis bought in 1957), the big kick was roller-skating. After a local rink closed for the evening, Presley and his entourage would come in, skate, eat hot dogs, and drink Pepsi-Cola till dawn. When skating palled, Elvis started renting the entire Fair Grounds amusement park, where he and his friends could ride the Tilt-a-Whirl, Ferris wheel, roller coaster, dodgem cars (Elvis's favorite), and eat hot dogs and drink Pepsis till dawn. Until quite recently, Presley has been in the habit of hiring a local movie theatre (the Memphian) and showing rented movies, favoring the films of actresses he has dated. The Memphian has no hot dog facilities but provides plenty of popcorn and, of course, Pepsis. Now that he is married and an expectant father, he does not get out so much at night, but the daytime is as glamorous, as exciting, as ever.

On a day not so long ago, when Presley happened to be staying at Graceland, the house was crowded with friends and friends of friends, all waiting for old El to wake up, come downstairs, and turn them on with his presence. People were wandering from room to room, looking for action, and there was little to be found. In the basement—a large, divided room with gold records hung in frames around the walls, creating a sort of halo effect—they were shooting pool or lounging under the Pepsi-Cola signs at the soda fountain. (When Elvis likes something, he *really* likes it.) In the living room boys and girls were sprawled, nearly unconscious with boredom, over the long white couches, among the deep snowy drifts of rug. One girl was standing by the enormous picture window, absently pushing one button, then another, activating an electrical traverse rod, opening and closing the red velvet drapes. On a table beside the fireplace of smoky molded glass, a pink ceramic elephant was sniffing the artificial roses. Nearby, in the music room, a thin, dark-haired boy who had been lying on the cloth-of-gold couch, watching Joel McCrea on the early movie, snapped the remote-control switch, turning off the ivory television set. He yawned, stretched, went to the white, gilt-trimmed piano, sat down on the matching stool, and began to play. He was not bad, playing a kind of limp, melancholy boogie, and soon there was an audience facing him, their backs to the door.

Then, all at once, through the use of perceptions which could only be described as extrasensory, everyone in the room knew that Elvis was there. And, stranger still, nobody moved. Everyone kept his cool. Out of the corner of an eye Presley could be seen, leaning against the doorway, looking like Lash LaRue in boots, black Levis, and a black silk shirt.

The piano player's back stiffens, but he is into the bag and has to boogie his way out. "What is this, amateur night?" someone mutters. Finally—it cannot have been more than a minute—the music stops. Everyone turns toward the door. Well I'll be damn. It's Elvis. What say, boy? Elvis smiles, but does not speak. In his arms he is cradling a big blue model airplane.

A few minutes later, the word—the sensation—having passed through the house, the entire company is out on the lawn, where Presley is trying to start the plane. About half the group has graduated into the currently fashionable Western clothing, and the rest are wearing the traditional pool-hustler's silks. They all watch intently as Elvis, kneeling over the plane, tries for the tenth time to make the tiny engine turn over; when it splutters and dies, a groan, as of one voice, rises from the crowd.

Elvis stands, mops his brow (though of course he is not perspiring), takes a thin cigar from his shirt pocket and peels away the cellophane wrapping. When he puts the cigar between his teeth a wall of flame erupts before him. Momentarily startled, he peers into the blaze of matches and lighters offered by willing hands. With a nod he designates one of the crowd, who steps forward, shaking, ignites the cigar and then, his moment of glory, of service to the King, at an end, he retires into anonymity. "Thank ya very much," says Elvis.

They begin to seem quite insane, the meek circle proffering worship and lights, the young ladies trembling under Cadillacs, the tourists outside, standing on the roofs of cars, waiting to be blessed by even a glimpse of this young god, this slightly plump idol, whose face grows more babyish with each passing year.

But one exaggerates. They are not insane, only mistaken, believing their dumpling god to be Elvis Presley. He is not. One remembers— indeed, one could hardly forget—Elvis Presley.

The time is the early '50s, and the scene is dull. Dwight Eisenhower is president, Perry Como is the leading pop singer. The world has changed (it changed in 1945), but the change is not yet evident. Allen Ginsberg is a market researcher for a San Francisco securities company. William Burroughs is in New Orleans, cooking down codeine cough syrup. Malcolm X, paroled from Massachusetts's Charlestown Prison, is working in a Detroit furniture store. Stokely Carmichael is skinny, insolent, and eleven years old.

It is, let us say, 1953. Fred Zinnemann rehashes the past with *From Here to Etenity*, and Laslo Benedek gives us, in *The Wild One*, a taste of the future. This is a movie with good guys and bad guys, and the good guys are the ones who roar on motorcycles into a town that is small, quiet, typically American, and proceed to take it apart. Their leader, Marlon Brando, will be called an antihero. But there is no need for the prefix. He is a new, really contemporary hero: the outcast.

Soon James Dean repeats the theme with even greater success. But Dean's career was absurdly short. "You know he was dead before he knew who he was," someone said. The outcasts of America were left without a leader.

Then, one Saturday night early in 1956 on a television variety program, a white singer drawls at the camera: "Ladies and gentlemen, I'd like to do a song now, that tells a little story, that really makes a lot of sense—Awopbopaloobop—alopbamboom! Tutti-frutti! All rootie! Tutti-frutti! All rootie!"

Though nearly all significant popular music was produced by Negroes, a white rhythm and blues singer was not an entirely new phenomenon. Bill Haley and the Comets had succeeded with such songs as "Shake, Rattle and Roll," and "Rock Around the Clock." But the pudgy Haley, in his red plaid dinner jacket, did not project much personal appeal. This other fellow was something else.

He was not quite a hillbilly, not yet a drugstore cowboy. He was a southern—in that word's connotation of rebellion and slow, sweet charm—version of the character Brando created in *The Wild One*. Southern high school girls, the "nice" ones, called these boys "hoods." You saw them lounging on the hot concrete of a gas station on a Saturday afternoon, or coming out of a poolroom at three o'clock of a Monday afternoon, stopping for a second on the sidewalk as if they were looking for someone who was looking for a fight. You even see their sullen faces, with a toughness lanky enough to just miss being delicate, looking back at you out of old photographs of the Confederate Army. They were not named Tab or Rock, nor even Jim, Bill, Bob. They all had names like Leroy, Floyd, Elvis. All outcasts, with their contemporary costumes of duck-ass haircuts, greasy Levis, motorcycle boots, T-shirts for day and black leather jackets for evening wear. Even their unfashionably long sideburns (Elvis's were *furry*) expressed contempt for the American dream they were too poor to be part of.

No one writing about Presley should forget the daring it took to be one of these boys, and to sing. A hood might become a mechanic or a house painter or a bus driver or even a cop, but nobody would expect him to be a singer. If he tried it at all, he would have to have some of his own crowd playing with him; he'd have to sing some old songs his own people had sung before him; and he would have to sing them in his own way, regardless of what people might say about him.

"Mama, do you think I'm vulgar on the stage?"

"Son, you're not vulgar, but you're puttin' too much into your singin'. Keep that up and you won't live to be thirty."

"I can't help it, Mama. I just have to jump around when I sing. But it ain't vulgar. It's just the way I feel. I don't feel sexy when I'm singin'. If that was true, I'd be in some kinda institution as some kinda sex maniac."

These days, when asked about the development of his career, Elvis either ignores the question or refers it to "my manager." Generally speaking his manager is the person standing closest to him at the time. This is often Alan Fortas, officially the ranch foreman, a young man only slightly less stocky than a bull, with a history of hostility to reporters. When the Beatles visited Elvis in Hollywood, Fortas, not troubling to remember their names, addressed each of them as, "Hey, Beatle!" They always answered, too: nobody wants to displease Alan.

A more voluble source of information is Dewey Phillips. During Elvis's early career Phillips was probably as close to him as anyone except his mother, Gladys. Now retired, Phillips was then one of the most popular and influential disc jockeys in the nation. He still speaks the same hillbilly jive he used as a broadcaster.

"Nobody was picking up on the ole boy back then. He was a real bashful kid, but he liked to hang around music. They'd chased him away from the switchboard at WMPS, and he'd come hang around Q. That's WHBQ, where I was doing my show, *Red Hot and Blue*, every night. Weekends, he'd come down to Sun Records—he'd cut that record, 'My Happiness,' for his mother, paid four dollars for it himself—and Sam Phillips, president of Sun, finally gave him a session. Tried to record a ballad, but he couldn't cut it. Sam got Bill Black, the piano player, and Scotty Moore, the guitarist, to see if they could work anything out with him.

"After a couple of tries, Elvis, Bill and Scotty fixed up a couple of old songs, 'That's All Right, Mama' and 'Blue Moon of Kentucky,' so they sounded a little different. When Elvis began to cut loose with 'That's All Right,' Sam came down and recorded these son-of-a-guns. One night I played the record thirty times. Fifteen times each side. When the phone calls and telegrams started to come in, I got hold of Elvis's daddy, Vernon. He said Elvis was at a movie, down at Suzore's number two theater. 'Get him over here,' I said. And before long Elvis came running in. 'Sit down, I'm going to interview you,' I said. He said, 'Mr. Phillips, I don't know nothing about being interviewed.' 'Just don't say nothing dirty,' I told him.

"He sat down, and I said I'd let him know when we were ready to start. I had a couple of records cued up, and while they played we talked. I asked him where he went to school, and he said Humes. I wanted to get that out, because a lot of people listening had thought he was colored. Finally I said, 'All right, Elvis, thank you very much.' 'Aren't you gone interview me?' he asked. 'I already have,' I said. 'The mike's been open the whole time.' He broke out in a cold sweat."

According to Phillips, Elvis at this time considered himself a country singer. "Sam used to get him, Roy Orbison, Jerry Lee Lewis, and Johnny Cash down at Sun and play Big Bill Broonzy and Arthur Crudup records for them, trying to get them on the blues thing, because he felt like that was going to be hot. One of Elvis's first public appearances was at a hillbilly jamboree at the downtown auditorium. Webb Pierce was there, and Carl Smith, Minnie Pearl, a whole houseful of hillbillies. Elvis was nervous, said he wanted me with him. But Sam and I were out at my house, drinking beer, or we had something going, and I missed the afternoon show. Elvis came looking for me, mad as hell. I asked him what he'd sung and he said, 'Old Shep' and 'That's How My Heartaches Begin.'

"What happened? 'Nothing.'

"So that night I went along with him and told him to open with 'Good Rockin' Tonight' and not to sing any hillbilly songs. I introduced him and stayed onstage while he sang. He went into 'Good Rockin',' started to shake, and the place just blew apart. He was nobody, didn't even have his name on the posters, but the people wouldn't let him leave. When we finally went off we walked past Webb Pierce, who had been waiting in the wings to go on. I smiled at him and he said, 'You son of a bitch.'"

The sales of Elvis's records enabled him to get more bookings, and Dewey Phillips bought him an old Lincoln sedan for $450 so he could play out-of-town jobs. Appearing in Nashville at a convention of the Country and Western Disc Jockeys' Association, he was seen—"discovered"—by talent scouts for RCA Victor. In a moviehouse matinee in Texarkana, he was discovered by Thomas Andrew Parker, a latter-day Barnum out of W. C. Fields by William Burroughs. Parker, an illegal immigrant from Holland, had created a fictional canny background for himself: he had worked in his uncle's "Great Parker Pony Circus," dipped candied apples, shaved ice for snow cones, operated merry-go-rounds, even put in a stretch as dogcatcher in Tampa, Florida.

Astute techniques in these businesses had enabled Parker to rise in the world to a position of some prestige. The title "Colonel" had been conferred upon him by, as he put it, "a few governors." He was managing the careers of such big-name country entertainers as Hank Snow and Eddy Arnold. But in all his years as a promoter, he had never found so promotable a commodity as Presley. He had seen Elvis at, for his purposes, just the right time. The demand for Elvis's records prompted RCA to offer $35,000 for Presley, lock, stock, and tapes. Sam Phillips accepted.

"Elvis knew he was going big time," Dewey Phillips remembers, "and he needed a manager. That was late spring of '55. He was the hottest thing in show business, and still just a scared kid. He had got his mother and daddy a nice house, they had three Cadillacs, and no phone. He asked me to be his manager. I told him I didn't know anything about managing. Then Colonel Parker came to town. He knew what he was doing. He didn't talk to Elvis. He went out to the house and told Gladys what he could do for the boy. That Parker is a shrewd moo-foo, man."

Elvis's first appearances on network television, on the *Tommy and Jimmy Dorsey Show* in January and February 1956, changed him from a regional phenomenon into a national sensation. This might not have happened, the American public might simply have shuddered and turned away, had there not been a new group among them: teenagers, the enemy within. When the older generation, repelled by Presley's lean, mean, sexy image, attacked him from pulpits and editorial columns, banned him from radio stations, the teenagers liked him more than ever, and went out and bought his records. Entrepreneurs could not afford to ignore Presley. As one radio producer asked: How can you argue with the country's number-one recording star? Reluctantly, almost unwillingly, show business accepted Elvis. Ed Sullivan, who only a couple of months before had condemned Presley as "unfit for a family audience," now was obliged to pay him $50,000 for three brief appearances. However, Elvis was photographed only from the waist up, and his material was diluted by the addition of a ballad, "Love Me Tender," which oozed syrup.

Such attempts to make Elvis appear respectable were very offensive to the good old boys back in Memphis. Steve Allen, involved in a ratings battle with Sullivan, booked Presley, but assured the audience that they would see only "clean family entertainment." Elvis appeared and sang, standing still, wearing white tie and tails, with top hat and cane, but without a guitar. Just after the show went off the air, Dewey Phillips's telephone rang.

"Hello, you bastard," Dewey said.

"How'd you know it was me?" asked Elvis.

"You better call home and get straight, boy. What you doing in that monkey suit? Where's your guitar?"

So when Elvis made his next hometown appearance (it was on July 4, 1956) he reassured his people. The occasion was a charity benefit and Colonel Parker had turned down paying engagements so that Elvis could be part of the show. His was the closing spot, and he was preceded by more than a hundred performers, including the orchestra of Bob Morris and Aaron Bluestein, the Admiral's Band of Navy Memphis, a barbershop quartet called the Confederates, Charlotte Morgan's dancing Dixie Dolls, and innumerable singers, by no means the least of which was one Helen Putnam, founder of Fat Girls Anonymous, who dedicated "A Good Man Is Hard to Find" to Elvis.

After nearly three hours, with the audience so bored that it was on the point of having a religious experience, Dewey Phillips, who was master of ceremonies, said, "All right. Here he is," and there he was, his hair hanging over his forehead, a wad of gum in his jaw. He wore a black suit, black shoes, black shirt, red tie, and red socks, clothes with so much drape and flash that they created a new sartorial category, somewhere on the other side of corny. He sang all the old songs in the old way, from "That's All Right" to "Blue Suede Shoes" to "Heartbreak Hotel." He sang until he was dripping with sweat, and when at last he spoke, his words were a promise to his friends, a gift of defiance to his enemies: "I just want to tell y'awl not to worry—them people in New York and Hollywood are not gone change me none."

Then his voice became a growl, an act of rebellion: "You ain't nothin' but a houn' dog," he sang, and proceeded to have sexual intercourse with the microphone.

> They told me you was high class
> Well, that was just a lie—

If the police had not been there, forming a blue wall around the stage, the audience might have eaten Elvis's body in a eucharistic frenzy. They were his and he was theirs, their leader: it was an incandescent moment.

And the same time it was a climactic one. For as he stood there singing defiance at his natural enemies—those with power, prestige, money—the Humes High School hood, the motorcycle jockey, was gone, and in his place there was a star, with power, prestige, money. A few months from now at about three o'clock one morning, he would be standing with one of his hired companions outside the Strand Theatre on Main Street in Memphis when a couple of his high-street classmates would drive past, not going much of anywhere, just dragging Main. They would slow their car as they came alongside the Strand; they would see it was Elvis; and then, without a word, they would drive on. "A few years ago," Elvis said, "they would have spoken to me."

Elvis had tried to go on being himself. When Paramount offered him a movie contract with a clause forbidding him to ride motorcycles, he said, "I'd rather not make movies." They let him keep his motorcycles. All that was really necessary was that he stop doing his thing and start doing theirs. His thing was "Mystery Train," "Milkcow Blues Boogie." Theirs was "Love Me Tender," "Loving You," "Jailhouse Rock," "King Creole."

Then he was drafted. The army cut his hair, took away his fancy clothes, and Elvis let them. His country had served him well and he was willing to serve his country. He is nothing if not fair-minded.

While he was stationed in Fort Hood, Texas, Elvis moved his parents to a rented house in the nearby town of Killeen. His mother, who had been doing poorly for more than a year, worsened, and on August 8, 1958, Elvis put her on a train to Methodist Hospital in Memphis and requested the customary special leave.

It was refused. When Gladys's doctors, at Elvis's request, advised his command of the seriousness of his mother's illness they were told, in effect, "If it were anybody else, there'd be no problem. It's standard procedure. But if we let Presley go everybody will yell special privilege."

Days passed while Gladys Presley sank lower and lower. In spite of constant urging from Elvis and the doctors, the leave still was not granted. Finally, on the morning of August 12, Elvis decided that he had had enough. "If I don't get a pass by two o'clock this afternoon," he said, "I'll be home tonight."

The doctors reasoned with him, urged him to remember that he set an example for millions of other boys. But Elvis had made up his mind. A Humes High boy can be pushed only so far. They could only advise the command of Elvis's plans.

So naturally, the pass came through. The army is not that dumb. Elvis had the same rights as any other American boy.

Back in Memphis Elvis fought his way through the crowds of newsmen outside the hospital. He was in his mother's room for only a few minutes; then he came out, walked down the hall to an empty waiting room, sank into a chair and cried.

His mother had been the one, perhaps the only one, who had told him throughout his life that even though he came from poor country people, he was just as good as anyone. His success had not surprised her, nor had it changed her. Shortly after Gladys Presley was buried, her husband and son were standing on the magnificent front steps at Graceland. "Look, Daddy," Elvis sobbed, pointing to the chickens his mother had kept on the lawn of the hundred-thousand-dollar mansion. "Mama won't never feed them chickens no more."

He never really got over his mother's death. He treasured for many years, in his office at Graceland, a lighted, fully decorated, artificial Christmas tree, a souvenir of the last Christmas the family spent together. He had the tree cared for all the time he was in Germany, where the army had put him safely away.

Elvis liked Germany, and both he and his father found wives there. When his tour of duty was ended, he came out with sergeant's stripes. The whole thing was fictionally celebrated in *G.I. Blues*, a happy movie with a multimillion-dollar gross. One Elvis Presley film followed another: *Flaming Star, Wild in the Country, Blue Hawaii, Girls! Girls! Girls!, Kid Galahad, Follow That Dream, It Happened at the World's Fair, Fun in Acapulco, Viva Las Vegas, Kissin' Cousins, Roustabout, Girl Happy, Tickle Me, Harem Scarem, Frankie and Johnny, Paradise—Hawaiian Style, Spinout, Easy Come, Easy Go, Double Trouble, Speedway, Clambake.* They all have two things in common: none lost money, none is contingent at any point upon reality.

But this is not quite true; there is one reality that they reflect. In *Fun in Acapulco*, Elvis walks into a bar that is full of Mexicans, all of whom have good teeth. A mariachi band is playing. Elvis comes in on the chorus, and carries away the verse. Everyone applauds. The men smile and the girls turn on to him. They all think he is a hell of a fellow. One expects that at any moment he may produce a model plane and lead them out onto the lawn.

Elvis has fulfilled the American dream: he is young, rich, famous, adored. Hardly a day passes in Memphis without a politician wanting to name something after him. So far nothing has been found worthy of the honor. Presley has become a young man of whom his city and his country can be truly proud.

And he may not even know whether he misses the old days, the old Elvis. At Graceland, through the powder-white living room, past the gilded piano, there is a door that looks out onto the swimming pool. If you had been standing there on a recent afternoon, you would have seen Elvis, all alone for a change, riding his motorcycle around the pool, around and around and around.

THE MEMPHIS SOUL SOUND

The *Esquire* piece stung Presley, as I'd intended. "Elvis asked me about it," Dewey told me. "I said I didn't know nothin'." A few months later, Presley was working before a live audience for the first time in eight years, making "The Boxing Ring Special," broadcast in December 1968. Maybe he would have done it anyway.

———————

While writing "Furry's Blues" I had begun to envision a book about older blues artists, men like Bukka White, Gus Cannon, Fred McDowell. Writing about poor old black men seemed safe—the Uncle Remus syndrome, I suppose. I sent the Furry piece to many magazines, all of whom said nice things but declined to publish it. The *New Yorker*'s rejection slip read, "The enclosed has a pleasant tone, we felt, but does not appear to be our peculiar kind of nonfiction piece."

Publishing the Elvis story in *Esquire* made me a professional journalist, something I'd never wanted to be. After a conference with a subliterate editor at the *Saturday Evening Post*, a periodical that symbolized much of what I hated about America, I found myself doing a piece for them about the music created in such Memphis studios as Stax and American. I went to these places at the right time. I began to specialize in funerals.

Before the altar at the Clayborn Temple African Methodist Episcopal Church in Memphis, Tennessee, there are three white coffins. Outside, in a freezing drizzle, hundreds of people with umbrellas are trying to shove past the ones who have stopped at the church entrance to buy the glossy eight-by-ten photographs being sold there. The photographs show six teenaged boys, one of them white, the rest Negro, looking like a team of bright young pool hustlers in silk suits with short, double-breasted jackets and black shirts with long roll collars. The name of the group is printed at the bottom: THE BAR-KAYS.

The photographs cost a dollar, but inside you are given an eight-page illustrated program. "OBSEQUIES," the cover announces in gothic print, "of the late Carl Cunningham, Jimmy Lee King, Matthew Kelly." Then there is another of the Bar-Kays' promotional pictures, with no indication which of them is which. Everybody knows that Carl is the one smiling in the center, and Jimmy is the one with glasses, kneeling down front. Matthew is not in the picture, because he was not a Bar-Kay, but the Bar-Kays' valet.

James Alexander, the plump boy standing at the left, was not on the plane that crashed a week earlier, killing several people, including the Bar-Kays' employer, singer Otis Redding. Ben Cauley, with a lip goatee, kneeling opposite Jimmy King, was the only survivor. The other two Bar-Kays are in Madison, Wisconsin. Phalon Jones, with the nicely processed hair, is at a local funeral parlor, and Ronnie Caldwell, the lanky white boy, is still in Lake Monona, where the crash occurred.

Inside the program, on facing pages, there are individual photographs and biographical sketches of Jimmy King and Carl Cunningham. Jimmy, the group's guitarist and leader, "constantly sought to produce the degree of excellence in his performance that would bring kings to their feet and comfort and solace to men of lowest degree." Carl was a drummer, and "the music which poured from his soul reached the hearts of thousands of souls around the world. The rhythm of his drums still beats out a melody which lingers on and on." Matthew, the valet, is not pictured, but does receive his own, rather stark, biography: "His formal education began in the Memphis School System and continued until God moved in heaven and pronounced that his pilgrimage through life had ended."

The old-fashioned church, with tall stained-glass windows and an overhanging semicircular balcony, is packed to the walls with mourners. A very fat nurse is on duty, and pretty girls in ROTC uniforms are acting as ushers. As the white-gloved pallbearers come down the center aisle, the Booker T. Washington High School Band, seated up in the choir loft, begins a slow, shaking rendition of "When Day Is Done," and all the relatives, friends, and fans of the Bar-Kays stand in silent tribute.

In a square on Beale Street, just a block away, the figure of W. C. Handy, molded in brass, stands in the rain. Since the Civil War there have been many funerals of young men who died in the pursuit of their music. In the old days they died of train wrecks, shooting scrapes, or unmentionable diseases. Now there are other hazards, but the ritual, the honor, remains the same. At the Clayborn Temple, an usher with creamed-coffee skin dabs at her long-lashed eyes, and somehow you cannot help thinking that the Bar-Kays might have lived out their lives and become old men without achieving anything to equal this glorious traditional celebration.

The official eulogy is presented by one of the church elders, a white-haired gentleman who speaks briefly and eloquently, and closes with a memory: "When I was a boy on Beale Street, we had no electric streetlamps. It was the era of the gaslight, and every evening towards dark the lamplighter would come along in his cart. Frequently night would overtake him as he proceeded slowly down the street, so that as you looked after him, he would vanish in the blackness, and you could not see where he was, but by the glowing light of the lamps, you could see where he had been.

"Now these boys have gone from us into the darkness where we can no longer see them. But when we hear a certain melody and rhythm, when we hear that *soul sound*—then we will remember, and we will know where they have been."

The early blues musicians were relatively unsophisticated performers, playing unamplified guitar, harmonica, and such primitive instruments as the jug and the tub bass. Professional songwriters, like W. C. Handy, and early recording companies, such as Vocalion and RCA Victor, capitalized on the initial popularity of the blues. But the Depression brought an end to the profits, and the Memphis music business did not revive until after World War Two, with another generation of blues men. They played amplified instruments and for the first time attracted a sizable white audience. A record producer has labeled the early blues "race" music, but the wider appeal and newly added heavy back beat caused the music of Muddy Waters, John Lee Hooker, and Howlin' Wolf to be called rhythm and blues.

Elvis Presley in his earliest recordings combined the music of the country whites with rhythm and blues, and therefore probably deserves to be remembered as the first modern soul singer. As one contemporary soul musician has said, "Country and western music is the music of the white masses. Rhythm and blues is the music of the Negro masses. Today soul music is becoming the music of all the people."

Presley's reign was followed by a period of weak, derivative rock and roll, lasting from the late '50s through the early '60s, until the advent of the Beatles. The Beatles themselves, in the beginning, were not essentially different from the better white pop groups, such as Dion and the Belmonts. But the progress of their music toward greater complexity prepared the way for public acceptance of the candid lyrics and experimental techniques that have always been part of the Memphis sound.

The "new freedom" enjoyed by the pop community was present on the 1920s' recordings of Furry Lewis and Cannon's Jug Stampers; it was there on the early Sun records of Elvis Presley and Howlin' Wolf; and it exists now on the Stax/Volt recordings of Sam and Dave, Otis Redding, and the Mar-Keys. The Mar-Keys, whose rhythm section records alone under the name Booker T. and the MGs (Memphis Group), work as the Stax/Volt house band. The Bar-Kays were hired and trained by Stax to be the road band, because the Mar-Keys, almost constantly busy recording with the company's artists, limit their public engagements to weekends and special occasions, such as Otis Redding's appearance last summer at the Monterey Pop Festival.

At the festival, that celebration of the psychedelic/freak-out/blow-your-mind pop culture, it was sometimes difficult to tell the musicians from the dervishes. The Who exploded smoke bombs and demolished their instruments onstage. Jimi Hendrix, having made a variety of obscene overtures to his guitar, set fire to it, smashed it, and threw the fragments at the audience. But, as one journalist put it, "the most tumultuous reception of the Festival" went to Otis and the Mar-Keys, all of them conservatively dressed and groomed, succeeding with nothing more then musicianship and a sincere feeling for the roots of the blues.

These basic qualities have characterized Memphis music from the beginning, but they had never before raised it to such a position of leadership. In the next few months, Otis would be voted the world's leading male singer by the British pop music journal *Melody Maker*. The same poll would rate Steve Cropper, the Mar-Keys' guitarist, fifth among musicians. *Billboard* magazine named Booker T. and the MGs the top instrumental group of the year, as did the National Academy of Recording Arts and Sciences (NARAS), and the National Association of Radio Announcers, which also selected the MGs' hit single, "Hip Hug-Her," as the year's best instrumental recording. NARAS voted Carla Thomas, a Stax vocalist, the most promising female artist of the year. The US armed forces in Vietnam named her their favorite singer.

Earlier in the year, Otis, the Mar-Keys, Sam and Dave, Carla Thomas, and other Stax/Volt artists had completed a successful European tour, out of which came a series of powerful live recordings. The Beatles wanted to record an album at the Stax/Volt studios, but security problems made it impossible. The album was to have been produced by guitarist Cropper, who, according to George Harrison, is "fahntahstic."

The technical ability possessed by the Memphis musicians can be acquired, but their feeling of affinity with the music seems to be inbred. The Memphis soul sound grows out of a very special environment.

The Mar-Keys, and Booker T. and the MGs, are listed as honorary pallbearers on the program, along with the Heat Waves, the Tornadoes, and the Wild Cats. The Bar-Kays were proteges of the Mar-Keys, and the relationship was like that between older and younger brothers. Carl Cunningham had grown up at Stax, having been a fixture in the place since the day he came in off the street with his shoeshine kit. Stax bought him his first set of drums.

Now Booker and two of the MGs were sitting down front in a side pew, just behind the families of the dead Bar-Kays. I had seen none of them since the crash, and when the eulogy ended and the band began to play the recessional, I slipped down the aisle to where they were seated. Booker, at the end of the pew, saw me first. Booker has a college degree and drives a Buick. One gets the impression that he has never made any sort of mistake, not even an inappropriate gesture. As I approached, he extended his hand, the one nearest me and nearest his heart. We squeezed hands silently, and then he passed by, followed by Steve Cropper. Steve looks like a very young Gary Cooper. He produced the records of Otis Redding, who was to be buried the next day. Steve is an enigma. He shook my hand briefly but warmly and said, "How's it going?" He is white, as is bassist Donald "Duck" Dunn. Duck, short and plump, seems more of a good ole boy than anyone at Stax, but he is the only one who has been influenced by the hippies. When he came back from Monterey he let his red hair and beard grow, and now, with his little round belly and cherrylike lower lip, he looks like a blend of Sleepy, Happy, and Dopey. We shook hands and walked together up the aisle. At the front door Duck reached into his pocket for a cigarette and said, in the manner of southern country people who express their greatest sorrow as if it were an annoyance hardly worth mentioning, "Been to one today, got to get up and go to another one tomorrow."

Two weeks before, Otis Redding and Steve Cropper had been sitting on folding chairs, facing each other, in the dark, cavern-like grey-and-pink studio at the Stax/Volt recording company. Stax is located in a converted movie theater on McLemore Street in Memphis, next to a housing project. The marquee is still there, with red plastic letters that spell SOULSVILLE, USA. The sign was changed once to read STAY IN SCHOOL, but the kids from the project threw rocks at it, so it was changed back again.

Otis Redding grew up in a housing project and left school at fifteen, but now when he came to the studio he was in a chauffeured Continental. Still, he had not forgotten who he was, where he had come from. The boys from the project knew this, and called Otis their main man. When he got out of the long white car and started across the sidewalk, he took the time to say, "What's happening?" to the boys in bright pants, standing at the curb.

"I was born in Terrell County, Georgia, in a town called Dawson. After I was one year old we moved to Macon. I've stayed in Macon all my life. First we lived in a project house. We lived there for about fourteen years. Then we had to move out to the outskirts of the city. I was going to Ballard Hudson High School, and I kind of got unlucky. My old man got sick, so I had to come out of school and try to find some kind of gig to help my mother. I got a job drilling water wells in Macon. It's a pretty easy job, it sounds hard but it's pretty easy. The hardest thing about it is when you have to change bits. They have big iron bits that weigh 250 pounds, and we'd have to change them, put them on the stem so we could drill—that was the hardest thing about it.

"I was almost sixteen at this time, just getting started singing. I used to play gigs and not make any money. I wasn't looking for money out of it then. I just wanted to be a singer.

"I listened to Little Richard and Chuck Berry a lot. Little Richard is actually the guy that inspired me to start singing. He was from Macon, too. My favorite song of his was 'Heebie Jeebies.' I remember it went, 'My bad luck baby put the jinx on me.' That song really inspired me to start singing, because I won a talent show with it. This was at the Hillview Springs Social Club—it's not there anymore—I won the talent show for fifteen Sunday nights straight with that song, and then they wouldn't let me sing no more, wouldn't let me win that five dollars anymore. So that . . . really inspired me.

"Later on I started singing with a band called Johnnie Jenkins and the Pinetoppers. We played little nightclub and college dates, played at the University of Georgia and Georgia Tech. Then in 1960 I went to California to cut a record, 'She's All Right.' It was with Lute Records, the label the Hollywood Argyles were on. It didn't do anything. I came back to Macon and recorded a song I wrote called 'Shout-bama-lama.' A fellow named Mickey Murray had a hit off the song recently, but it didn't sell when I did it. It kind of got me off to a start, though, and then I came to Memphis in November 1961.

"Johnnie Jenkins was going to record, and I came with him. I had this song, 'These Arms of Mine,' and I asked if I could record it. The musicians had been working with Johnnie all day, and they didn't have but twenty minutes before they went home. But they let me record 'These Arms of Mine.' I give John Richbourg at WLAC in Nashville a lot of credit for breaking that record, because he played it and kept playing it after everybody else had forgot about it. It took nine months to sell, but it sold real good, and—and I've just been going ever since."

Otis is playing a bright red dime-store guitar, strumming simple bar chords as he sings:

> Sittin' in the mornin' sun,
> I'll be sittin' when the evenin' comes—

The front of the guitar is cracked, as if someone has stepped on it. As he sings, Otis watches Steve, who nods and nods, bending almost double over his guitar, following Otis's chords with a shimmering electric response.

> Sittin' in the mornin' sun—

"But I don't know why he's sittin'," Otis says, rocking back and forth as if he were still singing. "He's just sittin'. Got to be more to it than that." He pauses for a moment, shaking his head. Then he says, "Wait. Wait a minute," to Steve, who has been waiting patiently.

> I left my home in Georgia,
> Headed for the Frisco bay—

He pauses again, runs through the changes on his fractured guitar, then sings:

> I had nothing to live for,
> Look like nothing's gonna come my way—

"I write music everywhere, in motels, dressing rooms—I'll just play a song on the guitar and remember it. Then, usually, I come in the studio and Steve and I work it out. Sometimes I'll have just an idea, maybe for a bass line or some chord changes—maybe just a feeling—and we see what we can make out of it. We try to get everybody to groove together to the way a song feels."

When Steve and Otis have the outlines of a song, they are joined by the rest of the MGs. Booker and Duck come in first, followed by drummer Al Jackson. Duck is telling Booker about his new stereo record player. "I got me a nice one, man, with components. You can turn down one of the speakers and hear the words real clear. I been listening to the Beatles. Last night I played *Revolver*, and on 'Yellow Submarine,' you know what one of 'em says? I think it's Ringo, he says, 'Paul is a queer.' He really does, man. 'Paul-is-a-queer,' bigger'n shit."

Booker sits at the piano, Duck gets his bass, which has been lying in its case on the worn red rug, and they begin to pick up the chord patterns from Steve and Otis. Al stands by, listening, his head tilted to one side. Duck asks him a question about counting the rhythm, and Steve looks up to say, "In a minute he'll want to know what key we're in." Duck sticks out his lower lip. He plays bass as fluently as if it were guitar, plucking the stout steel strings with his first two fingers, holding a cigarette between the other two. Booker sits erect, his right hand playing short punctuating notes, his left hand resting on his left knee. Otis is standing now, moving around the room, waving his arms as he conducts these men, his friends, who are there to serve him. He looks like a swimmer, moving effortlessly underwater. Then something happens, a connection is made in Al Jackson's mind, and he goes to the drums, baffled on two sides with wallboard. "One, two," he announces. "One-two-three-four." And for the first time they are all together, everyone has found the groove.

The Mar-Keys drift into the studio and sit on folding chairs behind another baffle, one wall of which has a small window. They listen, sucking on reeds, blowing into mouthpieces, as Otis and the rhythm section rehearse the song. When Steve calls, "Hey, horns! Ready to record?" they are thrown into confusion, like a man waked in the middle of the night. They have nothing to record; there are, as yet, no horn parts. Steve and Otis develop them by singing to each other. "De-de-da-dee," Steve says. "De-de-da-*daaah*," says Otis, as if he were making a point in an argument. When they have the lines they want, they sing them to the Mar-Keys, starting with the verse part, which the Mar-Keys will forget while learning the parts for the chorus. After a few tries, however, they know both parts, and are ready to record. "That feels good, man, let's cut it."

During the rehearsal, one of the neighborhood kids, wearing blue jeans, an old cloth cap, and Converse basketball sneakers with one green and one yellow lace, has slipped into the studio. He sits behind a cluster of microphones, unnoticed by Otis, who passes directly by him on his way to the far corner of the room, where he strikes a wide, flat-footed stance facing a wallboard partition. Otis can hear but cannot see Al Jackson, holding one stick high as if it were a baton, counting four, then rolling his eyes toward the ceiling and starting to play.

After "Dock of the Bay" was recorded, Steve and Booker added guitar and piano fills. The song boomed into the studio from a speaker high on the rear wall, and Booker played precise little bop, bop-bop figures, while Steve followed the vocal with an almost quivering blues line. The speaker went dead, then the engineer's voice came: "Steve, one note's clashing."

"Sure it is," Steve tells him. "It was written to clash." Which, in point of fact, is not true, since nothing has been written down so far. "Let's do it once more," Steve says. "We can do that bridge better. I can. First part's a groove."

Inside the control room, Otis and Duck are talking. "I wish you all *could* go with me to the Fillmore on Christmas," Otis says.

"Man, so do I. I got some good fren's in San Francisco. We could rent one of them yachts."

"I got one already. Three bedrooms, two baths, sumbitch is nice, man."

"My ole lady'd kill me," Duck says.

When the recording is finished, Steve and Booker come into the control room, followed after a moment by the little boy in Converse sneakers. The tape is played back at a painful volume level. Steve and Otis stare deep into each other's eyes, carrying a kind of telepathic communication. The little boy, looking up at the speaker the music is coming from, says, "I like that. That's good singin'. I'd like to be a singer myself."

"If you got the feelin', you can sing soul. You just sing from the heart, and—there's no difference between nobody's heart."

"That's it," Otis says when the record ends.

"That's a mother," says Booker.

Nearly every man at Stax dresses in a kind of uniform: narrow cuffless pants, Italian sweaters, shiny black slip-on shoes. But now, standing in the lobby, there is a tall young Negro man with a shaved head and full beard. He is wearing a Russian-style cap, a white pullover with green stripes, bright green pants, black nylon see-through socks with green ribs, and shiny green lizard shoes. In a paper sack he is carrying a few yards of imitation zebra material, which he intends to have made into a suit, to be worn with a white mohair overcoat. His name is Isaac Hayes. With his partner, David Porter, Hayes has written such hit songs as "Soul Man" and "Hold On, I'm Comin'" for Stax singers Sam and Dave. Porter, dressed less spectacularly in a beige sweater and corduroy Levis, is sitting at a desk in the foyer, not making a phone call.

"Come on," says Hayes. "Let's go next door and write. I'm hot."

"I can't go nowhere till I take care of this chick."

"Which chick is this?"

"You know which chick. You think I ought to call her?"

"What the hell do *I* care? I want to go write."

"Well, she's occupying my mind."

"Let's go, man, let's go. I'm hot."

Porter shrugs and follows Hayes to an office next door where there are three folding chairs, a table littered with old issues of *Billboard* and *Hit Parader*, and a baby grand piano with names and initials carved into it. Hayes sits down at the piano and immediately begins to play church chords, slow and earnest. As he plays he hums, whistles, sings. Porter hums along. He has brought with him a black attaché case, and now he opens it, takes out a ballpoint pen and several sheets of white typing paper, and begins writing rapidly. After about three minutes he stops, takes a pair of shades from his pocket, puts them on, throws back his head, and sings: "You were raised from your cradle to be loved by only me—"

He begins the next line, then stops. "Don't fit, I'm sorry." He rewrites quickly and starts to sing again. Then Hayes stops playing, turns to Porter, and says, "You know what? That ain't exactly killing me right there. Couldn't we get something going like: 'You can run for so long, then you're tired, you can do so-and-so—'"

"Yeah," Porter says. "Got to get the message in."

The door opens, and a small man wearing a black suit, black hat, and black mustache comes in, leading a very thin girl in an orange wig. "You got to hear this," the man says, nodding toward the girl, who is visibly shaking. "Are you nervous?" Hayes asks her. "Just relax and enjoy yourself. Don't worry about us. We just two cats off the street." The girl smiles weakly and sits down.

Porter is writing "Forever Wouldn't Be Too Long" across the top of the page. Then,

> My love will last for you
> Till the morning sun finds no dew
> 'Cause I'm not tired of loving you—

He stops, puts down the pen, and yawns: "Naw, I had something flowin' in my mind."

"How long you be working?" the man in the black suit asks.

"'How do I know?" Hayes says. "We don't observe no time limits."

"Yes," says Porter, "Hayes will probably be here all night. He don't observe no time limits."

Hayes laughs, Porter stomps his right foot once, twice, Hayes strikes a chord, Porter closes his eyes and shouts: "Cross yo' fingers." He sings, bouncing, the chair squeaking, getting louder and faster, as if he were singing a song he had heard many times, and not one he was making up in an incredibly fluent improvisation. The girl smiles, then breaks into a giggle. When Porter stops, he groans. "Man, we should've had a tape recorder, I'll never get that feeling again. Damn! That's a hit! 'Cross Yo' Fingers!' That's a hit title!" He turns back to his writing paper and begins to reconstruct the lyrics.

Hayes looks at the girl. "So you're a singer?" She gulps and nods. The wig, high heels, a tightly belted raincoat only make her seem thinner and more frightened. "Would you like to sing something for us?"

She swallows and nods again. They pick a song, a key (Hayes asks, "Can you sing that high?"), and she begins to sing. At first her voice trembles, but as she sings it grows stronger. She shuts her eyes and moves softly back and forth, as her voice fills the room. Porter stops writing to watch her. She is so frail looking that one expects her to miss the high notes, but she hits them perfectly each time, as her voice swells, blossoms. Finally she stops, on a long, mellow, vibrating note, opens her eyes, and gulps.

Porter applauds. "Wasn't-that-beautiful," he says.

"Where did you go to high school?" Hayes asks the girl.

"Manassas."

"Man—I went to Manassas. How'd you escape the clutches—When did you graduate?"

She looks away and does not answer.

"Haven't you graduated? How old are you?"

The girl mumbles something.

"What?"

"Seventeen," she whispers.

"Seventeen? A voice like that at seventeen? Old Manassa. Damn, you can't beat it." Hayes begins singing the Manassas alma mater song. Porter joins in. They get up and start to dance. Porter takes the girl's hands, and she joins him, singing and dancing. They all whirl around the room, as the man with the mustache closes his eyes and smiles.

Stax's only current rival in success is American Studios, on Thomas Street in North Memphis. American has recorded hits by artists as various as Wilson Pickett, the soul singer; Sandy Posey, the country-pop singer; King Curtis, the funky tenor player; Patti LaBelle and the Blue Belles, a girls' singing group; Paul Revere and the Raiders, a white rock group; and the Box Tops, a band of Memphis teenagers whose first record, "The Letter," outsold even the "Ode to Billy Joe" to become the year's number-one pop single.

There is no sign outside American, but no one seeing the long sweep of charcoal-gray exterior would expect the place to be anything but a recording studio. American was created in 1962, when a Stax engineer, Lincoln "Chips" Moman, left and formed his own company with Donald Crews, a farmer from Lepanto, Arkansas. Moman, who started out as a house painter, has been described as "the living embodiment of the

Memphis Sound." He has tattooed on his right arm the word "Memphis," on his left a big red heart. Although he produces most of the records cut at American, he has a reputation for never being at the studio. Donald Crews, who has never produced anything that could not be grown in rows, is almost always there, and he greeted me as I came in. "Used to be a receptionist around here," he said, "but she took to singin', and now we don't have one anymore." With a wave he indicated two gold records on the wall. They had been awarded to Sandy Posey, the ex-receptionist, for her first two recordings, "Born a Woman" and "Single Girl."

I told Crews that I was writing about the current revival of the Memphis sound, and I wanted to understand it better. He told me that he wanted to, too. "The music business is a mystery to me," he said. "We've had good luck with it—had more than twenty records in the charts this year—but I don't know how we done it. Only thing I've noticed is, down here we're all independents. All the Memphis studios have been Memphis owned. In New York, or even Nashville, they're spending Warner Brothers' money, or CBS's money, but when we produce a record down here, it comes out of our own pockets. That makes a little difference. Who you ought to talk to is one of our producers. I believe Dan Penn is in his office upstairs."

I found Penn, a young blond man wearing blue jeans and bedroom slippers, at his desk playing a ukulele. He told me that he had come to Memphis from Vernon, Alabama, after working for a while as staff guitarist in a studio at Muscle Shoals, because he wanted to produce hit rock and roll records. One of his first was "The Letter."

"Dan," I said, "what is it about Memphis?"

"It ain't Memphis," he said. "It's the South."

"Well, what is it about the South?"

"People down here don't let nobody tell them what to do."

"But how does it happen that they know what to do?"

He twirled the ukulele by the neck, played two chords, and squinted at me across the desk. "It ain't any explanation for it," he said.

Downstairs, I was stopped by a little Negro boy wearing Converse basketball shoes. He looked even scruffier than the one who had been at Otis's session. "You Wilson?" he asked.

"What?"

"You name Wilson?"

"No," I said.

"I thought you was Wilson."

"Sorry," I said, and started out the door.

"Hey," the little boy said, "take this." It was a small grey business card, with an address and the inscription, "Charisma Project."

I was outside before I thought to wonder where the boy had gotten the card. It was a coincidence, because I was headed for the Charisma Project, but he could have found the card at any of a dozen places. James Dickinson, the project's founder, has worked at nearly all the local studios. Under his direction the project has created theater, recordings, and the annual Memphis Country Blues Festival, which in recent years has given work to some of the finest old Delta musicians. Dickinson alone in Memphis combines the talents of a musician, songwriter, producer, and historian. And it was Dickinson who gave me, at last, a definition of soul.

The front office of the Charisma Project, located in an old white house on Yates Road in East Memphis, is crowded with sound equipment and antique instruments—a zither, a pump organ, a bass recorder, a drum with one head bearing a hand-painted view of Venice. Dickinson said that his involvement with Memphis music began after an incident that took place when he was twelve years old. "I was downtown with my father. We came out of the Falls Building into Whiskey Chute, and there it was—Will Shade, Memphis Willie B., Gus Cannon, and their jug band, playing 'Come On Down to My House, Honey, Ain't Nobody Home But Me.' I had had formal piano lessons since I was five years old, and all of a sudden here was this awful music. I loved it instantly. I had never known that music could make you feel so good. I started seeking out soul musicians, learning what I could from them. My first teachers were Piano Red, Butterfly Washington, and, a little later, Mance Lipscomb." By his late teens Dickinson was fronting his own band, sharing billing with such early giants of rock as Bo Diddley.

He spent several years playing organ, guitar, and piano at recording sessions in Memphis and Nashville, but since the formation of the Charisma Project he has concentrated on events such as the blues festival and on producing records. "Memphis is the center of American popular music," Dickinson said. "The market goes away at times, but it always comes back, because music that is honest will last. You hear soul music explained in terms of oppression and poverty, and that's certainly part of it—no soul musician was born rich—but it's more than that. It's being proud of your own people, what you come from. That's soul."

> I'm a Soul Man
> Got what I got the hard way
> And I'll make it better each and every day
> I'm a Soul Man

The Porter and Hayes song had just become the nation's number-one hit, earning a gold record for Sam and Dave, who would be singing it in Memphis on Saturday night. With Carla Thomas, they were to headline the twentieth edition of the Goodwill Revue, a charity music concert sponsored annually by radio station WDIA.

In 1948 WDIA became the nation's first radio station with programming exclusively for Negroes. WDIA described itself then as "The Black Spot on Your Radio Dial—50,000 Watts of Black Power." Now the station has broadened its focus, and the word "soul" has been substituted for "black."

From the beginning WDIA has been involved with projects to aid the community it serves. Proceeds from such events as the Goodwill Revue help to provide and maintain boys' clubs and recreational centers in poverty areas, Goodwill Homes for juvenile court wards, and a school for handicapped Negro children. Perhaps because of its strictly philanthropic nature—many artists perform without pay, and all WDIA employees, even those who perform, must buy a ticket—the Goodwill Revue has become a sort of love feast of the soul community.

In an annual message to the station's friends, the general manager said, "In sponsoring these shows, WDIA is merely providing you with a means of expressing your own generosity." But this year the station was also providing the audience with an opportunity to enjoy its own music at a time when there was more reason than ever to be proud of it.

In previous years, the first half of the program, traditionally reserved for gospel music, has been at least as important as the latter, secular half. But the audience has grown steadily younger and less interested in the old-time religion, and now the gospel groups play to a half-empty house. The revue was being held in the Mid-South Coliseum, and a scanty crowd, sitting on wooden folding chairs, their feet resting on cardboard matting laid out over an ice-hockey floor, listened coldly to the Evening Doves, the Harmonizing Four, the Gabriel Airs, and the Spirit of Memphis Quartet. Only one group, the Jessy Dixon Singers, led by tall, handsome, white-gowned coloratura Adrea Lenox, created much enthusiasm, with rousing, stomping choruses of "Long as I've Got King Jesus, Everything's All Right."

During the intermission, nine Negro policemen who had been sitting behind the big roll-out stage took their folding chairs and went out front, where they could hear better. The Coliseum was nearly filled to its capacity of fourteen thousand for the opening acts (dancers, minor singing groups) of the revue's second half, but the audience did not come to life until the appearance of a great figure in the history of soul music—Muddy Waters. Wearing an iridescent aquamarine/sapphire silk suit, huge green-and-white jeweled cuff links, and matching pinky diamonds, Muddy walked onstage, sang the opening bars of one of his earliest recordings, and was greeted by a roar of welcoming applause.

> I got a black cat bone, I got a mojo tooth
> I got a John the Conqueror root, I'm gone mess with you
> I'm gone make all you girls lead me by the hand
> Then the world will know I'm a hoochie coochie man

The loudspeaker system crackled and spluttered while Muddy was on, but everyone knew the words. During the performance of the next singer, Bobby Bland, the first four rows to the right of the stage began to sway together and to sing, or hum, along with the music, long-held notes in four-part harmony, even anticipating the chord changes. The four rows were filled with the Teen Town Singers, a group of "about sixty talented youngsters" from high schools and junior colleges in the Memphis area, some of whom each year are given scholarships from Goodwill Revue revenues.

When Carla Thomas was eighteen, she was a Teen Town Singer. That year she wrote and recorded a song called "Gee Whiz," which made the top ten on the popularity charts and made her a star. She has seldom been without a hit since, and now as a mature artist she is known as the "Queen of the Memphis Sound."

Her material has matured with her, but her first song at the Revue went back to the beginning. She stepped into a pink spot, a big, beautiful brown girl wearing a white brocade dress flowered with pearly sequins, and sang one of her early successes, "B-A-B-Y." The Teen Town Singers sang along on every note, inspired by the knowledge that any of them might become Royalty of Soul.

When Carla's father, Rufus Thomas, a WDIA disc jockey with several record successes of his own (his hit, "Walking the Dog," created one of the dance crazes of the '60s), joined her for a duet, the atmosphere was like that of a family reunion. Rufus and Carla sang, "'Cause I Love You," the first song Carla ever recorded, and the first hit, however small, to come out of the Stax/Volt studios. The audience loved it, clapping on the afterbeat, and they might not have allowed them to leave the stage if Sam and Dave had not been scheduled to appear next.

Sam Moore and Dave Prater, along with Carla and the other Stax artists, had taken soul around the world, and now they were bringing it back as number one, the world's most popular music. Their singing combines all the historical elements of soul music—gospel, blues, rhythm. "They'll go to church on you in a minute," a Stax executive has said, and it is an apt description of what they did at the revue.

With their band, in black pants and turquoise balloon-sleeved shirts, strung out across the stage behind them, Sam and Dave, dressed all in white, singing, dancing, shouting, exhorting the congregation like old-fashioned preachers, created a sustained frenzy of near-religious ecstasy. "Now doggone it, I just want you to do what you want to do." "Put your hands together and give me some old soul clapping." "Little louder."

"Little bit louder." "Do you like it?" "Well, do you like it?" "I said, Do you like it?" "Well, then, let me hear you say YEAH!"

It was nearly midnight when, with their coats off, shirts open and wringing with sweat, they got around to the song that seemed to say it all, for soul music's past, present, and future.

> So honey, don't you fret
> 'Cause you ain't seen nothin' yet
> I'm a Soul Man

The next night, Otis Redding, the King of Memphis Soul Sound, and the Bar-Kays, who would have helped to shape its future, would be dead. It would be, as the Beatles called it, "a bitter tragedy." But the strength of soul music has always been the knowledge of how to survive tragedy. Remembering another great soul star, Otis Redding once said, "I want to fill the silent vacuum that was created when Sam Cooke died." Now Otis's death has left an even greater vacuum. But someone will come along to fill it. He may even be here already, walking down some street in Memphis, wearing Converse sneakers.

THE GILDED PALACE OF SIN: THE FLYING BURRITO BROTHERS

The record played most often around the Rolling Stones' office in the fall of 1968 was the Byrds' *Sweetheart of the Rodeo*. Gram Parsons, a young man I'd never met from my birthplace, Waycross, seemed to have turned the well-known folk-rock outfit into a kind of country-rock band.

In spring of 1969, Parsons, who'd left the South Africa–bound Byrds when the Stones told him nobody played there because of its apartheid policies, released an album with his new band, the Flying Burrito Brothers. I was still waiting for a letter from the Stones, and it was pleasant to have the chance to write about something close to home.

Gram Parsons, the head Burrito, stares out of the cover photograph of *The Gilded Palace of Sin* album wearing a suit made by Nudie of Hollywood, who specializes in the outfits with spangled cactuses and embroidered musical notes worn by such traditional country and western performers as Porter Wagoner and Buck Owens. But Parsons's suit is decorated with green marijuana branches, and there are naked ladies on the lapels.

Wonderful as this is, it seems even more of a wonder when you know that Parsons comes from Waycross, Georgia, especially if you happen to know what Waycross, Georgia, is like.

Jerry Wexler of Atlantic Records, sitting around his Long Island house one night with Bert Berns, trying to come up with a real down-home song for Wilson Pickett, suggested that they write one about Waycross. "I figured there couldn't be any more down-home place than that," Wexler explained later. "Waycross, Georgia, would have to be the asshole of the world."

––––––––––––––

Waycross, population approximately twenty thousand, is located sixty miles from the Atlantic Ocean, thirty-six miles from the Florida state line, about fifteen minutes via alligator from the Okefinokee Swamp, close to the heart of Wiregrass, Georgia, a territory which may well be the deepest part of the Deep South. Memphis, Birmingham, Atlanta are southern; but they are nothing like Waycross. People around Waycross think of Atlanta the way you and I think of the moon—a place which, though remote, might possibly be visited someday by us or our children.

Wiregrass, the territory which includes Waycross, encompasses nearly ten thousand square miles of pine-and-palmetto forest, grading almost imperceptibly into the Okefinokee, in Seminole the Land of the Trembling Earth. The forest floor, carpeted with sweet-smelling dry brown pine needles, laced with creeks and rivers, becomes more unsteady under your feet, until another step, onto land that looks the same as the place where you are standing, will take you too far, the ground gives way, and you are sucked down into the rich peaty swamp, which, though it supports great pines, will not support you. Many men have walked into the Okefinokee, where even the pretty little plants eat meat, never to be heard from again. There is more water than land, and the huge cypresses towering overhead form the walls of corridors through the brown water, which is clear in the hand and good to drink.

The people of Wiregrass—dealers in, among other things, pine trees, tobacco, peanuts, sugar cane, moonshine whiskey, trucks, tractors, new and used cars, Bibles, groceries, dry goods, and hardware; in isolate farms on swamp islands; in turpentine camps deep in the woods, like Dickerson's Crossing, Mexico, the Eight-Mile Still; in unincorporated settlements like Sandy Bottom, Headlight, Thelma; in towns like Blackshear, Folkston, Waycross; from banker to bootlegger—all share two curses: hard work and Jesus. Wiregrass must be one of the last places in the world where the Puritan ethic still obtains, making an almost unrelievedly strenuous way of life even more grim. Before smoking tobacco was known to be a health hazard, it was frowned upon by many people there, simply because it gives pleasure. Although Waycross has the Okefinokee Regional Library and once had a world movie premiere (a swamp picture called *Lure of the Wilderness* starring Jeffrey Hunter), culture exists there only in the anthropological sense. The social life of the community has two centers, with, in general, mutually exclusive clientele: churches and roadhouses. There is violence, illicit sex, drunkenness—in a word, sin—in south Georgia, but they have not become behavioral standards. The ideal still is to be a hard-working, God-fearing, man or woman, boy or girl.

So here we have Gram Parsons, from Waycross, Georgia, with shoulder-length hair, and dope and pussy on his jacket. Parsons's first record, as far as I know, was *Safe at Home* by his earlier group, the International Submarine Band. The album, "a Lee Hazlewood Production, produced by Suzi Jane Hokom," included songs associated with Johnny Cash, Merle Haggard, Big Boy Crudup, and Elvis Presley, as well as a couple of country classics ("Miller's Cave" and "Satisfied Mind") and four Parsons originals. The music was fairly straight country and western, with piano, bass, drums, rhythm, lead, and steel guitars. It was an honest, pleasant, but not strongly exciting album.

Next, Parsons joined the Byrds, staying with them long enough to make *Sweetheart of the Rodeo*, the country album recorded in Nashville, which, though not a complete success, was one of that year's best records. When Parsons left the Byrds he formed the Flying Burrito Brothers.

The Burritos' first album, with roughly the same instrumentation as Parsons's two previous ones, has perhaps less surface charm than *Sweetheart*, but is the best, most personal Parsons has yet done. *The Gilded Palace of Sin*, unlike *Safe at Home* and *Sweetheart of the Rodeo*, is about life in the big city, where even a pretty girl, as Parsons warns on the first track, can be a "devil in disguise." "Sin City," the second track, predicts destruction for the city, "filled with sin," where the slickers in their "green mohair suits" advise you to "take it home right away, you've got three years to pay." But, the song cautions, "Satan is waiting his turn":

It seems like this whole town's insane
On the thirty-first floor
A gold-plated door
Won't keep out the Lord's burning rain

The two following songs, "Do-Right-Woman" and "Dark End of the Street" by Dan Penn of Memphis, the only ones on the album which Parsons had no hand in writing, are given new depth of meaning by their juxtaposition with what preceded them. "Do-Right-Woman" is especially outstanding: though obviously quite different, it is in no way inferior to the original Aretha Franklin recording. "My Uncle," the last track on side one, does honor to the great tradition, equal to the tradition of southern war heroism, of hillbilly draft dodging. It is delightfully good-humored "protest" in the best, healthiest, most direct, and personal sense:

I'm heading for the nearest foreign border
Vancouver may be just my kind of town
'Cause I don't need the kind of law and order
That tends to keep a good man underground

The second side opens with a return to a mood like that of "Sin City," except that the emphasis is on how out of place "this boy" feels, very much as in the old gospel song, "This World Is Not My Home." "Wheels" ends with a plea to "take this boy away." In "Juanita," the next song, "an angel . . . just seventeen, with a dirty old gown and a conscience so clean" finds him abandoned and alone "in a cold dirty room . . . with a bottle of wine and some pills off the shelf" and brings back "the life that I once threw away."

"Hot Burrito No. 1," which follows, is perhaps the best song Parsons has yet written, and he has written some very good ones. A rather old-fashioned rock and roll song, it might have been recorded in 1956 by the Platters, except for one line, the most effective on the album, "I'm your toy—I'm your old boy," which no one but Parsons could sing so movingly. "Hot Burrito No. 2," an uptempo secular love song, breaks the gospel-honkytonk taboo, which is just as strong as the black blues-in-church taboo, when Parsons sings, "You better love me—Jesus Christ!"

The next-to-last song is the only repeat from an earlier Parson album. "Do You Know How It Feels to Be Lonesome" from, ironically, *Safe at Home*, is the statement of a young man who must feel at home nowhere, not in the big city or in Waycross, Georgia. "Did you ever try to smile at some people," he says, "and all they ever seem to do is stare?"

"Hippie Boy," the final song, an updated version of Red Foley's "Peace in the Valley," is recited by Chris Hillman, possibly because his accent is less countrified than Parsons's. It tells a story with a moral: "It's the same for any hillbilly, bum, or hippie on the street . . . Never carry more than you can eat." The album's ending somehow summons up a vision of hillbillies and hippies, like lions and lambs, together in peace and love instead of sin and violence, getting stoned together, singing old-time favorite songs. The album closes with a fine, fractured chorus of "Peace in the Valley," with whistles, shouts, and rattling tambourines.

Perhaps Parsons, coming from the country, feels more deeply than most the strangeness and hostility of the modern world, but he speaks to and for all of us. Gram Parsons is a good old boy.

THE 1969 MEMPHIS BLUES SHOW: EVEN THE BIRDS WERE BLUE

The following piece is a time capsule. Many people in it are dead: Furry, Fred McDowell, Johnny Woods, Bukka White, John Estes, Robert Wilkins, Nathan Beauregard, Trevor Koehler, Lee Baker, Bill Barth, Charlie Freeman, and John Fahey, among others. The threatened I-40 through the park plan was thwarted by heroic Memphians. At the time, though, it looked inevitable. The survival of the blues didn't. Early in the century, blues had been a brief fad. In 1969 it seemed to be, possibly, coming back to life. We needn't have worried, except that blues, like war, is too serious a matter to be left to the professionals. As is the case with boxing, you always have to worry where it's going. But blues appears, from the perspective of a new century, to be a permanent part of the American musical landscape. It speaks to too many people for it to die.

Some people, however, it doesn't speak to. When *Rythm Oil* was published, this piece was nixed by the editor, an aging British woman who knew nothing about the blues. I didn't care, I had bigger problems. Still do. It's all part of living with the blues.

At about five o'clock in the afternoon on the second day of the Memphis Country Blues Festival, the old blues artists Fred McDowell and Johnny Woods were huddled together on folding chairs at the front of the stage at the Overton Park Shell, just getting into "Shake 'Em On Down," when a gang of men began moving a long series of big black amplifier crates from one side of the rear stage to the other. Hearing the clatter, Woods stopped playing harmonica and cast a worried glance backward over his shoulder. "I thought it was a big ole train a-comin'," he said. The crates were stamped WINTER because they contained the many amplifiers of

Johnny Winter, the Columbia Recording Company's $300,000 cross-eyed albino Texas electric blues baby, and I mention them because they will serve adequately as a symbol of what nearly killed the Memphis Country Blues Festival in its fourth year.

To understand the blues festival, you must know that Fred McDowell, the best living Mississippi bluesman, has been for most of his life a share-cropper, sometimes making a year's profit (after paying his bossman for rent and equipment) of as much as thirty dollars; and that Furry Lewis, who is virtually all that remains of Beale Street, worked for the City of Memphis for decades, collecting garbage, sweeping the streets, and then retired without a pension. No matter how they could play and sing, they were still just a couple of old niggers. They and others like them had been recorded on labels like Bluebird and Vocalion in the early days of race records; then, with the Depression and the WWII recording ban, they were forgotten. Through the days of the first electric blues bands, the Sun Records era of Elvis Presley and Jerry Lee Lewis, the late fifties rhythm and blues, and the rock revival of the sixties, the old men whose music provided the foundation for it all were ignored. When they were not ignored, they were exploited.

Just about the only people who ever really cared for the old Delta bluesmen were a few vintage southern beatniks. Although struggling for their own survival, they recognized a spiritual tie and responsibility and saw to it that the old men worked whenever possible. Charlie Brown, poet, hermit, actor, snake trapper, entrepreneur, was probably the first to hire the old men for public appearances, at the Bitter Lemon and Oso coffee houses in Memphis in the early sixties.

On the scene at about this time was a New Yorker named Bill Barth, one of the strange breed of northern musicologists, like Sam Charters and the Lomaxes, who spend their lives looking for the blues without ever quite finding it. Barth did unearth several lost blues artists, however, and in 1966 he and Charlie Brown produced the first Memphis Country Blues Festival, though it was not called that. It was just the blues show then, and it was rained out, but everyone came back a week later and the show went on, with Bukka White, B. B. King's cousin and teacher; Nathan Beauregard, who is supposed to be, at 106, the world's oldest blues singer; Rev. Robert Wilkins, a converted bluesman who became one of the finest gospel singers; and Fred McDowell and Furry Lewis.

There were also such white members of the Memphis musical underground as Lee Baker, a guitarist; Sid Selvidge, a country-folk singer; and Jim Dickinson, who is, among other things, a blues singer. The show started late, there were too many acts, most of whom stayed on too long; but the old men of the blues were given respect and, more important, applause; and the young musicians who were there showed that they cared enough about the blues to really learn it, not just to ape the lifestyle and the licks. The first Memphis blues show was, in spite of its faults, a fine thing.

Perhaps that is why the second blues show was such a disappointment. Nineteen sixty-seven was the year of the hippie tidal wave; the world was awash with dope and flowers. Charlie Brown, after a difference of opinion with the Memphis Vice Squad, had gone to Miami. The blues show took place, but somehow things were not the same. The Lee Baker Blues Band had become Funky Down-Home and the Electric Blue Watermelon; Lee/Funky, one of the young musicians who supposedly cared about the blues, played while seated on a motorcycle, wearing a dress, with flowers in his hair. The bizarre atmosphere affected even the old bluesmen. Generally unaccustomed to playing cold sober, they—some of them—managed this year to perform while falling-down drunk. A large audience, prompted by enthusiastic reports of the first concert, came to witness what was, with minimal exceptions, an embarrassment.

A few musicians refused to play the second blues show because it was such a circus, but by 1968 things had settled down somewhat, and most of them were back. The third blues show, the Funky Down-Home Memorial Concert (Funky was a guest of Uncle Sam at the Federal Narcotics Hospital in Lexington, Kentucky), included newly discovered Mississippi bluesman Joe Callicott and attracted a good amount of outside interest. *Billboard* and the AFM paper *Musician* carried stories; London Records cut an album, of semiprofessional quality, on the old blues players.

This attention was generated partly by the cresting popularity of the Stax/Volt and American Studio's Memphis Sound and partly by a widespread renewal of interest in the blues. Such white halls as the Fillmore had begun to hire B. B. King and his imitators; groups like Canned Heat had blues hits; the Rolling Stones recorded "Prodigal Son," a song regularly performed at the Memphis blues shows by its author, the Reverend Mr. Robert Wilkins. Before the next blues show took place, Robert Wilkins, Furry Lewis, and Bukka White had played the Electric Circus, a psychedelic New York boîte. The old blues had become, on a larger scale than ever before, worthy of exploitation.

As it happens, 1969 marked the 150th birthday of the City of Memphis, if you forget the years when, following a series of yellow fever plagues, the city's charter was revoked; so naturally the chamber of commerce made plans for a sesquicentennial celebration. Bill Barth, who in his well-meaning but slipshod way had remained the blues show's prime mover, suggested that the celebration include an expanded version of the blues show, and the city, desperate for good publicity since the death of Martin Luther King, agreed. An office in city hall was made available so that a representative of Barth's Country Blues Society and a chamber of commerce promotion man could coordinate the event.

Developments soon became impenetrably scrambled, but in outline several basic trends could be discerned. First, while Barth was expecting money from the city for his festival, the city intended to have its own festival and created a philanthropic organization, the W. C. Handy Foundation, to camouflage the show's Babbitt-like Boost Memphis advertising purpose. (Barth's shows, good or bad, always had one purpose: to earn a little money for the old bluesmen. All earnings over expenses were split between the musicians. At the 1968 show, each man had received $150, which might equal five years of sharecroppers' wages.) Endowed with $20,000 from the chamber of commerce, the city's man began negotiations to contract such noted blues artists as Louis Armstrong and Marguerite Piazza.

Meanwhile, anticipating money from the city, from nebulous recording deals, and from mysterious "backers," the Country Blues Society's man sent contracts to practically everyone who owns a guitar. The Rolling Stones, Taj Mahal, Canned Heat, the Flying Burrito Brothers, Johnny Winter, Blind Faith, George Harrison's protege Jackie Lomax, Jo Ann Kelly, the list went on almost forever, were invited to appear for expenses and fifty dollars a day, and a surprising number agreed. National Educational Television made plans to tape an afternoon's concert for its musical series, *Sounds of Summer*. The Memphis Country Blues Festival had become a very hip thing to do.

But as time went on and Barth, who had been on the road with his band, the Insect Trust, returned to Memphis with no money, it became less attractive to most people. The roster changed daily as one act after another remembered pressing obligations elsewhere.

By the festival weekend, the schedule of events had settled down into its final state of confusion. The city's First Annual W. C. Handy Memorial Concert was to take place Sunday evening, June 8, at the Memphis Mid-South Coliseum, a sports-and-entertainment arena, with such staple Memphis acts as Rufus and Carla Thomas, the Bar-Kays, Booker T. and the MGs, and such outside acts as the World's Greatest Jazz Band and, inexplicably, Johnny Winter, whom the city's promo man had picked, together with a couple of token old bluesmen from the list of acts contacted by the blues society. (The Armstrong-Piazza negotiations had been halted, not by a sudden outbreak of taste and sensibility, but by the fees those performers demanded.) The Fourth Annual Memphis Country Blues Festival would begin Friday night, June 6, at the Overton Park Shell, with a concert devoted primarily to the old blues artists; Saturday afternoon, National Educational Television would tape a special concert including acts from both the city and blues society festivals; Saturday night, there would be a modern blues show, featuring Johnny Winter, who agreed to perform since he would be in town anyway. The Country Blues Festival would close with a concert of gospel music Sunday morning.

In some of the blues festival's advance publicity, a Friday afternoon concert had been promised. That time was given instead to a rehearsal of the NET concert. The show's acts, better than twenty of them (lucky that so many had dropped, or there'd have been fifty), arrived late in the morning at the Shell, an open-air concrete theater, location of many free municipal events, children's plays, and charity concerts. Over the years, the Memphis blues show regulars have become a kind of family; they greet each other with candid warmth, sometimes, as Furry greeted

Funky, old jive to young, "Lee! When you get out?" There were two great white vans full of television equipment behind the Shell, and strange men wearing khaki shorts, blue knit golf shirts, and little yellow canvas hats, waltzing around a forest of cameras and microphones, muttering to each other in alien accents. The musicians tacitly agreed that such was the price of success.

Spectators were admitted, at a dollar a head, to the Shell's weathered wooden benches. There were many good things on the program for them to enjoy, but the delays caused by technical difficulties the NET people encountered made waiting under the hot, empty blue sky for the next thing to happen excruciating. During a particularly long delay, I went to the back of the Shell, heard music across the park, and walked over the road through a formal flower garden to look out over a wide green sweep of playground. Hundreds of kids, all colors, boys and girls together, led by a lady in a blue-and-white park commission uniform, were singing and dancing, whirling in two or three great circles, then in dozens of tiny, tightly spinning ones. It was like wandering into a Brueghel.

Overton Park is a green oasis close to the center of Memphis, a city whose beautiful old trees and houses are fast being destroyed by progress in the guise of, among other things, huge asphalt-paved shopping centers and hundreds of cleverly named cheap food joints. (Mahalia Jackson's Glori-Fried Chicken.) On this afternoon in the park, people at the zoo, the art school, the art gallery, the golf course, on the bicycle paths, and the birds, cats, chipmunks, and squirrels in the woods were proceeding as usual, oblivious to the expressway, Interstate Route 40, that was scheduled soon to tear the park in half.

Back at the Shell, the NET men were calling it a rehearsal, and the blues show was about to begin. This year's show was "respectfully dedicated to Joe Callicott's memory." The Mississippi singer-guitarist who'd made records in Memphis in the twenties had made it to only one blues show. He had been "rediscovered" for just one year, during which he had played in New York but had not been recorded. He left behind, the festival program stated, "only a small portion of the music he knew."

As if to make up for Joe's absence, there were some new old faces. Besides the regulars Nathan Beauregard, Fred McDowell, Bukka White, and Robert Wilkins (Furry Lewis, appalled by the NET rehearsal, had wandered away into the park), the show included McDowell's neighbor Johnny Woods, Sleepy John Estes and his neighbor Yank Rachel, and a slide guitar player named Lum Guffin, who sounded like Elmore James if James had been a better singer. The regular old white boys Baker, Selvidge, and Dickinson were there, too, as well as Barth's outfit, the Insect Trust.

The attention the old blues have received lately seems to have a revivifying effect on the players, even those who have not been directly touched by it. They sounded, on this night, better than ever. Fred McDowell and Johnny Woods opened the show with a set of blues, breakdowns, shuffles, and boogies, many of which were old at the time of the First World War. McDowell, probably the best living bottleneck guitarist, has recorded more than most of the old bluesmen, but Woods has only recently cut his first tapes. To call Woods's playing funky is to be guilty of gross understatement; he is the funkiest harmonica player who ever came up from the farm. He sounds like Sonny Boy Williamson, Sonny Terry, Howlin' Wolf, and a large, dying animal, all at once.

It is interesting to know how old much of Woods's and McDowell's material is, but you do not have to know its age to enjoy it. One of the pleasanter things about the Memphis blues shows is that none of the old blues players is presented for his historical value. All of them, even the 106-year-old Nathan Beauregard (skeptics grant him a decade less), can still play blues. And while some of them may at times have difficulty staying in tune, none of them has ever been so completely and hopelessly out of tune as, say, Big Brother and the Holding Company were at Monterey.

Beauregard, who is blind, was led slowly across the stage by his seventy-eight-year-old nephew, seated, given his guitar (a new Japanese electric), and incredibly, this withered mummy began to play and to sing about a girl who would "call you honey, call you pie." Beauregard is, in an odd way, inspiring. During most of the festival, when he was not playing he sat with his nephew at the rear of the stage, listening to the music, his face like a death mask with its closed eyelids, protruding cheekbones, and slight smile.

Bukka White, at fifty-nine the youngest of the old bluesmen, followed Beauregard. When B. B. King first came to Memphis, he lived with his cousin Bukka, whose bottleneck playing motivated B. B. to achieve the sustained ascending tones that in part characterize his style. Bukka vigorously plays a big National Steel Standard and sings, talks, and growls magnificently incomprehensible "sky songs." Part song, part reminiscence, part tall-story, they are called "sky songs" because Bukka "just makes them up out of the sky." *Down Beat* gave five stars, its highest rating, to a two-volume collection of Bukka's sky songs on the Arhoolie label. At the festival, Bukka received a standing ovation Friday night and every other time he played.

Sleepy John Estes and Yank Rachel, the guitarist and mandolin player who made records in the 1920s, '30s, and '40s, and whose songs have recently been recorded by Taj Mahal, were accompanied in their first Memphis blues show appearance by Jim Dickinson, who is in his twenties, on piano. Such meetings of old and young musicians have provided some of the blues shows' better moments.

They give the young players a chance to learn, of course, but at times they give the old men some surprises. During a lull in the NET rehearsal, Dickinson and Johnny Woods, seated together on a piano bench, had played an impromptu duet on "Shake Yo' Boogie." Nathan Beauregard's nephew, who happens to be a retired gravedigger, watched from behind the piano, and when they finished, spoke to Dickinson. "I haven't heard no *colored* man play piano like that in twenty years." Estes, Rachel, and Dickinson went back twenty years and more for a set of country dance hall tunes, with Estes singing lead and Rachel, on electric mandolin, playing brilliant doubletime passages with Dickinson.

The surprising thing about Lum Guffin, who was also making his first Memphis blues show appearance, is that no one has recorded him. Though he is supposed to have played on Beale Street in the 1920s, his present style is patterned closely after that of Elmore James. Of the many guitarists working this vein, Guffin has to be among the very best. He is adept at fingerpicking, but his slide work is outstanding. Guffin's "Dust My Broom" showed him to be superior to James as a singer, and his one festival appearance on Friday night's show seemed all too brief.

The Insect Trust, Bill Barth's eight-piece blues rock jazz band (Barth plays blues, the rhythm section plays rock, the horns play jazz), seemed at times neither to know nor to care where they were going but were almost always fun to listen to, and once in a while were really impressive, especially when Trevor Koehler, a fine young baritone saxophonist, was featured. Koehler played interesting, energetic, coherent solos, and even when he dipped into the post-Coltrane piggy-noise bag, never lost his sense of humor. The Insect Trust do not exactly play blues, but they have roots, and besides, it's Barth's show.

Robert Wilkins made some very good blues records in the 1920s, but in the '30s he was "sanctified" and since then has sung only for the Lord. His blues show appearances have been consistently excellent, and each has revealed a new development in his music. At the first blues show, Wilkins played acoustic guitar accompanied only by his "baby son," who must be six feet tall, on tambourine. "Big son" joined the next year, on electric bass. Then Rev. Wilkins started playing electric guitar. This year there were two additions: another, nonfamily, electric guitarist, and Wilkins's niece, whose looks and voice added fuel to the rumor that the Wilkins family carries an extra gene that produces attractive, talented gospel artists. Wilkins's present group must be regarded as one of the best gospel bands, the equal of the Staples Singers, with better material than the Staples, much of it original. Their "Soldiers in the Army of the Lord" was one of the highlights of the festival. Rev. Wilkins says that he does not know who the Rolling Stones are, but he is pleased that they have recorded one of his songs.

This year marked the return of Lee Baker/Funky Down-Home, who appeared with his new band, Moloch. Baker's past lapses of taste have not prevented him from becoming an electric blues guitarist in the very front of the second rank. (In the first rank there are a few black men and no white boys at all.) Moloch is a tight, grooving blues band. They accompanied, oddly enough, Sid Selvidge, a singer in the tradition of Jimmie Rodgers, Hank Williams, and Roy Acuff, though his roots go back to white country hoots and hollers. No other singer in Selvidge's field has such a powerfully precise voice. In fact, Selvidge's singing may be too good for today's taste; you can understand every word he sings.

He does not sacrifice any feeling, however; he has a fine, passionate falsetto, and is the best yodeler since Dale Evans.

Friday night's concert, except for Furry Lewis's absence, may have been the best at any of the Memphis blues shows. The participants went home to bed, singly and in groups, and arrived early the next day for the NET concert.

They might as well have slept late. The show started one and one-half hours late (more technical difficulties), and the first three acts—Rufus Thomas, the Bar-Kays, and a white singer named Brenda Patterson—had to repeat their performances because the cameras weren't working the first time. This was particularly difficult for the Bar-Kays, whose act, with its jumping, shouting, stomping, and hard-down funky playing, leaves them hardly enough energy to stagger off the stage.

The show's other acts included all the ones from the previous evening except Lum Guffin, who disappeared, and Rev. Wilkins, who, when presented with a contract by the NET men (still in the golfing outfits), took one look at them, knew they were not sanctified, and refused to sign. There were also three or four acts from the long list contacted by the blues society. John Fahey, a music MA from the University of California and a longtime friend of Barth, was introduced as "a young man who has made the blues into a semiclassical form." His playing wasn't bad, but it had little warmth. Fahey has made some good guitar-picking records on the Takoma label, but on stage he sounded twice as old and feeble as Nathan Beauregard.

Fahey played forever and was replaced by Jo Ann Kelly, a pretty blonde girl from England, who did a brilliant impersonation of Charlie Patton. Kelly must be among the funkier items in England; bringing her to Memphis, however, was like bringing coals to Newcastle.

While the blues society was making contact with the dozens of acts who nearly all decided not to come, it hired a group of local nightclub and recording musicians to serve as house band for the festival. As things turned out, there was no one for the house band to accompany, so they played alone, billed as the Soldiers of the Cross. The group does not play together regularly (they happened to have been working on an album with Albert Collins, the Texas bluesman, as the festival approached), and they did not rehearse before the festival, but each of them is such a skilled and seasoned professional that their performance was one of the festival's best.

Charlie Freeman, the guitarist, was the founder and original lead guitarist of the Mar-Keys. He has recorded with artists as various as Slim Harpo, Brother Jack McDuff, P. F. Sloan, and Jerry Lee Lewis. Both Freeman and the group's drummer, Maurice Tarrants ("Tarp," the Georgia Outlaw), have been with Jerry Lee Lewis's road band. Jim Dickinson, who sang with the group, has worked for years in Memphis and Nashville as an engineer, producer, singer, and session musician. He has had records on, among other labels, Sam Phillips's Sun Records, and some national music writers have called him the best living white blues singer. All the group are, as Tarp informed a pretty little Japanese groupie, "old-time Memphis heavies."

Their first song was St. Louis Jimmy Oden's "Goin' Down Slow." The sound balance at the NET rehearsal was so bad that Dickinson, screaming to make himself heard, developed a bad case of hoarseness, which fit very well with the lyrics of this song. "People, write my mother—tell her what bad, bad shape I'm in," Dickinson sang, and he really did sound as if he were dying. It was a perfect meeting of life, however unhealthy, and art: the real blues.

John D. Loudermilk, a Nashville songwriter ("A Rose and a Baby Ruth") who happened to be in town, sang a few songs, accompanying himself on guitar and harmonica. Wild-Child Butler, from Montgomery, Alabama, was perhaps the festival's most unusual performer. He looks, talks, and behaves just like a blues singer, and might even be a blues singer, except that he is apparently tone deaf. Fred McDowell and Johnny Woods played toward the end of the show. Their set was interrupted briefly by the movement of Johnny Winter's amplifiers across the stage. Winter himself was, as he had been since the day before, at a Memphis hotel, watching television.

The NET show, which would last two hours on television, had taken more than eight hours to tape. But the Memphis blues show's atmosphere has always been easygoing, like an all-day church meeting with dinner on the grounds, and people found ways to amuse themselves during delays in the concert. When nothing was happening, they wandered around, sat under the trees with friends, eating watermelon, drinking gin and tonic from old-fashioned green glass water jugs, turning on in their various ways. There was almost always something interesting to look at, young girls revealing startling new areas of skin, a Goodyear blimp that suddenly materialized and just as suddenly vanished, an old beatnik with the word JAZZ tattooed on his left shoulder. Just a good old down-home freak show.

Many of the blues show regulars had feared that all of the selfish outside interests, the overblown and half-assed preparations, the hype, in a word, surrounding this year's festival would destroy it altogether. The Memphis blues show was not conceived as a pop festival—it was started the year before Monterey—and its modest successes had never depended on huge crowds, publicity, and superstars. But Friday night's concert had been excellent, the NET show had been survived, and Sunday's gospel concert was not really very important. If Saturday night's "modern blues" show could escape disaster, the Memphis Country Blues Festival could be called a success.

But as night fell, the unsavory atmosphere that had hovered like a cloud over this year's blues show drew near and, before morning came, drenched the Overton Park Shell. Groups on the make, attracted by the hype, crawled out from under God knows what distant rocks and slithered up to Bill Barth. "We're the Jefferson Street Jug Band/Crazy Horse/the Permanent Brain Damage," they said. "We've come from five hundred/a thousand/nine million light years to be on your show. You gotta let us play." Barth, assailed by a vision of himself in Ed Sullivan's clothes, naturally said yes to all of them.

The show was not completely bad. An electric blues band from New Orleans called Nectar halted momentarily the downward musical trend. A few of the older musicians played, but no one paid them much attention. Furry Lewis, who more than any other living man exemplifies Memphis's musical history, a wonderful musician and entertainer, did two songs in a very subdued manner and then went away.

There were a lot of acts, each more out of place at a blues show than the one before; but it was left to Johnny Winter to provide the great climax of the evening and the festival.

Like so many people these days, Johnny Winter appears to know and to be able to reproduce every blues lick ever played. Maybe, when he was down in Beaumont fronting Little Johnny and the Jammers, he actually played blues. A cross-eyed albino boy, playing in those sweaty Texas joints—he must have played some blues. But in Memphis, he set up thirteen mammoth Sunn amplifiers (seven for him, six for his bass player), and though he played for over an hour, one blues lick after another, frequently several at once, he didn't play real blues.

By now there must be in the world a million guitar virtuosos; but there are very few real blues players. The reason for this is that the blues—not the form but the blues—demands such dedication. This dedication lies beyond technique; it makes being a blues player something like being a priest. Virtuosity in playing blues licks is like virtuosity in celebrating the Mass, it is empty, it means nothing. Skill—competence—is a necessity, but a true blues player's virtue lies in his acceptance of his life, a life for which he is only partly responsible. Johnny Winter can play rings around Furry Lewis; the comparison is ludicrous. But when Furry Lewis, at Winter's age, sang, "My mother's dead, my father just as well's to be," he was singing his life, and that is blues. When Bukka White sings a song he wrote during his years on Parchman Prison Farm, he is celebrating, honestly and humbly, his life. Most of the young guitar virtuosos do not have lives; they have record collections. Of course, they do have lives, if they would look inside and discover them. But it's much easier, and certainly more fashionable, to sing someone else's life, someone else's blues.

As Johnny Winter blasted away, I sat at the Shell, thinking about all these things, until I felt very depressed. Then I walked away into the park, through the flower garden and down into the playground that would soon become a giant expressway. The birds in the trees, kept up by the noise long past their sleeping time, were making soft fluting complaints. In my mood, there seemed to be some connection between Winter's amps, the expressway, the blues show, and the little birds, but I was too tired to figure it out.

The saga of the 1969 blues shows ends on an anticlimactic note. A few diehards, mostly old blues show regulars, met at the Shell Sunday morning, had a brief round of gospel singing, then packed and went home. Luckily, the city's First Annual W. C. Handy Memorial Concert drew two hundred customers Sunday night to the Mid-South Coliseum, which seats fifteen thousand. Luckily, because it appears that success may be a greater threat to the Memphis blues shows than the years of neglect the blues and its artists have suffered. If the grandiose plans for this year's show had been realized, Friday night's concert might have been sabotaged like the others.

Still, the recent wave of outside interest in the old Delta blues has not been entirely harmful (a few of the old men have made some money), and it might even have a positive effect, if those interested in the blues cared enough to temper their enthusiasm with understanding. Rock acts, in the interest of belatedly paying some dues, might stage a benefit concert in Memphis, for which the city might foot expenses, with the proceeds going to the old men. If the city wanted to do the right thing, it might start a blues archives, with good tapes and historical data on this vitally important music.

That is what might happen. But neither the city of Memphis nor the pop-music industry has ever really cared for old niggers and their music, and they are not likely to change now. The blues fad may have died away by next year, in which case Memphis will probably have its ordinary neighborhood blues get-together. On the other hand, next year the blues may be bigger than ever. In that case, the old men and the few who love them and their songs may have even less to look forward to.

DIXIE FRIED

The penultimate line of the next piece shows my unending determination to get things wrong. Once again we must consider one James Luther Dickinson, a personality more present in Memphis today than many who think they're still alive. As the new century commenced, I met Diann Blakely, a poet living in Nashville. I visited her in Nashville, doing research on her bones and skull, and while we were in Nashville, Dickinson asked me to write liner notes for his new CD, a reissue of the record he made in 1970. Diann's apartment was strange, I felt uncomfortable, but in the end I gave Dickinson what he asked for. He paid me with *The Complete Billie Holiday Columbia Recordings*. I already had a copy, but I thought that was nice of Jim.

You might think it would be easy to write liner notes for a record that was made to be played on your own record player. You would, however, be wrong.

In 1971, Jim Dickinson didn't have a decent record player. I don't know whether he does now, in this savage new millennium. I know I don't. In 1971, though, thanks to my mother's generosity, I had the same setup Miles Davis had, an Acoustic Research amplifier, a pair of AR-3A speakers (with their still-unsurpassed midrange), a Dual turntable, and a Sony reel tape player. Dickinson would bring over the tape of *Dixie Fried* and we'd listen to it. Then he'd go off and work on it some more.

———————

In a way, I was to blame for the whole thing. The day after Otis Redding died, I met the Atlantic Records producer Jerry Wexler, and we became close friends. A couple of years later, when he expressed dissatisfaction with the house band at Criteria Studios in Miami, I suggested he call Dickinson and see if he could hire the Dixie Flyers, a new Memphis band Dickinson had formed with the guitarist Charlie Freeman and some other local session players. As it turned out, Wexler could and did hire them, and to Miami they went.

I was then writing a book about the Rolling Stones, whom I met in 1968. After seeing homicide up close at the Stones' free concert at Altamont, the climactic event of the 1960s, I went to live in London for several months and came back to Memphis pretty crazy. In a largess of lunacy I drove to Miami, thinking that there I might be able to stay sane enough to write the book. Fat chance. This account would be robbed of its proper interest if I didn't tell you that some of the musicians on *Dixie Fried* were reduced at one point to digging for the drugs (previously buried by themselves) in the backyard by the light of Sam the Sham's motorcycle.

I didn't mean any harm! As Furry Lewis used to say, we just carryin' on fun. He also used to say, *Some people think the worried blues ain't tough—I declare if it don't kill you, it'll handle you mighty rough.* That's what happened. Some of us it killed, some it has only handled rough. So far. All I'd wanted was for Wexler to have the best musicians and Jim and Charlie to be bigtime players with Atlantic, whose records we had all grown up loving. Clyde McPhatter, LaVern Baker, Joe Turner, Ray Charles, Champion Jack Dupree, and all those great jazz records— you couldn't go any further uptown than Atlantic in the world of real people's music.

The Dixie Flyers didn't last long, but they did a lot. Among the artists they recorded with were Brook Benton, Jerry Jeff Walker, Carmen McRae, Little Richard, Dion DiMucci, Aretha Franklin, Ronnie Hawkins, the aforementioned Domingo Samudio, Taj Mahal, Sam and Dave, Delaney and Bonnie, and Petula Clark. The McRae, Hawkins, and Sam records are classics, and if the Dixie Flyers had never done anything else, they gave Atlantic Aretha's "Thrill Is Gone."

But Wexler didn't get what he'd wanted, a tidy little rhythm section in the MGs mold that would reliably cut hits with various artists while having instrumental hits on their own. The band couldn't agree on a direction. Dickinson and Freeman wanted what Dickinson has described as "a cross between Led Zeppelin and the Band," while other band members wanted to play like a polite jazz combo. Dickinson lasted, barely, through Petula Clark. I'm not sure how long the rest of the band stayed in Miami, but by the end of summer 1970, Charlie and Jim had come back to Memphis, as I had, wounded warriors all. Somehow the Dixie Flyers album transmuted into a solo Dickinson record.

Jim had reached the point where, as he said recently, "I could do what I wanted—but I no longer knew what I wanted to do." I remember the period as a siege.

––––––––––––––––

I arrived in Memphis from Georgia at the end of the 1950s, a teenager besotted with music. It took me a while to discover that the town was crawling with music-mad young men. The first one I met, I suppose, was Jim—James Luther—Dickinson, like me a student at Memphis State. A Baptist boy, as his name indicates—Dickinson's mother played piano at the Poplar Avenue Baptist Church—he'd transferred from Baylor University in Waco, where he studied drama with the renowned Paul Baker. Early in our acquaintance Dickinson told me about something he called "my aesthetics paper," an essay he wrote for a Baylor course.

The essay rendered a fictional account of an American Indian making a totem pole. The Indian had seen a vision, quite a specific one, and he worked feverishly, chopping and carving, in order to finish the totem pole before the idea got away from him. While he worked, a small, white cloud in the distant west began gathering moisture, swelling and darkening as it drifted steadily eastward toward the Indian. Hours passed while the cloud developed into an enormous black thunderhead that at last burst above the Indian, drenching him to the bone as he labored on. Finally the totem pole was finished, and he fell asleep, exhausted, cold, and wet.

When he woke up, the sky was bright and clear, sheer blue. The sun was warm. The object he had constructed lay before him, a magnificent sight, a truly remarkable totem pole. And yet, impressive though he had to admit it was, somehow it wasn't . . . quite what he'd had in mind. The storm he'd tried to ignore had entered into the process, altering his vision, changing his work irrevocably. He'd made a fine, perhaps even great, totem pole, but it wasn't exactly right; it wasn't the precise work, in the totem pole genre, he'd intended to create.

After all that work, that frenzy, what a letdown. Still, many other tree trunks lay around, waiting to be transformed into the pole he'd envisioned, the pole of his dreams. He selected another one and started again to chop and carve. Beginning to perspire with concentration and effort, he didn't see, in the distance, a small white cloud heave into sight. . . .

Forty years have passed since I first heard this story, and my reaction remains unchanged: a teenager with such subtle understanding of the artistic process possesses something akin to genius. One would have to go a long way to find a better metaphor than the young Dickinson devised.

In the early 1960s Dickinson ran the Market Theater in Memphis's farmers market, an empty stall where he put on plays and musical performances. Memphis in those years was developing a young musical community that included puppeteer and percussionist Jim Crosthwait, singer Sid Selvidge, guitarists Lee Baker and Gimmer Nicholson. Only now, more than forty years later, does it become apparent how perfectly suited Dickinson's technique was for his time and place. His approach is dramatic; he uses musicians the way directors use actors. Memphis provided musicians who were unique characters. Crosthwait was stopped by traffic police in an alcohol check and asked to walk a chalk line. He walked it on his hands, and they let him go. Selvidge was called the best singer since Frank Sinatra by a writer for the *New York Times*. Nicholson, a Red Cross disaster specialist who died of cancer in December 2000, made one classic CD; the story of Baker, a murder victim in 1996, is the stuff of multigenerational and multiracial tragedy.

Without the Dixie Flyers, Dickinson, like the Indian with his totem pole vision, was alone. It was something to see, a man with influences from

Antonin Artaud to Tex Ritter endeavoring to make a coherent statement of his Weltanschauung in Memphis at the start of the drug-crazed 1970s. I've heard Dickinson say that success is becoming, throughout life, more like yourself. In putting together *Dixie Fried*, Dickinson dug deep into his roots. Even the package was symbol laden. Dickinson appeared on the cover wearing his father's wedding suit, holding his grandfather's cane and top hat, standing—barefooted to display his web toes, of which he is ordinately proud—on the Dickinson carriage stone from the old Arkansas family plantation. The pose he strikes satirizes Edward Hull "Boss" Crump, Memphis's self-proclaimed "Great Benefactor." It's a way of saying, "We don't care what Mr. Crump don't allow—we gone barrelhouse anyhow."

For the songs also, Dickinson went back to his origins, among other places. "Wine" is the Night Caps' "corruption" (Dickinson's term) of "Wine Spodee-Odee"; he performed the song in high school. "The Strength of Love" is by John Hurley and Ronnie Wilkins, who wrote "Love of the Common People" and other classics. "Louise" was chosen because it reminded Dickinson of our friend Mike Alexander, who had recently blown his brains out with a double-barreled shotgun at the Alamo Plaza on Summer Avenue in Memphis. (Such events were part of the thunderstorm that accompanied the making of the album.) The version of Dylan's "John Brown" Dickinson knew was the Staple Singers'. Dickinson's version closed the first side of his album definitively. The Vietnamese war was still raging, but Dickinson observed in my hearing that the song isn't about war, it's about a mean woman.

"Dixie Fried" was the last song recorded for the album. I was at the session, and I remember thinking that the limit of insanity had been reached. And yet there's a kind of poise about it, as if an equilibrium has been regained after wild, out-of-control careering. "The Judgement" was written by Dickinson as a prophetic message, you might say, to then-president Richard Nixon. On that track Charlie Freeman plays celestial lead guitar, accompanied by "Clarinet Charlie" Lawing and the redoubtable Dr. John, Mack Rebennack, on piano. Dickinson found "O How She Dances" on a tape at the University of Texas music library in 1961. The song, or piece of eccentric material, was performed by New Orleans dentist and musicologist Edmund Souchon. Dickinson and Crosthwait used to do it at the Bitter Lemon, a coffeehouse in Memphis. Crosthwait's talking drums provide an ironic commentary to the track on *Dixie Fried*.

Dickinson met Bob Frank, the then-young Memphian who wrote the ancient-sounding "Wild Bill Jones," when Frank wandered into the Market Theater one night over four decades ago. He has lived for years in San Francisco, where he's still writing good songs. "Casey Jones" is Furry Lewis's take on the true story of the brave engineer. It was ripped off by Waylon Jennings for his "Waymore's Blues," but Waylon did it legally, or close enough. Anyway, Furry probably didn't write it all himself. The song provides a thoroughly satisfying conclusion for the record, true to Furry, to Memphis, to Dickinson's peculiar vision. Other tracks were cut for *Dixie Fried*, but the ones I've described, in spite of their diversity, somehow cohered.

The record was called, for a long time, *So Ready from the Creeks*, a phrase in Lord Buckley's version of Robert W. Service's "Dangerous Dan McGrew." As the months dragged on and Dickinson's vision became less pastoral, he thought of a play on the name of the defunct band. The name came from the turn of the century trolley from Memphis to the Raleigh Springs spa north of town, the Dixie Flyer. By the time Dickinson had the album finished, the Flyers had long ago crashed and he felt Dixie Fried.

When the record came out, I was listening to it one afternoon at Wexler's house in Miami. With Wexler and me was Mack Rebennack, who played guitar and piano on the album. "You can say what you want to," Mack said at one point, "but that sonofabitch is sellin' that song."

Wexler stood up and faced the speakers, spreading his arms. "If Bob Dylan made this record," he said, "they'd call him the risen Christ."

Nick Tosches, in his book *Country: The Twisted Roots of Rock 'n' Roll*, called *Dixie Fried* "one of the great musics of the century."

Some people liked the record a lot, but it wasn't around long. "You're not a man till you've been cut out," Dickinson said at the time, valiant as ever.

———

Over forty years and more, Dickinson has created a remarkable body of work, as solo artist, sideman, and producer. Musicians with whom he's been associated include denizens of the Sun, Stax/Volt, American, Sonic, and Muscle Shoals Studios, as well as the Rolling Stones, Chuck Berry, Alex Chilton, Screamin' Jay Hawkins, Toots Hibbert, the Replacements, Sleepy John Estes, Ry Cooder, and Bob Dylan. Dylan, who for a time used Dickinson's version of "John Brown" on the soundtrack played before his concerts, called Dickinson "my brother" on the Grammy Awards show in 2000 as he accepted a Grammy for *Time Out of Mind*, on which Dickinson played keyboards. Dickinson has lived to see his sons Luther and Cody succeed with their North Mississippi All-Stars, a superb blues and boogie band. Dickinson himself has a new album, *Free Beer Tomorrow*, threatening to escape. And *Dixie Fried* is reincarnated and ready to warp the minds of a new generation. Things could be worse. At least, unlike many of our friends, we're still here. For the moment.

BLUES FOR THE RED MAN

In October 1969 the Stones, with new member Mick Taylor, came over for an American tour. I flew to Los Angeles to see them, met Gram Parsons, and as Max Shulman said, "Bang! Bang! Bang! Bang! Four shots ripped into my groin, and I was off on one of the strangest adventures of my life." At the end of the tour I went to England with the Stones, returning months later to Memphis, where I was arrested on drug charges. (My mistake was having a few hemp plants in my vegetable garden.) Then I went to the Ozarks, holed up in a cabin, and meditated on music and death while in the world outside the most precious heroes kept falling.

> A few of the very bravest men in the tribe constitute a small group known as the "Contraries." As the name suggests, these men always do the opposite of what is said; i.e., they say "no" when they mean "yes," approach when asked to go away, and so on. In battle, they are possessed of a special magic, a "thunder bow," which causes them to accomplish acts of extraordinary bravery. One is called to the society of Contraries by a special vision, and thereafter he eats alone from special dishes, lives in a red lodge, and associates with ordinary people infrequently and in a distant manner.
>
> —Elman R. Service,
> *A Profile of Primitive Culture*

He wanted to be buried under a tree beside the White River in Arkansas, where he loved to camp and fish and get high and turn bright red, but you almost have to be born there to be buried there, and Freeman was born in Memphis. "They don't call it Bluff City for nothing," Freeman said.

Freeman (C. F. Freeman III, 31, Musician) boasted that no one could say Freeman I, II, or III had never been drunk. When his father died drunk in East Memphis, trying to see how fast his car would take Dead Man's Curve, Freeman was one month away from entering the world.

Freeman's mother was a waitress. She married again, a man named Red, a Baptist who worked for the Firestone Tire and Rubber Company. Red and Freeman found little to share.

Freeman's health was delicate. He suffered from rheumatic fever, asthma, nervous complaints, like Brian Jones, like many another gifted child. Doctors prescribed medicinal substances. Freeman discovered that he liked taking medicinal substances. He took as many medicinal substances as he could for as long as he lived.

Much of Freeman's early cultural life, the life of the spirit, centered around his neighborhood movie theater, the Normal on Highland Street. There he was a member of the Roy Rogers Fan Club and later an usher, riding to work on his moped, wearing a motorcycle jacket. His local heroes were Speed Franklin, Griff Rimmer, and Donny Creel, zip-gun hoods, but his idol was Lash LaRue. Watching Lash LaRue, Freeman imagined himself turning renegade to ride the owlhoot trail, to be revealed only in the end as the hero. When Lash LaRue came to play the rodeo at the Memphis Mid-South Fair, Freeman planned to join him and go on the road. Before Freeman could apply, LaRue was arrested by the Memphis police for possession of stolen goods, namely typewriters and sewing machines.

When Freeman was an adolescent, Memphis was a dry town, run by the fundamentalist religious groups and segregationists who represented just what Freeman was interested in rebelling against. But across the river, in the awful Arkansas rice-and-cotton-field bottoms, in West Memphis, the most dismal flat truckstop town in the country, in what looked as if it might be the last nightclub in the world, the Plantation Inn, Freeman and every other punk alive were doing what the neon sign said, HAVING FUN WITH MORRIS.

The bouncer at the Plantation Inn was a beefy Golden Gloves boxer named Raymond Vega. At his best, wearing gloves, Vega would run out of gas in the third round. At his worst, tight and in a cummerbund, he could be knocked across the dance floor and into the tables by a slender youth in a short-sleeved blue button-down collar shirt. No one kept order at the Plantation Inn, and the clientele included killers. Dago Tiller, for example, had literally snatched a woman bald-headed. Her picture was in the newspapers.

Freeman survived one of the frequent Plantation Inn brawls by standing in the middle of the dance floor kissing a girl named Bobbie Sue until the battle was over. Bobbie Sue and Freeman both went to Messick High School, in the same neighborhood (one-family houses, small lawns) where Freeman had ridden his moped. Sometime, years before, Freeman had been given a gun and a guitar, possibly by an uncle on his father's side of the family, and at Messick he started a band, inspired by the Largoes, the band at the Plantation Inn. The Largoes were Guitar Friday, Blind Oscar on organ, two tenor saxes, a bass player, and a drummer named Big Bell. The singer was called Wild Charlie or Tennessee Turner and wore heavy eye makeup and dark red nail polish.

Freeman's band included Duck Dunn, Don Nix, and Steve Cropper, who would later play with practically all the people in the world who were musicians and many who were not. They had come together from two groups, both of whom had played the Messick High School assemblies. Calling themselves the Royal Spades, they began to find work at the St. Michael's and Little Flower C.Y.O. dances and at roadhouses like the Starlight Supper Club, Neal's Hideaway, and Curry's Club Tropicana. Steve Cropper played rhythm guitar, wearing a harmonica on a wire rack around his neck, singing Jimmy Reed songs. This was in 1958 or 1959. At the Rebel Room in Osceola, Arkansas, the stage was separated from the customers by a screen of chicken-wire. The band discovered the reason in the middle of their second set, when the fists, bottles, and chairs began to fly. Freeman was happy that night. He had a band that played no better than the Largoes in an even worse place than the Plantation Inn.

The tenor sax player in the band was Charles "Packy" Axton, whose mother, Estelle, owned with her brother Jim Stewart a recording studio called Satellite Records, later to be renamed Stax, from the first two initials of their names. The availability of the studio, in an old movie house on a black street (at first it was behind a Dairy Queen, and Packy had to sell hamburgers between takes, but never mind), led the band to try making a record and to change their name, from the marquee that was still on the building, to the Mar-Keys. They tried and failed to cut several songs, among them one called "Last Night." Finally "Last Night" was recorded, but by somewhat different personnel from the original Messick band.

When Freeman finished high school he could read music well and was a more than competent player, much better than he had to be to play roadhouses. He accomplished what he had attempted in his Lash LaRue days by leaving town to go on the road with the Joe Lee Orchestra, the best legitimate band traveling out of Memphis. They sat down and played written arrangements. Freeman had left the Mar-Keys for better things. Then one night in Chicago, Freeman said, "I heard the record and the guy who played it said, 'That was the number-one record in the country, "Last Night," by the Mar-Keys.' I thought, That's my band. I better go home."

Freeman reassembled the band, and they played a few places in and out of town while waiting for the drummer, Terry Johnson, to graduate from Messick. Then they were on the road in a bus, a group of teenaged white boys with a number-one rhythm and blues hit, among the first Anglos, as Sam the Sham said at the funeral, to play the chitlin circuit. Mrs. Axton, Packy's mother, and Carla Thomas, who at eighteen, black and beautiful, had recorded the studio's first hit, "Gee Whiz," went with them, but the air in the bus soon became too thick, and the ladies went home, leaving the Mar-Keys and the chitlin circuit to fight it out among themselves. This was in 1961. Before the Rolling Stones had begun to get into trouble for playing nigger music to whites, before the Rolling Stones existed, the Mar-Keys were appearing at the Regal Theater in Chicago. Not even Elvis Presley had attempted the things the Mar-Keys got away with. Freeman jumped off the stage at the end of the show, landing on his knees, playing the guitar high over his head.

It is not certain just when Freeman started to turn red. He turned red when he got high, and he had been getting high most of his life. Turning red was not the half of it. When Freeman was in Milwaukee with the Mar-Keys, one of his girlfriends in Memphis received a call from him which began, "Baby, you may not believe this, but I'm up in the corner of the phone booth looking down at myself."

On their second national tour, in St. Paul, the Mar-Keys (they had a new piano player now, a Yankee named Bob Brooker whom they called Bear and did not especially like) had a fight onstage during which someone hit the Bear with a chair. That broke up the band, although groups including most or some or none of the original Mar-Keys still made appearances around the country. The originals were on various cuts on some of the albums, *Last Night*, *Night Before Last*, and *Do the Pop-Eye*, but most of the tracks were cut by Steve Cropper, who did not go on the road, and the studio musicians who had been playing with him, from whom Booker T. and the MGs emerged. Freeman played sessions and club dates around Memphis. There was at this time a thing known as a Charlie Freeman contract, the terms of which were that the promoter hired a band called the Mar-Keys with Freeman and God knew who else. Freeman collected the grand or two the promoter was paying, and the other musicians got ten dollars or fifty dollars or whatever they could get. But this was not a satisfactory state of affairs for Freeman, playing occasional gigs. It was very different from being on the road following a hit record.

Freeman missed the madness of the tour, he missed turning red and leaping off the stage each night, he missed the exhilaration. Freeman loved exhilaration, and when you are booked into an insane gig on the roof of the concession stand of a drive-in movie in a strange town, under some unfamiliar sky, and you start to play and Packy, not hearing anything, thinks the mike (one mike for seven instruments) doesn't work, and he's saying, "Hey! This fucking mike's broke," his voice coming through loud and strong on all the little speakers hanging inside all the cars on the lot, "Somebody fix the fucking mike," and the people begin to honk their horns in protest, so you play louder, and Packy, coming up to the mike to take a solo, steps back just far enough and falls off the roof, and—it's just fucking exhilarating, that's all.

Freeman loved the road; even being in Texas, where he always got into trouble, was better than not being on the tour. One night at LuAnn's in Fort Worth the Indian waitress Freeman had been sleeping with sat down at the bandstand in front of Freeman and raised her dress. Underneath she was wearing nothing but the pistol with which she intended to kill him, and this was her way of letting Freeman know it. He escaped as usual, but he used to say, "People from Tennessee should stay out of Texas. Remember Davy Crockett and the Alamo." Freeman saw the Alamo once. All over the walls, top to bottom, tourists had written, FUCK YOU.

Freeman was arrested twice in Texas, both times when he was with Jerry Lee Lewis. He had tried, when the Mar-Keys' contracts declined, to adopt a more normal way of life. He had enrolled at Memphis State University, where he made good grades, even attended meetings of the philosophy club, but it didn't last. Freeman had an offer to join Jerry Lee Lewis, the Ferriday, Louisiana, Flash, the Killer, one of the original Memphis Sun Rock and Roll Immortals. "I might have become a pseudo-intellectual," Freeman used to say, "but I went on the road."

Freeman was with the Lewis band between Fort Worth and Dallas in a place called Grand Prairie the first time they were arrested. They were coming back to their motel with seven hundred pills, two hundred for Jerry, five hundred for the band. It was Freeman's birthday, and the cops let him take along the drink in his hand on the ride downtown. They spent the night in jail, posted bond in the morning, and went to Canada for their next show. They were too busy to appear in court. They might drive to Canada and then to Miami for a matinee the next afternoon.

Months later they came back to Texas, feeling sure that their trouble with the law would have been forgotten. During the last show at Panther Hall in Fort Worth the cops started coming in, and by the end of the show the band was surrounded. Freeman put down his guitar, took the Seconals out of his pocket, swallowed them, and told a girl who was standing by the stage to wait right there, he'd be back in a minute. Then he walked up to a sheriff and shook his finger in the man's face. "Look here," Freeman said, and the sheriff slapped the handcuffs on him.

Walter Cronkite reported the arrest on the *CBS Evening News*, and Freeman was pleased. He escaped again and stayed on the road, living to freeze almost to death in a blizzard between Sioux Falls and Omaha. Freeman and two of Lewis's other musicians fell asleep in the front seat of a white Fleetwood Cadillac, wrapped up together for warmth, staying there in the minus-thirty-degree weather from 9:30 until 8:00 the next morning, when a snowplow found them. They were a couple of days in the Omaha hospital thawing out, taking glucose in the arm, but soon Freeman was flaming red again, dancing atop the piano bench, the drummer dancing on his snare and tom-tom, Jerry Lee dancing on the piano keys, all of them wired out of their minds. At the big finish Freeman dived off the piano bench onto his knees, playing the guitar high over his head. It was like traveling with a circus.

But two years with the same circus were about all that Freeman could stand. He came back to Memphis, got married, and started playing sessions at the local recording studios, cutting everything from radio and television commercials to albums with Chuck Berry, Slim Harpo, and Bobby Bland. Freeman was tall and thin, and when he left the road he looked, with his black shirts, bouffant hair, lip goatee, and shades, like a super-cool pimp. Living in Memphis again, he went hunting and fishing regularly for the first time since his uncles had taken him when he was a boy, and his hair fell lank and his beard grew in dark wisps. Freeman began to look Indian. He claimed his mother was part Choctaw and his father was part some other kind of Indian. Anyone who saw Freeman, bloodred, walk into a studio and throw a brace of fresh-killed stewing squirrels on the console, or saw him shoot with his shotgun a hole in the ceiling of the studio, knew he was, if not an Indian, at least a real renegade riding the owlhoot trail.

In spite of himself, Freeman rose in his profession. A recording band collected around Freeman and Tommy McClure, a bass player who'd been in Freeman's old outfit, the Roy Rogers Fan Club at the Normal Theater. An album they cut with Texas blues guitarist Albert Collins was nominated for a Grammy, and Jerry Wexler, the Atlantic Records executive and producer, hired the band to work in Miami as the house rhythm section at Criteria, one of the world's best recording studios.

Billed as the Dixie Flyers, they cut records with Sam the Sham, Ronnie Hawkins, Lulu, Petula Clark, Little Richard, Dion, Brook Benton, Aretha Franklin, Carmen McRae, Delaney and Bonnie, Taj Mahal, Sam and Dave, Jerry Jeff Walker, and the Memphis Horns, the remainder of the horn section from the Mar-Keys, the band Freeman started in high school. Freeman went on, as he had all his life, taking as many dangerous drugs as he could get. A Synanon therapist who happened to meet him described Freeman as "a Mozart of self-destruction." He passed out on the studio carpet at times, but he would scrape himself off the floor, strap on his guitar, and Wexler, who produced many of the Dixie Flyers' Miami sessions, would stand in the control room transported: "Listen to that Charlie Freeman," he'd say. "High as a kite and playing like a bird."

He had long been the only man besides Keith Richards, the world's only bluegum white man, who played the songs of Chuck Berry, the archetypal rock and roll guitarist, worse than Berry himself. For Ronnie Hawkins and Sam the Sham he played rock and roll that becomes space jazz, taking solos that sound as if the strings are sliding off the guitar. On ballads like "Breakfast in Bed" with Carmen McRae and "The Thrill Is Gone" with Aretha Franklin, Freeman's playing has such grace and feeling that one note can break your heart, if your heart's in the right place.

But there was too much ecstasy in the mixture; the Dixie Flyers were too volatile, like all Freeman's bands. They blew up. Freeman moved in the rare high atmosphere where music lives and breathes and the record company gasps for air. Coming out of the studio in Miami after hours and hours of drink and dope and music, he was seen to look at the sky, look at his watch, and say, puzzled, "Hell, man, it's eleven o'clock in the afternoon."

The Dixie Flyers left Miami at the end of 1970. They recorded and toured in America and Europe with the singer Rita Coolidge, but she started traveling with Freeman's friend, Kris Kristofferson, and in March 1972 the Dixie Flyers disbanded.

In the last months of his life Freeman played very little. He went places, Los Angeles, Woodstock, looking for work, not asking, just hanging out, staying cool, making himself available. He was too proud, too Indian, to do more than that. Even the most jaded musicians, who had played with everyone from Perez Prado to the Rolling Stones, sat in awe of his presence. They listened to his stories, threw knives with him, tried to get as red as he did, went into comas, woke up and went back to their mundane pursuits on a more sober level, leaving Freeman, the legends' legend, high and dry.

He came back to Memphis and moved into Orange Mound, a black ghetto adjoining his old high school neighborhood. Even in Memphis he could find no work. "They know where I am, they can call me," he said, when he did not have a telephone. His wife, Carol, went to work as a waitress, and Freeman went fishing. He went to Jack's Boat Dock on the White River so often that Jack offered him a job as a guide. When a neighbor scolded him for sitting on the porch drinking while Carol cut the grass, Freeman held up his magic fingers and said, "These hands were never meant to touch a lawnmower."

Finally, after the sheriff had come for the cars and Freeman had taken to sitting all day in his grandfather's old chair, shooting a pistol into the fireplace, Freeman decided to return to the bad-luck state of Texas. Tommy McClure, the bass player, was in Austin working with Marc Benno, a Texas guitarist who'd joined the Dixie Flyers when they were with Rita Coolidge, and they asked Freeman to come. He had looked for work in all the best places; now it was time to confront the worst. "I should've had a feeling about Texas," Carol said.

Freeman went to Austin and began playing with McClure and Benno. On his fourth night there he passed out, as he had on the three previous nights, as he did nearly every night, from taking as much as he could of whatever there was to take. Only this time, he didn't wake up. He was declared dead on arrival at Breckenridge Hospital at 2:11 PM, January 31, 1973. The primary cause of death was listed as pulmonary edema.

Freeman died wearing his favorite jeans and red plaid flannel shirt, even his favorite red underwear. He had his arrowhead, his gold guitar pick, and his grandfather's knife in his pocket. He died with his boots on. Remember the Alamo. FUCK YOU.

Like Lash LaRue in the movies, Freeman was revealed in the end to be a hero. They put him on an airplane in a crate, and at Memphis Funeral Home just before two o'clock on Saturday afternoon there were sprays of flowers, all kinds, all colors, along the walls and in great banks behind the steel-gray coffin, where Freeman, dressed in the gold-embroidered blue robe he'd worn onstage at the Albert Hall, was laid out on white satin. There were flowers from all the studios and record companies that had not been able to give Freeman any work toward the end of his life.

The pews were filled with Freeman's relatives and friends, including musicians from all the bands he had played in and even the engineer from the Memphis studio he'd shot up. The president of the musicians' local came, but he had to leave before the service started.

A Baptist preacher who had never seen Freeman alive found the grace to praise his "ministry in song" and closed by saying that to those who knew him, Heaven seemed closer now because Freeman was there, a thought that many of his friends must have found to be true but not comforting. Fred Ford, also known as Daddy Goodlow, one of Freeman's closest friends and one of the greatest living jazz reed players, a big black man in a black suit, looking with his long gray beard and large dark eyes like a great African minister of wisdom and death, praised Freeman for his strength and his sense of humor. "If he were here he would say, 'Be strong,'" Ford said, "and it seems like he is smiling."

Actually, Freeman wasn't smiling. His lips, pale under the pale lip rouge, were swollen slightly inside the corners where the undertaker had stapled them together. Still you could tell that he had smiled once with satisfaction before he nodded out, Freeman's smile of victory that you saw just before his head dropped.

They took his old acoustic guitar, draped with red roses, out of the coffin, closed the lid, and carried the coffin in a long procession away from the river to the edge of town, where the land starts rolling eastward, to the graveyard where a hole had been dug for Freeman's body. The funeral party crowded around the opening of fresh yellow clay. The preacher read from his book, said that he had a wedding at three o'clock, and left. Sam the Sham, wearing his gold earring and a denim jacket, said a few words that remained to be said about Freeman. "When Freeman was good he was the best, when he was bad he was the worst," said Sam, who has been known to brandish a weapon in a studio himself. "If all the people were pallbearers who wanted to have that honor," Sam said, "the handles on this coffin would be a mile long." All around the grave people were crying: Freeman's relatives, musicians, dope dealers, criminals, madmen, tears streaming down their faces. It was quite a sight.

Sam closed with a prayer, and the crowd dispersed quickly. The sun was bright, but the wind was chilling.

"I bet it's cold in that hole," Sam said as we drove back to town.

"Freeman's not in that hole," somebody said.

"I didn't say he was," Sam said in his beautiful gypsy voice. "I said I bet it's cold in there."

Tomorrow Sam was leaving Memphis for Los Angeles, his current home. I took him to the place where he was staying and listened to tapes of his new songs while he packed. Sam had picked up an old valise that he'd left at the Sun recording studios since 1966, and he went through it, packing his gold records of "Wooly Bully" and "Little Red Riding Hood," throwing away old fan letters, motel bills, a business card from a limousine rental service. "The limos of youth," I said.

"They have a way of turning into rattletraps," Sam said.

He was going across town to see a girl he'd wrapped in furs a few years before, so we said goodbye. McClure and Benno, who had driven up from Texas, came over to my place later. We drank and took things and talked about the Normal Theater and the Plantation Inn. I remembered the night at Freeman's house in Miami when McClure was carrying his right hand in a sling after having smashed it against a wall, Sam was preparing to terrorize the studio with a revolver, and I, after traveling for lifetimes with the Rolling Stones in such places as England, Alabama, and Altamont, was phosphorescent blue and undergoing attacks from giant golden spiders. I drove to the studio that night with Freeman and guitarist Duane Allman, the Midnight Rider. We were talking about our beautiful bandit friend, Mike Alexander, who played bass in Duane's first band, and who, the month before Duane's fatal motorcycle wreck, would take a shotgun and blow the top of his head off in Memphis at the Alamo Plaza hotel. Now Mike, Duane, and Freeman were all dead.

"Freeman wasn't no Indian. He put it off on the Indians. Freeman was just crazy," McClure said, his mad eyes swirling into mine. It was surprising to see any of us still alive.

Early in the morning McClure and Benno left, heading back to Texas. I locked myself out of the house, broke a window, climbed in, and passed out.

When I woke up I took some medicinal substances for my mind and body and started to write, listening to a record by Freeman's original favorites, Roy Rogers and the Sons of the Pioneers:

> The Red Man was pressed from this part of the West,
> It's unlikely he'll ever return
> To the banks of Red River where seldom if ever
> Their flickering campfires burn.
>
> Home, home on the range,
> Where the deer and the antelope play,
> Where seldom is heard a discouraging word
> And the skies are not cloudy all day.

BEALE STREET'S GONE DRY

My own enlightenment came in Cleveland, Mississippi. I was leading the orchestra in a dance program when someone sent up an odd request . . . Would we object if a local colored band played a few dances?

. . . We eased out gracefully as the newcomers entered. They were led by a long-legged chocolate boy and their band consisted of just three pieces, a battered guitar, a mandolin and a worn-out bass.

The music they made was pretty well in keeping with their looks . . . The strumming attained a disturbing monotony, but on and on it went, a kind of stuff that has long been associated with cane rows and levee camps. Thump-thump-thump went their feet on the floor. Their eyes rolled. Their shoulders swayed. And through it all that little agonizing strain persisted. It was not really annoying or unpleasant. Perhaps "haunting" is a better word, but I commenced to wonder if anybody besides small town rounders and their running mates would go for it.

The answer was not long in coming. A rain of silver dollars began to fall around the outlandish, stomping feet. The dancers went wild. Dollars, quarters, halves—the shower grew heavier and continued so long I strained my neck to get a better look. There before the boys lay more money than my nine musicians were being paid for the entire engagement. Then I saw the beauty of primitive music.

—W. C. Handy, *Father of the Blues*

At the first Rock and Roll Hall of Fame banquet, in January 1986, some months after Cleveland had been chosen as the site for the Rock and Roll Museum, Sam Phillips, whose Sun Records had made known to the world the music of Elvis Presley, Jerry Lee Lewis,

Charlie Rich, Johnny Cash, and Roy Orbison—among many others—introduced Carl Perkins with the words, "It's a late date to be saying it, and I mean no disrespect to the people of Cleveland, who I'm sure are a fine people and *spir*achul people—but Cleveland ain't ever gonna be Memphis."

He was booed by an audience too young and ignorant to know or care what Memphis, the Mississippi Delta, the South, have meant to music.

Before the first ten years of the twentieth century were over, W. C. Handy had started writing and publishing songs based on the blues he heard on Memphis's Beale Street. In the 1920s and '30s, the original blues performers themselves, men like Will Shade, Gus Cannon, Robert Wilkins, Furry Lewis, and Robert Johnson, set the tone: "Cocaine habit is mighty bad, it's the worst old habit that I ever had." The '40s found Memphians Jimmy Lunceford, Buster Bailey, and the elder Phineas Newborn, the latter two sidemen with Duke Ellington and Lionel Hampton, carrying the tradition forward with swing and boogie-woogie. It has been suggested that Carl Perkins's "Blue Suede Shoes"—the first record to reach the top of the pop, rhythm and blues, and country charts—represents one of the most important steps in the evolution of American consciousness since the Emancipation Proclamation. Perhaps it was an even more important step, because the proclamation was an edict handed down from above, and the success of "Blue Suede Shoes" among Afro-Americans represented an actual grassroots acknowledgment of a common heritage, a mutual overcoming of poverty and lack of style, an act of forgiveness, of redemption.

At a distance of sixty-three years, several generations, it can be seen as the prelude to a tragedy, the murder of Martin Luther King, one of the '60s assassinations from which the country still has not recovered.

In 1959, having graduated from Sidney Lanier High School for (white) Boys in Macon, Georgia, I moved with my family to Memphis. I knew little about the place other than that it was on the Mississippi River and had an association with the kind of music I liked. I soon learned that Memphis was, if anything, even more "Southern" and puritanical than Macon, with no liquor served by the drink and almost no integration. Restaurants, taxis, hotels, parks, libraries, movies, all were segregated. Blacks still sat in the back of the buses. Whites who wanted to hear black music went to an all-white club called the Plantation Inn across the river in West Memphis, Arkansas, and listened to a singing group called the Del Rios or to Loman Pauling and the Five Royales. My first experience on Beale Street was being thrown out of a Ray Charles concert at the Hippodrome for sharing a table with some black classmates from newly integrated Memphis State University. There were tables for blacks and tables for whites, but no mixing allowed. "What you mean, pattin' these nigger girls on the ass?" a cop asked me. "I haven't patted anybody on the ass yet, sweetheart," I said, finding myself seconds later face-to-face with the gravel in the alley. Living in Memphis, off and on, for twenty-five years, learning the blues, I would come to know those alleys, that downtown gravel, well.

An essay I wrote in the mid-1970s for *Beale Street Saturday Night*, a documentary album by James Luther Dickinson, provides a snapshot, now fading, of Memphis as it was then. Beale Street these days is not exactly thriving, but you can go there on certain nights and hear great music from the likes of Herman Green and Calvin Newborn. The following, though, is how it used to be.

Once a friend came to dinner at my house in Memphis, Tennessee, bringing two girls on holiday from London, new friends he had met on his way across town. Some people, I hear, have rules about mealtimes, banning serious conversation and the throwing of food, but at my house the only rule is that there are no rules. So while we were eating and getting drunk I asked my friend's English friends if they were enjoying Memphis. The girls, who were paying for their holiday by working as waitresses in a bad Memphis Italian restaurant, were enjoying Memphis hardly at all, and what they enjoyed least was their customers telling them how good life is down among the magnolias on the Mississippi.

It took some time to describe the disgusting ignorance of people who don't know how bad their lives are. By the time the girls had finished answering the question, I had finished dinner and was about three-fourths done getting drunk. Maybe more than three-fourths. I told them that in this century, Memphis, Tennessee, has changed the lives of more people than any other city in the world. I used, I regret to report, the phrase "cultural influence." The girls, one of whom kept falling asleep from some pills some of the benighted people of Memphis had given her, wanted to know whether I preferred Memphis to Paris, London, Rome, and then left to wait tables. I never had a chance to tell them that, like it or not, they had shopped at supermarkets, eaten at drive-in restaurants, slept in Holiday Inns, and heard the blues because people in Memphis had found ways to convert these things into groceries.

I know now, because I am more sober, that none of us can say what city has in our time most affected people's lives. Los Alamos, New

Mexico, and Los Angeles, California, both have been influential, and so have St. Louis, Missouri, and Peking, China. But after the yellow fever plagues that all but destroyed Memphis at the end of the last century, people there created from the shell of an antebellum southern town a new city with new traditions.

The ninth-century tradition among the Indians, the first inhabitants we know about in the place that would one day be called Memphis, was to live in small villages and hunt with spears and clubs in forests of giant chestnut, elms, many kinds of hickory, and oak, for buffalo, deer, plentiful game, birds, and fish. The sixteenth-century tradition among the Spanish in the same place was to feed the Indians alive to dogs. There were too many Indians then for that tradition to last, but in the end there were too many white men, Spanish, French, English, and American, killing as they came. The Chickasaws sold the land in 1818 to the United States government for five cents an acre. The next year, Generals Andrew Jackson and James Winchester and Judge John Overton, land speculators from Nashville who were already the de facto owners of most of the land before the government bought it, laid out plans for the city of Memphis. Jackson had granted squatters right on his land to many of his old troops, and he sold out before the old soldiers learned that their land was to be incorporated and Jackson's gift to them would be taxed. Jackson went on to be president and to send the Indians to Oklahoma.

In the next twenty-five years, Memphis grew from a flatboat town, a collection of waterfront shacks, to a steamboat town with strange grand houses built away from the river beside huge magnolia trees. On Front Street, a mule could still step in mud up to his shoulders.

During the Civil War, after the heroic, twenty-minute Battle of Memphis, the Union Army was headquartered on Beale Street, where local blacks, most of them freed slaves who feared the local whites, began to gather. The war did not destroy Memphis, as it did other cities, like Atlanta. The fine old houses were untouched, but the city became stagnant. The rich felt little in common with poor whites, less with blacks. No sewers were built; why should the rich buy indoor plumbing for the poor? So there came the yellow fever, again and again, like the plagues of white men on the Indians, until the land was once more worthless enough to arouse greed.

In 1878, when yellow fever struck Memphis for the third time, most of its fifty-five thousand people left. About six thousand whites and fourteen thousand blacks stayed; only 30 percent of the whites, but 90 percent of the blacks, survived. There was considerable weight of opinion, especially amongst the writers of newspaper editorials in river towns to the north, that Memphis should be burned as a breeder of pestilence. Memphis did surrender its city charter, recovering it in 1893, after building sewage disposal and running water systems.

Memphis was a town again, but just the shell of one, a blank page on which Clarence Saunders wrote "Piggly Wiggly". Like Thomas Edison, who after the war developed a means of transmitting electric current to kill the roaches in the Main Street rooming houses where he lived, Saunders with the supermarket was a man with a plan. Fortune's Jungle Garden, a restaurant too small to hold the crowds after the opera, took food out to customers who would eat and drink in their carriages under the trees late at night. When Ed Crump came to Memphis from Holly Springs, he was just one more speculator, another man with a plan. W. C. Handy and a number of other people around this time began writing down and publishing blues songs. These men and their plans prospered. Crump became mayor of Memphis in 1909, and the melody lingers on. Through the 1920s Crump controlled West Tennessee, had great power in the state legislature, and carried disproportionate influence in the United States Congress. When asked for whom they would vote, Memphians said, "I'm not sure—Mr. Crump hasn't made up my mind." The depression of the 1930s helped few people anywhere, but it was Franklin Roosevelt's hostility to city bosses, along with the efforts of brave locals like Lucius Burch and Edward Meeman, that made certain Mr. Crump's decline. By then Crump was past his prime, and no politics was local.

Beale Street was also past its prime, but it wasn't local, either. There was enough left in 1956 that Count Basie, playing in town, could hear Phineas Newborn Jr. at the Hippodrome. The street had lost its bloom, but there were still a lot of stores, most of them pawn shops. In the years since, "urban renewal" has erased the black parts of the surrounding neighborhood. The path of Martin Luther King from the Clayborn Temple African Methodist Episcopal Church to Beale Street has been scraped clean, bound by curbs, and planted with grass.

What happened to King in Memphis was murder, but what is the word for the fate of Eli Persons? In 1917 Persons was charged in Memphis, on what evidence no one knows, with the rape and beheading of a sixteen-year-old white girl. Law officers gave him to a crowd of more than a thousand whites, who decided not to lynch Persons, since hanging was too good for him and not enough to satisfy the girl's mother. They built a bonfire with Persons tied to the central log, burned him to a crisp, cut out his heart, and rolled his head down Beale Street.

Memphis is called the Bluff City because it is on the highest spot on the Mississippi River between the Ohio River and Natchez, but the bluff is near its lowest point at the foot of Beale Street. The *Kate Adams*, the *Viney Swing*, the other great steamboats, are gone, but the river is still wet, a witness, never silent, which never accuses but sometimes condemns. Beale Street begins at the river, struggles up the bluff, across the I. C. tracks and Front Street, past empty sockets and dry rot of urban blight. The quiet voices of men down the street trading for cotton do not reach our ears, and even the ghosts of the girls of the original Gayoso Hotel seem to be asleep.

The grand old Orpheum Theatre, with its resident phantom, stands at Beale and Main, just beyond the killer mall. Across Main Street both sides of Beale have been bulldozed, a new bank and a new public utilities building have been constructed, and all traces of the past have been destroyed up to Lansky's Men's Wear, the place where Carl Perkins and Elvis Presley learned how to dress cool. In Lansky's window are striped shoes and a lemon-yellow suit with scalloped lapels.

Crossing Second Street, coming to pawn shops where mesh screens protect empty, boarded-up display windows, you notice that no one else is on the street. Passing the place that used to be a Chinese opium den, you see no one. A. Schwab's department store, Art Hutkin's hardware store, the Engelbergs' pawn shop, are about all that survive of human commerce to Third Street, the beginning of the blocks that made Beale Street "the greatest place on earth," Thomas Pinkston said, "until they ruint it."

In the early decades of this century, before Beale Street was ruint, Memphis was the murder capital of the country, and Beale Streeters did more than their part to secure the title. One night in 1909 a saloon-keeper named Wild Bill Latura walked into Hammitt Ashford's black saloon, announced that he was going to turn the place into a funeral parlor, and with six bullets shot seven patrons of the establishment, killing five. Beale Street was dangerous, but there were no Beale belles and no cocaine down on the old plantation. That same year Sam Zerilla opened the Pastime Theatre, soon followed by the Palace Theatre, built by Antonio Barrasso and the Pacini brothers. On Thursday nights the Palace presented special shows for whites.

Now not only is the Palace gone but also the Monarch, Hammitt Ashford's, P. Wee's, and all the whorehouses of Gayoso Street. At Myrtle Street, near the end of Beale, you can throw a half-empty beer bottle through the window of 706 Union Avenue, where Sam Phillips made the first recordings of Elvis Presley, Jerry Lee Lewis, Johnny Cash, Charlie Rich, and Howling Wolf, and chances are no one will even see you. It is a short walk across Nathan Bedford Forrest Park to the University of Tennessee medical school, where many people from Beale Street have been dismantled by students to be buried in three-foot boxes. They don't get many Beale Street cadavers now, because most people from Beale Street are dead or gone, or both. The hotel and office buildings of downtown Memphis that once looked down on Beale Street do not see even the little that is left, because all the old downtown hotels and many other buildings are empty. Through the wisdom of its civic leaders, Memphis is once again nearing the point of being worthless enough to attract money. When that happens, watch out. As Sleepy John Estes said, Memphis has always been the leader of dirty work in the world.

THE KING IS DEAD!
HANG THE DOCTOR!

What, you might ask, does a piece about Elvis's doctor have to do with the blues? In some ways the following piece is the hardest I've ever had to write. In March 1978, I fell off a mountain in North Georgia, breaking my back. I had by then been writing a book about the Rolling Stones for nearly ten years and was well strung out on CNS depressants: muscle relaxers, soporifics, and painkillers. The broken back multiplied the problem; after that I was really in pain. A year later, I had a drug dependence that dwarfed Tennessee. The two people who warned me were Jim Dickinson and Paul Bomarito. I knew they were right, that I was approaching the point where the toxic dose is smaller than the therapeutic dose. Twice I attempted to stop taking drugs, as they say, cold turkey, and twice had grand mal epileptic seizures. Dickinson suggested I see Nichopoulos. My friend Joella Bostick, crazy but shrewd, also knew Nichopoulos well and admired him, and so I made his acquaintance.

That, you might think, would be enough to gain entry for this piece in a blues book. Certainly, considering the innate sadness of the material—a decent Greek doctor from Alabama tries to help a good ignorant old boy from Mississippi entertain his dumb-assed fans. But it doesn't stop there. Not hardly. I did the piece for *Playboy*, who rejected it, deciding they had no interest in telling the world Elvis *didn't* die of drugs.

Before that rejection, though, I had to, first, not die of drugs myself, and second, write the piece. I hadn't worked in months, and when I tried, I found that I could no longer write. It was without question the worst time of my life. I walked around dead. You can't write unless you can hear the words in your head, and my head wasn't talking. I didn't have the blues, I had a terminal illness. Slowly, after months of trying to force myself to work and failing, I gave up and God started speaking to me again. At first there were only faint whispers, but the voice grew stronger.

The piece wound up being published in an anthology titled *The Elvis Reader* with its pages in the wrong order. I only wish I were joking. Before seeing the book, I had a copy sent to Memphis deejay George Klein, the president of Elvis's senior class at Humes High School. When I saw him, George said, "Man, was that piece you wrote screwed up somehow? It was really hard to follow."

As Dr. Nick and I drove out of Memphis, we passed one of the green and white traffic signs with a guitar pointing the way to Graceland and the likeness, sideburns clearly outlined, of Elvis Presley. Dr. Nick, driving a yellow Cadillac that Presley had given him, looked out at the cold spring rain. "For a long time," he said, "I didn't realize the full extent of the part I was playing in this thing."

We were going to Anniston, Alabama, to spend a few days with Dr. Nick's mother. It was the first chance we had found to talk since the Tennessee State Medical Examiners' hearing, several weeks earlier, where Dr. Nick had been charged with misprescribing to twenty patients, including Elvis Presley.

"One day Father Vieron came to my office," Dr. Nick said. The Reverend Father Nicholas Vieron, priest of the Greek Orthodox church attended by Dr. Nick and his family, has known Dr. Nick for twenty-five years. "He told me that he thought I was doing myself an injustice, I was doing my practice an injustice, my patients, my family, by being gone so much. That Elvis could have any doctor he wanted and didn't really need me all the time. That I shouldn't devote so much time to him. 'Why do you need to be there? Why can't it be somebody else on all these tours that you go on?'

"I gave it some serious thought. This was in 1975. The tours had changed, they'd really gotten laborious. It used to be that after a performance, Elvis enjoyed having some of the fans who would hang around the hotel come up and talk to him, just to get a feeling of people in that area and what they thought of the show and to feed his ego some. This would take two or three hours. I thought it was good for him, because it occupied his time, kept him happier. But some of the bodyguards resented it, because it meant that they had to stay on duty. If he'd get ready for bed, go on and have his supper, then they could go on out to the bar and do their thing.

"So, somehow we got away from doing that, and it really got to be a drag, because a lot of that responsibility after the show—who's going to be with him and talk to him for two or three hours—a lot of times would fall on me. And this was day and night after night. My nights were just horrible. I would go to bed when he'd go to bed, and then he might sleep two or three hours and wake up wide awake, and I'd have to go in and try to get him back to sleep. Then he might sleep two or three more hours, or he might sleep four or five hours. But the average was he'd sleep two or three hours and wake up, two or three hours and wake up. It was hard for me to fit into that schedule. On a tour, I had very little time when I could go and do anything. If he woke up and I wasn't there, he'd go bananas. It got to the point where I was working eighteen or twenty hours a day, sleeping in cat naps.

"It was also causing me an awful hassle at the office. The other doctors were bitching about me being on a constant vacation. How could I expect to come home and want time off? I'd have to work double, I'd have to make up the night calls I missed. And yet it was the same sons of bitches that would derive the benefit from it. The money I got from Elvis went to them, went into office practice. I had a hell of a time with all this.

"So when Father Vieron came in that day, I'd already given it a lot of thought. But Elvis had problems when I didn't go, and he'd carry somebody else. There were a couple of tours, one Vegas tour and maybe a couple of other tours, where the shows didn't go too well because he was oversedated. A lot of times when the other doctors would go, it would be hard for them to keep the medicine with them. He always wanted to keep something there by his bed in case he'd wake up. He'd wake up and think he wasn't going back to sleep. He'd be half asleep, and he'd reach over and take whatever was there. Maybe three or four or five sleeping pills. The next day, try to get him up, no way to get him up. There were several times when he was a robot onstage. He'd done these songs so many times, a lot of people didn't realize it, but hell, he might not wake up till halfway through the show or after the show was over. Tell him things that he did, and he just wouldn't remember. After having gone through a few experiences with that, and some really bad ones, it was the consensus of the Colonel and the promoters that things were under better control when Elvis was with me than when he was with some other people. That they'd rather have me on the tours, and it got down to the fact that they weren't going to have any more tours at all if I wasn't going.

"I thought, Is it really my place to look at the business aspect of this relationship? Is it really my place to worry about what his promoters and business people are worried about, like, 'Is he going to be able to make the next show? Are we going to have to cancel it? Is he going to be too groggy to do the show?' It was a dilemma for me. It felt like this was going beyond the bounds of doctoring, and yet it wasn't, because his welfare, his health, were involved, and it's hard to separate that aspect of it from the business aspect.

"But the kicker, my turn-on, was the crowds. People would say, 'Don't you get tired of seeing the same damn show over and over again? How can you sit through the same songs all the time?' You don't hear half the songs. But you're watching these thousands of people who are mesmerized by this human being up there, and watching their expressions, their jumping up and down. The real feeling of accomplishment comes from knowing that he was able to do so much for so many. People would carry away something that would last them for weeks and months, for a lifetime."

But at the medical examiners' hearing, when asked what he would do if he ever found himself in a situation like that of being Elvis Presley's physician, Dr. Nick said, "I'd get out of it, if I had the option."

Near Corinth, Mississippi, about a hundred miles from Memphis, we stopped for gasoline. With his fluorescent mane, olive complexion, and distinctive, rugged features, Dr. Nick is easy to recognize. It occurred to me that being in Mississippi this year with Dr. Nick could resemble being there some years ago with Dr. Martin Luther King. Dr. Nick has received many threats of violence, and a bullet thought to have been intended for him struck a doctor who was sitting behind him at the Liberty Bowl football game in Memphis on Thanksgiving Day 1978, even before he had been accused in print and on television of killing Elvis Presley.

It had been raining off and on all morning. It would soon be eleven o'clock, but it still seemed early, like a winter morning just before sunrise. We bought soft drinks in cans and drove on, the wipers pushing up dirty trickles of mist.

Before we left Memphis, Dr. Nick had said, "Ask me anything." I asked him how he got to know Elvis Presley. He remembered the first time he treated Presley, who was at the time newly married and staying at his ranch near Walls, Mississippi. On a Saturday afternoon early in 1967, George Klein, a friend of Presley whose fiancee, a nurse, worked for Dr. Nick, called Dr. Nick to the ranch to attend to Presley. "He had a movie to start Monday, and he'd been real active the last couple of days riding his horses," Dr. Nick said. "The movie was going to have a lot of action in it, and he was having a difficult time walking because of the saddle sores and blisters he had developed. He thought that there might be some way he could get an immediate cure so he could go on out there. I don't know if he thought I was a faith healer, or what."

Dr. Nick convinced Presley to postpone making the movie for a few days and helped to notify Colonel Parker and the film company of the delay. Then Dr. Nick left, but he was called back to the ranch twice that afternoon, once to answer a question of Presley's "that he could have asked me over the telephone," and once again even though Presley "didn't have any problem. He just wanted to talk. I don't remember what the talk was about. That was the first encounter. I didn't realize at that encounter that this was the way he was. That this was going to be a way of life. But it was typical of him; throughout our relationship, there would be times that he could handle something over the telephone, but he'd rather for you to come out and talk to him about it. He'd want me to fly out to California. He'd make up some ridiculous problem. There wasn't anything wrong, he just wanted somebody to talk to.

"Things got a lot easier for me when he moved to Memphis. After his first major illness, he felt more secure here from a medical standpoint than he did seeing different people on the West Coast. His first major illness was caused by an acupuncturist out there who was not giving him acupuncture. He'd have a syringe with Novocain, Demerol, and cortisone that he would inject, and he'd tell Elvis this was acupuncture. We discovered this when we had to put Elvis in the hospital in '73. We almost lost him then.

"From that time till the time he died, except for a few skirmishes we had, he became very dependent on my opinion. He wouldn't feel like he was show-ready unless he was involved in a certain program. We'd start going through the routine of what we needed to do about his weight, what we needed to do to build up his endurance. We needed to be sure that he'd seen his dentist, that he'd gotten his ingrown toenails clipped so he didn't get in trouble onstage. We had to be sure we had things like a nasal douche, a little glass cup that we'd put salt water in to clean out his sinuses. We had Ace bandages and adhesive tape in case he pulled a groin muscle. He was always having trouble with a sprained ankle, and we took ankle corsets, making sure we had two or three. Sometimes he'd be on such a strict diet that somebody would go to these hotels a day or two ahead of time and prepare his special diet food for him. On a couple of tours he didn't eat anything but diet jelly. He'd get the hots about something like that, some fad. At the time, it was terrible. We wanted him to lose weight, but he's got to have the energy to perform, and it's hard to build up physical endurance without eating properly.

"Actually we had better control over his diet on the road than we did at home. At home we had the problem of everybody mothering him—scared if they don't carry up a dozen ham biscuits, fix six eggs and a pound of bacon, the poor little boy won't get enough to eat or else he's gonna get mad at them and they're gonna get fired because they didn't fix the usual thing. A lot of times I'd go by at mealtimes just to eat part of his food, so he wouldn't eat too much.

"When he started spending nearly all of his time here, it was sort of a daily thing. On the way home, I'd stop by and see how he was and kill two or three hours there, then get my ass chewed out when I got home: Where had I been?"

"What made you inclined to stop by there on a daily basis?"

"He'd get his feelings hurt if I didn't. I just enjoyed talking to him. I'd get busy and say I'll go by there tomorrow instead of today, and then tomorrow I'd be busy too and still wouldn't go by there, and the next thing I knew I'd get flak, like, 'Why are you mad at Elvis?' People that he liked, he just liked to be around them, and if you weren't around him, he'd want to know why you weren't.

"We'd usually have sort of a family gathering, have supper all together and break bread. His father would be around, Priscilla was around for a while, some of the guys who were working there. Then that was put to a halt. I'm not sure whether it was Priscilla's doing or a joint thing between Priscilla and Mr. Presley. A lot of guys would go there just to freeload, and Priscilla was into this thing that she wanted some privacy with him. She didn't want to have somebody around every minute of the day. But he couldn't be satisfied unless he had five or ten people around all the time."

"How did he take Priscilla's leaving? Was he crushed by it?"

"He was hurt I think mainly because of the circumstances. That she got involved with her karate instructor, and he's the one who pushed her into that. I think he was more mad at Mike Stone than at Priscilla. He thought they were friends and that Mike stabbed him in the back. Yet on the other hand he was gone so much of the time touring, he was with other women, and he had such a guilty conscience about being gone so much and doing so many things that he was doing, that he encouraged her to get involved with other activities and other people. That way he wouldn't feel so guilty.

"He seemed to have to have female companionship. Not on a sexual basis, just female companionship. Because he missed his mother so much—because of his not having that relationship, he enjoyed relationships like the one with Mrs. Cocke, the nurse. It was a kind of maternal relationship."

"Did Elvis get along with his father?"

"He had a lot of respect for his father. He and his father didn't see eye to eye about a lot of business things that they did together. He kind of let his father run his business, give him something to do. Elvis was always spending more than he was taking in, and it was always driving his father crazy. If Elvis spent all the money in his bank account, he figured he could do another tour and make more.

"I remember one time that we were talking about how rough our parents had it back in the Depression, how they had a hard time making ends meet. We talked about the number of hours our parents worked, and how little they got out of it, and he told this story about his daddy. Once when they were living in Mississippi, they'd gone without food for a couple of days, and Vernon went to some grocery store or food market and stole some food, and he got caught and went to jail for several days. Elvis made me promise that I'd never say anything about that. He said, 'Nobody knows about this. I don't want anybody ever to know this, it would really hurt my daddy if people knew.' Right after Elvis died, it was in one of those damn—*Midnite*, or the *Enquirer*—a lead story, 'Elvis's Father in Jail.' That was when everybody was selling everything they could get."

"When you met Elvis, he was already depending on sleeping pills to go to sleep?"

"Since he started in the music business, he was taking at least two or three sleeping pills, sedatives, nearly every night. Take it on down to the last few years, on the road, it was so important to him to get rest and sleep so he could be perfect for the next day. He felt like people had to travel so far and pay so much money to see his shows, he wanted everything to be perfect."

"Did the problem you had controlling the amount of medication Elvis took worsen as time went on?"

"No, it never really worsened, in the sense that there was a perpetual problem of taking more and more all the time. It was an episodic thing. There were times when he'd get by with almost nothing, times when he'd take normal amount, other times that he'd take more—I'm talking about sleep medication or tranquilizers—depending on what he was going through. There were times when he wanted to sit up and just read. He wouldn't take anything for sleep. He'd sit up and read for two or three days and not take any kind of medicine other than maybe a decongestant or his vitamins. This to me is not an addict.

"They talk about the importance of records of what was done, when the same person was doing the same thing day in and day out. You know this one person as well as you know yourself. You know what you've been through with him. You know if he's been having a bad night, if the speakers were bad and he's upset about it, or some song didn't go off right, or the guitar player broke a string, or something created in his mind a bad show. It was always worse in his mind than it was in anybody else's. He was such a perfectionist that I would know when it was going to be hard for him to sleep and hard for me to sleep because I'd be busy all night long trying to get him to sleep. Instead of seeing him every three or four hours, I'm going to be in there every two hours. There have been many nights when I fell asleep across the foot of the bed waiting for him to go to sleep."

"Do you think he was happy, in the sense of being satisfied with where he had been and where he was going, when you knew him?"

"I think he was happy, up to that point, but he had greater expectations—things that he wanted to accomplish. He in no way had fulfilled his hunger for either knowledge or improving himself as a performer in films or on the stage as a singer. He had a lot that he hadn't touched.

"He had some problems with his health. His blood pressure was a little elevated. He was most of the time overweight, he had problems with his colon that contributed somewhat to his protruding abdomen, he had some liver problems we thought were related to his Tylenol intake. He had some back problems and neck problems. He was a compulsive water drinker. He had to have a gallon of ice water with him all the time. A lot of his puffiness was—he'd take in more than he could get rid of. I never could figure out why he drank so much water. It's a psychological hangup for some people. I guess a psychiatrist could explain it.

"He liked the short cuts to everything. He always thought there had to be a quicker way to do everything than the logical, practical way. He was talking one time about how nice it would be if he could go to sleep for a few days and then wake up and lose all his excess weight. He said, 'Why don't you do that? Just keep me asleep for a week or two weeks or something, and let me lose some weight, and then wake me up?' I said, 'It's not practical, Elvis. Your bowels still have to function, we can't do that.'

"So he goes out to Vegas and talks Dr. Gahnim [Elias Gahnim, official ring physician of the Nevada Boxing Commission] to do it. He was out there three weeks, kept him knocked out asleep, had him on some sort of papaya juice diet, and he came back all bloated up, he was taking in more papaya juice than he was taking in on a normal diet. That really clobbered his colon. You need physical activity for your colon to function properly. His was already nonfunctioning because of his laxative abuse, and all he did was sleep for three weeks."

"Why would he abuse laxatives?"

"He abused laxatives because he stayed so constipated. A lot of things contributed to it. Finally his colon, just like any muscle that you don't use, lost its ability to contract. The normal colon is about this big around," Dr. Nick said, gesturing with his doubled fists together. "Elvis's colon was about the size of your leg. You can imagine how much stuff was in it. Whether it was gas or water or shit or whatever, it occupied space. He thought he had control over things. He thought when he'd lose control that he could regain it again any time he wanted to."

"Was his death totally unexpected to you? Did you have any kind of previous indication?"

"No, his death was not completely unexpected. Several of us had seen Elvis close to death's door before. We always worried about it. In town, one of the aides was supposed to sleep upstairs in the room next to his in case he got up in the middle of the night, so they could go in and check on him. But unfortunately, the night of his death, the aide was Ricky Stanley, and he was drugged out on something and instead of being upstairs he was downstairs. That morning, Elvis had called down to Ricky to go get him something, he had trouble going to sleep, but they couldn't get Ricky up. Elvis's aunt and the maids had gone down to try to get Ricky up, and he's completely in another world. So Elvis called my office, eight o'clock in the morning, and I wasn't there yet. But Tish Henley, the nurse who lived at Graceland, was there, and Elvis talked to her. Tish told her husband where there were a couple of sleeping pills, to put them in an envelope and give them to Elvis's aunt, and Elvis sent his aunt over to Tish's house, and she carried them back over there to him.

"At the time when I was trying to resuscitate Elvis, in the ambulance, I was so out of it, what was going on—I should have realized that he'd been dead for several hours at that time. Except that when I got there, [Presley aide] Joe Esposito told me that Elvis had breathed. If he had just breathed, then there might still be some hope. What had happened was that when they moved Elvis, turned him over, he sort of sighed. He had fallen straight forward like he was kneeling on the floor, but with his head down."

According the police report, Elvis Presley was found at about 2:30 PM on August 16, 1977, face down on the red shag carpet of his bathroom floor, "slumped over in front of the commode . . . his arms and legs were stiff, and there was a discoloration in his face." The bathroom adjoined Presley's bedroom in the white-columned mansion at Graceland, the thirteen-acre estate in Whitehaven, Tennessee, where he had spent most of his life since the early days of the career that had taken him out of poverty and made him the highest paid entertainer and possibly the most famous human being of his time.

A Memphis Fire Department ambulance and Dr. Nick were called. Dr. Nick arrived and boarded the ambulance as it was leaving Graceland to take Presley to Baptist Memorial Hospital, ten minutes away in Memphis. On the way there and in the emergency room, cardiopulmonary resuscitation attempts were made without effect. At 3:30 PM, Dr. Nick pronounced Elvis dead.

In the state of Tennessee, when someone is found dead, the local medical examiner must investigate. Dr. Jerry Francisco, the Shelby County (Memphis) medical examiner, was informed of Presley's death by Dr. Eric Muirhead, chief pathologist at Baptist Hospital. Dr. Nick had returned to Graceland and received consent for an autopsy from Elvis's father, Vernon Presley. The fact of Elvis's death had been made public, and a crowd had gathered at Baptist Hospital, creating a traffic jam outside the emergency room. Francisco agreed that the autopsy should be performed at the Baptist Hospital morgue rather than across the street at the medical examiner's morgue.

The preliminary, or gross, autopsy was completed before eight o'clock that night. In a press conference afterward, Dr. Francisco made the "provisional diagnosis" that Presley had died of cardiac arrhythmia: his heart had lost its regular beat and then stopped. To determine the precise cause of the attack, Francisco said, "may take several days, it may take several weeks. It may never be discovered." Francisco also said that the preliminary autopsy had revealed no evidence of drug abuse. The medical examiner's office reported to the Homicide Division of the Memphis Police Department that Presley had died a natural death.

A few days before—incredible timing—a book had appeared, titled *Elvis: What Happened?* Written by three former bodyguards of Presley and a writer for the tabloid press, the book told of Presley's desire to have his wife's lover killed, described his "fascination with human corpses," and called him "a walking drugstore." The book also told of Presley's attending the 1964 funeral of Dewey Phillips, who died in 1968. Still, Presley's sudden death, coming at the same time as the allegations of his drug abuse, caused many to speculate, in spite of the medical examiner's statements, that he had died from a drug overdose.

On October 21, 1977, Dr. Francisco, after having reviewed Presley's complete autopsy report and other data including reports from four toxicology laboratories, issued his final opinion. Francisco said that Presley died of hypertensive heart disease resulting in cardiac arrhythmia, and that the death had not been caused by drugs. The next day, the Memphis *Commercial Appeal* carried a story listing ten drugs said to have been found in autopsy samples of Presley's blood at Bio-Science Laboratories in Van Nuys, California. The story was titled, "Near Toxic Level of Drugs Reported in Presley's Blood."

For over twenty years, Elvis Presley had been famous, but he had not been well known. The details of his private life, of passionate interest to many, were known to very few. These few—the "Memphis Mafia," employees who were Presley's friends or relatives—had surrounded him during his life, guarding his privacy with almost total silence. *Elvis: What Happened?*, the three fired bodyguards' lament, had broken the stillness, but with Presley's death and the revelation that he had left almost his entire estate to his daughter, there were among the Mafia few indeed who did not take part in a Babel of Elvis memories. Almost everyone had a story to tell or at least a book to sell.

The books included *My Life with Elvis,* by a secretary; *A Presley Speaks,* by an uncle; *The Life of Elvis,* by a cousin; *I Called Him Babe,* by a nurse; *Elvis, We Love You Tender,* by Presley's stepmother and stepbrothers; *Inside Elvis,* by a karate instructor; and *Elvis: Portrait of a Friend,* by one of Elvis's numerous best friends. The movies would come later.

The books told and retold the story of Elvis Aron Presley, the Depression-born son of Mississippi sharecropper Vernon, who, with his eighth-grade education, misspelled the biblical name Aaron on his son's birth certificate. Elvis's stillborn twin brother, Jesse Garon, was much discussed, and many attributed his death to the unusual affection between Elvis and his mother, the former Gladys Smith, whose actual middle name was Love. "She worshipped that child," a friend said, "from the day he was borned to the day she died."

The little shotgun house, built by his father and grandfather, where Elvis was born; the single room where Elvis and his family first lived in Memphis; the housing project where they lived during Elvis's years as an outsider at Humes High School; all have become standard parts of the legend. So have the Crown Electric Company, where Elvis worked for forty dollars a week after his graduation from school, and the Memphis Recording Service, where Elvis paid four dollars to record on an acetate disc two songs, "My Happiness" and "That's When Your Heartaches Begin," as a present for his mother. Sam Phillips, the owner of the recording studio and Sun Records, heard Elvis, gave him the chance to make a record for release, and the rest is history, the kind of history that sells.

The first Elvis Presley record was released in 1954; his first movies were released in 1957; the next year, as the career for which she alone had prepared her son was just getting started, Gladys Presley died. Though Elvis made three films a year for ten years after her death, he did not appear in public concert again for over twelve years. He kept for the rest of his life a pink Cadillac that he bought for his mother and kept for many years the tree from their last Christmas together.

There are some interesting photographs of Elvis and Gladys—one of Elvis kissing Gladys while holding a pair of jockey shorts to her bosom, another showing Elvis holding Gladys's head, a handful of her hair, looking into her eyes, curling her lip in a smile, but not a smile, an earnest look . . .

What must Elvis have seen, looking into Gladys's eyes? God visited Gladys Presley with the mysteries of birth and death, and the life of Elvis was the result, the realization of her awe-filled vision. It was her image of him, idealized beyond reason, that the public—his public—accepted.

> He is dressed like a prince, the diamonds glitter, the cape waves; he is tall and athletic, and in the cunning play of lights (all that pale blue and crimson) he seems as unreal as the ghost of a Greek god, the original perfect male. Who cares if he's made up? if the lights are deceiving? if the tune of "Thus Spake Zarathustra" makes you fall for the trick? The fact remains that he is, that he floats through countless dreams, and that whatever he was, or wherever he is going, he is now, at this moment, the living symbol of freedom and light.
>
> —W. A. Harbinson, *The Illustrated Elvis*

Elvis was buried at Graceland beside his mother. "What has died," one editorial writer suggested, "is the adolescence of an entire generation. It is the memory of several million people's first intimation of freedom that was in the white hearse."

The anniversary of his death promises to become a holiday like Christmas or the Fourth of July, when each year more Elvis products are served up. One year after Presley's death, a Canadian writer, in a piece called "The Last Days of Elvis," listed eleven drugs found in Presley's body by the University of Utah Center for Human Toxicology and quoted a pharmaceutical guide regarding contraindications and the dangers of drug interactions. The story contained allegations of a conspiracy of silence including the Memphis police, the *Commercial Appeal*, and Presley's doctors, none of whom were named.

About a year later, *Elvis: Portrait of a Friend* was published. It was produced by an ex-employee of Presley named Marty Lacker and his wife, Patsy, with the help of an editor of veterinary publications. The book contained chapter titles like "The Doctor as Pusher" and

"Prescription for Death" and left no doubt that the death-dealing doctor was Dr. Nick.

———————

George Constantine Nichopoulos was born in 1927 in Ridgway, Pennsylvania. His parents, Constantine George (Gus) and Persephone Nichopoulos, both came from villages in Greece. At sixteen or seventeen, Gus came to New York City and worked as a busboy. In 1925, on a six-month return visit to Greece, he met and became engaged to Persephone Bobotsiares. In January 1927, after working with a cousin in a restaurant in Ridgway and saving his money, Gus married Persephone in Greece and brought her to Pennsylvania, where, in October, their son was born.

In 1928, with the help of Persephone's brother in Greenville, South Carolina, Gus started running a restaurant in Anniston, Alabama. When he retired, more than forty years later, Anniston celebrated Gus Nichopoulos Day. There were not many Greeks in Anniston, a handsome town of about forty-five thousand people, on rolling hills in eastern Alabama, and the Nichopoulos family was in many ways exemplary. Since Anniston has no Greek Orthodox church, the Nichopouloses regularly attended a local Episcopal church. Gus, who died in June 1979, had been a Shriner, a 32nd Degree Mason, an Elk, a Rotarian, a State Farm Valued Customer, a greatly beloved citizen. Persephone still lives in the white frame house where she and Gus reared their son, who came to be called Nick, and his sister, Vangie, six years younger.

Nick walked a few blocks to the Woodstock Grammar School and then to Anniston High School. His parents allowed him to play football only if he studied music, and there are photographs of him standing on the front lawn at home, wearing short pants, holding his violin under his chin. He is a dark, serious little boy. From the time Nick was quite small, he worked in his parents' restaurant. He was a first-string fullback and halfback on the Anniston Bulldogs football team. He became an Eagle Scout. He couldn't decide whether he wanted to be a priest, own a restaurant, or be a doctor.

In 1946, Nick graduated from high school and joined the army, which put him to work for eighteen months in a hospital in Munich. When he got out of the army, he entered the premedical course of study at the University of the South in Sewanee, Tennessee, graduating in 1951. That fall, he entered medical school at Vanderbilt University but left after one year to study for a PhD at the University of Tennessee in Memphis. While going to school in Memphis, Nick met Edna Sanidas, a pretty blonde girl whose father also owned a restaurant. Nick and Edna were married in 1954. The next year, their son Dean was born. In 1956, Nick went back to Vanderbilt Medical School, and in 1959 he graduated with an MD degree.

In 1963, after serving his internship at St. Thomas' Hospital in Nashville, Dr. Nick brought his family (now there were also two daughters, Chrissie and Elaine) to Memphis and started working in a partnership called the Medical Group. He had worked there four years when he met Elvis Presley.

After he pronounced Presley dead, Dr. Nick stepped out of the emergency room into the room where Presley employees Billy Smith, Joe Esposito, Charlie Hodge, David Stanley, and Al Strada were waiting. Billy, Presley's first cousin, had been as close as any friend Presley ever had. "Dr. Nick started to speak to me and he couldn't talk," Billy told me at the medical examiners' hearing. "That's how much Elvis's death hurt him. Dr. Nick loved Elvis. He did everything he could to help Elvis. How can anyone think Dr. Nick would hurt Elvis?"

Ten days after Presley died, the *Commercial Appeal* published an exclusive interview with Dr. Nick. In it Dr. Nick said, "I spent many hours a day thinking about different things to do to help him . . . It's going to take some time to lose some of those thoughts and I think everybody's lost . . . We keep thinking that he's here someplace. It's hard to accept."

A year later, Dr. Nick talked briefly about Presley on a local television show, but otherwise he said no more. While friends and relatives of Presley, no longer on his payroll, signed contracts for books and movies, Dr. Nick, almost alone, kept silent. There had been around Elvis Presley a hierarchy of silence, and Dr. Nick was very near its top.

Meanwhile the Elvis memories, finding an audience, began to resemble the music business, sometimes described as a self-devouring organism that vomits itself back up. In New York City, Charles Thompson, a Memphis-born television producer, was reading about Presley. *20/20*, the ABC television news program for which Thompson works, was new and had to have some hot stories if it were to compete with its opposite number, CBS television's popular *60 Minutes.*

Thompson had worked as a field producer at CBS, leaving when ABC beckoned partly because he and CBS had not seen eye to eye on a story about Billy Carter's supposed violations of federal energy regulations. Thompson had wanted to do the story, but the powers at CBS had thought there was no story, or none worth putting on television. It wasn't Thompson's first such disagreement with an employer. In 1970, when Thompson was working for a television station in Jacksonville, Florida, he did a story on pollution that accused the station itself of polluting and got himself fired.

Thompson had graduated from high school in Memphis, studied journalism at Memphis State University, worked at the *Commercial Appeal.* In the middle 1960s, Thompson did two tours with the navy in Vietnam, serving as liaison with the marines, calling in air strikes. He saw a good bit of action, and when he came back home had troubling nightmares of mangled bodies, burning children, and seemed to see the dark side of issues.

When Thompson learned, the day it happened, that Presley had died, he expected, so he said later, that "by night they would say it was drugs." He was surprised when they didn't, but when he read the Elvis books, among them Marty Lacker's accusation of Dr. Nick, his expectations were at last fulfilled. Thompson's reportorial sixth sense told him, This is good, this is a story. "King dies of drugs from court physician" is good. The King is dead! Hang the doctor! Still, Thompson admits that he came to Memphis for a "top-to-bottom investigation on Elvis" with nothing more than a hunch. "I didn't have anything," he has said.

In looking through the Presley file at the *Commercial Appeal*, Thompson came upon the Bio-Science toxicology report that had been quoted in the "Near Toxic" story. Thompson says he showed the report to a doctor at Baptist Hospital, who said, according to Thompson, "Jesus Christ, it's obvious. The son of a bitch died of drugs."

At least one doctor at Baptist Hospital says that Thompson showed him the report. He told Thompson that in his opinion, Presley's drug problems had been primarily with laxatives and steroids. The doctor advised Thompson, should he have questions about Presley and drugs, to call Dr. Nick. In July of 1979, by his own count, Thompson tried three times to question Dr. Nick, who did not return his calls. Armed with that fact and the toxicology report, Thompson told the doctor who'd suggested he talk with Dr. Nick: "I think I've got a homicide."

Thompson brought James Cole, his brother-in-law, who like Thompson had worked for the *Commercial Appeal*, in to help research the story. Cole learned that a routine audit of prescription records in Memphis was going to be conducted by the Tennessee Healing Arts Board and telephoned the board's office in Nashville, the state capital, "to find out what was going on." He talked with Jack Fosbinder, the board's chief investigator, who told him that an audit of the first six months of 1979 was in progress. Cole told Fosbinder, so he has said, "We suspect Elvis may have died a drug death. Maybe you should look back into 1977."

In August of 1979, after Charles Thompson's three failed attempts, Thompson's New York colleague, ABC television news performer Geraldo Rivera, came to Memphis to talk to Dr. Nick and failed six times. The *20/20* team had no such trouble talking with the state Health Related Boards' investigators. On September 6, Thompson, Rivera, and Cole came to Dr. Nick's office after a meeting with the investigators, who had told them that Dr. Nick was about to have formal charges brought against him. On this, his seventh try, Rivera succeeded.

In the interview, Rivera asked Dr. Nick various questions about Presley, leading up to the big charge: "The records indicate that, especially in the last year of his life, you prescribed certain medications to Elvis Presley in quite extraordinarily large amounts. Why?"

"I can't comment on that," Dr. Nick said, "and I don't believe that it's true."

"The records we have, doctor—and I'll say this as gently as I possibly can—indicate that from January 20, 1977, to August 16, 1977, the day he died, you prescribed to Elvis Presley, and the prescriptions were all signed by you—over five thousand schedule two narcotics and/or amphetamines. That comes out to something like twenty-five per day."

"I don't believe that."

"Well, is it something that you'd like to refresh your memory on, or is it something you deny?"

"I deny it."

While all this television business was happening, I knew nothing about it. I had my own worries. They led me to Dr. Nick. On March 24, 1978, I had fallen from a granite boulder on a north Georgia mountainside, breaking my back, bruising my brain, learning more about pain than I cared to know, finally developing a drug dependence only slightly less grand than that of the late (and no wonder) Howard Hughes.

After a year I tried to stop taking the drugs my doctors prescribed. I tried twice and twice had grand mal seizures, full-scale epileptic brain-fries, blind, rigid, foaming at the mouth, fighting off unseen enemies, screaming, turning into a hydrophobic wolf. A neurologist tested the impulses coming from my head, told me they were abnormal, and advised me to have my brain injected with radioactive dyes, which I declined to do.

About this time, a friend, a patient of Dr. Nick's, advised me that one night soon I was going to be dead before I was asleep, and advised me to see Dr. Nick. On July 5, 1979, I told Dr. Nick all the above.

"This is interesting," he said, "but what do you want from me?"

"I've been given this room full of drugs," I said. "I don't want to go on taking drugs, and I don't want to be epileptic. What are my chances?"

I filled a bottle, bled, coughed, inhaled, exhaled, held still, bent over, dressed, and waited, sitting on a metal table in a cold little room. Dr. Nick came in, shook his head, and said, "Looks like you've lived through a nightmare."

I've survived, I thought. It was news to me. Dr. Nick sent me into his office to wait for him. On the wall beside the door there was a large photograph of Elvis Presley, signed and with the inscription, "To my good friend and physician, Dr. Nick." The office was thick with things that obviously were gifts from Dr. Nick's patients. Among them were many small frog figures, so that the office looked like a Greek gift shop being taken over by swamp life.

Dr. Nick came in. We talked about diet and exercise. I hadn't drunk a glass of milk in years and hadn't exercised since running for a helicopter at Altamont. I mentioned that I had worried my family, and Dr. Nick said he would call and reassure them. He gave me no drugs, sent me to no specialists, but he let me know that I was going to be all right. I was a bit dazed, trying to get used to the idea.

On September 13, 1979, the ABC television network presented the *20/20* show titled "The Elvis Cover-Up." One of its most characteristic touches was an interview with a retired pharmacist from Baptist Hospital, where Presley's stepbrother, Ricky Stanley, picked up a prescription of Dilaudid for Presley from Dr. Nick the night before Presley died. The pharmacist said that having sold Presley the fatal dose weighed mightily on his conscience. No one bothered to tell the man that no Dilaudid was found in Presley's body.

After "The Elvis Cover-Up" was shown, I saw Dr. Nick socially two or three times. He had been presented with a list of charges by the board of medical examiners—not pathologists but doctors who, to help maintain professional standards in the state, examine the practices of other doctors—but he wasn't interested in talking about the case. "The lawyers don't want the medical examiners to get the idea that we want to try this thing in the media," Dr. Nick said. His accusers had no such reluctance.

On January 13, 1980, Dr. Nick's hearing before the board of medical examiners began. Because of Tennessee's "sunshine" requirement that proceedings of this kind be held in public, the hearing took place in the Memphis city hall. Public interest in the case was believed to be great, and attendance was expected to be heavy, but it had not been thought necessary to hire the Mid-South Coliseum.

Whatever else the hearing may have been, it was a physical ordeal. The weather was seasonable for January, cold and sometimes wet. The sessions lasted from Monday through Saturday, starting each morning at 8:30 and adjourning usually ten hours later.

The audience, smaller than anticipated, averaged about a hundred people. It included Elvis fans of many descriptions, from old ladies in E.P. baseball jackets to a pair of effete young male twins who had come from Ohio to see Dr. Nick swing. Also in the audience were Dr. Nick's immediate family and many of his friends, among them his priest, Father Vieron. There were reporters, print and broadcast, local and international, and the photographers were like ants at a picnic. ABC television's numerous lights, cameras, sound recorders, and crew, including Charles Thompson, James Cole, and Geraldo Rivera, were a constant presence, on hand to take postcards of the hanging.

Behind the chamber's wooden railing sat the state's attorneys and interrogators, Dr. Nick and his lawyers, the five medical examiners, and the referee, or hearing officer. Police in plain clothes stood against the rear wall, staring at the audience.

The start of the hearing was delayed by the glare of the television lights. As the medical examiners shielded their eyes, the hearing officer insisted that the lights be moved: "We're going to be here a week, and we can't have everybody go blind."

The charges against Dr. Nick were, first, gross incompetence, ignorance, or negligence; second, unprofessional, dishonorable, or unethical conduct; and last, dispensing, prescribing, or distributing controlled substances "not in good faith" to relieve suffering or to effect a cure. On the first day of the hearing, the state's attorneys called ten of the twenty patients of Dr. Nick listed in the charges to testify. Tennessee has no statute protecting the privacy of exchanges between doctors and patients; Dr. Nick's patients had to testify or go to jail. The patients—among them an investment banker, a record promoter, a landscape gardener, a restaurant cashier, a doctor's wife, and two ex-heroin addicts—were questioned before the public and the press concerning their most intimate problems, which included alcoholism, insomnia, divorces, abortions, obesity, cancer, and bereavement. After each person's name in the charges there was a list of prescriptions from Dr. Nick, each list showing a decline in the amount of medicine prescribed. Contrary to the usual pattern in malpractice by overprescribing, Dr. Nick made no charges for prescriptions and saw his patients often, giving frequent physical examinations. Every patient who testified praised Dr. Nick.

After the patients had testified, the state called Dr. Nick himself to the witness stand. His lawyers insisted that he should not be forced to testify for his accusers; that he would take the stand and submit to cross-examination, but as part of his defense, not the state's prosecution. The hearing officer took the position that the hearing was not a criminal court, and that no statute prevented the state from calling Dr. Nick. The first day ended with Dr. Nick's lawyers intending to seek a ruling on the question in chancery court.

But on Tuesday the defense relented. A chancery court suit might take years; so Dr. Nick, wanting to settle the larger issue, took the stand. He discussed his prescribing practices, talking about each patient in the charges. Count number fifteen, Elvis Presley, received the most attention.

Responding to questions from the state's attorneys and the medical examiners, Dr. Nick described the progress of his relationship with Elvis Presley. He told of his efforts, with the help of Memphis alcohol and drug abuse specialists David Knott and Robert Fink, to save Presley's life and restore him to health after his nearly fatal overmedication by the fake acupuncturist in Los Angeles. After Presley learned that Drs. Knott and Fink, who had been called in by Dr. Nick, were psychiatrists, he refused to see them.

Keeping drugs from other doctors away from Presley was a continuing problem, Dr. Nick said. He attempted to consult with other doctors who saw Presley, "trying to get some continuity in his treatment," but Presley, without telling Dr. Nick, saw doctors in other towns, some of whom sent him medications by mail. Presley employees were instructed by Dr. Nick to turn over to him all medicines from other doctors so they could be discarded or replaced with placebos.

In 1973, following Presley's "acupuncture" treatments, Dr. Nick said, "I thought he was addicted. I do not think he was an addict." Although he made extensive use of placebos in treating Presley, Dr. Nick said, Presley "had a lot of chronic problems . . . degenerative changes in his back and neck . . . that you couldn't treat with placebos." Still, there were times when Presley could not be persuaded to take any medicine at all.

Before a Las Vegas opening that Presley considered most important, he refused to take even antihistamines, saying, "This one's on my own."

On "The Elvis Cover-Up" program, Geraldo Rivera had accused Dr. Nick of prescribing five thousand drug doses to Presley in the last six months of his life. The board's revised list of charges made it twelve thousand drug doses in Presley's last eighteen months. Perhaps the single most important point in Dr. Nick's testimony was his statement that the drugs were not for Presley alone but for the entire company, as many as a hundred people, who worked with Presley on the road. Presley appeared with a male vocal group, a female vocal group, a rock and roll rhythm section, and a large orchestra with strings. Dr. Nick, after learning from a few tours' experience what he was likely to need, came prepared to care for everyone from the equipment handlers to the flute player, including the record producer with the kidney transplant.

"I carried three suitcases full of equipment," Dr. Nick said. "I had everything you'd expect to find in a pharmacy—all kinds of antibiotics for people who were allergic to penicillin, I had expectorants, I had decongestants, I had just what you can imagine you'd use every day in your office. I carried a laryngoscope, I carried some long forceps in case he aspirated, I carried these little bags for breathing, I carried suture material, adhesive tapes, splints, everything that you would expect a first aid stand to have, plus what a physician would have."

The suitcases were kept locked and in Dr. Nick's possession. When he was away, a nurse kept the suitcases and dispensed drugs only according to Dr. Nick's specific orders. Twice during the last six months of Presley's life, Dr. Nick's car was broken into and drugs for tours were stolen and had to be replaced. The Memphis Police Department had been notified both times.

The drugs were bought in Elvis Presley's name because otherwise Vernon Presley, his son's bookkeeper, wouldn't have paid for them. A longtime acquaintance of the Presleys has said, "Vernon would cringe when he had to spend money. You could actually see him cringe." Dr. Nick wrote prescriptions in his own name before a vacation trip to Hawaii with Presley, some of his associates, and their families because "I knew that if I had charged him for the medication that I was taking along, his father would blow a gasket." Presley gave away fleets of cars, fortunes in jewelry, houses, hundreds of thousands of dollars, but his father could never stop pinching pennies. It was all part of the unique dilemma of being Elvis Presley's physician.

Dr. Nick acknowledged the absence of written records of Presley's treatment, saying, "The reason some of these things were not kept in the office or someplace was that people were always perusing his charts. It was difficult to have any confidentiality with his records, whether it be in my office or the hospital or wherever. I certainly wish now there were records. That would certainly be helpful. I think that if he hadn't died, the end result as far as his improvement during this period of time is answer in itself."

Dr. Nick said that he had received with Presley's help a bank loan to pay for his house, and that he was repaying the loan with interest. He had never charged Presley for visits to Graceland. Speaking of the per diem fee Presley paid the Medical Group for Dr. Nick's time on the road, Dr. Nick said, "It's difficult to pay for services that last eighteen hours a day.

"My objective was to help him," Dr. Nick said, "because I thought that he helped so many people—not physically or monetarily, but—to keep him rolling and to go to his shows and see what reward all these people got—it's an experience that you'd have to go through."

In spite of Dr. Nick's talk of rewards, the state's assumption seemed to be that Presley was, as Geraldo Rivera had said on *20/20*, "just another victim of self-destructive overindulgence" who had "followed in the melancholy rock and roll tradition of Janis Joplin, Jimi Hendrix, and Jim Morrison." The idea of Presley following in the tradition of Joplin, Hendrix, and Morrison defies chronology, sociology, musical history, and common sense, but neither "The Elvis Cover-Up" nor the hearing had any connection with common sense.

On the second day of Dr. Nick's testimony there was a bomb threat. Years of effort to keep Elvis alive had earned Dr. Nick threats and accusations, cost him many thousands of dollars in legal fees, and brought shame to his family. "You killed Elvis!" people driving past Dr. Nick's house yell at him, or his wife, or his children.

The medical examiners didn't appear to sleep while he testified, as some of them seemed to do at times when other witnesses testified, but Dr. Nick's testimony had the effect of making the witnesses for his defense anticlimactic. The first of the three doctors who were expert witnesses for the state was a pharmacologist who had never treated any patients, the next said that drug addiction should be cured in two or three weeks, and the last testified that he refused to treat patients who smoke. None of them had any firsthand knowledge of Dr. Nick's patients. Each of the experts perused the charges, saying where he thought Dr. Nick had gone wrong.

Then the defense began. It was late Wednesday afternoon. The party had been going on for three days. There was time this afternoon for the defense to present only two witnesses. Both were ex-girlfriends, one of Presley, one of Joe Esposito. Both were good-looking, and though they verified important matters—Dr. Nick's treating Presley with placebos and intercepting drugs from other physicians—their very glamour made them seem out of place; they seemed to be comic relief.

On Thursday the defense called sixteen witnesses, among them doctors, members of the Presley staff, Health Related Boards investigators, a coordinator from the Medical Group, and a patient, a department store executive who told how Dr. Nick helped him overcome the addiction to narcotics he developed while hospitalized for months following a car wreck. The coordinator testified that the Medical Group had fifteen thousand patients, thirty-five hundred of whom were Dr. Nick's. The twenty patients listed in the charges represented one half of 1 percent of Dr. Nick's patients. By choosing at random and comparing six of Dr. Nick's full working days at the Medical Group, it was shown that he prescribed controlled substances to only one out of every twenty patients.

The Health Boards investigators admitted meeting and exchanging information with the *20/20* staff before the charges were delivered to Dr. Nick. One of the investigators testified that the recommendation for the state to file charges against Dr. Nick was made without consulting even one licensed physician. Later, James Cole would admit that he gave the investigators the tip on the Presley "drug death" in the first place.

The Presley employees testified that Dr. Nick cared for all the people who worked with Presley, not just Presley himself. They verified that Dr. Nick gave Presley no medication in an uncontrolled manner, that Presley at times left town to get drugs he couldn't get from Dr. Nick, and that Dr. Nick had instructed them to intercept all drugs coming to Presley from other sources.

Dr. Nick had testified that in 1975 he had arranged for a nurse to live at Graceland "so we could better control and dispense medications." The nurse, Tish Henley, testified that she often took away from Presley medications that did not come from Dr. Nick, and that she sometimes, under Dr. Nick's orders, gave Presley placebos. At no time was dispensing drugs left up to her discretion. After tours, she said, copious amounts of leftover drugs were destroyed.

Some doctors to whom Dr. Nick referred Presley testified that Presley had showed no signs of narcotic or hypnotic abuse. Dr. Nick was said to show a remarkable interest in patients he referred to other doctors. Dr. Lawrence Wruble, a gastrointestinal specialist, said that at one point he and Dr. Nick had told Presley to stop doing two shows a night in Las Vegas or they would stop being his doctors, and from that time Presley did only one show. Wruble spoke highly of Dr. Nick's care and concern for Presley. Dr. Walter Hoffman, a cardiologist at the Medical Group who has known Dr. Nick since he was a graduate student, described him as "more empathetic than any practitioner I have ever known."

During the hearing's first days, the audience had been divided between Dr. Nick's supporters and detractors. By Thursday afternoon, the troops were tired. Some of us had settled down to being simply reporters with battle fatigue. When the hearing stopped for the day, I had a question for Geraldo Rivera, who was sitting amid his crew beside an empty seat. After "The Elvis Cover-Up" story, Rivera had done a follow-up in which he said that if Presley's autopsy report were released, the information in it—

"'. . . would send at least one doctor to jail,' yeah, I remember," he said.

"Were you talking about Dr. Nick?"

"Yes, but I didn't understand. I didn't know about all his other patients. I didn't believe Elvis was getting drugs in the mail. I'm beginning to see another side of Dr. Nick. He was definitely no scriptwriter. He made mistakes with Elvis, but I think he's a good man. I just feel bad about his family. I see them looking at me, and I can tell what they're thinking."

"It's obvious they hate your guts," I said pleasantly.

On Friday morning, Dr. Jerry Francisco, the Shelby County medical examiner, took the stand and repeated his conclusion that Elvis Presley died of cardiac arrhythmia brought on by high blood pressure and hardening of the arteries. Presley's heart was twice the normal size for a man of his age and weight, his coronary arteries were occluded, and he had a long history of hypertension.

Dr. Francisco said that the amounts of drugs in Presley's body did not, even in combination, indicate the likelihood of a drug overdose. The circumstances of his death also indicated that drugs were not at fault. If Presley had taken an oral overdose of drugs shortly after 8:00 AM on the day he died, he might have been in a coma by 2:30 PM, the time he was found, but he would hardly have been stiff and blue, dead for several hours. The typical victim of an oral drug overdose dies a lingering death in a comfortable position, not pitched forward on a bathroom floor.

Dr. Francisco was followed by Dr. Bryan Finkle, an English toxicologist, now director of the University of Utah Center for Human Toxicology. Dr. Finkle, who has worked in forensic toxicology at New Scotland Yard, testified that the concentration of drugs found in Presley's body was not sufficient to affect Presley's respiration or the amount of oxygen in his blood. Dr. Finkle said that although he had been quoted on "The Elvis Cover-Up" program as saying that drugs may have made "a significant contribution" to Presley's death, he had not been informed, when a member of the *20/20* staff telephoned him, that he was being interviewed or that his statements "would be construed in such a fashion."

Dr. David Stafford, a toxicologist at the University of Tennessee Center for the Health Sciences, said that he had tested Presley's autopsy samples for thirty or forty drugs and had found nothing consistent with the diagnosis of a toxic drug dose.

The last defense witness—what idiots some lawyers are—not a doctor, testified that Dr. Nick, by caring enough to seek an opinion from a second surgeon, had saved the leg of his old maid aunt.

After lunch on the last day of testimony, portions of "The Elvis Cover-Up" program were shown to the examiners, and the lawyers for both sides made their closing statements. The defense said that the collaboration between ABC television and the state's investigators concerning Dr. Nick "allowed the media to punish him unmercifully—without any justice—from September 13, 1979, through January 18, 1980." It was pointed out that Dr. Nick profited from no one's drug dependence, that even patients who took advantage of his trust to obtain drugs had, over the length of time in the charges, been withdrawn from drugs. Dr. Nick had at times, for a variety of reasons, kept incomplete records, but that situation had been corrected before the charges against him had been filed. Dr. Nick, the defense said, "is a fine, compassionate, sensitive physician."

The prosecution said that regardless of Dr. Nick's good faith and intentions, we live by standards, and Dr. Nick had violated the standards of his profession. He prescribed too many drugs, in inappropriate amounts, for too long a time. The examiners were called on to revoke Dr. Nick's license "until such time as the board can be sure that his practice is consistent with good medical practice."

On Saturday, January 19, 1980, the board voted on the charges against Dr. Nick. Of the first two charges—gross incompetence, ignorance, or negligence; unprofessional, dishonorable, or unethical conduct—the board unanimously found Dr. Nick innocent. But he had violated certain relatively minor regulations. He had discarded, without keeping records, drugs whose fate must be recorded. He had also allowed certain patients to receive too many drugs, even though in the long run he had withdrawn them from drugs. The medical examiners found Dr. Nick guilty on ten of the charges of improper prescribing in the complaint.

One patient to whom Dr. Nick was found guilty of improper prescribing was Elvis Presley. However, one of the examiners said that the guilty verdict was only for faulty record-keeping and commented that he had found "no evidence that Dr. Nichopoulos was negligent in his care of this patient." Another of the examiners said, "I think we have to consider the extraordinary circumstances under which he was operating. He was under the gun. I think he exercised considerable restraint in trying to control the medication. There are very extenuating circumstances, and I certainly agree that there was no involvement by Dr. Nichopoulos in any way in the death of Elvis Presley."

The board suspended for three months Dr. Nick's license to practice medicine, and he was put on probation for three years. The sentence, after "The Elvis Cover-Up" allegations, seemed to some people absurdly light. To others, it seemed unnecessary chastisement of an excellent physician.

At least, Dr. Nick thought, he had run the gauntlet, it was over. He had told what he had done, the medical examiners had made their ruling, and it was a relief to have the matter settled at last.

So Dr. Nick thought until he realized that the matter wasn't settled at all. No one had gone to great lengths in reporting the testimonies of Dr. Nick or the witnesses for his defense, but in March 1980, *Memphis*, the local slick-paper magazine, published an article called "The Elvis Expose: How ABC Unearthed the Story, the Real Story." It said that Dr. Nick at the hearing had described Presley as a "ranting drug addict." Without irony it quoted Charles Thompson as saying, "They haven't said anything that disagrees with our first report ('The Elvis Cover-Up') last September." It took no notice at all of the testimonies that the drugs Dr. Nick ordered in Presley's name were not all for him. This is not surprising, since the writer of the article, Tom Martin, a Federal Express employee who writes in his spare time, attended the hearing only on Friday and Saturday mornings and was not present to hear any of the other testimony. It was as if Dr. Nick and the other defense witnesses had never spoken.

The article described with complete acceptance Thompson's personal inclination to believe that Presley died of drugs, James Cole's telling the Health Related Boards' chief investigator about Presley's "drug death," and presented the ABC team in much the same light that they, in one of their various motions to have Presley's autopsy report released, had shone on themselves: "We think that we behaved toward Dr. Nick with the highest courtesy and consideration. We are confident of the truth, honesty, and fairness of what we have broadcast and believe there are no grounds for charges of unfairness, false portrayal, prejudice, exploitation, or sensationalism."

Except for the Greek newspapers, calendars, and bric-a-brac, Dr. Nick's mother's house in Anniston is exactly like my grandparents' house in South Georgia, down to the African violets in the breakfast room. Being there is my idea of Greek Orthodox Heaven: nobody forces you to do anything, and there is so much delicious food you don't have a chance to get hungry.

We arrived on a Friday; Saturday afternoon we took a break from Mrs. Nichopoulos's wonderful cooking and ate sandwiches from the Golden Rule Barbecue. After lunch we went to the Highland Cemetery to visit the grave of Dr. Nick's father, who died in June 1979, before the scandal broke. Dr. Nick had told me that one strong bond between him and Presley had been the respect they both had for their parents. I was sure Dr. Nick was glad that his father hadn't died suffering with him the humiliations of the last year.

Later, in the late afternoon at the house Dr. Nick had left to find his future, he reminisced further about the days when he spent so much time taking care of Elvis: "I'd spend two or three hours a night taking care of his eyes. Elvis had glaucoma. He used to dye his eyelashes, and I think that may have had something to do with it. And he'd get these bacterial infections on his skin—you know, Elvis didn't bathe."

"No," I said, "I didn't."

"He'd take sponge baths, but he wouldn't get wet. He took these pills from Sweden that are supposed to purify your body."

I remembered Billy Smith, Presley's cousin, testifying at the hearing that on the morning of the day Presley died, after they had played racquetball, Presley had cleaned up, and Smith had dried his hair. It was nothing unusual to Presley or to Billy Smith, but I wondered whether many people would ever understand the strange life of Elvis Presley, the sharecropper's millionaire son, the pauper who became the prince. He may have been uneducated, he may have been uncultured, his favorite food may have been peanut butter and mashed banana sandwiches, but he was still the King, and the King didn't open jars, or dry his own hair, or take baths like the common folk. Not even Mick Jagger keeps a cousin on hand to dry his hair, but Mick Jagger's mother never worshipped him or cared for him as lovingly as Gladys Presley had cared for Elvis.

Elvis had been the King, and now he was just a dead junkie, and many people thought the one at fault was Dr. Nick.

The next day, when we left for Memphis, it was misting in Anniston, with just a few raindrops. As we drove, the rain stopped, the afternoon grew warm, the sky was clear and blue. We opened the sunroof and listened to tapes of Elvis singing. Then the weather changed again, and by the time we reached Memphis it was cold, and the sky was overcast, gray, and bleak.

On May 16, 1980, the Shelby County grand jury indicted Dr. Nick on fourteen counts of illegally prescribing. Each count is punishable by a prison sentence of two to ten years and a fine of as much as $20,000. Dr. Nick is free on bond and awaiting trial.

A local official, a friend of both Presley and Dr. Nick, told me, "They'll ruin him. It's not that they could do it; they're doing it. The prosecutors don't care what good he's done. They'll put him in jail if they can, and if they can't, they'll bankrupt him. They'll get him on a technicality or keep indicting him on slightly different charges until they break him."

"It's like a medieval ducking trial by ordeal," said a doctor who also knew both Presley and Dr. Nick. "If Dr. Nick drowns, he's innocent."

GRACELAND

Memphis is the Fourth Chickasaw Bluff, bluffs that were home to the Chickasaw Indians. They sold it to Andrew Jackson, James Winchester, and John Overton for five cents an acre. Right here where I'm sitting there were buffalo, and there is a historical record of that. Memphis is a gaggle of neighborhoods, a patchwork of problems. If you descend south from Memphis, down Elvis Presley Boulevard, you get to Whitehaven, where Graceland is, then you get to Southaven, where Al Green's church is. None of this fits together, and that's a constant concern. The redemptive thing about it is that I was able to come back to my neighborhood, buy my house, and be surrounded by the dearest, kindest people. People forgive each other in Memphis. But we won't forgive Graceland.

One afternoon in the early 1980s I found myself in a souvenir shop across the street from Elvis Presley's Graceland. They had lots of interesting items, among them oil portraits of Elvis and Lisa Marie on black velvet, but my eye was caught by a set of tumblers bearing a photo representation of the front page from the *Memphis Press-Scimitar* for August 16, 1977, with its headline, A Lonely Life Ends on Elvis Presley Boulevard. What the hell do you drink out of that, I wondered. Hemlock?

People obsessed by Elvis tend to be weird, and I never met one yet with a healthy sense of humor. To illustrate the difference between Elvis fanatics and the unimpaired, when Billy Gibbons of ZZ Top visited Graceland, he found it so funny that they threw him out, after which he had bumper stickers made up saying "I Was Asked to Leave Graceland." Billy has a sense of humor.

By the time that ill-fated visit occurred, Priscilla Presley had clamped down on Graceland with a death grip, and the souvenir shops, all taken over by Elvis Presley Enterprises, had cut some of the more arresting items out of their inventory. Nevertheless, Elvis was making more in death than he ever had in life, and Graceland was paying for itself for the first time in its existence.

Graceland was built in 1939 by Memphis physician Thomas Moore and named for his wife's great-aunt Grace Toof, who had willed them the land, thirteen acres in the suburb of Whitehaven, just north of Mississippi. In 1957, when Elvis bought it for $100,000, its most recent use had been for services by the Graceland Christian Church. It would be the first place in Memphis, since the Presleys came there in 1948, where Gladys Presley, Elvis's mother, would have room to raise chickens, and raise them she did.

After Gladys's funeral, Elvis and his father returned to Graceland. Standing on the front steps, Elvis pointed to the chickens in the yard. "Look, Daddy," he said. "Mama won't never feed them chickens no more."

Gladys never trusted Elvis's manager, the man she knew as Colonel Tom Parker. When, in the mid-1980s, Parker's true identity was revealed—he was Andreas Cornelius van Kujik, from Holland—a member of Elvis's Memphis Mafia asked him why he'd never said he was a Dutchman, and Parker replied, "You never asked me." The sentimental Parker, told that Elvis had died, said, "This don't change nothin'."

It all makes one wonder what Elvis thought of the Beverly Hillbillies. On second thought, the Beverly Hillbillies by comparison are fairly mundane. Consider: all of Elvis's uncles worked for him. His father had done prison time for changing the amount on a check a man gave him for a hog, not the act of a genius.

Yet it can't be denied that Elvis possessed, or was possessed by, a kind of genius. Still he was, for all his life, deeply ignorant and aware of it, living on cheeseburgers, BLTs, and fried peanut butter and banana sandwiches because he was afraid to order things he didn't know how to eat.

Graceland, perhaps more than anything except his music (it's a sel-dom-remembered fact that Elvis recorded more songs by Ben Weisman, who wrote "Rock-a-Hula Baby" and "Do the Clam," than any other songwriter) embodies Elvis's aesthetic. A fifteen-foot white satin couch, blue shag carpet on the ceiling—a palpable if unspeakable style.

I once met the interior decorator who designed Elvis's Jungle Room. I will not mention his name since he seems to consider this accomplishment something akin to being Oprah Winfrey's diet coach or Noriega's dermatologist. The thing that made our meeting memorable was the presence of a mutual friend who insisted on telling the story of what happened one night when the decorator was working on the Jungle Room.

In order to appreciate the story, you must know that Elvis, paranoid as President Nixon, had television cameras all over Graceland, so that whatever you were doing, he might at any point be watching you on one or more of the three TV sets he had at the foot of his bed. You should also know that Elvis had a number of dogs that ranged freely over Graceland's interior. One of these was a chow chow with the black tongue and disposition typical of the breed. Finally, you should bear in mind that while Elvis could afford a lot of expensive stuff, nobody at Graceland knew how to make it work.

That was the case with the back door leading out of the Jungle Room—it was heavy, dragged on the floor, and was hard to shut. Plus, the decorator turned out the lights, and it was dark in there, so when he tried to leave, with the chow chow gnawing at his leg, he shut the door with all the haste he could muster, not noticing that the dog's head was caught between the door and the jamb. If Billy Gibbons had done what he did, Billy would have had bumper stickers printed up that said "I Killed Elvis's Dog." Strangely enough, the decorator didn't even get fired. With his Jungle Room profits he later built a million-dollar studio on Union Avenue in Memphis.

The actor Chris Ellis, who gets beat up in *My Cousin Vinny* and plays Deke Slayton in *Apollo 13*, has for years celebrated Elvis's Death Day, a major Memphis festival, by creating commemorative T-shirts bearing incisive caricatures of the departed King. Sometimes they are rather inoffensive, like the one showing a corpulent Elvis resting on a cloud, with the legend, "I Found a New Place to Dwell." On one occasion, however, Ellis inveigled a girl in whom he had a romantic interest and a male friend to go with him to Graceland for the Death Day vigil in the Meditation Garden, the holiest of Elvis sites, where the bodies are buried. (When the Moores owned Graceland, that part of it was the barbecue pit.) What made it interesting was that the T-shirt Ellis was wearing, his latest commemoratif, showed a particularly fat and ugly Elvis with the caption, "I Killed Elvis—He Choked on My Dick."

Because the vigil is a candlelight service, no one noticed the shirt until Ellis was, like, right next to Elvis's grave. Then, as he tells it, he was set upon by two lesbians in red satin Elvis baseball jackets. One of them told him, "If you're looking for trouble, you came to the right place." To which Ellis, never at a loss for a *riposte*, said, "I'm not looking for trouble. I'm looking for another one of those killer blowjobs." Then he ran for his life, as did the young woman he'd brought along. Luckily he'd left his friend in the car with the motor idling. "I probably shouldn't have run off and left my date, though," he said later. "I never did get anywhere with her after that."

MOSE ALLISON

Over the vast desert of time where I was lost after returning in 1984 to my native Georgia, I scraped by partly by envisioning a trick to make it topical and getting assignments. At this time the magazine business was committing suicide. But there were pockets of energy. Mercenary soldiers, lonely sex freaks, blues fans. Blues fans seldom agree on what's really blues. Mose Allison was soon to become seventy, so I looked him up.

> If you describe on a map a circle with its center at Moorhead, Mississippi, the place where the Southern cross the Yellow Dog, lying within a hundred-mile radius are not only Como and Hernando, but also Red Banks, Helena, Lyon, Leland, Rolling Fork, Corinth, Ruleville, Greenville, Indianola, Bentonia, Macon, Eden Station, West Point, Tupelo, Tippo, Scott, Shelby, Meridian, Lake Cormorant, Houston, Belzoni, Bolton, Tunica, Yazoo City, Lambert, Vance, Burdett, and Clarksdale, whence come Gus Cannon, Roosevelt Sykes, Son House, Jimmy Reed, Muddy Waters, Fat Man Morrison, Charlie Patton, B. B. King, Albert King, Skip James, Bo Diddley, Emma Williams, Howlin' Wolf, Elvis Presley, Mose Allison, Big Bill Broonzy, Willie Brown, Jimmie Rodgers, Robert Johnson, Booker T. Washington White, Otis Spann, Bo Carter, James Cotton, Tommy McClennan, Jasper Love, Sunnyland Slim, Brother John Sellers, and John Lee Hooker. Also within this radius are Greenwood, where Furry Lewis was born, and Grenada, where John Hurt died.

> —Stanley Booth,
> *Rythm Oil: A Journey Through the Music of the American South*

Last November 11, Mose Allison, the composer-pianist-singer, turned seventy. It seemed a proper time to look in on him and see how life as a senior citizen is for the man once called—forty years ago in an album title—Young Man Mose.

I found out there are problems. One problem is, he's not acting his age. He's running and exercising, playing international gigs, has a new album, and is on the lookout for tunes. Another problem, he's still, in his phrase, "the man without a category." Is he a jazz player? Yes. Is he a blues man? Yes. "To me," Allison said, "it all comes from the same place."

Though he left there over half a century ago, the accent and the—soul?— of the country are still very much part of Allison. Tippo, population two hundred, Allison's birthplace, is forty-five miles from Moorhead on Mississippi highway 8, between Effie and Needmore in Tallahatchie County, deep in cotton territory. Tutwiler, in the same county, is where W. C. Handy saw a man at the train station playing a guitar with a knifeblade and singing the words, "Goin' where the Southern cross' the Dog."

The man was singing about two railroad lines, the Southern and the Yazoo and Mississippi Valley, known also as the Yazoo Delta—and, in the poetic parlance of the common people, the Yellow Dog. Right then and there, Handy said, "life took me by the shoulder and wakened me with a start."

Jazz and blues didn't exist as musical genres in 1903, when life awakened Handy. According to Allison, they really should never have been separated: "Up until recently, all the great jazz players have played the blues. Louis Armstrong played and sang the blues all the time. So when the country blues players were discovered later, people started to discriminate between that type of blues and the kind of blues jazz players played. You don't hear too much classic blues playing today when you hear jazz but all the great jazz players did it."

As Allison explained to me, his birthplace was outside Tippo proper: "The place where I was born, my grandfather's farm, is called the Island because Tippo Bayou encircles it. People had to ford the bayou to get in and out. They built a bridge when I was growing up, but there hadn't been one before. It was always called the Island, about an eighty-acre farm, completely encircled by Tippo Bayou.

"My grandfather had a player piano, and the story is that my father taught himself to play piano by lookin' at the piano roll, the keys goin' down and everything. He just evidently had a good ear and he taught himself to play, he played at parties and things. He played around the house some when I was a kid, I'd hear him—'Twelfth Street Rag,' 'Sweet Sue,' stuff like that. He could never figure out why I didn't try to play that way. When I started playin' boogie-woogie he didn't know what I was doin'.

"My younger brother did what I was supposed to've done, he stayed down there and farmed, went broke. [laughs] He's still there, but he's not farmin' anymore, he had to quit farmin'. That crunch in '83 when interest rates were 15 percent and commodity prices went down, a lot of them got caught. There's very few small farmers in the Delta now. He didn't lose his land, he still rents it out, but he had to get a job. So, that's what I was supposed to've been, but I never did like it."

He did his share of it, though—as a boy he plowed mules, picked and chopped cotton, cut and hauled hay: "I'm probably one of the few remaining blues singers with *that* experience."

Allison, who minored in philosophy at LSU, explained to me about personal destiny: "It's part genes and part memes. Are you hip to memes? That's the things you get culturally, y'know. Genes are what you get biologically, memes are what you get from the cultural background. There was music in the house all the time, my old man played piano, as I said, and I took to it right away. Lately I've been readin' a lot about the brain, and one of the studies they've done with birds shows that a bird can't sing his song unless it hears it—there's about three days in there when the bird has to hear its song, or it'll never be able to sing its song. It's just a matter of being triggered. The potential is there, and it's just whether or not you get triggered. I got triggered by my dad bein' musical and hearin' music a lot.

"I had a cousin who was a jazz fan, she had records of Louis Armstrong, Fats Waller, Earl Hines, people like that, so I got all of it at an early age. She was my first cousin. She was older than me but she lived in Mississippi, and she was goin' to college when I was a teenager, but she had records. I remember even before we had electricity, the wind-up Victrola. My folks went to dances all the time, they used to go over to the riverboat, and go to dances on it, so I got access to it at an impressionable age, and it just took, you know. Then you have to figure in whatever X principle there, the natural talent, if you have any and so forth. Which you spend your whole life trying to prove. Trying to decide whether you have any, or whether you're just clever. It's hard to tell. [*laughs*]

"My father had an older brother, but I had a bunch of aunts, and most of them got married, so I had uncles like that, but my grandfather was married three times, and he had three different bunches there. My father was on the second wife, Texana. I always wondered about her, nobody knows anything about her much. She died when my father was a baby. So, who knows, I always figured the musical talent might possibly have come right through her. My father looks like her. But, talkin' about Tutwiler, there's a movie in Tutwiler called the Tut-Ro-Van-Sum. 'Cause of Tutwiler, Rome, Vance, and Sumner. I was talkin' to Muddy Waters about it, he grew up in Tutwiler, y'know. I said, 'You know about the Tut-Ro-Van-Sum?' and he said, 'Man, I used to go to the Tut-Ro-Van-Sum, used to sit in the balcony on Saturdays.' So it's a possibility that me and Muddy Waters could have been in the Tut-Ro-Van-Sum Theatre at the same time. Course, I'd be down in the white section and he'd be up in the balcony. Watchin' Hopalong Cassidy or somethin'."

One of Allison's earliest influences was what he calls a "jyuck box." (His Delta inflections give the u in juke a short sound—rhymes with book—while reversing the process with the expression boogie-woogie.) The juke box was at, of all places, a gas station. Your reporter is from the rural south but had never encountered this phenomenon.

"There was a juke box at the . . . filling station?"

"Right, that was just sort of a hangout."

"And people would come by and drink Co'-Colas and play the juke box?"

"That's right, and beer, that was the beer place, they had beer there, and they had craps, so it was sort of like the local hang. This was in

Tippo, at the crossroads. On Saturdays, it was like overwhelmed with all the black labor in the area. I remember goin' over there and listenin' to the jyuck box at the service station when I'd go over and take a break. It had mostly country blues—I remember people like Roosevelt Sykes and Big Bill Broonzy. I've got a blues line that I consider the quintessential blues line, that nobody can identify. I heard it on the jyuck box in Tippo, Mississippi, and I think it was a woman—I suspect that it was Memphis Minnie. But nobody's ever been able to identify this thing for sure, and I've talked to blues scholars and bluesmen, B. B. King, John Lee Hooker, Junior Lockwood, and all these people—most of them have heard the line, but none of them remember who did it. Now, the line is, 'Papa's in the jailhouse, Mama's drinkin' wine, sister's on the corner doin' the bo'-hog grind.' The bo'-hog grind, man, that's where it's at, that's the whole damn thing, right there. You got to be a country boy to know what the bo'-hog grind is, anyhow. I told John Lee Hooker one time, 'Man, I saw you doin' the bo'-hog grind on the David Letterman show,' and it broke him up.

"When I was listenin' to the jyuck box in Tippo, it was like Tampa Red and Memphis Minnie and the people who preceded Muddy Waters and B. B. King. I learned a lot of those tunes, I used to play 'em at parties y'know, 'Let Me Play with Your Poodle,' 'My Little Machine,' 'Diggin' My Potatoes' by Big Bill Broonzy, I dug all that stuff when I was a kid, and Louis Jordan, he was always on the jyuck box. It's amazing how many people Louis Jordan has influenced. I heard an interview by Sonny Rollins recently and he was talkin' about Louis Jordan."

"The original rock and roll?"

"I always tell people that the original rock and roll band was Tuff Green in Memphis. Tuff Green and his Rocketeers. I used to go to the Mitchell Hotel, man, they used to sneak me in there, '47, '48."

Memphis in the postwar years had too many great musicians to name here. Andrew "Sunbeam" Mitchell's hotel was the stopping and jamming place. There are players in Memphis who still remember the impact of visits by the likes of Charles Brown and Oscar Dennard, both classically trained pianists who could play in every key. Allison met men like saxophonist Bill Harvey, B. B. King's first musical director, and heard the legendary Phineas Newborn Sr. Orchestra at the Plantation Inn in West Memphis.

In 1945, Allison had entered the University of Mississippi. "I started out in chemical engineering," he said. "I figured that was a good thing to do to see the world. I think I remember readin' somethin' about chemical engineerin' when I was comin' up. I did that for the first semester, and then I went to the army. I was gonna be drafted so I joined the army for eighteen months. This recruiter sold me this bill of goods about if I would join, I'd be able to stay with my buddies. So me and two friends from Ole Miss joined the army for eighteen months and three days later they went off to North Carolina to the Quartermaster Corps and I went to basic training at Fort McClellan, Alabama. I found out later that was where Lester Young did his basic training. It was about as dismal a place as you can find."

The army, where Allison played with the 179th Army Ground Forces Band, wasn't a complete waste of time. "When I went to the army and started playin'," Allison said, "I ran into guys that had been around a lot. I was in the army with a trombone player, one of the best in the world, Tommy Turk. I had learned to write arrangements at Ole Miss. There was a guy, a musician, one of my early gurus, named Bill Woods, a piano player and a saxophone player, from Charleston, Mississippi. He was one of the first guys who took any interest in me, and he was a good arranger. So when I went over to Ole Miss and started playing with the Mississippians, I started writing arrangements for the band. It was like, three trumpets, five saxophones, the whole nine yards. Arranging was easy for me to do once I got started. In the army I kept at it, and I met some guys who were arrangers, and they would help me with things. By the time I got out of the army I'd written a whole book of arrangements for the Mississippians. I think they've still got some of the charts down there. When I came back I did a couple of semesters of economics."

Allison kept returning to Beale Street, where he saw blues artists who affected him profoundly: "The Beale Street Auditorium, where they had big shows, that's where I saw the original Sonny Boy Williamson. He was on a show called *Smart Affairs of 1949*—it was in '48—Larry Steele and his Sepia Revue, with the dancin' girls and the big band and comedian and the whole thing. I went just for the show, and—I don't think he was even advertised—he walked on by himself, toward the end of the show, and played a few blues numbers, just playin' harmonica and singin' by himself, and it just floored me, man. The power of it—I thought, oh, man, yeah—it got me right back into takin' the blues seriously.

"Then I left Ole Miss and ended up with an English major, down at LSU. My first gig was in Lake Charles, my first six-night gig. That was the first trio gig that I played."

Allison was graduated from LSU with a BA in English in spring of 1953. He had been playing clubs in the South for years, and he continued that for a while longer, getting what he calls "on-the-job training." I'd read that he had first worked in New York with Al Cohn, and I asked how they'd met.

"I met Al Cohn's wife in Galveston, Texas—the wife he had at the time," Allison said. "She was a singer named Marilyn Moore. She did sort of a Billie Holiday thing. I was workin' in Galveston, this was about '54, I guess, '55. I met her at a session, she sang and I played behind her. She told me if I ever came to New York to look up Al, and she gave me the number and everything. So, eight months later, or whenever I did decide to go to New York, I called Al up and he had me out to his house, man, to dinner and the whole number, and we played, and so forth, and he started gettin' me on whatever he could get me on. He wasn't workin' that much at the time, he was mostly writin'. But not too long after that, he and Zoot started workin' a lot more, and when they started workin' at the Half Note, downtown on Spring Street, I used to work with them all the time down there and I worked gigs just with Al and just with Zoot. Al was definitely one of my first benefactors up in New York. He put me on whatever he could. He got me on my first record date. The first record I made was the thing with Al and Bobby Brookmeyer and Nick Stabulas and Teddy Kotick. I don't remember what label it was or nothin', but it was a good record. Every now and then somebody turns up with it."

Allison started recording as a leader with the small jazz label Prestige, went to commercial giant Columbia for three years, then found a home at Atlantic for a decade and a half. His first album under his own name came from a series of short piano themes that he called *Cotton Country Suite*. The record company thought somehow the word cotton wasn't commercial, and now not even Allison uses the original title: "*Back Country Suite*—I had been collecting those little pieces over the years—actually the thing that inspired that was Bela Bartok, at LSU. I heard him for the first time, one of his things, the piano suite, *Hungarian Sketches* or somethin', just a piano playin' fairly simple tunes, but they were so evocative, that gave me the idea. I said, well, hell, I can do that with my background, the music I grew up with, I ought to be able to come up with somethin' like that. So I collected those little pieces for the next two or three years, and when I got to New York I had it together and I made a tape of it over at that Thirty-Fourth Street loft—Thirty-Fourth right between Second and Third—two Mississippi guys were the ones that ran it, friends of mine, so I used to play there all the time. I made a tape of the thing there, and I took the tape around, and I didn't get any takers for the first few months. Then one night I was at a party where [jazz pianist] George Wallington was playin', he had an apartment up there on the West Side, and I played some of the pieces from *Back Country Suite* for him. He said, 'Look, man, I can probably get you a record date at Prestige,' 'cause he knew Bob Weinstock. So he took me 'round to Prestige, and they signed me right there, to do six albums in two years, two hundred and fifty dollars an album. So that's how that came about, I gave George the publishing end of it—he had a publishing company, Jazz Editions—which I've regretted ever since. I finally got it straightened away after a long time, and after a lot of money. But that happens to everybody, it takes a while to find out. George is dead now. His brother took over Jazz Editions, and that's who I had to sue to get my rights back. But foreign copyright laws are different, so Jazz Editions still has the right to collect half my money in foreign countries on tunes like 'Parchman Farm' and 'Young Man Blues.'"

"Speaking of that, what did you think when the Who cut that?"

"I got a check in the mail from Jazz Editions for $7,000. I thought, 'Man, what the hell is this? This must be some mistake.' I'd been gettin' twenty dollars and thirty dollars, and I couldn't figure out what had happened. I didn't know anything about 'em [the Who]. I had heard about the Rollin' Stones. I ran into the Rollin' Stones, I played on a show with them in about '66. [Actually August 7, 1964.] At a place called Richmond, outside of London, on a soccer field. It was a blues festival, and all these English blues people were there. That's when Brian Jones, the blond guy, was still alive, and he was the star then, Mick Jagger wasn't the star. I had never heard of 'em, they had to be brought in in a covered van, I didn't realize that kind of thing was going on, it was amazing the adulation those guys were gettin'. And when they did their show, I couldn't believe it, Brian Jones would go out and shake his locks, man, and all these teenage girls would go crazy. Ten, fifteen thousand people there, it was frantic. It was new for me to see that that was happenin', and people were sayin' what did I think about it, I said, well, it's better than Lawrence Welk and Guy Lombardo, hellofa lot better than the *Hit Parade*. But it was a few years later, I guess, that the Who did the thing, the first time I ever made any money off a record.

"I've made a few bucks from some of my songs that the rockers have done, but as far as my records go, they've never paid out. None of my records have ever gotten out of debt. I owe all the record companies money. I was with Atlantic for seventeen or eighteen years [actually from 1961 to 1976, but it seemed longer] and made a lot of records for 'em, and I got my first royalty check from Atlantic last year. Because of a reissue they did, they had to pay me a coupla hundred dollars royalties or sump'm. But all the time I was with 'em I never made any money except what I got in advance."

"In 1996 you did that thing with Van Morrison and Georgie Fame." [*Tell Me Something, Songs of Mose Allison*, Verve]

"Yeah, right, and I'm still tryin' to get the money. I've gotten paid for just a fraction of what it's sold, man. I don't know what I'm gonna do, but I gotta do sump'm, it's been about eighteen months now since it came out, by all reports it's sold over two hundred thousand copies, I've gotten paid for thirty thousand."

"You must have enjoyed your years with Atlantic, though."

"Oh, yeah. I loved [Atlantic Records producer] Nesuhi Ertegun, man. You mentioned Jerry Wexler, he was the one tryin' to get me to go do somethin' commercial all the time, I used to hate him. He was always tryin' to get me to go down to that place down there where they had that rock and roll band, Muscle Shoals, tellin' me how I could start sellin' records and all that. So—whenever he comes on the programs as some kind of scholar or sump'm, I always snigger a little. I used to hang with Nesuhi a lot, he was my man for a long time. In fact, he's the one who kept 'em recordin' me even though I wasn't sellin' any records. I was sorta like the mascot there for several years. They kept comin' up with these suggestions, and I kept ignorin' 'em. But I was able to do pretty much what I wanted to do."

Until he wasn't. In the eighties nobody was rich enough to afford a mascot. Allison for several years was without a label, until in 1981 he was signed to Elektra/Musician, where he made two albums, *Middle Class White Boy* and *Lessons in Living*. The association led to his affiliation with Blue Note, a venerable jazz label with four Allison titles currently in release. The latest one, *Gimcracks and Gewgaws*, was released in January 1998, which more or less brings us up to the present. With chronology for the moment satiated, we return to philosophy, aesthetics, metaphysics.

"I did an interview with Ray Charles recently," I said to Allison, "and it kind of gratified me to hear him bring this up, 'cause it's something I've thought many times—you get to where you think, 'Maybe it's just me, maybe I'm the only person who feels like this.' He started talkin' about people we listened to comin' up, whoever it was, Johnny Mercer or Jo Stafford or Frank Sinatra or Billie Holiday—Ray made the point that with these people, you heard one note, and you knew who it was. Instrumentalists too. Coleman Hawkins, Lester Young, Pee Wee Russell—one note and you know it's Pee Wee Russell. Ray was saying, 'I don't know—if you know some people around today like that, tell me, 'cause I'd like to check 'em out, but I don't hear it.'"

"Everybody's singin' that same song," Allison said, "and they should be singin' it, because it's true. I just saw Nat Hentoff bein' interviewed. He was sayin' the same thing. He said, Man, these young guys, they can play anything, they've got all the technique in the world, but none of them have any personality, and it's really a shame, it's a loss, because there's no real personal expression. A lot of players, a lot of young journalists, man, they never heard of anybody. Haven't even heard of Charlie Parker, a lot of 'em, you know."

"Record companies are trying to sell what they put out this week, and to hell with the rest of it."

"That's the only saving grace about Europe, they take a look at the whole thing—they still dig guys, eighty-year-old players over there, and they know a lot about the early music."

"In Europe they know better what art is. In America jazz is not art."

"It's the commercial thing. And New York is like one-upmanship. I saw Lester Young on his last gig in New York. At the Five Spot on the Bowery, it was on a weeknight, and there were like ten people there, the waiters were makin' noise with the chairs, and all this stuff, and he wasn't gettin' any respect, and he was playin' beautiful. He sounded beautiful. Next week, Ornette Coleman was there, they were lined up around the block, you couldn't get near the place. That pretty well sums it up. They wanta know what's new, what's the latest thing, what's up—"

"Who's in, who's out, who's gonna tell ya what it's all about—"

"Yeah."

"What is blues? What is jazz? What's the difference?"

"Blues is the seedling, and jazz is something sprouted off of it. There's different definitions of jazz and blues. There's a sociological definition of jazz, which is the music developed by African Americans in New Orleans in the twenties or whatever. My technical definition of jazz is, the music that is conceived, felt, and performed simultaneously."

"The act of improvisation."

"Right. Now, that eliminates all the jazz players who are just simulating somebody else, or if you play somethin' that you've played over and over, and you know that you're playin' it, that's not jazz either. Jazz is those moments when you really are thinkin' it, feelin' it, and playin' it. That's sump'm that jazz players pursue every night, with varying results. Jazz, blues—it's passion, it's a type of unlettered passion.

"I actually prefer Muddy and John Lee and those guys, 'cause to me they have that Delta sound, that deep sound. I remember some early stuff by T-Bone Walker—he was one of the first ones that had a band, had those good three horns or whatever it was, he did some things with a small band that I really dug. To me the epitome of that Delta sound is Muddy Waters with Little Walter. 'I'm goin' down in Louisiana . . . baby behind the sun . . .' They play twenty-four hours of Muddy on his birthday at KCR up here."

"I've heard the reason you live in New York is for the radio."

"That's it. That's about the reason, 'cause you can hear music on one of these radio stations that you won't hear anywhere else in the world. I hear things every day, almost every day. I've heard things I would never have heard in my life, if I hadn't been listenin' to the radio here.

"I never heard a thing by Muddy that I didn't like. Lester Young and [Thelonious] Monk are probably my two favorite jazz people. I was on a flight with Pee Wee Russell one time. We were sittin' together, and we were talkin' about the difference between American and European audiences, and Pee Wee said, 'Well, the European audiences are housebroken.' That knocked me out. It's pertinent, too. I noticed that with the festivals. American festivals for a while, they were always havin' fights, people gettin' drunk and all that kind of stuff, and throwin' trash all over ever'thing, and you don't get that so much in the European places, at least the ones I've been to."

"Did you know Monk?"

"Yeah, I opened shows for Monk lots of times. Monk's manager, Harry Colomby, was a good friend of mine and he was helpin' me when he was gettin' Monk off the ground—he's the one that got Monk the first gig at the Five Spot, the thing that really got Monk goin'. And he got him the records contract at Riverside. Harry Colomby was a high school history teacher on Long Island, but he had the taste, and he started managin' Monk, and that's what he was doin' when I met him. Monk never played a bebop lick in his life, and he's always considered the father of bebop or sump'm, and he never played any of those bebop changes, that everybody played for years, the turnarounds. Some guys, that's all they played, just bebop cliches, one after another. But Monk never did that. I always regard Monk as an eccentric traditionalist. Some of his stuff was right out of New Orleans. He was a great guy, you talkin' about a gentleman and a scholar, that really applies to Monk. He had his moments, they had to take him to Bellevue now and then, but it was all connected to bad things, he'd just get in a slump now and then. I was never around him when he was like that. Monk would say somethin' ever' now and then that was really off the wall but you got to thinkin' about it and you'd say, man, there's somethin' to that."

"What role, if any, does race have in blues?"

"When I first came to New York, hardly anybody had ever even heard of Muddy Waters and John Lee Hooker or any of those people, and there certainly weren't no blues clubs. This was in the late fifties, and there was still a lot of experimental jazz then. Nobody knew anything about the blues, so I was a sort of novelty to 'em. There was always those people who were sayin' that I wasn't doin' it like the classic blues people, and there was always somebody sayin' that a white southern college boy shouldn't be tryin' to do that anyhow. [Race] was always in the background. The first time I played in Chicago, on the South Side, *Jet* magazine called me up, and when I told them I'd gone to LSU, they said well, were you the first black guy that went to LSU? I said, I think there's sump'm you oughta know.

"It's one of those reoccurring things that's been hovering over my career the whole way. It doesn't bother me. When [a reporter] said that [about Allison stealing the black man's music], I decided I better go ahead and deal with it. Because I was in London, and man, if there's anybody that's stolen black music, it was a lot of 'em in London at the time.

"Not too many black guys ever came on to me with that stuff. It was mostly the white hangers-on, and people who felt like they had some sort of priority on it. In Chicago one time I got run out a black club by white detectives. They claimed they were doin' it for my own good, they said, you'll get your throat cut down here. Some of the players that were my connection to the club were from Memphis. I was in there sittin' in. That element is always lurkin' in the background, but I had so many supporters, great black players who dug what I was tryin' to do, that kept me from gettin' bothered by it. But that tune ['Ever Since I Stole the Blues']—I wanted to make a comment on that whole number there, 'cause I got to thinkin' when she said that, well, what would it have been like if I had actually stolen the blues? What would happen? 'They even closed down the barbecues.'"

"You said you no longer do the 'cotton-sack' songs. But then you record 'Dixie.' Do you do 'Dixie' in clubs?"

"I did 'Dixie' at the Village Vanguard one night. That was a few years ago. I did it in 6/8 time. I felt like I was doin' the boogie version of 'Dixie.' But I knew there would be people, whites and blacks sayin', Aw, you shouldn't do that. There'll be black people who think you ought not to play it at all, and white people who think you shouldn't mess with it like that. I figured I'd get some static for doin' it that way, but the main reason I did it was 'cause the bridge to 'Dixie' is unlike any bridge, and I felt like it'd make a great bridge for players to play on. I like to dig up those old things and do them in a completely different way."

Mose's daughter Amy has an album on Koch, *Amy Allison: The Maudlin Years*, a critical success. She is now recording with a band called Parlour James. "Amy does sort of ironic things," Allison said. "One of her songs is 'Now That You Got What You Wanted, It Ain't What You Wanted at All.' I'm hopin' she'll be able to make a livin' at it pretty soon.

"When I met Charles Brown, he told me he had to wash windows for three or four years or sump'm, and he said the thing that got him back into playin' was he was washin' a window at a house one day, and they had a real nice piano inside, and he just went in and started playin' it, and decided he had to get back goin', y'know. His dad was named Mose. I didn't meet him until a few years ago, and I was playin' in Seattle one night, and he walked up and said, 'Mose Allison, Charles Brown.' I said, 'Snuff-dippin' mama,' and he said, 'What makes yo' lip hang so low?'

"You were talking about what caused the blues to happen and how'd it all get started, and there's somethin' that I didn't point out yet that I believe is important in this whole thing, and that's humiliation. All the best players have been humiliated, you know. I've found myself, when I've been humiliated in my career, it's always motivated me to play better. It makes you more determined."

WIREGRASS

When, in 1984, my book finally emerged from its mossy cocoon ("That took longer to write than the Bible," Keith Richards said) I left Memphis, where I'd lived twenty-five years, and returned to Georgia.

I must have fallen asleep as we drove in the shiny new black 1947 Ford sedan along the white sand road into the slash pine forest, because the first thing I remember is opening my eyes to see the red swamp water that had overflowed the ditches, covering the hubcaps, drowning the engine, leaving my parents and me marooned in a sea the color of old blood. A smiling black man named Frank Porter came out in a gum truck, a big flatbed vehicle used for hauling barrels of turpentine, and towed us to a hill. In the Okefinokee territory, a hill is a place that's not underwater.

I was five years old, and I had come to live in Wiregrass, where it seemed I would never be sad. Even after Frank Porter tried to stab my grandfather, I loved the swamp country. At times there I was afraid, but nothing in the woods was as frightening as what I would find in the world outside.

Each weekday morning, Wiregrass was awakened by a short, rotund man named Butler, whose yodeling yoo-hoos seemed part of the pre-dawn fog, along with the slave-code shouts the woods hands gave as they trudged from the shotgun shacks of the quarters to the stable where the mules and horses were kept, where the gum-drenched wooden wagons waited. Some days I would go out with them, riding my buckskin pony while the hands chipped faces—scraped the bark from pine trees—or dipped gum—gathered turpentine. Other times I would go alone into the woods, carrying a light lunch to be filled out with such plant foods as pine nuts and palmetto shoots. I washed my hands in the red water with the dark green leaves of po' man's soap and spent mornings watching a sundew plant devour a fly or opening pitcher plants to release the still-living insects trapped inside.

Years would pass before I understood what was happening in Wiregrass, where life went on as if emancipation had never been proclaimed. The black workers, many of whom had been brought in from Mississippi by the owner of the turpentine company, were paid in cash and in scrip, a kind of play money that could be used only at the company-owned commissary. Almost all of them were in debt to the company, making them its property. Men from other turpentine camps came in the night to steal them, family, furniture, and all, and my grandfather would find the rustled families and bring them back. The system was hard on everybody but me. All I knew at the time was that I loved the place I lived and the people there. Among the woods hands were men with names like Cat, Slick, Shoejohn, and Dollbaby. One of the black women was called Mony because she had once said, when asked how she was, "I don't feel good. Feels like I gots de mony," meaning pneumonia.

Mr. MacDuffie, who ran the commissary, was a philosopher and the author of many wise sayings, such as "One man's just as good as another one and a whole lot better." Speaking of automobiles, Mr. Mac said, "Brand new's the best model." Fired numerous times for being found in the woods, where he was supposed to be checking the hands' work, sitting in the wagon wearing carpet slippers, Mr. Mac was still employed by the turpentine company in Wiregrass when he had the first of a series of strokes that killed him. I was a teenager then, no longer living at home, but the company owner's son and I brought the partially paralysed Mr. Mac a hospital bed from a nearby town. "Aren't you going to thank these boys, Mac?" asked his wife, a fine, religious woman. "They're just like your other friends, they've been praying for you."

Mr. Mac, well read in the classics, especially Shakespeare and the Bible, fixed us with a baleful glare and said, "The prayers of the wicked availeth little."

Ambition, first my parents' and then my own, would take me away from Wiregrass—to other towns and cities, other countries. I came to know love, hate, friendship, betrayal, mansions, jails, poverty, and wealth. But at last my exile would end, and I would return to the scenes of my childhood.

This time I approached Wiregrass from the northwest, not stopping except for fuel until I could see Georgia. I was headed for the coast, but after driving through such garden spots as Sylvester, Ty Ty, Enigma, and Willachoochee, I detoured south to the place where I had lived nearly forty years before. The old house was still there, and so were the trees I had climbed and fallen out of. The pay-building where Frank Porter made his almost lethal move was deserted, and all the workers were gone, their quarters long ago sold for twenty-five dollars apiece. The commissary was padlocked, the stable had been torn down, and a spot that once rang with shouts was silent except for the wind sighing through the pines.

The red water still ran in the ditches, the palmetto and gallberry bushes were still there, but the humor and sorrow, the passing shadows I knew as a child, existed only in memory. I had come back alive, though, and that in itself was a miracle.

My daughter, the six-year-old starlet, Rock and Roll Ruby, was waiting for me at my parents' house on St. Simons Island, so I left Wiregrass again, knowing that the ghosts would be there whenever I wanted to visit. The important thing was that the stories remained, and now it would be my job to tell them.

FASCINATING CHANGES

This piece was written before Phineas Newborn Jr. died, but it ran in the *Village Voice* as one more obituary. I don't like it, as a poet once said, but I guess things happen that way.

As Charlie Freeman's body was being lowered into the grave, under that cold gray sky, I stepped closer to Fred Ford, the large, white-bearded black man who had spoken at the Memphis Funeral Home.

"This is not the time," I said, "but I think Atlantic would like to do the Phineas Newborn album Charlie wanted to produce, sort of as a memorial."

"Give me a number where I can call you."

I took a card from my notebook and jotted my number on the back. That was Saturday, February 3, 1973. Monday, Fred called. "Do you know what you gave me?"

"I'm not sure," I said.

"You wrote your number on the back of a ticket that said 'Club Handy Benefit Dance for Bill Harvey—to Buy Him a Leg.' I went on the road with Bill Harvey and the Harlem to Havana Revue when I was fifteen years old. I'll keep that the rest of my life."

It must have been sometime that night I said to Fred, "I can't believe I'm sittin' next to the man who barked like a dog at the end of Big Mama Thornton's 'Hound Dog.'"

"Yeah," Fred said, his large, dark eyes looking into the smoky neon depth of the cinderblock Fabulous Club Gemini. "I was gonna meow like a cat, but it was too hip for 'em."

I knew almost nothing about Phineas Newborn except that he was a jazz pianist whose records I'd seen reviewed in *Down Beat* in the 1950s. He'd had some problems, been under lock and key in New York and California in the late '50s and the '60s, and now he was back in Memphis, living at his mother's house on Alston Avenue, south of Crump Boulevard.

At the Gemini, Phineas played with a junkie drummer and a kid bass player. Sometimes the drummer nodded, and the bass player didn't listen, but Phineas was phenomenal.

I have known only one other person like Phineas Newborn, a Japanese karate master who lived for a time in Memphis, where he had a girlfriend. One night he and a young student were at his girlfriend's house when her old boyfriend happened by. "You know," the karate master said to the student, smoothly changing the subject from whatever it had been, "I can hit you—kill person behind you." He gave his chest a modest touch. "I can do." Phineas Newborn is just like that. We will return to this point. In fact, we will not depart from it.

Phineas Newborn, I would learn, was to some people a living symbol of African American genius, the ultimate product of a tradition whose roots are mysterious and deep. His family life and American music were one and the same, with a cast including Elvis Presley, B. B. King, Count Basie, Benny Goodman, Charles Mingus. His style resembled that of Secretariat, or the young Muhammad Ali. He could think of things to do that no one else had ever done, and then he would do them. He had, another Memphis pianist once observed, "a boogie-woogie left hand, a bebop right hand, and this . . . third hand." But it was not simply unsurpassed technique that made his work so affecting: his music derived power from its own emotional range—the outer-space comedy of "Salt Peanuts," the nostalgic humor of "Memphis Blues," the rhapsodic sadness of "The Midnight Sun Will Never Set," the majesty of "The Lord's Prayer."

The day after hearing Phineas at the Gemini, I phoned Atlantic vice president Jerry Wexler to tell him that Phineas was playing better, if possible, than ever. That afternoon Wexler went to a Newport Jazz Festival promotion party at the Rainbow Grill, where he told the guests that "people these days talk about Atlantic and rock and roll, but it's really a jazz label—and I want to report that Phineas Newborn is cookin' in Memphis." People stood and cheered. "Wein wants to book him," Wexler told me that night, "and so does D'Lugoff, who says he'd like to manage him." When I told Fred Ford, he said, "Have mercy."

The next time I saw Phineas—Junior, "Gates," Little Red, "a five-foot-four, 140-pound genius" who could, as Fred Ford says, "reduce a three-thousand-pound piano to smolderin' ashes"—he and Fred were coming in the back door of Memphis's Ardent Studio, Phineas in a snap-brim, Fred in a Russian fur cap, both wearing dark overcoats. Both ready for the Fifty-Second Street of their boyhood dreams. In the control room the engineer, seeing Phineas approach the Yamaha grand, without knowing who he was, rolled the tape. Phineas began playing "Memphis Blues," stepped on the damper pedal, and sat down. In that order. "Who is that?" the engineer asked.

Phineas and Fred stayed in the studio for over an hour, with Fred, whose own sax had he said been indisposed since September, fighting a cold and unfamiliar baritone while Phineas coaxed cascades of advanced harmonics from the facile Yamaha. When they stopped for a break, Phineas paused in the door of the control room to light a Pall Mall. "Thanks," Fred said, accepting a cigarette and a light. "You sho do play some fascinatin' changes."

Phineas plays with such total ease that mere mortals, watching him, are mesmerized into thinking they can do it too, and leap on the set. Years ago at jam sessions at Andrew "Sunbeam" Mitchell's Club Paradise on East Georgia Avenue, Phineas would baffle leapers by changing the key a half step each chorus. "Horn players would play a few notes, jam the mouthpiece tighter, try again," Fred said, laughing like Uncle Remus talking about Brer Rabbit.

The reply to the New York offers was that for the moment Junior would stay in Memphis. I was elected spokesman, and here are the notes of the message I sent to Atlantic:

I talked to Fred. He and Phineas appreciate everyone's interest and are working hard on their two-album set. I think we may get some of that to listen to soon. On the live gigs, as far as money is concerned, I understand Phineas couldn't consider leaving town for less than $2,500 for a five-day week. He's doing fine, he's not destitute, and he's not eager to up and go to New York. He was up before, the hot jazz star, and it had bad results for him—nervous breakdown—so Fred is being very protective, which is understandable, but they are recording and working hard.

This was, though I didn't know it then, too much like asking for a rain check. On September 23, 1973, I wrote Wexler again:

Enclosed you will find something that I have never sent you, namely, a demo tape. The tape is of Phineas Newborn Jr., playing impromptu solo piano, and he has no peers. No one, not Art Tatum, not even Blind Tom, compares with him for unpredictability, inevitability, ingenuity, power, and range of imagination. Yet it is never far from ragtime and the blues, the roots of his music.

Blind Tom, Thomas Greene Bethune, a Georgia slave born in 1850, is supposed to have known five thousand pieces of music and been able to listen to a brass band, a grind organ, a whistled tune, and then repeat the music on the piano, even if he heard them all at once. I kept preaching to the converted because lots of people had enjoyed the way Charlie Freeman played, and he died out of work like Dewey Phillips. Watching Memphis's most brilliant products die out of work had made me fervent.

I knew, too, that Wexler had doubts about Phineas's mental state, because he kept asking, "Can he take care of business?" I gave glowing reports of Phineas's playing and said nothing about other aspects of his behavior, such as his close association with the psychiatric ward at Veterans' Hospital and his reaction to women—I do not think the word *aggressive* is too strong.

January 9, 1974. Today is Wednesday. Saturday night about eight o'clock Phineas was admitted to John Gaston Hospital with multiple cuts, bruises, broken bones. He had been living in a halfway house on Vinton, near the red-light district. Earlier Saturday night a blonde girl, hair in a ponytail, wearing slacks, came to see him there. "Phineas," she said, "I want you to come with me, there's somebody I want you to meet." He was in bed, but he got dressed and went out with her. A short while later he came back, just barely alive.

When I got hold of Fred he volunteered nothing, let me tell him what I'd heard, let me ask questions: "These people any particular color?" "The opposite." "What kind of people would do that?" "Animals," Fred said.

That night Fred and I drove around Memphis with my rifle in the car as we'd done once before when one of us was being measured for a frame by a mutual acquaintance. I soon realized that Fred had been fishing: he knew no more about who had done Phineas harm than I did, and Phineas wasn't going to tell. Nesuhi Ertegun heard what had happened to Phineas—in those days Atlantic was Wexler and Nesuhi and Ahmet Ertegun—and sent a check for $2,500.

———————

January 16, 1974. Just back from Alston Avenue, a street of small single-family dwellings where, in the white frame house at no. 588, I met Phineas's mother, a little red woman in a green dress and a red sweater, a short orange pencil stuck in her graying, slightly processed hair. The front room was crowded, pictures of Phineas and his father and brother Calvin on the piano. She moved the footstool, covered with clean laundry, so I could sit down, and she sat on the piano bench. I gave her the check. She looked at it and said she didn't know whether her son would accept it. I told her how I came to have it, and she told me about when he was in Europe playing and his agent and his wife were in Florida laying out in the sun. "Phineas came back and told the agent, 'Don't book me no more'—but the agent wanted to send him on these long hikes, and his wife starts after him, 'You don't want to work,' and his agent is mad because he wants money, and he's sweet on his wife. Then Phineas goes to Europe the second time and comes home to find every stick of furniture in the place gone except the piano.

"So he has been used and misused, and he's very wary of people— sometimes he don't even trust me, won't even take a chance on me, and I scratched and went to the cotton fields and paid up to five dollars a lesson so he could take lessons, because I was his first fan. Because I took such pleasure in his playing. He'd play, and he'd ask me, 'How does that sound, Mama?' and I'd say, 'It sounds good, son, play it again,' and he'd bap it again.

"But for the last few years he has been emotionally disturbed. When I came in the hospital the other day and saw the shape he was in, all beat up, I had to hold back my tears. I turned aside and told myself, This is no place to cry, and held his cigarette. My hand was trembling, but I held it for him. I told the woman administrator down there that I wanted to move him to the Veterans' Hospital—she said, 'Aren't you satisfied with the care he's getting here?' And I said yes. I looked her right in the eye—I can look them right in the eye—and said I am very grateful for what you've done. But first of all, my son went to the army. He has earned the care of the VA hospital. And second, no matter how long he has to stay there, he can stay and get treatment and it won't cost anything—and a nurse standing there said, 'That's reason enough.' So I called the Ford Funeral Home and told them not to send a hearse or a long funeral car but to move Phineas, and they did, and I went down to pay them—called their names, been knowing them, Congressman Ford and all of them, all their lives—and they said, 'Oh, no, we can't let you pay, this is a gift to Phineas.' I said, 'God bless all you thugs.'

"So I will get what he needs—I remember when he was little, he asked me, 'Mama, will you buy me a bicycle?' and I didn't know where we would find the money, but I got him one. When he sees me looking like this he won't say a word, but I go out there all spruced up, he'll say, 'You look good, Mama—you look like you used to when Daddy was alive.' He is emotionally disturbed. But I know he can play the piano. He knows all the tunes, he don't need no music. On his worst day, he can play piano. Not everybody knows how he is. But I do. I know him. And I love him. And I will see that he gets what he needs, and sometimes things more than he needs, just because he wants them. Because once upon a time, he was my good child. And he is still my good child. I sat beside his bed and told him, Put your hand in Mama's. Play C—D—E—F—G in Mama's hand. He played the notes against the palm of my hand, and I said, You'll be all right, son. You going to play again."

———————

In the early decades of the twentieth century, James Newborn, a slender, dark-skinned black man, owned a farm near Jackson, Tennessee. But he preferred preaching, wood carving, and photography, leaving the fields to his fifteen sons, the fruit of his first marriage. According to the unpublished autobiography of his grandson, Calvin Newborn, James had another family with the woman who became his second wife: "Papa had a natural instinct for polygamy."

Although he saw no value in education, nine of James Newborn's sons went to high school, one becoming a Los Angeles chiropractor, another graduating from Tennessee State College and serving as bandmaster at Memphis's Geter High School for over thirty years. Phineas, the oldest, wanted to play drums. But his father, who considered secular music the work of the Devil, would neither buy any nor let him earn the money to buy some. Resenting this and his father's treatment of his mother, Phineas left home to live with an aunt in Jackson. One day he was trimming a hedge when who should stroll past but the russet-hued, glowing Rosie Lee Murphy. Her father, Willie Murphy, who farmed in nearby Whiteville, Tennessee, was called Son Twenty because his mother, nicknamed Twenty, had been her parents' twentieth child.

Rose was going to nursing school, living in a dormitory. She and Phineas courted, married, and moved to Memphis. The Depression was just beginning. Phineas and Rose lived in one room in Orange Mound, a black neighborhood near the State Normal Teachers' College, where Phineas went every day on his bicycle to work as a cook's helper. He was also playing drums at night with local musicians. At the end of 1931 Rose went back to Whiteville to have her first baby.

"Phineas brought a radio from Memphis," Mama Rose remembers. "As long as that hillbilly music like 'She'll Be Comin' Round the Mountain' played, Junior listened and bucked his eyes. But when Bessie Smith . . . started out singin' them slow blues, he'd let out a howl." There was family speculation that the baby was marked for music. Or, to put it another way, that Phineas's wicked pursuit of the Devil's music had put the baby under a curse.

But Phineas, determined, missed no chances to hear and play music. "When them bands would come uptown," Mama Rose said, "we'd catch that streetcar. Wasn't but seven cents each. We'd go and take that baby to that show." Count Basie called the Newborn infant Bright Eyes because his eyes would light up when the music began.

Calvin, the second and final child of Phineas and Rose, came fifteen months after Junior. The family moved nearer to downtown Memphis and Beale Street, where Phineas played for the Midnight Rambles at the Palace Theater with bands like the Chickasaw Syncopators, led by Memphian Jimmie Lunceford, who asked Phineas to go on the road with him. It was a real opportunity, but Phineas let it go. His dream was to have a family band with his sons.

Unable to read music himself, Senior bought a piano and, when Junior started school, had him take lessons from Miss Georgia Woodruff, his first-grade teacher. After initial complaints—"Mama, it's hard." "If it wasn't hard, I wouldn't have to be paying for it."—Junior played for the love of it. "I listened to Fats Waller and Art Tatum . . . and they encouraged me. My father was the one who let me know about the association of the pianoforte with orchestrating and general musical composition. The idea influenced me so much I developed quite a fondness for the piano." During years of study—the first twelve volumes of exercises— Junior had to repeat one lesson.

"I told him," Mama Rose said, "'Look, we are poor people, and I can't afford to pay twice for this same page.'" Mama Rose never had to tell him again. "He loved it. And the girls would drive up on they bikes, and he'd be paddlin' on that piano, and they would come on in, and I'd go in the kitchen, come back, Calvin have one them gals' head layin' in his lap, but Junior still be playin' the piano. He loved music, and he loved the piano. But Calvin was—cowboys, and shine shoes, and go to the cotton field. Went to the cotton field one time pickin' with the neighborhood girls, came back, and he was tellin' Junior, 'Yeah, man, Ellis May and Ruthie Jean and all of us was out there, man, we had a lot of fun, you ought to go with us tomorrow.' Junior told him—just kept playin'—'I'll take your word for it.'"

Calvin started studying piano in turn, but "Babe," Mama Rose says of Calvin, was "kinda slow. He's kinda bad. Want to do everything but practice."

Calvin and Junior, intrepid adventurers, inspired by the aura (ADULTS ONLY) of the Midnight Rambles, at the end of an afternoon's playing in a park near home, wandered away down the railroad tracks to Beale Street, where they ate hot dogs, listened to a jug band and a blind blues singer, watched the movies at the Palace, hid under their seats till the Rambles commenced, and were rewarded with jokes, jazz, dancing girls. "I knew then," Calvin writes, "I wanted to be in show business."

Though that evening ended with frightened boys confronting worried, irate parents, Senior soon had his sons back at the Palace. He came home from a tour with the Lionel Hampton Orchestra bringing their latest hit, "Hey! Ba-ba-re-bop!" and the story of Hamp's teaching it to his parrot. Junior and Calvin played the song at the Monday night amateur contest, where the master of ceremonies was Rufus Thomas. They won first prize, performing as a piano duet, with Calvin also singing and dancing.

Calvin, following his father's advice and his own inclination, "budded as a dynamic showman, while Junior became a budding piano virtuoso. After being embarrassed by Junior, I lost interest in the piano and reverted to guitar. Dad asked Riley B. B. King to take me to Nathan's pawn shop on Beale, and I purchased a guitar for five dollars."

Already able to read classical piano music, Calvin sought lessons from a white guitarist, who refused to teach him, saying he would drive white students away. Tommy Dunlap, a friend of Senior's, began giving Calvin lessons. The first song he learned was "Steel Guitar Rag."

Meanwhile Junior was gaining a local reputation, performing "Rustle of Spring" at the LaRose Elementary graduation exercises and "The Lord's Prayer" at the Mount Vernon Baptist Church. He already knew by heart things like "Rhapsody in Blue."

The boys had not been long in high school the night Lionel Hampton—who named Junior "Gates"—came back to town. They met Hamp's pianist, Oscar Dennard, a young genius from St. Petersburg and the only man, woman, or child in anyone's memory who ever cut Junior. At the grand piano in the lobby of Sunbeam Mitchell's hotel, the traveling musician's home away from home, the two boy-sized beboppers battled for over a quarter of an hour with their left hands alone. Oscar started the set with nursery rhymes—he had a way of applying Bach's three-part inventions to "Three Blind Mice." Calvin: "After meeting him Junior woodshedded all day and went out jamming every night for quite some time."

Junior was studying now with Professor W. T. McDaniel, bandmaster at both Manassas and Booker T. Washington high schools, and playing with both school bands, the Rhythm Bombers and the Bookerteasers. He learned bassoon, French horn, trumpet, alto and baritone horns, tuba, drums, glockenspiel, saxophones, and other reed instruments. Calvin mastered trombone, baritone horn, piccolo, and flute. Between them they took on the entire range of western musical instruments. "He and Calvin can play any instrument," Mama Rose said. "Calvin, or Junior, could play anything but the harp. And they went out and took some harp lessons."

Memphis musicians still talk about the afternoons in the 1940s when a black boy, standing just tall enough to reach the piano keys, came into O. K. Houck's Union Avenue music store, where no one knew him, and played to perfection the sheet music, all of it, stacks each day. When the bandleader Phineas Newborn came in, the store's music teachers would tell him about the prodigy, but he said that his group was satisfied with their piano player. Then one day Newborn came in and the boy looked up, still playing, to say, "Hello, Daddy."

Junior said that he joined his father playing with Tuff Green and the Rocketeers when he was fifteen, but Calvin insists that he started playing with them and Junior when he knew only the "Steel Guitar Rag"—or about three years after Junior started studying piano—so Junior must have been quite a bit younger than fifteen. Another local legend holds that Junior played piano on B. B. King's first sessions when he was so young he needed special permission to join the musicians' union, and since the recordings were made in late 1949, Junior would then have been seventeen.

The initial B. B. King session, produced in a quonset hut by Sam Phillips for Modern and RPM owners Saul, Les, and Jules Bihari, employed Senior and Junior, Tuff Green, and Ben Branch, the tenor player, who would enter history as one of the men talking with Martin Luther King when King was shot. Senior didn't play on B. B.'s second session, but Calvin joined Junior, Branch, Green, Willie Mitchell, Hank Crawford, and the drummer Tel Curry. Ike Turner played piano when Junior didn't. B. B.'s next recording unit would include George Coleman—that's Coleman's propulsive alto on "Woke Up This Mornin'." Memphis swarmed with giants in those days.

Senior played with heroes like Gatemouth Moore, who, according to Mama Rose, "used to sing the blues at the Brown Derby till the hair stand up on your head," and the formidable tenor saxophonist Leonard "Doughbelly" Campbell, who died returning to Memphis from Texas in a car wreck that killed two other musicians but only broke Senior's arm. Calvin says the broken arm made Senior's feet stronger. He went back with Lionel Hampton for a while after that, and when he left Hamp hired two drummers.

Junior had spent his sixteenth summer on the road with the Saunders King Orchestra and would travel with the Ruth Brown-Willis "Gator Tail" Jackson group, while Calvin, who played piccolo with the Bookerteasers and baritone horn with the Letter Carrier's Band, toured with Roy Milton. The boys' out-of-town excursions were unfortunate necessities to Senior, who had grown more determined as years passed to have a family band. The chance had come in 1948, when Senior's band started a residency at Morris Berger's Plantation Inn in West Memphis, Arkansas. There were eight instruments—Senior, Junior, Calvin, Honeymoon Garner on organ, Kenneth Banks on bass, two tenors, and trombone. The trombone player, a freshman at Booker T. Washington named Wanda, also sang. Soon she and Calvin were playing trombone duets. Movie stars like Pat O'Brien and John Carradine, big-time broads like Eva Gabor, musicians like Tommy and Jimmy Dorsey, crossed the Mississippi to see and hear the Phineas Newborn Family Showband. Calvin: "That was where we really grew musically, the Plantation Inn." Calvin remembers playing every night from 9:00 to 4:00, but Mama Rose says the schedule wasn't quite that demanding.

After a year or two, the Newborn band moved to the Flamingo Room, formerly the Hotel Men's Improvement Club, upstairs at Hernando and Beale, where a really dedicated (or perhaps deaf) thief robbed the cash register one night while everyone else was transported by Junior's playing. The band took a sabbatical from the Flamingo to travel with Ike Turner and Jackie Brenston, whose "Rocket 88" was on the record charts. Also on the show were the Four Ames, who became the Four Tops, Moke and Poke, and Redd Foxx and Slappy White. Playing the Regal in Chicago, the Apollo in New York, the Howard in Washington, the Palladium in Los Angeles, they traveled in an old Greyhound bus that nearly went over a cliff in Arizona when the brakes failed. Stranded in New Orleans, they played at the Dew Drop Inn for room and board until their booking agency sent them return fare to Memphis and the Flamingo. For the next couple of years they mostly stayed put except for summer residencies at resorts in Hot Springs, Arkansas, and Idlewild, Michigan. The Michigan engagement led to successful club gigs in Cleveland and Detroit. Senior's dream must have seemed within his grasp.

Calvin, married by now to trombonist Wanda, had become such a showman that Flamingo owner Clifford Miller booked guitar battles. "You'd have guitar players to come in and battle me," Calvin has said, "like Pee Wee Crayton and Gatemouth Brown, and I was battlin' out there, tearin' they behind up, 'cause I was dancin,' playin,' puttin' on a show, slidin' across the flo' . . ."

One night, probably in late 1952, a teenaged white boy "came in there, didn't have on any shoes, barefooted, and asked me if he could play my guitar. I didn't want to let him, I don't usually—I didn't know him from Adam. I'd never seen him before. In fact, he was the only white somebody in the club. He made sure he won that one. He sang 'You Ain't Nothin' but a Hound Dog' and shook his hair—see, at the time I had my hair processed, and I'd shake it down in my face—he tore the house up. And tore the strings off my guitar so I couldn't follow him." The boy turned out to have a name even more rare than Phineas Newborn—Elvis Presley. He became friends with the Newborn family, and

Mama Rose has recollections of going off to church with Senior, leaving Junior and Calvin with a fresh-cooked ham in the kitchen, and coming home to find that Elvis had been there and left only the hambone. Elvis often remembered the Newborns with Christmas cards and presents, and on the day he died, Junior, touring Japan, dedicated that evening's concert to his memory.

After graduating from Booker T. Washington in 1951, Junior entered Tennessee State Agricultural and Industrial College, a black school in Nashville. The head of the music department recommended that he transfer to Juilliard, where he could concentrate on music, but Senior refused to let Junior go. This may have been the single most destructive event in the life of Phineas Newborn Jr. (There's a thesis: the southern father, Abraham/the southern son, the sacrifice. Or as Furry Lewis used to say, the Only Forgotten Son.) Resentful, Junior left school after the second year, returning to Memphis, spending a year at Lemoyne before receiving an army draft call.

Stationed at Fort McPherson, Georgia, Junior played French horn and tenor saxophone in the Third Army Headquarters Band. (He also wrote arrangements for a show in which, among other things, a man juggled wheels with his feet while Junior played "Wagon Wheels.") Back in 1952, Count Basie, playing in Memphis, had heard the grown-up Bright Eyes, and when the Basie band played Savannah, Junior renewed acquaintances with the Count. By now Junior's style—based on the music of pianists like Art Tatum, Fats Waller, Nat Cole, and Bud Powell, instrumentalists like Charlie Parker and Lucky Thompson, as well as Memphis keyboard legends like Struction and Dishrag, with his group the Four Cup Towels—was fully developed. He played, at least as fast as any pianist ever had, block-chord solos and unison runs with both hands and both feet, showing complete mastery of keyboard and pedal techniques. Basie, Junior recalled, was "fascinated."

Released from the army in June 1955, Junior, still in uniform, came to the music store his father had opened on Beale Street and chanced to meet a large gentleman Mama Rose introduced as "Mr. Howling Wolf," whom Calvin had been teaching to read music. The Phineas Newborn Family Showband were reunited, but not for long. Later that year, John

Hammond, the music critic and record producer, came to Memphis with Basie and his band when they played the Hippodrome on Beale Street, and met Junior. In 1956 Basie set up a telephone conference call with Junior, Hammond, Willard Alexander the agent, Morris Levy the promoter, and Benny Goodman. "They decided it was best for me to record and then proceed to start playing outside of New York," Junior said. "I worked Philadelphia, Newark, and several other places, and finally opened at Basin Street." Junior played opposite Clifford Brown and Max Roach. *Esquire* devoted a full page to a review comparing his performances to the debuts of Louis Armstrong in 1924 and Bix Beiderbecke in 1925.

All of which represented to Phineas Senior the death of the dream that had given purpose to his whole life, because he went along only as a spectator. Playing with Junior, Calvin, and their Memphis schoolmate George Joyner (who later became Jamil Nasser) was not Senior but Kenny Clarke, whom many regard as the original modern jazz drummer. December found the Newborns back in Memphis, where W. C. Handy—blind and too weak to play at his annual pilgrimage to the Blues Bowl black high school charity football game—passed the trumpet to Junior, who played accompanied by five marching bands.

Signed for five years to the Alexander agency, Junior, with the quartet, played top clubs on both coasts and in Canada, including twelve weeks of the first year at Birdland opposite some of the strongest players in jazz. Senior's pride in his sons could not take away the pain of not playing with them. When the quartet appeared at the Newport Jazz Festival, master of ceremonies Father Norman O'Connor asked Senior, in the audience, to stand. "I knew that Dad wanted to be there onstage playing with us," Calvin says, "I could feel his sadness."

Having opened at Carnegie Hall, the agency's "Birdland Show of 1957," which involved among others Basie's band, Sarah Vaughan, Billy Eckstine, Lester Young, Stan Getz, and Chet Baker, Phineas's quartet played Symphony Hall in Philadelphia, then headed north. "After performing in Montreal," Calvin writes, "I got backstage and noticed Bud Powell butting his head against the wall."

———

The late 1950s was a strange time for jazz and for America. President Dwight Eisenhower's favorite musical organization was Fred Waring's Pennsylvanians. His favorite writer was Zane Grey. Henry Miller, D. H. Lawrence, William Burroughs, Jean Genet, J. P. Donleavy, Vladimir Nabokov, and pubic hair were obscene. Charlie Parker and Art Tatum died, then Lester Young and Billie Holiday, who was arrested in her hospital bed. Miles Davis received what the *Amsterdam News* termed "a Georgia head-whipping" for standing outside the Greenwich Village nightclub where he was working. Art Pepper drew two-to-twenty in California for his third drug bust. Young, Holiday, Gene Ammons, Dexter Gordon, Stan Getz, and Chet Baker, among others, also did time for drug offenses. Bud Powell, in mental institutions five times from 1945 to '55, was not alone with his problems.

The Birdland 1957 tour ended without Calvin, who received a draft notice, but Phineas carried on, with Little Rock guitarist Les Spann struggling to master Calvin's parts. Eventually Calvin was given an honorable discharge and returned to society as unadaptable to army discipline. Meanwhile Phineas, with Charles Mingus, had duetted in clubs and recorded the soundtrack to a movie, John Cassavetes's *Shadows*.

Phineas's first album, on Atlantic, with Calvin, Oscar Pettiford, and Kenny Clarke, was followed by a series on RCA Victor, United Artists, and Roulette, no fewer than nine albums from the period 1956–60, featuring him in settings from large string orchestras to left-hand only. (One night at the end of the '50s, Phineas honored Oscar Dennard by letting him finish the set at the Red Rooster on 136th Street in Harlem. Not long after that, Dennard toured with the New York Jazz Quartet in Europe, Russia, and Africa. In Egypt he contracted typhus and died in a matter of days.) It would be laughable, were human life and loss not involved, to read some of Phineas's early notices. *Young Men from Memphis* with Junior, Calvin, Frank Strosier, George Coleman, Louis Smith, Booker Little, George Joyner, and Charles Crosby, received three stars—"good"—in *Down Beat*. Three stars were hard to get. Martin Williams gave Billie Holiday's *Lady in Satin* two and a half, calling the album "a mistake." Williams deplored the lack of "logic" in Junior's playing, as if rejecting the Fauves because of inaccurate color. Junior, possessor of a dry, mordant wit, while playing elucidates the history of jazz piano as he makes ironic comments on it. The New York critics, ignorant of Junior's work with the likes of B. B. King and Jackie Brenston—and ill-equipped, even had they known, to perceive value in such "rhythm and blues" performers—came to the consensus that no one with that much technique could have any soul.

John Mehegan, pianist, teacher, and *Herald Tribune* columnist, observed in *Down Beat* that

> Phineas has recently astounded the jazz world with what appears to be a technical virtuosity found only in the top echelon of classical pianists. However, there are little or no dynamics or shading in his playing . . . he seems to know little of the orchestrative qualities of the keyboard in relation to chords and sonorities . . . Phineas is not in any sense of the word a funky player . . . To be blunt, Newborn exhibits a highly nervous lateral emotion that is never relieved and becomes an incessant mannerism that would seem an ideal sound tract for a *Tom and Jerry* cartoon. A heavy moss of classicism clings to his playing which prevents any real jazz feeling from emerging.

The absurdity of a white piano teacher from New York telling Phineas Newborn about real jazz feeling is delicious. Reviews from such people could do harm even when they were good. Phineas's RCA Victor album with strings, *While My Lady Sleeps*, worthy of comparison with the Charlie Parker and Clifford Brown sets with strings, received this compliment from *Down Beat*: "As a pop-mood music package, this is worthwhile listening." I was fifteen years old when I read that, and it didn't send me out into the streets looking for the album. Other pianists redressed the balance somewhat—Oscar Peterson called Junior the best of the pianists younger than himself (thereby eluding comparison); Ray Bryant, in a *Down Beat* blindfold test, said of Phineas, "His technique is fabulous; he can get over the piano as good as or better than anybody in the business today." Teddy Wilson said, "He has a fabulous technique, and it will be interesting to see what direction he goes in the next few years because he certainly has the equipment at the keyboard." But then Junior would release a record, like *Fabulous Phineas*, with its definitive "Cherokee," and *Down Beat* would offer two and a half stars—better than fair, less than good. Even Leonard Feather's accolade—"the greatest living jazz pianist"—is devalued by the knowledge that he said the same thing about Bernard Peiffer and later wrote that he might also have said it of Oscar Peterson after an outstanding performance.

While playing at the Cafe Bohemia in Greenwich Village, Junior reencountered Dorothy Stewart, a girl he'd known at Booker T. Washington, who was now living in New York. They soon married and had two daughters, but didn't stay together. Calvin describes seeing the marriage end with "two men forcing Junior into a parked car" as Phineas, having a breakdown, was being taken to Bellevue for observation. On release he drank himself into Kingspark State Hospital, from whence he returned to Memphis, and the two brothers, once so close, would not see each other for nearly ten years.

Calvin began working with Lionel Hampton, then joined Earl Hines. His wife, who had become a narcotics addict, had convulsions and died in her sleep, and Calvin began using heroin himself. By this time Junior was in California, working Los Angeles clubs and starting a series of albums with such musicians as Frank Butler, Paul Chambers, Louis Hayes, Leroy Vinnegar, Roy Haynes, Ray Brown, Elvin Jones, Sam Jones, Philly Joe Jones, Teddy Edwards, Howard McGhee, and Shelly Manne. His divorce had become final, and he found another woman with whom he lived and had a son.

One day in 1965, Calvin, still in Manhattan, dividing his time between playing and stealing to score heroin and cocaine, received a surprise visit from his father, now the drummer with Hall A. Miller's Animal Circus. Phineas Senior neither drank, smoked, cursed, nor chased women. His only vice and greatest pleasure was playing drums. But his heart was failing, he told Calvin, doctors had said he had to quit. Calvin the next day played in the circus band, where he learned that Senior had "a spectacular act making the elephants dance to his drumbeats." Later that year

Senior, unable to stop himself, sat in with Junior in Los Angeles, walked off the stage, and dropped dead.

Junior's problems continued:

CLINICAL RECORD

NEWBORN, Phenias [*sic*]

VAC Brentwood Hospital, Los Angeles, California

1-18-68

History of Present Illnesses

Prior to the present commitment this patient was discharged in July of 1967 from unit 3 L.A. County General Hospital at which time he was to seek outpatient treatment. After a period of 3 weeks he discontinued taking his medication and ceased contact with his private physician and he reportedly resumed drinking about October 2, 1967. It was at this time that he began to show recurrent symptoms of mental illness when he was described as making bizarre movements with his hands exhibiting extreme suspiciousness and remaining mute most of the time. He had expressed the belief that he and Jesus Christ were related in a direct fashion and said he was married only once: to his mother. There was only one child: himself. The pattern of his illness pertains to his work as a Jazz Musician. When work is irregular or non-existent and he is at loose ends he gets to drinking rather heavily and his behavior develops into hostility to authority and apparently his mental symptoms exacerbate. His history of mental illness dates back however to 1958 in New York where he was committed from Belview [*sic*] Hospital. He in no way recognizes he is or has been mentally ill.

This 36-year-old committed Negro veteran entered Brentwood VA Hospital in a withdrawn, hostile suspicious state and continued in this general state for most of his hospitalization. He spends a great deal of the time withdrawn but playing the piano with obvious skill and appropriateness musically. He was confined to house-keeping detail in an effort to get him doing something besides going into his piano playing constantly. Last month he went on passes to his home and on evening passes to meetings of Recovery Incorporated. He has begun to socialize a bit more and appeared to be stabilizing. All he needs is an altercation with his common law wife and he is thrown back into inappropriate laughter and withdrawal and hostility. He plans on signing a contract for a piano bar performance in the local area, was put on trial visit status as of 1-12-68 to return for follow-up in two weeks.

J.L.S., M.D.

12-2-68

Hospital Summary

This 37 [*sic*] year old nonservice connected patient, musician by profession, has spent close to eight years in the hospital. On his admission and a large part of his hospitalization, his illness was manifested by either delusions, paranoid thoughts or else withdrawal behavior, escaped from reality in playing the piano.

Dr. F.P.

12-16-69

The patient was readmitted on 4-24-69

ADDENDUM: Patient has now again recovered from his episode and will go to live with his mother in Memphis, Tenn. Patient was given a Regular discharge effective 3-17-71.

A.P.S., M.D.

"His wife called me one time—said, 'Mama Rose, I cooked him a steak, made him a salad, then he goes in the bedroom, sees clothes on the bed, says, "Move these clothes."' She told him, 'Come in here and help me with these dishes.' Junior lays low, don't say nothin,' and she calls him again. He says, 'I'm a piano player, not a dishwasher.'

"I told her, 'Listen. I cook him steaks. I make him salads. I wash the dishes.'

"'But they say the way to a man's heart is through his stomach.'

"I said, 'They muss a been talkin' about a white man, honey. The way to a Newborn's heart is by shakin' them sheets.' I told her, 'Get in there and shake them sheets.'"

CLINICAL RECORD

NEWBORN, Phineas, Jr.

VAH, Memphis, TN 38104

10-11-72

Nature and Duration of Complaints

(Include circumstances of admission)

Bizarre behavior for the last several weeks.

History

This 41-year-old separated black man from Memphis, Tenn., was admitted to Ward 2-C, Psychiatric Service, VAH, Memphis, Tenn., on 9-23-72. His mother swore a lunacy warrant for his admittance to the hospital. Mr. Newborn is a musician and he has never come home very early at night but lately Mrs. Newborn, patient's mother, said the patient stayed all night on the streets near their house talking to himself and staring into space. People in the neighborhood literally got scared of him, so Mrs. Newborn said she didn't have any alternative but to bring charges against him. Mrs. Newborn, patient's mother, further stated that Phineas was a full-term normal baby. At school he was average student, never failed. After high school he enrolled in Memphis State University [*sic*] to study music. He spent 2 years at college and got carried away wth his music and quit college. While he was in school Phineas was always a shy loner, and he was kind of slow in getting acquainted with the girls. He said he admires the girls but he preferred to be alone. From 1952 to 1955 he was in the Army stationed at Ft. Jackson, S.C. [*sic*] His rank was PFC. Apparently he did not have any problems while in the service.

He played the piano at different night spots in Memphis. He made pretty good money but he drank a lot. Apparently always his only best friend was his mother. Mrs. Newborn does not know whether he has been taking any drugs. Lately Phineas would not sleep at all, and he would not eat. He would stay up almost all night. The patient was married twice. His first wife was born in Memphis and they grew up in the same neighborhood. His agent books him in New York for concerts. His first wife read his name in the newspaper and decided to go to see him. Several months later they were married.

Patient's mother said she never agreed with this marriage because her daughter-in-law was several years older than her son, and she had an 11-year-old child from a previous marriage. His wife left him because of his mental illness. They lived together several years and have 2 daughters. She left him and took all the furniture in the house, left only the piano. Mr. Newborn then left for California. He met another girl and they were going together for 3 years. A little boy was born before they got married. This marriage also did not work. Patient's mother said that Mrs. Newborn was very selfish and sadistic. She would keep him locked up all the time in a mental institution. He was in VAH, Brentwood, Los Angeles, Cal., several times.

J.H., M.D.

As the dates indicate, I met Junior when he was an inpatient—the hospital must have let him out to play the Gemini.

Admission Date
6-12-73

Discharge Date
8-14-73

Summary

This 41-year-old black male was admitted to Ward 2C of the Psychiatric Service of Memphis VAH on 6-12-73 because he had struck his mother. He has had no recent female relationships. On 6-14-73 the patient was transferred to Ward 1C to be involved in the behavior modification program. He was initially angry at his mother for putting him in the hospital and at the hospital program for insisting that he be involved and perform. He was always silent in groups and rarely talked about himself. The only time he was happy or productive was when he was playing the piano, and he seemed to use this to feel good about himself and to gain the approval of others without the necessity for closer involvement. It was arranged that he board at the Halfway House for pyschiatric patients and in addition attend the Day Treatment Center program for one-half day during the week days. He was going to be encouraged to work on his piano. His mother agreed to furnish whatever money was necessary to make it possible for him to start in the program. He was therefore given a discharge 8-14-73. He is considered mentally competent and able to work. His prognosis is poor.

J.H., M.D.

The Halfway House is the one where Junior was living when he was assaulted.

Admission Date	Discharge Date
1-7-74	1-17-74

Summary

This patient was referred from John Gaston Hospital. Apparently he was attacked and beaten on the day of admission. The patient was unwilling or unable to give a past history or circumstances under which he was injured. The patient remembers absolutely nothing about his injury, what happened, or where. He was noted to have injuries of both hands, arms and had forearm casts on both arms. He was diagnosed as having a trimalar (cheekbone) fracture and when it was discovered he was a veteran he was referred to the VA Hospital. Examination revealed the nose to have crepitation on the lateral side of the dorsum of the right nose. A definite fracture could be palpated, however, the bones were in good alignment. Several lower incisor teeth have been either evulsed or extracted. There were also some teeth missing on the maxillary alveolare. The patient was admitted and after proper laboratory work he was taken to surgery where on 1-17-74 his trimalar fracture was reduced with a #22 urethral sound introduced through a skin incision over the lateral brow and into the intratemporal fossa. The fracture was elevated and an audible pop was heard. It was felt that this fracture was stable at this time. However, the next morning it was noted that this fracture was down again. The patient was then taken to surgery where open reduction and interosseous wires were placed at the zygomaticotemporal, zygomaticofrontal and zygomatico-athmoidal sutures. In view of the patient's psychiatric ailments his postoperative period was complicated somewhat. The patient removed his protective dressing over his face and pulled the packing out of his maxillary sinus. However, it was felt that all had been done for him and that due to his poor cooperation we could not get an excellent repair of this fracture. The patient was discharged OPT NSC to return in one week.

M.G., M.D.

On the evening of the day he was discharged, Phineas went to Ardent Studio with Fred Ford and recorded the triple-speed left-hand *tour de force* "Out of This World" that would appear on his 1975 *Solo Piano* album. Hearing the performance while looking at the X-ray photograph of Phineas's broken hand is enough to make you think that Little Red, like Jerry Lee Lewis, is a bit more than human.

One rainy afternoon in October, I think, of 1974, Mark Myerson Jr., an Atlantic representative from New York, had visited the little house on Alston. Phineas was still in bed—it was about three o'clock—and Mama Rose, greeting Mark, a well-mannered young man whose father engineered classic Duke Ellington and Frank Sinatra sessions, returned the check from Atlantic for $2,500 that I had given her. Mark took it without understanding but with perfect grace, listening to Mama Rose and nodding, discreetly putting the check away.

Into the front room, with its dilapidated piano, overstuffed furniture, many framed photographs, and bric-a-brac—a little china-colored angel playing tenor saxophone—came Junior, wearing a red shawl-collar dressing-gown, smoking as always, looking at the floor. After introductions, Junior was asked to play.

"Play Mama's favorite," Mama Rose said. "Play 'Please Send Me Someone to Love.'"

"If you want to hear that, you play it," Junior said. "I'll play something I wrote." Whereupon he sat at the piano, with its forty-four dead keys, played his Coplandesque composition "Shelly's Suite," named for his older daughter, and a number of other songs while it rained hard, torrents of notes and weather, and we listened. As Piano Red used to observe, "When the music spirits hits you, it hits you hard."

At length Atlantic issued another, larger, check to Phineas in payment for the album *Solo Piano*—not the double album Fred Ford had envisioned, but the twenty-years-overdue solo album—which received a Grammy nomination and many excellent reviews. Some good things resulted, but for the most part life went on as it had in Memphis. I was living in a house with a vintage snooker table, and at times Fred and Phineas would come over and Fred and I would shoot snooker while we listened to records and Junior ambled around restless because I had no piano.

I was still, six years after the events had transpired, writing about the Rolling Stones at the end of the '60s. By now so overcome with shame at my inability to finish the book that I could no longer face the Stones, I stayed at home on July 4, 1975, when they played Memphis. With me were an old friend named Susan and her young son Daniel, who were visiting for a few days. Memphis was hot and humid, and as if things weren't crazy enough, a plague of bb-sized beetles attacked the three prize plum trees in my backyard. I stood in the heat picking them out of the bark with the point of a knife. Daniel helped me for a while, which I appreciated, but then even the good-hearted ten-year-old decided it was a fool's errand and left me to my futile task. The trees would die overnight.

Into this less-than-idyllic scene descended my friend and sometime Rolling Stones pianist Jim Dickinson and his wife. Dickinson wanted me to come along and see the Stones, but he wouldn't say so, and I wanted to see them, but couldn't bring myself. Soon Fred and Phineas showed up, Junior at once taking a shine to the striking auburn-haired Susan, who, having been married to a drummer, had already had more conversations than she'd wanted with over-friendly musicians. She went into the kitchen, followed by Phineas, followed by me. Busy at the counter, Susan ignored Phineas, and he exited into the backyard where the Nazi bugs were gassing the plums.

Leaving the Dickinsons downstairs with Fred, who was saying, "I have seen the time I could call six and have it come up, tell the dice what to do," Susan and I went up to my office, sat on the couch, and passed the time until we heard footsteps on the carpeted stairs. I looked around the doorjamb to see who was coming up and spied Fred on the landing. "Where Junior?"

Insufferable Yankee editors have explained to me how offensive it is to quote southerners speaking as we speak. Fred said *Where Junior* not because he didn't know it's correct to say Where is Junior but because he knew I knew there wasn't time to say Where the fuck is Junior?

"I don't know, he went out in the backyard, is he not there?"

Fred was waving good-bye before I got the line out. I went downstairs, looked out back, saw no one, strolled through the living room past the Dickinsons, Jim looking now like a man on a hopeless mission, on to the front porch, and scanned the neighborhood. Junior was standing on a porch a few doors down, reading a newspaper, while in the front yard a young, shirtless, white boy, maybe a year or two older than Daniel, looking rather perplexed, clipped a boxwood hedge. He had watched a small red man amble down the sidewalk, turn in at his house, go up on the porch, and start reading his family's newspaper. The boy's perplexity did not decrease when he saw Fred Ford, the Chocolate Santa Claus, striding toward him. Fred stopped at the walkway and said, "Little brother?" Phineas kept reading. "Time to go." Boy still clipping. Junior, silent, folds paper, drops it where he found it, again passes boy—clip, clip, clip, eyes rolling—and together Ford and Junior walk to where Fred's borrowed four-door sedan is parked at the curb. Fred unlocks the front door, steps back for Junior—who reaches in, unlocks the back door, opens it, gets in, sits back as if to say, "Home, Jeems"—as Fred, shaking his head, slams the front door, goes to the driver's side, gets in, starts the engine, and pulls away, with Junior's posture in back seat asking—axing—the musical question, Who is the world's greatest classical-jazz piano player?

———————

Later that month at a Club Paradise concert, the mayor's office honored Junior with a citation "for outstanding and meritorious service" and Mama Rose with a key to the city. The concert reunited Junior with Calvin, who had been living in Los Angeles, detoxing on methadone and playing with Hank Crawford, by now a distinguished Ray Charles

Orchestra alumnus. Any doubts in Calvin's mind about his ability to hold his own with, or against, his brother should have been removed by the time they finished "Cherokee," the last song of the evening. Phineas's playing is affected by, depends on, the nature of the occasion, the stature of the musicians accompanying him, the quality of the audience's intelligence and understanding. On this night his home community expressed pride in the Newborn family, and Junior and Calvin showed why it should be proud. That the concert was not recorded is a disaster and shows how proud of the Newborns the Memphis community really was.

In the next year, Phineas played in San Francisco and did occasional club gigs and concerts. *Solo Piano* was having a good effect, and in 1977 this unfortunate man, considered by VA physicians unable to live an unsupervised life, toured Japan all by himself. A Pablo album, *Look Out! Phineas Is Back!* with Ray Brown and Jimmy Smith, was released that year. In 1978, *Centerpiece*, a remarkable album featuring Calvin "Newborne" and Hank Crawford, came out, and Junior finally returned to New Yark, where he played the Village Gate. Robert Palmer's *New York Times* review said, "He is back, healthy and playing superbly."

In July 1979 Phineas returned after twenty years to Europe. We went not because we were needed but because Irvin Salky, a Memphis lawyer who had booked the engagements and was prevented by illness from going with Junior, paid our expenses, so Fred Ford and I went along. Phineas first played at the Montreux Jazz Festival; the opening concert, billed as the Piano Summit, featured him alone, playing duets with Jay McShann, Hank Jones, and John Lewis, and in a double-Bosendorfer trio with Herbie Hancock and Chick Corea. At the end of the last set, Hancock and Corea were reduced to beating on the wood of their Bosie because Little David the Giant Killer, the Albert Einstein of the piano, had the keys sewed up. The next night Junior played an impromptu but memorable jam session with Ray Brown and Dannie Richmond.

Phineas's last concert of that European visit was at a jazz festival in Juan les Pins. Backstage, Count Basie's guitarist Freddie Green, seeing Junior, said, "Where is Calvin? He's the greatest guitar player in America." We stayed on to relax for a few days in the south of France, and Junior enjoyed being among the many beautiful naked people. He dressed up in his tux every morning so the girls would ask who he was. Fred began to call him "the Count." I'd go down to Fred's room and he'd say, "You seen Drac?"

Months later I heard that Atlantic's attempts to release the Piano Summit had been stymied by representatives of some of the pianists who'd played with Junior. If this is true, it's understandable, because none of their careers would be enhanced by the evidence of how completely they were outplayed. "Hank Jones is the only one who even put up a fight," Fred said. "And Phineas just let John Lewis off easy 'cause John such a nice guy."

But each triumph left Phineas sitting on the couch in his mother's living room. At some point in the early 1980s, I called Phineas, said, "How are you?" and was told, "I'm just vegetating."

Over the next decade, Phineas played a week or so each year in New York City, mostly at Sweet Basil in Greenwich Village. He played at festivals in the United States and Canada in the last couple of years, but his opportunities to work were not many and not close together.

In April 1988, in order to check up on Phineas for this story, I went back to Memphis. As I walked up on the porch of the little house on Alston, Phineas opened the door. I said hello to Mama Rose and to Calvin, who for over a year had been alcohol- and drug-free, attending Lemoyne College, and writing his book.

Phineas and I hugged each other when I came in, but he seemed a bit restless. I sat on the piano bench, Mama Rose and Calvin on chairs, and Junior asked if I wanted a beer. It was two o'clock, early for me to take a drink, but I said sure. He brought a tallboy for me, one for himself, and sat on the couch. I started talking about Memphis in the 1940s, when Big Phineas, Al Jackson Sr., and Tuff Green had bands. They had been before my time, and I asked how many players they included.

"They had four-five horns on the front line," Calvin began.

"Don't tell nobody you wrote it," Junior said. "*I* know you wrote it—like these folks at the Church of God, all apeshit coons—"

"Tuff and Al had about ten pieces," Calvin continued.

"In those days it was getting' back to Germany, testin' some mo' of that shit," Phineas went on. "Just like they told you Jesus was Jehovah was a leper, you know."

"They played big-band arrangements," Calvin said, "—had that Count Basie sound."

Junior barked with the medical reports' inappropriate laughter that made everyone who heard it ask, Is it mocking? Is it hostile? Why is this man laughing?

"When," I said, "did the record store open?" and Junior, as if in answer, began singing "Silent Night."

"Was the store open before Junior went in the army?" Calvin asked his mother.

"Yeah it was open," Junior said. "I went there in my *old soldier* suit—"

"What year was you in the army, Mister Soldier?" Mama Rose asked.

"I didn't ever get out of the army. Got my dog tags on me right now," Junior said, reaching inside his collar. He was dressed for the stage as always in a dark blue suit and striped foulard. "United States 52372651," he read.

"How old were you when you started playin' with your daddy's group?" I asked, pressing on.

"Oh, 'bout fifteen," Junior said, but he must have been younger. "I was that age when I built that other rockin' chair back there—"

"Little rockin' chair," Calvin laughed.

"You wasn't but a year old when your daddy built that," Mama Rose said.

"I liked to burn up this one," Junior said, talking about the couch, "tryin' to get me some pussy while I was smokin' a goddam cigar—"

"Shut up!" Mama Rose said. "Anybody can act silly."

"What sort of material did the Memphis bands play?" I asked.

"Blues every time," Junior said.

"No they didn't play no blues every time," Mama Rose said. "They played all types of music. Whatever them bands was playin' in New York City and upstate New York, that's what Tuff and Phineas and Al Jackson and them would play."

"They had a lot of good arrangements," Calvin said. "They played a lot of jazz then, now it's considered jazz, but back then it was just good music. They had good arrangers in the bands like Onzie Horne and Slim Waters."

"They were readin' musicians," Mama Rose said. "They weren't just out there slappin' their hips and carryin' on, they'd read that music. When the bands would come in town from other places, they'd meet down at Sunbeam's and they would jam together, you know."

"They used to rehearse right here," Calvin said. "In fact I remember the first time they asked Junior to play piano. Then they asked me to play guitar. I played 'Steel Guitar Rag.' I didn't know but one song."

Junior, on his way to the kitchen for another Bud, reached past me to play the opening bars one-handed. Calvin and I talked about the brothers' early playing experiences, with Junior interjecting to ask me for a cigarette and to recall that he had "played a 4-H Club Convention and didn't get but fifty cents. Fifty cents."

Mama Rose was answering a question about her brother-in-law David Newborn, the music teacher, when Phineas asked, "Did David kill Goliath? I'm curious about what the church people have been talkin' about, you know—"

"Shut up when I'm talkin'!" Mama Rose told him.

It is just this sort of ironic repartee—what Phineas calls off-Broadway humor—that has earned him such poor marks from the VA physicians, perhaps the one group less capable of understanding him than the jazz critics.

"Tell me 'bout when you met W. C. Handy," I said, trying to keep the conversation going.

"Oh, I never met W. C. Handy," Phineas said.

"Yes he did," Mama Rose said.

"I happen to be Christ myself, and Christopher was his maiden name—"

"Shut up, boy," Mama Rose said. "He met Handy, he met all of them, 'cause we carried him with us, and he grew up and he'd follow 'em, his daddy would take him, he met all the musicians—"

"I ain't never grew up, I ain't nothin' but a nigger you know—"

"Dizzy Gillespie, Count Basie, Lionel Hampton, Roy Milton, all of them seen him. So, yeah, he met Handy, don't pay him no 'tention, that's his Bud—"

"Bud didn't do it to me. That pussy poisoned my ass, why I like bootys Bud my goddam self," Phineas said.

"What's the most important aspect of being a writer?" student Calvin asked.

I gave a long speech to say persistence, during which I mentioned that when I started I'd thought that I might fail but that I could at least die trying. Phineas laughed then, not the bark but a good solid laugh.

Calvin and I went on talking, about writing and our lives, while Junior went out for cigarettes. Both of us had come near to death, courted it, many times.

"You was lookin' at it the wrong way," Mama Rose said. "That's the weakness of your faith and all."

That was true, but it had nothing to do with Phineas, who has never had a moment's lack of faith. He has been hurt by the faithlessness of others, but his faith is steadfast. "Had to pay my wife a hundred and fifty dollars a month child support for years," he said when he was back on the couch.

I mentioned an award that Lemoyne music teacher and killer saxophonist Herman Green had given to Mama Rose, and she said, "I'll tell you somebody else who made me feel good—B. B. King." She told about going with her niece to hear King at the Paradise and get King's autograph for her sister.

"I asked the security, 'I want to see Mr. Riley King.'

"'Well, he's resting. Who should I tell him?'

"'Mrs. Phineas Newborn Senior.'

"B. B. hopped up, he said 'Let her in!'

"I go on in, he signs my sister's autograph and all, he says, 'We go way back.' Says, 'You 'member when you was there at my house, and they took the draperies off the wall?'

"I said, 'You know I 'member, child.' He had bought some draperies from L. D. Price department store, and he wasn't payin' on them, and the man came and took the draperies down from the window, and we sittin' there.

"He said—'I wanted to give up.'

"He was on the radio. [sings] 'B. B. King, the Beale Street Blues Boy.' And Martha, his wife, she workin' at the laundry. And she would tell him—listenin' to other folk—he need a job. And B. B. tellin' the old man and me, 'Yeah, Martha's disgusted, man.' Phineas said, 'It's money in it—if you can ever get to it.'

"B. B. told me that night at the Paradise, 'Mama, I wish she'da had the sense like you.'

"I said, 'Don't look like I have much. But I'm rich, boy.' 'Cause, see, I loved the same thing. We'd go, when they was dancin,' and I'd dance and dance and enjoy that music. And sometimes we wouldn't have a cryin' quarter when we got through. But I enjoyed the music. But this woman listened at 'em, 'B. B. need a job.'

"B. B. told me, 'The last time I saw Big Phineas'—you know, the old man passed in California—he said, 'His feet was swollen, and Mama I gave him a hundred dollars. 'Cause I can't forget—I'd have give up.'

"One time I told the old man, 'You Newborns, you just scared of money and money's scared of you.' He said, 'Well, I see you ain't left me.' I said, 'No, well, I told that preacher, For better or for worse, but I got to admit a lot of the time it's been worse'—He said, 'But you still here.'

"He was a good person. We were talkin,' my mother and I, and I said, 'Mama, that Bible says, Cast yo' bread on the water. In many days it will return,' and I said, 'and Rosie Newborn say it'll have butter and jelly on it.'

"The old man cast his bread on the water, and people have been good to his sons, and good to me. I reap the benefit.

"Calvin was a good showman," Mama Rose went on, "but Junior never tried to sing or shake or nothin'. But he can play a piano. And what's amazin' to me, I don't care what condition he's in, I have seen him in a shape that I had a warrant and had him picked up, carried him to the hospital. And after they found out that he was Phineas—now the old doctor didn't know, but some young intern came in, and Junior sittin' there lookin' right ugly, walkin,' drinkin' water every two minutes—"

"Suppose they tell you you Jesus Christ and take you to the Church of God in Christ—" Junior said. The COGIC is a big black denomination headquartered in Memphis.

"And he picked up this chart, this young doctor. He said, 'Are you Phineas Newborn Junior?'

"Junior: 'Yeah.' He touched Dr. Brook—'Oh, this man is a genius, this man is this, blah blah, he can play a piano—'

"Junior raised up, touched him, said, 'Look—don't tell that doctor that, he never will let me out, you know a genius is not but one step from a crazy man,' and sat back down."

"If a rabbit got an asshole, what it cost a bear to get some pussy?" Phineas said, went to his room, climbed in with his clothes on, pulled the covers over his head, and crashed.

I stayed a while longer, reminiscing with Calvin and Mama Rose— about the days when Aretha Franklin, "only so high," would walk past on the way to her father's New Salem Missionary Baptist Church—until Calvin had to get ready to play at a Beale Street nightclub. It was Mama Rose's birthday.

I drove up Crump Boulevard past Elvis Presley and remembered seeing Phineas a dozen years ago standing on that corner, rumpled, unshaven, but radiating power, like Clark Kent after a bad kryptonite binge. I thought of seeing him five years ago at a piano bar on Beale Street, drinking Scotch in silent fury while a white girl played and sang "San Francisco." I remembered a passage in George Lee's *Beale Street* about the cornet player Sam Thomas, the street's original bandleader, and later I looked it up again. "He was the first of a great line of musicians that sprang up on Beale Street," Lee wrote, "and his early activities did much to lay the foundation upon which was built up one of the world's greatest music centers. In view of this contribution, of his great ability, and of the fact that thousands of dollars were made by others on music that he arranged and composed, it seems an unusually cruel blow of fate that he finally died, broken and disheartened, in the Shelby County Insane Asylum."

Reading about Thomas put me in mind of a procession of vanished Memphis music characters—among them the original Bar-Kays, Jimmie Lunceford, Gus Cannon, Will Shade, Bill Harvey, Nathan Beauregard, Fred McDowell, Sleepy John Estes, W. C. Handy, Buster Bailey, Memphis Minnie, Leonard Campbell, Tuff Green, Al Jackson Senior and Junior, Frank Floyd, Howlin' Wolf, Memphis Piano Red, Charlie Freeman, Furry Lewis, Elvis Presley, Bill Justis, Dewey Phillips, Tommy Cogbill, Booker

Little, Sonny Criss. I thought of Lucky Thompson, sleeping on the beach on St. Simons Island and on a park bench in Savannah, and of King Oliver, dying in Savannah, writing to his sister, "The Lord is sure good to me here without an overcoat."

"I cried, Lord have mercy, what evil have I done?" Furry used to sing, "Look like the blood in my body done got too low to run."

I wondered what evil Furry had done, or gentle Lucky, or stoic Joe Oliver. According to Junior's medical reports, he hallucinated, drank to excess, thought he was Christ—but while I saw him depressed, detached, and ironic, I never in fifteen years knew him to hallucinate. He drank too much at times, but only from boredom, and as for his occasional come-die noire insistence that he was Christ, it seemed to me very Christlike. Phineas had no doubt that the Kingdom of God is within him—it flowed from his fingertips. Phineas, like the Fool in *Lear*, sent back shibboleths to believers in a manner that shook their faith—the one about having one child, himself, with his mother was classic textbook stuff: the Id talks back. Betrayed, neglected, Phineas struck back with ironic humor. What a wicked man.

Another year passed, and a friend called to say that Phineas had a couple of tumors. Soon after, he was dead.

Before we went to Europe in 1979, I'd asked Phineas what he considered the most important thing for a young musician to keep in mind.

"Stay young at heart. That's the right idea as far as I'm concerned. Play young at heart. Play the way you feel. A thing of value outlasts a thing that has no value. Attempt to produce things of value as you go along. If it's worthless, it won't last; if it has value, it generally does—an eternity, almost, in minds and hearts."

THE GODFATHER'S BLUES

Toward the end of 1988, a radio reporter from Augusta, Georgia, called with news of James Brown. I'd seen Brown's wife's allegations that he had beaten and shot at her, but I knew nothing more about his predicament. "He's going to prison," the radio man told me.

"Bullshit," I said. "They won't put James Brown in jail."

On December 15, 1988, James Brown was sentenced to six and a half years in a South Carolina prison, but not for beating his wife. By the time I managed to talk with him, he had served two years and was set to get out a few months later. "I don't even want to get into it," he said. "These people railroaded me and put me into this thing, it wasn't never about no drugs. Police made a mistake and couldn't cover it up. Because they shot the truck up. I'm sittin' there talkin' to another policeman. Them people took advantage of me. I done fought this mother for two years. Two years later, I'm not gone fight it. If it'd helped me then, I'da did it. I did two years because I wouldn't plead guilty. I could've pleaded guilty and walked out in ninety days. That's the deal they made me. I wouldn't take it. I made one mistake. You can't beat the police—right or wrong. I made my statement. I'm happy with what I did.

"Two years later, y'all want me to be a hero. I'm gonna say it like it is. I have nothin' to say about the system. I told BET that yesterday. I have nothing to say about blacks and whites. I have nothing to say about nothing. I did two years for nothing, I did it from integrity, nobody come forward. All those organizations and groups, and I love you very much, thank you for wantin' to do it, but I got too much manhood about me to sit up and cry about it now, 'cause somebody want to use it for a steppin' stone."

Asked about his friend, Jacqueline Daughtry, Brown said only, "She's a good girl." But there was more to the story.

To hear James Brown at his best, you have to catch him in court. Hearing only his concerts and records, you miss the really soulful reaches of his voice. In the midst of his captors and tormentors, his voice becomes a wind tunnel of scars, raspier than Miles Davis's most muted solo, each suspiration of breath telling volumes of abuse borne by the black man in stoic silence.

The last time I saw him in court, on March 21, 1989, when he was called from prison to have outstanding charges dealt with, Brown didn't do much testifying. He sat on one side of the large, well-lit, South Carolina courtroom, his facial planes composed into an expression of resigned suffering, while the mother of Woodrow C. Laird, the prisoner ahead of Brown on the docket, told the judge what Woodrow had said when he left home: "'I'm goin' to get me some boots.' Just as wild-lookin' as he could be," she said. "Wild as a goat."

Laird, a graying white man who had previously been an inmate of the South Carolina state hospital and pleaded guilty to trafficking in marijuana, had led a chase through several counties in which a police car was destroyed. James Brown, convicted of a similar offense, though he'd caused no damage to anyone's property, had been sentenced to six and a half years. Brown's face revealed nothing as he heard the judge give Woodrow Laird—who, unlike Brown, had never quelled any riots or won any humanitarian awards and knew no presidents personally—four months in jail and five years' probation.

Just before the court went into session, Brown, dressed in a suit of small gray checks, a gray necktie, and a burgundy shirt, had slipped a left-thumb-and-index-finger OK gesture to his wife, who came in wearing a silver-gray dress and sat near the front of the spectator's gallery. Nearby were William Glenn, Brown's first cousin and oldest associate, and Danny Ray, his announcer for decades.

When the time came, Brown's attorney, Bill Weeks, a tall, clean-cut young white man, an ex-basketball player, told the judge, "Your Honor, Mr. Brown's hat is in his hand."

Brown had no additional time added to his sentence, even though he had tested positive for PCP and marijuana. "Please stay off drugs," said the judge, a man from the same area of South Carolina, near Barnwell, that Brown comes from. "Put your troubles behind you—you can do a lot of good."

At his Augusta sentencing, two months earlier, Brown had talked about wanting to be a model, "not only for children but for the country as a whole." He had worn a red shirt that day, too. What kind of lawyer lets his client go to court in a red shirt, I wondered. Albert H. "Buddy" Dallas, of Thomson, Georgia, Brown's primary lawyer, seemed weak-chinned and shifty-eyed, but I restrained myself from forming an opinion of him based on his looks. He was pleasant, accommodating—we walked around the Augusta courthouse together, he took me to the jail door where Brown's mother and other family members were waiting to speak to him. Then it turned out that Brown would not be allowed to talk with the press. The next day I called Dallas at his office to tell him that I had a lot of respect for his client and that I'd like to write about him, but I'd rather not write anything than do him harm. Later I began to think that was the worst thing I could have said to Buddy Dallas.

That morning in Augusta, Adrienne Brown, James's wife, was sentenced for drug and traffic violations. She received twelve months' probation and a $600 fine. Her lawyer said that "Mrs. Brown apologizes to the community for any embarrassment." Brown himself didn't exactly apologize, but he said he "didn't want Augusta to be embarrassed." Of his legal situation, he said, "I don't feel good about it."

One day several years before, outside Augusta's Richmond County Jail, hearing the cries and noises from within, Brown told journalist Gerri Hirshey, "You're hearing rage and frustration, and those are things I left behind."

The question is, in Augusta, Georgia, how far behind the past can be left. Just off Broad Street, across from the liquor store, stands a stone column, known locally as the Slave Pole. Men and women about to be sold were tied to it, so the story goes, and anyone who knocks it down will die.

———————

Leaving the Augusta court, I met Isaac Ford, a young, muscular black man lately fired from his job as an officer of the Augusta Police Department. Before it was over, he had provided me with lists of Augusta horrors, things only a cop could have seen or known about. The things everybody knew about were bad enough.

Later I met two other ex-APD employees. Between them and Ford I heard accounts of events in the APD central station ranging from pistol-barrel-sucking to homicide. Isaac Ford was a brave man who knew a lot about the Augusta law. One of the few men who might know more, James Brown, was forbidden by prison officials to speak with the press, even though the press—Tokyo phoning at 4:00 AM South Carolina time—kept trying.

———————

In his autobiography, *The Godfather of Soul*, James Brown says of his initial prison sentence (eight-to-sixteen years for breaking into cars when he was fifteen) "It reminded me of the days out in the woods when my daddy was gone . . ." Abandoned by his mother at four, alone in an unpainted shack without plumbing or electricity, Brown learned, before he could read or write or had a thought of singing and dancing in public, to do time.

Until well after the first half of the twentieth century, the forests of South Carolina and Georgia were filled with wealth for white men who could coerce blacks into wading water and dodging rattlesnakes and moccasins to scar and collect the resins bled from great pines, some of which had grown a foot a year for a hundred years. The blacks, paid in cash and scrip to the owners' commissaries, almost never avoided becoming indebted and were obliged to stay and work. Before James Brown was six, his father took him out of the woods, across the Savannah River to Augusta, which is not the same as freedom.

The site of Augusta is perhaps the most delightful and eligible of any in Georgia for a city [William Bartram wrote in 1776]. An extensive level plain on the banks of a fine navigable river . . . Augusta . . . I do not hesitate to pronounce as my opinion, will very soon become the metropolis of Georgia.

Augusta, Georgia's second oldest city and its capital from 1786 through 1795, is today the state's second largest metropolitan area, known best as the home of the Masters golf tournament or the Savannah River bomb plant, the country's single facility producing only tritium and plutonium for nuclear weapons. The site of the first black Baptist church, Augusta has the South's oldest newspaper in continuous circulation, the *Chronicle and Herald*. Woodrow Wilson and Ty Cobb lived there. George Washington and the Marquis de Lafayette found Augusta a pleasant place to visit. On the other hand, the lower portion of the city is bordered by Erskine Caldwell's "Tobacco Road." In 1935, the *Chronicle* investigated, discovered people living in the conditions Caldwell described, and recommended that the problem of such human scum's existence be solved by the judicious employment of isolation and sterilization. This is not unrelated to the problem of James Brown.

The Masters tournament had existed only four years, and the Atomic Energy Commission's Savannah River Project was not yet even a gleam in the eye of a mad scientist when, late in 1938, James Brown came to live with his aunt Handsome "Honey" Washington in her whorehouse at 944 Twiggs Avenue, where he saw, as he wrote later, "everything." Also living there was William Glenn, Washington's grandson, one year older than Brown. Both boys were Juniors; Glenn was called Big Junior, Brown Little Junior. "We were as close as brothers," Brown has recalled, "wore each other's clothes, shined shoes together, and sometimes slept in the same bed."

Augusta, which Brown refers to in his book as "sin city," was then and is now divided like Gaul into three parts: the upper-class whites in the big houses on the hill looked down, literally and figuratively, on the Harrisburg district, home of the poorer whites, and the Negro territory, called the Terry. The reality of black existence at this time, when Georgia vied with Mississippi for the national lynching championship, was that in any attempt to be something besides a subservient menial worker, one could hardly avoid breaking the law, and even that didn't make life easy. In spite of their relatives' diligent pursuit of prostitution, gambling, and bootlegging, Big and Little Junior searched the railroad tracks for coal to heat the house and shined shoes for rent money while dodging the police, who insisted that Augusta bootblacks be licensed. Still it was not until James had started school and been sent home for "insufficient clothes" that he began stealing to buy some decent garments and got into more serious trouble. The police caught him and another boy taking a battery out of a car and kept them in Augusta's Richmond County Jail overnight. When James returned home, William, who was about to join his mother in New York City, told him, "You got to get away from Augusta." But James Brown chose to stay, and so it happened that by the time he had reached sixteen, the minimum age for a driver's licence, he was in prison with a sentence set to last as long as he had then lived.

Brown has described his childhood as replete with torture—undeserved whippings from his father, whom he calls "dangerous"; beatings from his uncle; being electrocuted by three white men with an electric compressor while digging a water-filled ditch. He has said that the warden of the Juvenile Training Institute in Rome, Georgia, raised him. (The warden struck him only once, with an open hand, which by comparison must have seemed like a caress.)

Locked in his father's cabin in the pines, James had played a ten-cent harmonica; as an older boy in Augusta he had played organ and piano, sung gospel songs, performed for his classmates at school and on local amateur shows; at twelve he'd formed a singing group called the Cremona Trio, and in prison he sang with a gospel quartet. Still, his first love was sports; his heroes were Augustans Ty Cobb and Beau Jack; he boxed and pitched baseball left-handed, and when, after serving three years and a day, he was paroled, it was so he could pitch for the baseball team in Toccoa, Georgia, where he had spent his last year. "That's when I learned there's no such thing as law," he said. Being given a harsh sentence that was rescinded when the baseball team was faced with a crucial game embittered Brown, but what had perhaps a more profound effect on him was his exile from Augusta. The Richmond County Solicitor agreed to Brown's parole only on the condition that he stay away from the town where his family lived. "Years later, when I was living in one of the best neighborhoods in Augusta," Brown states in his autobiography, "I met Solicitor Haines's son and told him, 'Your father sent me away and didn't want me to come back, but I want you to know I don't hold it against him.'" Then he adds: "I think the boy was embarrassed."

Much of what Augusta resents about Brown is contained in that quote: he presumed to return, to live in a white neighborhood, to behave as if he, and not the empowered local whites, were "quality." The Old South doesn't like uppity, and Augusta is, or believes itself to be, the Old South.

The journey back to Augusta was not short. A young pianist in Toccoa named Bobby Byrd gave Brown a place to stay (in the Byrd family's small house with Byrd's grandmother, mother, sister, and four other family members) and an address to give the parole board. He worked first at a car dealer's and then, after wrecking a customer's vehicle—"one way or another," Brown's book records prophetically, "my troubles always seemed to involve a car"—at a plastics factory.

Brown carried on boxing (three fights in Toccoa—two wins and a draw) and pitching for the Toccoa baseball team. He remembers throwing a no-hitter the day after his marriage to a good Baptist girl named Velma Warren who'd heard him sing with his group, the Ever Ready Gospel Singers. After a few months, Brown joined Bobby Byrd's nameless secular group, which became the Flames, then James Brown and the Famous Flames, with a record on the King label, "Please, Please, Please," that would sell over a million copies. By then—the record was released in 1956—Brown had two sons; another would be born the next year, during which Brown played Harlem's Apollo Theatre and saw his mother, who'd been absent from his life for twenty years. When she smiled at him, he saw that she had lost her teeth. "I'm going to get your mouth fixed for you," he told her.

In 1958 Brown had another million-seller, "Try Me," and another, "Think," two years later. When his musical success began, he had been allowed to play Augusta as long as he spent less than twenty-four hours in town. In 1964, after integrating the Macon City Auditorium, Brown integrated Augusta's Bell Auditorium, both before the passage of that year's Civil Rights Bill.

In 1965, in the midst of a popular-music revolution, Brown cut his first international hit, "Papa's Got a Brand New Bag." At thirty-two years of age, Brown—known by then as "the hardest-working man in show business"—had become an institution. But he saw himself as just getting started. "I wasn't content to be only a performer and be used by other people; I wanted to be a complete show business person: artist, businessman, entrepreneur." He also had higher societal ambitions of a statesmanlike sort: he joined the NAACP, and visited Africa. People started calling him "Soul Brother Number One," which to Brown meant that "I was the leader of the Afro-American movement for world dignity and integrity through music."

He expanded in business, buying radio stations in Knoxville, Baltimore, and Augusta. In Boston the night after Martin Luther King was shot, Brown saw to it that his concert was televised, and counseled blacks to stay home. "Let's not do anything to dishonor Dr. King," Brown told the audience, at one point adding, "I used to shine shoes in front of a radio station. Now I own radio stations. You know what that is? That's black power."

After that President Johnson invited Brown to dinner at the White House and sent him to entertain US troops in Vietnam. Another epoch-making hit followed, "Say It Loud—I'm Black and I'm Proud," ending a year of characteristically contradictory apotheosis. In January 1969 he sang at President Nixon's inauguration; in February he attended James Brown Day in Augusta, an event promoted by the principal of the grammar school he'd left without graduating. Following this, Brown, who'd lived since the early 1960s in Queens, New York, decided to return to Augusta. Buoyed by a B'nai B'rith Humanitarian Award and a cover story in *Look* headlined "Is This the Most Important Black Man in America?," Brown—though plagued with divorce and paternity suits and IRS problems—went home.

Some of Brown's white neighbors were still protesting about his moving into a house on Augusta's exclusive, expensive Walton Way when, the following year, a sixteen-year-old black boy was killed in the jail, and blacks rioted. Georgia governor Lester Maddox found Brown at a gig in Flint, Michigan, and told him what was happening. Brown returned the next morning; on the air, in the streets, he pleaded for nonviolence. Amid rumors of an invasion by Ku Kluxers and Black Panthers, the Augusta airport and bus terminal were closed for a week.

A few months later, Brown got married to a woman from Baltimore named Deedee, by a probate judge in Barnwell, South Carolina, who had never heard of Brown and told *Jet*, "I married them out there on the front porch. I got a real nice front porch. I marry most of my colored couples out there unless it's raining, then we come inside."

In the 1970s, Brown's life, like many American lives, seemed to suffer from the "malaise" of which President Carter spoke. Brown played Vegas, visited Nigeria, recorded his third *Live at the Apollo* album, but he seemed to be searching for significance; he played a rock festival for crippled children, was honored by then governor Carter for his work with state drug programs, and released an anti-abuse song called "King Heroin." His tax problems continued; the Apollo closed, his oldest son died in a car wreck, and Brown went into semiretirement. His decision to spend more time with Deedee and their two daughters resulted in a second divorce. In 1978 the Apollo reopened; on July 16, Brown had just finished his second show there when he was arrested on a contempt charge arising from a civil suit against one of his radio stations. "I'd come out of prison to do right," he said, "and still wound up in jail." Brown sank into a, *comme on dit*, funk—ended, he says, by a rededication of his life to God.

The 1980 film *Blues Brothers* brought Brown back to public attention. He toured parts of Europe and did club and television appearances.

On Groundhog Day 1982, Brown was on *Solid Gold* and met Adrienne Rodriguez, who would become the third, and possibly the last, Mrs. Brown.

"It wasn't love at first sight," Brown said, "it was recognition at first sight. Our souls had met a long time before."

Brown followed the *Blues Brothers* success with the films *Dr. Detroit* and *Rocky IV*, the latter containing a new James Brown top-ten pop hit. In January 1986, with that song, "Living in America," still on the charts Brown was inducted into the Rock and Roll Hall of Fame. He spoke of it as the culmination of his career. Just over two years later, on the day after Easter, 1988, Brown was wanted by the police for trying to kill his wife.

My Augusta radio news friend had mentioned a woman who represented Brown in organizing a charity concert ordered by an Augusta judge as part of a sentence against Brown for a traffic offense. Though the concert was to benefit an agency for abused children called Helping Hands, the Leukemia Society, and the Fraternal Order of Police, it was boycotted by the police and very negatively portrayed in the local media.

A few days after Brown went to prison, I spent an evening in Atlanta talking with his friend Jacque Daughtry, who wore, as I'd heard, one pink and one blue cowboy boot and blonde hair down to the tag on her Levi's. Her story started over a decade before, with a young girl, bald from chemotherapy and pale, looking younger than her sixteen years, meeting James Brown at the Atlanta airport and telling him, "I want to be a singer and songwriter like you, but the doctors say I'm dying," and James Brown saying, "You don't have to do what they say. You can be anything you want to be if you believe in yourself and what you're doing."

Flash forward ten years: the girl, now a singer and songwriter, was working on a charity recording project with the Atlanta Falcons football team, none of whom knew that she, Jacque Daughtry, was the sick girl members of the Falcons had once visited in cancer wards. At this point the healthy Daughtry had a sick recording project—after two years and $25,000 worth of studio time, the record wasn't finished, the Falcons kept losing, no one could agree on which charity to endow, and the whole thing appeared a bottomless pit. Then Daughtry had a dream about James Brown, got in touch with his attorney, sent him a tape, and received a call from Brown, who said he'd sing the song and set a date for a recording session in Augusta.

So it happened that in 1987, on a stormy spring night "like something out of a horror movie," Jacque Daughtry found herself at a sound studio on Peach Orchard Road waiting for James Brown, who was over six hours late (detained in Atlanta, unbeknownst to Daughtry, by dental surgery). Close to despair, standing outside the studio so the musicians and personnel inside wouldn't see her crying, Daughtry saw two headlights "like Rudolph the Red-nosed Reindeer coming through the fog." When the car stopped, out stepped James Brown. "I told you I'd be here," he said.

Without another word, Brown went into the studio, put on headphones, listened, then asked, "Who *wrote* this song?"

Daughtry, in the control room, closer now to outrage, said, "I did. What's wrong with it?"

"If you wrote it, get out here." With Daughtry beside him at the microphone, Brown said, "Don't ever let anybody tell you there's anything wrong with your song. I just wanted to be sure *you* knew there was nothing wrong with it. You have just learned one of the most valuable lessons of your career."

The morning after the session, Daughtry, back in Atlanta, answered the phone.

"Jacque, it's me, James. What do you think about the record? Is it all right? Should we change anything?"

"He was just making me feel like somebody," Daughtry said, "like he did ten years before at the airport."

Far from being a fait accompli, the record still lacked a charity to benefit and a sponsor to pay for it. Finally the Leukemia Foundation was selected; Coca-Cola, that conspicuously affluent Atlanta phenomenon, donated expenses; and then came the idea to release the record at the halftime show of the Falcon's first 1987 home game—with James Brown performing. Brown agreed, but when Daughtry asked the Falcons to pay traveling costs for Brown and his musicians, they refused. Soon after that, Daughtry, at home and crying again, answered the phone.

"Whassaproblem?" James Brown asked, and offered—though he'd refused to play Nixon's second inauguration when the Republicans wouldn't cough up expense money—to pay the halftime show expenses himself.

On the day of the show, September 20, Brown made it from Florida, where he and his band were appearing, to Fulton County Stadium with seconds to spare, sang with Jacque Daughtry, and received a standing ovation. The Falcons won, something they would do only twice more that season. "It was magic," Daughtry said. "Sunny, seventy-two degrees, a breeze was blowing, there wasn't a cloud in the sky." But in the distance a thunderhead was forming.

It would take over a year for Daughtry to tell me the reason for the storm: that on the day of the Falcons show, after going from the stadium to Scottish Rite Hospital to visit a little girl, she and James Brown became lovers. "You and me were made for each other," she remembered him saying.

———————

The night we met, Jacque Daughtry and I talked for eight hours. Some of what she told me I found hard to understand, but that was because I'd never been to Augusta. Driving into Augusta from where I lived, on the Georgia coast south of Savannah, along the scenic route from Garnett through Estill to Fairfax and so on, one encounters a roadblock with guards dressed like a cross between state troopers and storm troopers. This is the Savannah River Project, the nuclear-trigger factory, where they have been dumping toxic waste in cardboard boxes into shallow landfills for over forty years, a place evacuated by strontium-90 laden turtles. In the daytime one sees giant tubes belching steam from what must be a big, angry core. At night one sees mysterious flashes of light like glimpses into the door of Hell. Whole towns were destroyed to create this spectacle. Each driver is issued a pass, each car's number of occupants is recorded, and for the next seventeen miles one drives above thirty-five miles an hour until reaching the exit roadblock and surrendering the pass. High spirits on the highway anywhere near this place are like bomb jokes in an airport. James Brown found the wrong neighborhood to put his business in the street.

———————

On July 5, 1987, Brown, in Augusta, had backed into a car and received a ticket for not having insurance papers. In September, a week before the Falcons' halftime show, he was charged with speeding and attempting to elude the police. That incident occurred a few days after Adrienne Brown's arrest on Washington Road near the Augusta National Golf Club. Stopped for speeding, she struck and kicked the doors and windows of a police car, incurring a charge of criminal trespass. Early in November James Brown was jailed in Aiken, South Carolina, for running into two parked cars, leaving the scene of an accident, and resisting arrest. People in the Augusta-Aiken area, many of whom already disliked Brown, began to think of him and his wife as public menaces.

Not long after the Falcons' show, James Brown listened to more of Jacque Daughtry's songs, asked if she'd like him to manage her, and was accepted. "He worked me to death, but he gave me balls, he gave me strength," Daughtry said. "And I saw this strong man become an exhausted, beaten child. He changed from a cocky, arrogant man to a pitiful child, begging for his life."

Brown's arrests shocked Daughtry, but she found more disturbing his fears for his own sanity: "I can't think straight," she remembers him telling her. "I'm afraid I'm losing my mind." At other times Daughtry said Brown seemed convinced that "somebody's tryin' to do me in," telling her "be careful what you eat and drink," and insisting that his phones and office were bugged.

Meetings were held with Brown, his manager-attorney Buddy Dallas, and veteran band members like guitarist Ron Lassiter and saxophonist St. Claire Pinckney. In these meetings the idea surfaced that Brown, who had been regarded in the music business as, if anything, too much of a disciplinarian, fining musicians for playing wrong notes, being unshaven, or needing a shoeshine, was being drugged, and he agreed.

On April Fool's Day, 1988, Daughtry, in Augusta at Brown's invitation as she often was around this time, staying in a room at the local Marriott Courtyard suites, went for a ride with Brown in his van. They stopped at a Washington Road car dealership, where some work was being done on a Volkswagen Rabbit Brown was buying for one of his daughters, and at a convenience store for soft drinks and candy. Then, driving down a South Carolina expressway, Brown asked Daughtry for a cigarette, declined one of her Winstons—"too strong"—and asked Daughtry to give him one of his wife's Kools from a package he'd seen behind the front seat. Before the cigarette was finished, Brown began to hear voices in the van. "They're comin' to get me," he told Daughtry. Wheeling away from the expressway into dense pine woods, Brown bounced the van off trees, knocking the back doors off, getting stuck as night fell. "He had a sawed-off shotgun pointed at me," Daughtry said. "That van was an arsenal. It was like Fort Knox. He didn't know who I was. He kept hearing things outside the van and talking about Vietnam, he thought he was in Vietnam. He told me to get in the back. What would you have done? I got in the back. I thought if I could make love to him I could get him calmed down.

"It would have been one thing if I'd said, 'James, take me out, bounce off of trees, let's have a hair-raising, death-defying ride and sex romp in the woods and see if we come out alive. And then spend the next three fucking hours trying to figure out how to get out of the woods.' Because it was past midnight, it was twelve-thirty or one o'clock in the morning. I don't to this day know how he got us there without killing us, but it was pitch black. When you turned your lights on, you couldn't see anything except pine trees, and he'd run over a sort of low cliff and flipped the van over on one side . . . you know, the thrill was kind of gone.

"That was the point when I realized that he was not a violent man. Anybody else would have fucking wrung my neck. Because I'm sitting there crying and screaming in fear and he looks over at me very calmly and he goes, 'Jacque. Shut up. Please. We gotta get out of here.' I'm thinking, Oh my God, we're gonna die, I'm gonna die with this man and they're gonna find out later that we died out in the middle of the woods. I didn't think, number one, that the man could get the van up. But he did. He's a hell of a driver, I must admit. Anybody else would never have gotten out of there. But he did it. He got his act together. He said, 'They did this to me. They did this to me, and they almost killed you.'"

April Fool's Day that year was on Good Friday; Brown did not return to his Beech Island, South Carolina, ranch until early morning, Easter Sunday. Before that day ended Brown had, according to his wife, shot holes in her mink coat and her white Lincoln and beaten her with a metal mop handle. She had the sheriff's department issue warrants for aggravated assault and assault with intent to kill but later declined to testify, as she had once before following an alleged incident in December 1984. She also filed for divorce, then changed her mind, as Brown had done twice. The Saturday after Easter, Mrs. Brown was arrested at Augusta's Bush Field airport and charged with illegally possessing eight grams of phencyclidine, an animal tranquilizer nicknamed PCP, a substance that is tasteless, odorless, and can be absorbed through the skin. The next month she was arrested in Bedford, New Hampshire, for setting fire to the Browns' hotel room and for having seven ounces of PCP. Nine days after that, James Brown was jailed in Aiken, South Carolina, on charges that included possession of seven grams of PCP, possession of a weapon, and assault on an officer after leading police on a high-speed chase. According to the sheriff, the PCP was in a nasal-spray bottle that fell out of Brown's coat. Two days later police arrested Mrs. Brown at the Augusta airport with half a pound of PCP in her bra.

During the summer of 1988, Jacque Daughtry worked on plans for a charity telethon, and James Brown went to Europe on tour. When he returned he seemed clear minded and in good general health, but after being hospitalized for further dental surgery—Jacque Daughtry met Adrienne Brown for the first time in Brown's hospital room—James Brown, "feeling funny from the medicine," went to an Athens, Georgia, drug-treatment clinic, staying only one night. He was still suffering from his operation but also seemed to be depressed. On one occasion he asked Daughtry to come to Augusta and then said he couldn't make it to the office. "I'm washed up," she remembers him saying. "I'm finished." Close associates observed a marked deterioration in Brown's condition when he came off the road; Brown, the master of control, found it impossible to deal with home life in a reasonable, restrained manner—a task at which other great men have failed.

In July, Brown, tried for the offense involving PCP possession, received a sentence of two and a half years' probation and was ordered to give a charity concert within the year. (That same month, a white police officer in the roll-call room at the Augusta Police Department shot a black officer dead at point-blank range and was charged at first with nothing, at last with involuntary manslaughter. A University of Georgia management study of the APD was ordered.)

On Saturday, September 24, James Brown, visiting his suite in an office park on Augusta's Claussen Road, found to his displeasure that some unauthorized person or people had been using his restroom. Indoor plumbing has a heightened significance for those raised without it. That may account in part for what happened next. Carrying an inoperative antique shotgun, Brown walked into a nearby room where an insurance licensing seminar was in progress and asked two women there to come with him to lock the restrooms. Although Brown threatened no one, a sheriff's deputy who happened to be attending the seminar slipped out and called the police. According to news reports, Brown left in his red-and-white pickup truck as Richmond County lieutenant Overstreet arrived, lights flashing. He followed Brown a mile down Interstate 20, where Brown stopped, driving away again when Overstreet got out of his car. Brown went to North Augusta, South Carolina, where he was pursued by police officers and Aiken County sheriff's deputy Donald Danner. Testifying in Brown's defense at the resulting trial, Danner said that Brown obeyed the command, given over his patrol-car loudspeaker, to pull into an abandoned lot at the corner of Martindale and Atomic Roads. According to Danner, he went to the truck, spoke to Brown, and reached in and turned off the engine. At this point the other officers arrived and started breaking out the truck's windows. Brown restarted the vehicle, backed up, then drove forward past the officers as they unloaded at least seventeen, maybe two dozen, hollow-point .45 bullets into the truck, flattening its front tires. Fearing for his own life, Danner said, he left the scene. Fourteen police cars followed Brown at a speed of about thirty miles per hour back to Augusta, where he drove into a ditch in front of a friend's house and was taken into custody.

At 7:25 the next morning, Brown, who had been released on a $4,000 bond, was again arrested in Augusta, driving his Lincoln Continental down Ninth Street. Arresting officer T. J. Taylor said that Brown "just had his hands up in the air while he was driving down the street. He was incoherent and couldn't hold his balance." Blood tests on Brown revealed the presence of PCP.

A few days later, Jacque Daughtry took James and Adrienne Brown to Anchor Hospital in Atlanta. ("Actually," Daughtry said, "I took them several times, because James had to go home for clothes, he was drooling, foaming at the mouth, it was awful. We kept stopping at McDonald's, at the Burger King, the Western Sizzlin'. At one place a little boy asked for an autograph and James pulled a gun on him. It was a nightmare.") Brown told admitting doctors that he might have a brain tumor but insisted he had no drug problem, and the hospital physicians agreed, allowing him to leave after four days. "Take care of my wife," Brown said. He left for a tour of Europe, and Mrs. Brown returned to Beech Island.

The next day, Daughtry took Mrs. Brown to Atlanta's South Fulton Hospital, where she was confined for a month.

On October 26, an Aiken County grand jury indicted James Brown on two counts of assault and battery with intent to kill (because of his driving forward past the police who were shooting at the truck) in connection with the September chase. Jacque Daughtry, asked to put together the charity concert ordered back in July by the Augusta court, devised Wrestle-Rock, a combination sports (if wrestling is a sport) and music event. The *Chronicle* said that a more appropriate punishment for trash like Brown would be to have him clean trash from the highway in a prison road gang, and at first Augusta Civic Center officials refused to allow him into the building.

On October 31, Augusta police came to James Brown's second cousin's house—Melvin Glenn, Willie Glenn's son, lived there with his family—on a domestic dispute call. When police arrived, no dispute was in progress, but at least five officers took Melvin Glenn into a back room, decided to arrest him, and were unable to do so without killing him. Augusta police chief Freddie Lott explained the death by saying that Glenn had been drinking and fighting with his wife and that he struggled with the officers. The night Glenn died, Buddy Dallas called Jacque Daughtry—curiouser and curiouser—and sent her down into the ghetto in a white limousine to see what she could do for Glenn's wife and family. "I saw the room where they killed him," she said. "There was blood all over, on the walls, the mattress, on the bed. They said he had a nosebleed. Must have been a hell of a nosebleed."

The Civic Center officials finally agreed to give Daughtry a date for the charity concert—Sunday afternoon, December 2, when everything would cost triple scale—although there was nothing else scheduled at the center that weekend. "Augusta gave me a thorough education in racial prejudice," Daughtry said.

"During November, I got death threats, somebody called up and offered me $150,000 not to have the concert, the police called me a nig-gerfucker, they'd come in my motel room when I was out, they knew everything I did. I found cocaine in my room and flushed it down the john." On the eve of the concert, the *Chronicle* reported sales of only fifty-six tickets. Daughtry, sensing disaster, took some of the musicians who'd be playing the next afternoon to an Augusta hospital so they could see a few of the children their work might help. There she met a fifteen-year-old black girl named Katina Bryant, who said she wanted to be a singer but couldn't because she was too sick. "Don't you believe it," Daughtry said. Later that evening, at a country church with James Brown, Jacque told him that she was the little girl he'd spoken to at the airport years before.

The concert was scheduled for two o'clock on that cold Sunday afternoon, but at 1:30 the Civic Center officials still had the front door locked. Daughtry opened the back door, letting in Boy's Club members and children's ward residents to whom she'd given tickets. That boosted attendance at the seventy-five-hundred-seat arena to under four hundred. The police stayed away, but a line of them, drawing triple-time pay, stood in front of the stage, scowling. Musicians from the Atlanta Rhythm Section, Hall and Oates, Lynyrd Skynyrd, and other bands, played bravely into the gloom, until Daughtry stopped the show. "I couldn't stand it," she said. "I asked, 'Could you turn up the house lights? There's a little girl here.' Nobody knew what I was talking about, because there were many little girls there. I brought Katina Bryant on stage, asked for two chairs, put my hand-mike in my lap, asked her if she'd sing, and she said yes. I thought if the whole thing was going to hell anyway, why not let a little girl's dream come true? She'd sung for me in the hospital, so I knew she had a beautiful voice. She'd had a blood transfusion less than an hour before, but she said she'd do it.

"'Aren't you afraid?' I asked her. She said, 'Why should I be afraid?' She told the audience, 'This is my friend. We're here for the children.' I'd told her about the boycott, and she asked, 'Why are they boycotting the children?' I said I couldn't answer that, and asked her to sing. She did the Whitney Houston song that goes, 'I believe the children are the future . . .' Then I asked her to sing 'Amazing Grace,' and she got a standing ovation. 'Katina Bryant has cancer,' I told the crowd. 'People like her are what this show's all about.' I looked down at those cops in front of the stage and there wasn't a dry eye among 'em."

James Brown, dancing as if he had no troubles, sang "Papa's Got a Brand New Bag," and the small crowd stood and cheered. Afterward he said, "We got to try . . . for those who can't help themselves. It's the children of the world that we have to help. That's the most important thing . . . it's the children that count."

Ten days later, a chilly Tuesday, James Brown awaited trial in the Aiken County jail. On Thursday he was convicted of aggravated assault and sentenced to six and a half years in prison.

"After he got me back to my car, that Friday before Easter," Daughtry said, "I started back to Atlanta, and I was several miles out of Augusta when here came James like a bat out of hell, blowing his horn, motioning for me to pull over. I did, and he ran up to the car. 'You forgot to tell me you love me,' he said. I had to laugh. My clothes were torn, I was a wreck, but he made me laugh. The next morning he called and said, 'My God, what have I done to you?'

"He called after that to say that he was wearing denims—he couldn't even say *denim*—and tennis shoes, because that was what I liked to wear. When I went back to Augusta, he had the radio set on this easy listening station, because he thought I liked it. I'm sitting there listening to 'Somewhere My Love,' wondering what is this man going to do for me next?

"I know what he did for me—he went to jail. I really believe if he had gotten to court, and he had just turned around and said, 'I know this is going to be very alarming to everybody in this courtroom, but I was set up,' it would have opened up the whole case. It really hurt me, because I realized then that there's no justice." Daughtry was utterly convinced of James's innocence.

"He's under a lot of medication and a lot of craziness," Brown's wife told the court in his defense, and they can hardly have doubted her. With Brown in jail, Mrs. Brown's lawyers and the court arranged for her a sentence of probation. "Justice Was Done," the ever-severe *Chronicle* titled its editorial on James Brown's sentence, but the one about Mrs. Brown's asked the musical question, "A Squishy-soft Deal?"

Jacque Daughtry found herself spending time with her new friend, Katina Bryant.

"At first it was partly a way of staying close to James, because children mean so much to him," Daughtry said. "I told Katina she could live and be a singing star and help other children, because James Brown showed me anything was possible if you really believe. I asked the judge who sentenced James, 'Why would you take all the good this man does out of the world?' I believed too much—one day Katina called and said she had something to tell me, and she wanted me to be calm. 'You're a very emotional person,' she told me. I asked her what it was, and she said, 'I'm going to Heaven. Soon. The doctors told me.' I started saying all over again how they'd told me that, but she stopped me and said, 'Just remember, around my mama, right up to the end, we have to pretend I'm gonna get well.'

"I wrote 'Katina's Song' and she used the last strength in that little body to sing it. The Kroger grocery stores helped put it out with all the proceeds going to children's hospitals, and the song was used in the Miracle Network telethon in 1990."

A year after the Wrestle-Rock show, the mayor of Augusta, Georgia, honoring Daughtry for her charity work, specifically "Katina's Song," gave her the key to the city.

On July 17, 1991, the governor of Georgia issued a proclamation honoring James Brown, who was described as a "personal friend." "It's just a pleasure to celebrate in the comeback of the legendary Godfather of Soul," Governor Zell Miller said, and denied that there was any irony in Brown's being honored by a state that had imprisoned him. "I know the inner man of James Brown. The inner man is a man who's compassionate, a man who's strong, and a man who's not going to stay down. Here he is, bigger and better than ever."

Miller asked Brown how he felt, and James Brown sang one of his best known lines: "I Feel Good."

ELEMENTARY EGGLESTON

Now for a glimpse into Purgatory. Like snowflakes, fingerprints, and marriages, friendships are unique. I never heard of one any stranger than the one shared by Bill Eggleston and me for over half a century. This piece takes us to the Lamplighter before the night when Bill pulled a pistol and became forever persona non grata.

"The murder is always in the past," William Joseph Eggleston said, leaning over the bar, speaking in a conspiratorial tone to my right ear. It was about eleven o'clock, and the Lamplighter, on Madison Avenue in midtown Memphis, glowed like a dim bulb. The three other men sitting on the black leatherette bar stools wore bill caps, two with slogans: "Everybody's goodlookin' after 2AM" and "This is my PARTY cap." Jim Reeves was singing, "Put your sweet lips a little closer to the phone . . ."

Eggleston and I were out of the Lamp's sartorial swing, me in Irish tweeds, him in a four-button glen plaid jacket, knee-high English riding boots, and a full-length Nazi SS overcoat. ("This town is no place to wear a Nazi uniform," one of his Memphis friends said, and another answered, "I should think it would be the safest place in the world.") Eggleston wears the coat not out of Nazi sympathies but a kind of fierce irony that seems remarkable in such a sweet-tempered man. When Hitler's name chanced to come up in one of our conversations, Eggleston quoted Sir Christopher Wren's epitaph: "If you seek his monument, look around."

Eggleston went on: "The first thing you know in the dream is that you'll have the killing hanging over you for the rest of your life."

"I never kill anybody I'd really like to kill."

"Me neither."

"Do you have precognitive dreams?"

"I have a thousand deja vus a day. But when I'm asleep, I'm in a world quite removed from me, with moving lights and perfectly contoured shapes. As a child I had a recurring fever dream with a fine thread of something, like a silver ribbon, running at a speed so high it looks like it's sitting still—then it starts getting a little messed up, then it goes into whole galaxies of confusion, then, at last, because there's no conceivable way out, it's a complete debacle. They're the worst ones."

"Nightmares?"

"Dreams. Sometimes the silver thread straightens itself out—feels pretty good."

In the Lamp's men's room, things bite you on the legs and light in your hair. "Shirley, could we have a couple of beers?" Eggleston had asked the dour, dumpling-shaped bartender as we came in.

"Don't wear my name out tonight," Shirley had said, moving slowly toward the cooler.

I came out of the men's to find Eggleston, having spilled his drink, asking Shirley for a Kleenex "to blow my nose." The front wall of the Lamp had been rearranged a few days earlier by a young man who'd attempted to drive a stolen rental car through it. "I guess he wanted curb service," Shirley said.

More people had come in. "Every day is a good day," a man at the left end of the bar, near the jukebox, was saying. A girl sitting near the middle of the bar said, "I can't help it if you don't like my gay friends" to the man in the PARTY cap. At the far right a white-haired man was finishing a beer. "I'm 'on have one more and go home," he said.

"All right, Vern," Shirley told him.

"Hard to believe how simply we started," Eggleston said as I sat down.

———————

Because of mental slowness, I had known Eggleston a number of years before noticing his resemblance to Sherlock Holmes. Eggleston shares, except that he is more handsome, most of Basil Rathbone's classic incarnation of the master detective: tall thin frame, tight jaw, economical mouth, aquiline nose, piercing dark eyes. The mutual characteristics extend to arcane knowledge—Eggleston, like Holmes, is a connoisseur of tobaccos, music, art, firearms, tailors, and cobblers, but has added some specialties that Holmes might have needed at the end of the twentieth century, such as the ability to take a television set apart and put it back together again, to build flawless loudspeaker systems, to produce videodiscs—one can almost hear Holmes describing Eggleston's *Stranded in Canton*: "A monograph, Watson, on certain peculiarities of phrase in the shoptalk of transvestites on Bourbon Street in New Orleans."

When we met, nearly thirty years ago, Eggleston, who had recently arrived in Memphis from the Delta—Sumner, Mississippi—was already, in his early twenties, reputed to be a "serious" photographer. Since then he has had Guggenheim and National Endowment for the Arts fellowships, lectured at Harvard and MIT, had his work displayed at museums and galleries such as the Victoria and Albert and the Corcoran in Washington, had a one-man show of color photographs at the Museum of Modern Art (only the second ever), and been described numerous times by critics and historians as the father of color photography. A couple of years ago, he was honored by Fuji at a Tokyo ceremony on the occasion of photography's sesquicentennial anniversary. When he accepted his award, Eggleston, who speaks little Japanese, sang, in English, "Heartbreak Hotel." Still singing—"I been so lonely, baby"—he went out to the sidewalk, where a Japanese woman he remembers as "very beautiful" looked into his eyes and said, "Oh, so lonely."

"How did you start?" I asked Eggleston. "What was your first camera?"

"A Brownie Hawkeye, when I was ten or so. Everything I photographed blurred, looked horrible. Then at Vanderbilt, my friend Tom Buchanan, with whom I'd discovered Bach's *Magnificat* the year before at boarding school, marched me to the store and made me buy a camera and developer."

"What kind of camera?"

"A Beauty Canter—Japanese version of a Leica M3."

"Do you still have it?"

"Swapped it for an Argus. I had my grandfather's Contax and Leica IIIA at home. My mother's father, Judge Joseph Albert May, took pictures for a hobby. He also had a camera that used five-by-seven glass plates. Because my father was in the Pacific Fleet, my grandfather brought me up until I was eleven, when he died. Wonderful man. Looked just like W. C. Fields."

Vern said, "Shirley, hon, lemme have just one more."

"Sure thing," Shirley said.

"You know, this is going to be harder with you than with somebody I just met," Eggleston had said as we sat down.

"But more interesting," I'd replied. Now the elegant Egg and I, catching Shirley while she was up, ordered refills and pressed on.

Eggleston is, to understate the case, not like most southerners, or most Americans. He takes a certain quiet pride in such things as never having owned a pair of blue jeans or done a push-up, and though he has an extensive—some would say alarming—collection of firearms, he shoots nothing but skeet and the occasional streetlamp. Well, and once in a while the walls of rooms, when engaged in metaphysical debates with romantic partners.

He and Rosa Dosset, the Mississippi Delta princess who became his wife and the mother of his daughter and two sons, have been confederates, so to speak—not to say united—for thirty years. As teenagers they roamed the countryside in matching baby-blue Cadillac convertibles.

For more than ten years, Eggleston has divided his time mostly between Rosa's hundred-year-old Mediterranean-style house on Walnut Grove Road in East Memphis and the similarly venerable white-columned midtown abode of his mistress, Lucia Burch. Rosa's family, in crass terms, was among the richest in the South, with thousands of farming acres, and Lucia's father is one of the most distinguished American attorneys, whose accomplishments include a key role in freeing Memphis from the political dictatorship of E. H. "Boss" Crump, as well as success in defending such diverse clients as Jimmy Hoffa, the labor union godfather, and Martin Luther King.

Of women, Bill once told me, "I like to stick to the big ones." This elevated view did not prevent him, however, from a liaison of several years' duration with a young Memphis ecdysiast. She used to call me at times when, for example, she had purchased steaks for dinner with Bill and he hadn't shown up. Her little apartment, like Rosa's and Lucia's grander establishments, displayed collections of classic cameras and museum-quality prints, all Eggleston jetsam, and featured entertainment of a high, if not especially intellectual, quality. Eggleston's long association with the ex-Warholite, Viva, has been documented by gossipmongers. She used to call me, too, and talk about how she wanted to have Bill's baby. I finally had to get an unlisted number.

Other women have come and gone during the course of our friendship. Once, in the seventies, he flew from Memphis to Florida and played the piano at a wedding of mine that preceded a marriage of one month's duration. Bill came along on the honeymoon; he and I drove a Cadillac with so many intelligent features that Bill said he wanted it to be the executor of his estate. My bride, an MD from Brooklyn who was attempting to be southern, drove a red Chevrolet pickup in the company of two sickly kittens and a parakeet. That was during the era when Bill and I drank "dry martinis" from ice-cold bottles of Gordon's gin. Actually, any brand would do.

Not always apparent to observers is that no matter what else goes on around Eggleston, the work continues. At the time of the Honeymoon from Hell, he and I had both bought Kodak's then-new instant cameras. When the hostility between my bride and me became so intense that it caused film to fog, we began pointing our cameras straight up, taking pictures of the heavens, the only sublimity available under the circumstances. Out of this came *Wedgwood Blue*, a limited-edition volume of Eggleston sky pictures.

Another aspect of Egglestonian reality that confounds the unwary is his view of politics, described by a liberal writer as "hopeless." Like any genuine aristocrat, Eggleston has no problem dealing with the ends of the social spectrum—in fact the only profound and consistent dislike I have ever heard him express is for the middle class. For a couple of years he and I shared a chauffeur, a young black man whose name was Bob something, but who was called Molasses. We enlivened our afternoons by having Molasses drive us, in Bill's words, "to terrorize my middle-class sister." The poor woman, wife of the most prominent Memphis architect, socially impeccable, would dissolve in horror hearing Bill tell Molasses, whom he had invited into the house, to "go wait in the car—you're not allowed in the house with white people."

Molasses, who was in on the joke, took special pleasure in telling unsuspecting people of all races, "I like bein' Mr. Bill and Mr. Stanley's nigger."

Once, parked in Rosa's Mercedes across the street from Graceland with Bill and his stripper passed out on the back seat, Molasses replied to a curious state patrol officer, "I ain't got no driver's license."

The officer, clearly aware of the intricacies of local society, told Molasses, "You be careful driving home. And when he wakes up"—pointing to Eggleston—"you tell him you don't have a license."

Eggleston has been compared to William Faulkner, a man with whom, as an artist, he has little in common, since Eggleston is a complete technical master, and much of Faulkner's work, for all its brilliance, is technically flawed. Still, there is this similarity: Faulkner, in his hometown of Oxford, Mississippi, was called "Count No-'count" (from "of no account," i.e., worthless), and Eggleston is likewise disrespected by most of Memphis. Even those outsiders who use his talents to advance their own ends seldom scruple to portray him as an out-of-control clown. The entrepreneur who promoted Eggleston's trip to East Africa at the end of the seventies spoke for publication about Eggleston's drinking and the project's lack of success without bothering to mention the hundreds of powerful images, many of them still unseen by the public, that resulted. The effete English editor who was speaking on a telephone which Eggleston happened at the time to be shooting unintentionally revealed, in describing the incident, his lack of awareness that Eggleston was attempting, with obvious difficulty, to get his attention.

"Nineteen fifty-seven or '58 I got a Nikon SP," Eggleston said. "Took it and an S2 to Mexico about '63."

"Why'd you keep taking pictures?"

"A photographer friend of mine at Ole Miss" (where Bill attended for nearly five years without bothering to take a degree) "named Eugene Fisher bought a book of Magnum work with some Cartier-Bresson pictures that were real fucking art, period. You didn't think a camera made the picture. Sure didn't think of somebody taking the picture at a certain shutter speed with a certain film. I was at Ole Miss because the head of the art department was a friend of my parents and their friends in the Delta. His name was Warren Brandt. After we'd done a few things, he said, 'Let's just skip the rest of this curriculum. Why don't you take the first basic course in art—drawing with charcoal and ink.' I was quite facile in that, as I was not in history or any other subject. Except I used to correct my English teacher occasionally for incorrect grammar. This was only about the second year that I was interested at all in photography. So he had me painting and we were doing all right."

"Were you doing representational things?"

"The things I was doing were like puzzles and lessons at the same time—intended half seriously. About that time somebody older, who knew, saw some of those things and told me what I already knew—that I was right about it—told me I was kind of advanced. And that was good, because I still go on today with those drawings and things."

The day before, Eggleston had shown me a five-by-forty-five-foot work in colored chalk on paper he'd recently completed.

"I had," he went on, "starting out, three sort of key figures, the third being the most important. First was Brandt, second was a man named Andrew Morgan, who's in Florida somewhere now. Another excellent teacher, who would support whatever I did on paper or canvas. But at this point I met Tom Young, whose best friend was Franz Kline. Tom was friends with people like Jackson Pollock and that group of artists in New York in the fifties. Tom happened to marry a girl from Mississippi and elected to leave that scene and bring up a family, so he came south to teach. He saw my first photography and the drawings I did then. We kind of worked together. He went to Pope, Mississippi—one of his wife's family owned several stores there, in what is virtually a ghost town now, and Tom converted one of them into a studio. We spent months together down there, just building strange things and doing drawings on nine-by-twelve-foot pieces of paper. All these people instilled in me, before I got to Memphis, say by the time we met, a terrific amount of confidence. Which would never have happened if I had not met them, if I had hung around the old guard of friends who never got out of the county, much less the state or the country, but who have libraries of thousands of books. That would have been the late fifties."

"In the early sixties, you and Rosa came to Memphis."

"She happened to take a few courses at Memphis State, so I happened to go over there and meet a few people. When I got to Memphis I couldn't find anybody—maybe you will recall, in the world of graphic arts there didn't seem to be any kind of father figure or teacher figure at all. Because they were like contemporaries you didn't have a tremendous amount of respect for. You remember the crowd we were in—Jean Morrison, Bill Christenberry—almost without exception, but Christenberry, from other fields than art. Photography wasn't even born yet. If you were lucky enough to have a photographic book, it was probably a compilation from *Life* magazine. A friend of mine bought *The Decisive Moment* and I took it from him because I discovered how good it was."

"I didn't see that book until much later. I saw Robert Frank's work because I read the *Evergreen Review*, which used some of his pictures on the cover."

"If I had known, I would have sought out Frank, but I didn't know about his work then, and Bresson was too far removed geographically. I think maybe it was better anyway because I got a thorough grounding in what I call painting or graphic theory—from people who were good at teaching. Brandt and Morgan were not recognized as important painters, but if they were interested in you, they could pass it on."

"It's interesting to look back at that time. When I was seventeen I read Hemingway's short stories and wrote not a word for two years. They stopped me cold. Some of them were sheer perfection. I couldn't see where you could go from there."

"That's the way I felt about Cartier-Bresson—I couldn't imagine doing anything more than making a perfect fake Cartier-Bresson. Which I could do, finally. But there came a point—must've had something to do with pulling up roots and coming to Memphis—because then I didn't have these mentors, and after a while I had to face the fact that what I had to do was go out into foreign landscapes. What was new back then was shopping centers and I took pictures of them."

"I remember being amazed at what you had done, looking at some of your first color stuff. It was the first color photography I'd ever seen that was equal in technical quality to advertising photographs. There was an enormous gulf between black and white and color photography at that time."

"Still is. What I set out to do was produce some color pictures that were completely satisfying. That had everything. Starting with composition. My first tries were ridiculous. I got some snapshots back, and I hadn't exposed them properly, they were awful, I threw them away. Composition was probably correct, but it was lost in the dismal technical failure.

"I'd assumed that I could do in color what I could do in black and white, and I got a swift, harsh lesson. All bones bared. But it had to be. Then one night I stayed up figuring out what I was gonna do the next day, which was go to the big supermarket down the street, then called Montesi's—why I don't know. It seemed a good place to try things out. I had this new exposure system in mind, of overexposing the film so all the colors would be there. And by God, it all worked. Just overnight. The first frame, I remember, was a guy pushing grocery carts. When they get the carts from the parking lot and push them back to the store so other people can use them. I had a picture of some kind of freckly faced, red-headed guy in the late-afternoon sunlight. Pretty fine picture, actually."

"Those pictures revealed the beauty of light. That it was capturable."

"And in color."

"Exactly. The color of light could be captured. With composition that made the whole thing more effective. It was a great historical moment."

"I got to one point where I thought I'd really go out on a limb, and I resorted to slides because I couldn't get any decent prints from negatives at the time. I could have if I'd known more about it. I took a picture of the Greenwood, Mississippi, Moose Lodge and had a dye-transfer print made, and I couldn't believe the damn thing. So that did it, it was proven, everything was proven, negative or positive would work."

"How'd the MOMA show come about?"

"It came out of a later experiment in using slides. I thought I had to do it. After a while I realized that because what was being produced was not prints but slides, blocks of carousels, I could put in my little suitcase from 1969 to 1971 or something. And John Szarkowski said it was a hermetic thing, and he was right. I'd done the black-and-white shopping center series, and the negative color experiment had lasted about a year—frankly, a lot of inspiration for the slide work came from seeing Joel Meyerowitz's slides in New York. It was around that time I met Garry Winogrand, Diane Arbus, Lee Friedlander. Those few people I sought out—it's almost but not quite like saying they're heroes, it's more like seeking out your fellows, kindred spirits."

"They are heroes, though."

"Of course they are. Friedlander's the greatest photographer."

"Of all?"

"Of course."

"Why?"

"He is a great master—nothing can come close to him in his field—black-and-white photography."

"But he took great color pictures thirty years ago."

"But that's not what he's about."

"Well, I guess his densest stuff is black-and-white."

"His work is the densest stuff we have. We're kind of lucky to get to go see it. It's the best there is right now, black-and-white or color. The best there is."

At this point, well after midnight, with the Lamp whirling about us, Eggleston took away my notebook and began to express his opinions by drawing. He drew a page, then I drew a page, both of us drawing with some heat, as if we were having a mute argument. Matters escalated when

Anne, the Lamp's diminutive, durable, strawberry blonde owner, came in and made available her secret stash of felt-tipped colored pens. The Lamp is a strange kind of bar where, when you need them, colored pens appear. We might still be there drawing had not our friend Dixie arrived. When I met Dixie, years ago, her first words to me were, "Wanna watch me tinkle?" The drawing having subsided, Dixie joined us at the bar.

"Do you remember, Bill," I asked, "one night when we were down by the river on the tenth floor of the Lowenstein Tower and I held you in my arms out over the balcony railing and then I climbed over the railing and I was holding onto the balustrades—"

"Ten floors up, like Buster Keaton on the railing—"

"I would open my hands and drop to the bottom and then I would climb back up and open my hands again and drop back down—just for fun. But since we've survived and glasnost is upon us, I think we have an even broader sphere for our shenanigans—"

"I feel more alive than ever."

"Put in the article, 'Dixie looks wonderful,'" Dixie said, giving her dark ringlets a toss.

"Why do we love the people we love?" I asked. "Why do we love Kandinsky and Dewey Phillips and Howlin' Wolf and Elvis Presley and Mozart and Robert Burns and Bach—because they taught us how to play."

"You can be sure of one thing," Eggleston said. "It doesn't come out worth a damn if you're not having a good time doing it."

SWEET DADDY

People don't realize that Memphis was not only the source of the blues but was also a great wellspring of jazz. Nobody ever looked more like a jazz musician than Fred Ford.

I remember driving around Memphis all night with Fred Ford and a loaded rifle. Our friend Phineas Newborn had been attacked and beaten nearly to death, some "friends" of ours had tried to set us up in a heroin bust, and Fred and I felt uncomfortable. That was a hard period, but we got through it. Now Fred, like Phineas, is on the other shore. I'll be there soon enough.

In the early nineties, Fred, the organist Robert "Honeymoon" Garner, and drummer Bill Tyus came to St. Simons Island, Georgia, for some gigs in the area. After a successful black-tie concert at the Ritz Theater in Brunswick, on the mainland facing St. Simons, we went to a cajun restaurant on the island for a late-night repast. While we waited for our meal, I began to reminisce about the food of my youth.

"What was always good to me was a big old pot of speckled butter-beans and purple hull crowder peas mixed, you know, with some little snap peas in there and a nice big chunk or three of fat meat, streak-o-lean, to season it up—and just about five or ten minutes before it gets done and that cornbread comes out of the oven, just lay a few little old baby pods of okra on top of the beans and peas, let them steam till they get just right—"

"Moon," Fred said.

"Yeah," Moon said.

"You know what Stanley been doin' all these years?"

"What he been doin'?" Moon asked.

"Passin'."

I've never had a greater compliment.

He was always larger than life to me, one of the few people I've known who genuinely possessed that quality, never any doubt about it. First, there was the way he looked: big black man, big white beard, big soulful brown eyes. He looked like somebody important, and he was. Sweet Daddy Goodlow, aka the Chocolate Santa Claus. Fred Ford was a natural heavyweight, I'd estimate about six feet tall, and as they say well covered. Once when the slender Memphis guitarist Calvin Newborn(e) was drinking, he threatened Fred, who simply chuckled—he had one of the world's finest chuckles—and said, "Have you ever heard of a monkey whuppin' a go-rilla?"

Fred's life was filled with ironies, one being that he was best known not for his superb reed playing but for his barking on Big Mama Thornton's "Hound Dog." Fred was present at quite a few historic events, including Johnny Ace's final game of Russian roulette. "It was no mo' than what you might call hoss's play," Fred said. Fred had his own language, or his own twists of language. He spoke not of a butter and egg man but "a big egg and butter man." Once we happened to be driving on Front Street in Memphis just after five o'clock in the afternoon; the street was aswarm with comely secretaries, and our heads swiveled this way and that, checking them out in silence. Finally Fred said, "*Mm. Dusty* pussy."

Before I met him, I saw him around Memphis for years, at American Studio, at the Holiday Inn Rivermont, always on the fringes of the music business—just about the coolest, most romantic-looking person I'd ever seen. No jazz musician who ever lived looked more like a jazz musician than Fred.

In 1979, Fred, Phineas, and I went together to Europe, where they played at the Montreux Jazz Festival and other places. I left Memphis in 1984, and in 1989 Phineas died. Fred almost made it into 2000, but couldn't quite.

He had, as he said, gone on the road with Bill Harvey at fifteen. He had been in B. B. King's first band, Johnny Otis's band, and Gatemouth Brown's. He recorded with those artists and others including Little Richard, Rufus Thomas, Lightnin' Hopkins, Junior Parker, Jerry Lee Lewis, Charlie Rich, Cybill Shepherd, Alex Chilton, and Lee Baker. Reuben Cherry's Home of the Blues label released several singles by Fred, including "Stardust" and "Secret Love," and Duke issued at least one, "Last Chance," a classic rendering of the changes to Errol Garner's "Misty."

The Charlie Rich connection is interesting, and worthy of investigation. Jazz player Rich, the only person in his Arkansas high school who read *Down Beat*, with his Wendy's money hired Fred to come out to his house every Tuesday night and play jazz. They were both misfits in Memphis music because of their extensive knowledge and excellent taste. Rich recorded this stuff, and someday Carpetbagger Records will probably sell it to us.

Fred also played for years at Mallard's, one of the restaurants in Memphis' Peabody Hotel, with "Honeymoon" Garner. They played together at a number of other places also, among them a series of shows in my present location of Brunswick, Georgia. When a well-meaning but decidedly unhip Brunswick fan referred to Fred and Moon as "boys," Fred asked the musical question, "Have you ever seen a boy with lips that could fill a number two foot tub?" Sometime after this, we were talking on the phone, and Fred said, "Y'know, when I was young, and we was hangin' out together and all, I was Sweet Daddy Goodlow. But now, man, I'm Bitter Father Badlow." He changed his mind later, though, and went back to being Sweet Daddy.

After the Peabody gig went away, Fred started playing at the Center for Southern Folklore on Beale Street. I saw him there in October of 1998 for the last time. He met me with an embrace, and I'm grateful I had the chance to see him. It was just before his cancer was discovered.

He would have been seventy years old in 2000—on Valentine's Day, the perfect birthday for such a sweet man.

A book could be written about Memphis saxophonists, from Leonard "Doughbelly" Campbell to Hank Crawford to Sonny Criss to Frank Strozier to Charles Lloyd to George Coleman to Herman Green to Andrew Love to Charlie Chalmers to Joe Arnold to Jim Spake to Ace Cannon to Packy Axton and on and on. I'm not sure about Campbell, who died a long time ago, but all the others I've named knew Fred and respected him. We were lucky to know him, and we shall not look upon his like again.

BOBBY*RUSH!*

Bobby Rush possesses that rare quality, a sense of humor. He's the kind of natural musician who can do anything, from plumbing to producing, and his stage shows are the wildest and funniest on the blues circuit. I met him in Memphis during the eighties but didn't write about him until the end of the nineties. He's proof the blues is still real, still here.

I

What it should be, really, a soft drink, soft but hard, loaded with caffeine. Bobby*Rush!* A brand name.

II

As the millennium approaches, the banquet table of the blues groans under the weight of the various available dishes, but some of the menu is fast food—empty calories, the kind that don't really satisfy hunger. Among a plethora of vacuous guitar virtuosos and vocalists simulating other people's styles there exist few originals.

Having watched the blues closely for more than forty years, I have no misgivings at putting Bobby Rush in the top rank of contemporary performers. I'm not saying he's the best, an absurd consideration in any case; I'm saying there's nobody around who's better, more authentic, or more entertaining.

In the following account, I try to avoid invidious comparisons between Bobby Rush—it's a stage name, and he likes it used in full—and great historical figures like B. B. King and John Lee Hooker, who have not made an exciting recording in years. Bobby Rush, in his mid-sixties, continues to make first-rate R&B records and to have the best stage show since Ike and Tina broke up. If my friend Mick Jagger were hip enough and wanted to revive his career—instead of endlessly dragging his scrawny ass around the planet regurgitating his greatest hits—he would cut Bobby Rush's "Jezebel." But he's not hip enough, nowhere near as hip as this senior citizen from Houma, Louisiana, southwest of New Orleans, within spitting distance of the Gulf of Mexico. Not Houma proper but a farm near there. Bobby Rush is the real thing, as country as a tree full of owls or a passel of possums. But he's also at least as up to date as Kansas City.

After admiring him from a distance for a decade and a half, I finally caught up with him at the eighth annual Springing the Blues Festival at Jacksonville Beach, Florida. He had not played there before—in spite of his long career, he has only recently emerged from the chitlin' circuit to start working municipal blues fests and other venues where the audience is predominately white. Having lived for years on the South Georgia coast, I've observed that Jacksonville audiences set a standard for lifelessness, so I thought this would be a good test of Bobby Rush's much-anticipated (by me) showmanship.

I met Bobby Rush at about one o'clock on a Saturday afternoon in early April. When I arrived at the Ramada Resort, where he was staying, he was in his room talking to a shapely blonde in jeans. It was business, but I noticed what I considered a telling detail: the Gideon Bible was open on the table. A glass wall looked out on the beach and the long sweep of grey Atlantic. Bobby Rush, appearing at least twenty years younger than his age, had on black tassel loafers, black socks, black jeans, and a black jacket trimmed with fake snakeskin. I was wearing a light tan Kuppenheimer sport coat I found at the Goodwill, resoled loafers trimmed with python, and a great many scars. Between us Bobby Rush and I had well over a hundred years of blues experience.

Since this meeting, we have spent many hours in conversation. A small part of our testimony follows.

III

"Until a few years ago," Bobby Rush told me, "nobody knew I exist. Not really. I'm probably the only one livin' who have did as well as I've done, and nobody know nothin' about me."

He has a valid point. For one thing, there's a conspiracy against people with a sense of humor. But we'll get to all that. Earlier, I had asked about his life as a child.

"My daddy was a preacher," he said. "He had a church in Houma and a church in Pine Bluff, Arkansas. He would preach at one church on the first Sunday and the other one on the third. As a kid, I was very involved in church, and going to church, but I never sung in the choir. I remember my first guitar, I made it out of a broom wire. I had a brick on one end and a bottle on the other end, it was like what they used to call a diddley bow. I'd go to church on a Sunday, and the choir would be singing, and I'd be singing, but not in the choir. The ladies would be shouting and everything. We'd get out of church about one o'clock and come home, and my dad would have to go back and preach most of the time in the afternoon. I wouldn't go back to church with him, I'd play the guitar outside my house. And the same people that had been shoutin' in church, man, they'd be boogie-woogiein' with me, havin' a ball. I was about ten or eleven years old."

"Had you seen somebody who inspired you to be a performer?"

"No, I hadn't. I've been a dreamer all of my life. I remember at six or seven, eight years old, workin' in the cotton field. One time my mother hit me in the head with a cup, because I was standin' in the field at eleven o'clock or almost twelve o'clock in the daytime, lookin' up at the sun, and the sun was just cookin' me. And I did not see the sun, or feel the sun. I wasn't aware that I was lookin'. My mind was gone into a deep thought, and I could see myself onstage. Doin' what I do now. I could visualize— when I was ten, me bein' twenty. I'm a big man, I done grew up, and I'm on the stage, like Muddy Waters or Howlin' Wolf or some of the guys I hear on John R.'s radio show. I didn't know what they would look like, but I could imagine in my mind that they were dressed in these long tails. See, there was a Prince Albert can that I could relate to. My daddy was smokin', and he smoked Prince Albert. There was a man's picture on it, that had a long frock coat. All I could relate to, bein' dressed to me, was—I'm this famous cat, and I look like this guy on Prince Albert. As a child, that was fabulous to me. I would set the Prince Albert can on a table and visualize with little capes around me, and I'd be tryin' to look as much like this man on this Prince Albert can as I could, dress-wise, because that represented stardom to me. I didn't know nothin' else to relate to. There was no one that I knew in my family that was famous or had the potential to be famous, that I could relate to. I could only go by when I'd hear a Muddy Waters record and things like that.

"I had an uncle, O. B., and he would go to shows and dances and come back and I would say, 'Uncle O. B. Tell me what you saw last night.' He'd say, 'Why you wanta know?' I'd say, 'Tell me how you walked in the place—what the star looked like—what he had on.' Now what I'm doin', is dreamin'. You follow me? I would make him tell me, finally—when he walked in the door what happened. When the star came to the stage, what happened. What the first song. What way he walked. How many steps he walked from the dressing room. I wanted to know everything he did, so I could visualize like I was there and put myself in his shoes. I would just sit there and dream and grow up, and I could see myself as a grown man. I was ten or eleven years old. I would go in and get some matches, scratch about four or five matches, put 'em out quickly, so the end of 'em would get black, and I would use that matchstem to paint my little mustache on. Then I could visualize. I had my little guitar, and I would stand in front of the mirror in the chifforobe. I was seekin' out, then, what it took to make me stand out."

"When you were a kid, you listened to WLAC?" The broadcasting service of the Life and Casualty insurance company, located in Nashville, featured white announcers like Gene Nobles, "Hoss" Allen, and John "R" (for Richbourg), who played black music and became regional celebrities. On clear nights WLAC reached as far south as Jamaica.

"I listened to WLAC, then I listened to all the country and western stations who were in my neighborhood, just local radio stations, and I listened to Roy Acuff and all that stuff, the Grand Ole Opry. My favorite song was a country-western song that went, 'You get the hook and I'll get the pole, baby—you get the hook and I'll get the pole, we'll go down to the crawdad hole.' I was the kind of child who, when I heard a song, if I liked the song, I put myself in the song. I could see myself with a fishin' pole—which I learnt later, he wasn't talkin' 'bout a fishin' pole—but to me as a child, I know about fishin', I know about the pole, I know about the crawdad hole, and the crawfish and mud and what have you. I related to it in that way. I found out when I got grown, he wasn't talkin' about fishin' at all. But as a child, you relate to what you know about.

"I was like that even when I went to church, I would get carried away—instead of me listenin' to the message, I would grab the message and put myself in the preacher's position, and I'd be goin' through the sermon like I'm preachin'. I'd be sittin' there rockin', and I'd be doin' what he's doin', but I'd be takin' it my direction. I used to go to movies, and I would be this person on the screen. I would be the preacher, I would be anything that struck my attention that I liked. And I would venture from him, and put myself in it, and I would do my own thing. That's kind of like what I did with music. I liked Howlin' Wolf's performances, and I liked Muddy Waters—I liked most people that I had a chance to hear, but I wasn't exposed to too many blues guys at that time. Comin' from my house, my father a preacher, you didn't listen to that much radio playin' the blues, you'd listen to gospel stuff. So I didn't have a chance, until his back was turned, to listen to those kind of things."

"Who were the first people you saw live?"

"Joe Turner—Big Joe Turner. I saw him at a place called Townsend Park in Pine Bluff, Arkansas. I think the next guy I saw was Jimmy Reed. And Little Walter. And then come Howlin' Wolf and Muddy Waters."

When Little Walter was in his band, Muddy Waters, verifying the authenticity of his sidemen, told an interviewer, "Little Walter got a bullet in he leg right now." Howlin' Wolf, who would have been the all-time winner, had there been such a competition, of the King Kong Lookalike Contest, would in those days crawl onstage on all fours, holding in one hand a hammer, in the other a hacksaw. Samuel Beckett and Harold Pinter, their dramaturgical coevals, had nothing on these thespians.

In 1953, at nineteen, the stagestruck Emmit Ellis Jr. moved to Chicago, becoming, not long thereafter, Bobby Rush. "I gave myself the name Bobby Rush out of respect for my dad, because he's a preacher, and I'm a junior."

"How did you select the name Bobby Rush?"

"I just went through names. I started to name myself Truman Roosevelt. 'Cause it sounds good. I would listen to the sounds of names—there was a cousin of mine who's named Bobby, and it had a ring, but Bobby's so common. I needed a name that had the first name and last name as a combination. What I mean about that, if you notice, everybody call me Bobby Rush. I tried to pick a name where you say one, you say the whole name, like one word. There's too many Bobbys, too common, and there's too many Rushes, too common, but Bobbyrush, there ain't but one of 'em. Bobbyrush. It's double entendre too, like, I'm in a hurry, I'm rushing, and quick to catch on, whatever you want to call it, slow but yet fast. But I thought about the name for a year before I adopted it for myself. Came out of the blue sky. Sonny Thompson aksed me one time, 'How you like your name?' I said, 'I love it.' And nobody never—since I adopted the name, I always tell my real name, it's no big secret, but people call me Bobby Rush, not Bobby, and I prefer people to call me Bobby Rush. You don't have to call me Mr. Rush. A lot of people who work for me call me by my last name, and that's okay, but I do want people to call me Bobby Rush."

"It's a great blues name, Bobby Rush."

"I think it is."

"You've made it a great name."

"I think it's got a little swing to it. You know, some presidents don't have—their names don't ring. You know what I'm talkin' about? I think President Eisenhower—that sound like a president. President Truman—man, that sound like you in control. Truman, like a true man. Hellofa name. President Clinton, it sounds weakish. It don't sound like a authority name. I guess names don't have anything to do with a person himself, but I was lookin' for that ring. To me, as a kid, T-Bone Walker was so powerful. *T-Bone Walker*. That sound like a blues player. *Muddy Waters*. Muddy Waters sound like you in the alley, man. *Howlin' Wolf*—come on, you can't beat this name. The *Wolf*. And what he do? *Howl*. Now, you know that's a name, man. I picked my name 'cause I have always been kind of a fast walker, fast talker, and had energy—Rush fits me because it's energyfied. Bobby *Rush*—You take a drink and it rush to your head. Speedy.

"When I started doin' what I was doin' as a young man, I wasn't doin' it to arrive at anything. I was doin' what I loved and what I felt in my heart. I guess it's kind of like makin' money at what I do, 'cause when I first started to doin' what I do, I wasn't doin' it to make money. I never thought about this could get me rich or get me famous. That wasn't in my mind. It was somethin' I wanted to do. It wasn't about the money. Then all of a sudden, a few years later, somebody said, 'Well, Bobby Rush, you can make money doin' this.' I said, 'You mean I could make money doin' what I love to do?' That was the second incentive. The first incentive was, I just wanted to do what I do because I like what I'm doin'. It wasn't about the money, it wasn't about arrivin' at anything. Later that came in play. But at the beginning, for the first, probably ten, fifteen years, I just wanted to be famous 'cause I could do what I wanted to do bein' famous. Not bein' rich and havin' all these things that come with riches. I never thought about it in those terms. What I thought about was that if I could be famous, then I wouldn't have to work as hard as some of the guys work at the steel mill or some other job, and yet I could do what I wanted to do. I'm a pretty good carpenter, and there are some other things I can do very well as a handyman and make a good livin', but that's not what I wanted to do. Music is what I wanted to do."

> I don't claim to be no gardener
> I don't have a green thumb
> But I'll dig around yo' little rose bushes
> Till yo' gardener come
> —"Handy Man"

In 1992 *Handy Man* would become the title of a Bobby Rush CD. But for years the young Bobby Rush pursued public appearances in Chicago clubs to the exclusion of recording or more extensive touring. Even for a professional entertainer he had, to understate the case, remarkable stage presence, or presences.

"Maybe '59, or it could have been '60, myself, Earl Hooker, Tina Turner, Ike Turner, used to work at a place in Rock Island, Illinois. Earl Hooker told me about this guy, so [the club owner] and I got to be good friends. I started to playin', I would go down and play every weekend, so the man said, 'Bobby, why don't you be my house band, come down and work for me Friday, Saturday, and Sunday, or any night you can do it?' So I said okay. Then he says, 'Your show is so good, you're drawin' so many people, we need a MC or a comedian.' I said, 'I got just the man for you.' He said, 'When can you get in touch with him?' I said, 'When I get back from the weekend.'

"This is on a Friday night. A gentleman in Chicago called Prettybop was a good comedian and a MC. Monday I went to him and said, 'I want you to go to Rock Island, Illinois, with me.' He's no longer living, he's dead and gone. He said, 'Okay, I will.' I said, 'What kind of money will you do it for me?' He said, 'Well, I'll go down there for twenty-five or thirty dollars, long as you pay my room.' I called the man up, said, 'Listen'—and I lied to the man, I said—'The man want fifty dollars and you pay for the room.' He said, 'Tell him I'll give him forty-five dollars and pay for a room.' I said, 'Okay, you have a deal.' I went back and told Prettybop, he said, 'Okay, I'll go.' It's like maybe Tuesday now. Come Thursday night, he calls me up and says, 'Bobby, I'm sorry, man, I just can't go, my wife—' I don't know whether she was pregnant or what have you, but anyway, his wife didn't want him to go. Here it is Thursday night and we're leavin' Friday mornin' early. I said, 'Well, think about it in the mornin'.' He said, 'Well, let me call you in the mornin'.' Next mornin' came, his mind still wasn't made up that he wanted to go. First he called me early that mornin', he said, 'I think I can go, call me back at eleven o'clock.' Well, eleven o'clock was a little tight for me. I called him back at eleven o'clock, and sho nuff he can't go.

"I don't know what to do now, 'cause I was gettin' about thirty-five or forty dollars a night, payin' my band like twenty dollars a night, as a bandleader. Now forty-five dollars—I'd pay him thirty dollars, and I'm makin' fifteen dollars a night on this man. 'Cause he don't know what I'm getting. 'Cause I'm the agent, or whatever. I said, I don't know what to do. Then I said, 'I got it!' My wife said, 'What's wrong?' I said, 'I got it!' She said, 'Tell me what you talkin' 'bout.' I said, 'I can't talk about it now, but I got it.' I had been doin' jokes and things on the bandstand, so I went to this Goodwill store and bought some overalls, I must have paid twenty or thirty cents for the overalls—it was less than two dollars for everything. I got me a big hat, a big shirt, and a big suit that you had to put a belt around, double it around you, big suit. I dressed cleanly under this suit. I put this suit on top of it—so I named myself the Tramp. The Tramp, that's all I said, the Tramp.

"I went to the club that night, I said, 'Ladies and gentlemen, we got a MC with us tonight, a comedian, he's emceeing the show, his name is Tramp. I'm goin' back there and we gone start the show.' I go back in the room, I said, 'Ladies and gentlemen, let's give a hand to the Tramp.' I walk out on the flo', I tell some jokes, stay on the stage fifteen, twenty minutes, doin' my routine, like a standup comedian, and just killed the people. I'm a born comedian, you can hear it in my songs. In the early days, I used to stop the band in the middle of the night and do a couple of standup jokes. Anyway, this particular night, I called my own self on, and just killed the people, things just went right. I said, 'Now, ladies and gentlemen, it's star time. You're here to see Bobby Rush, and here's Bobby Rush. Ladies and gentlemen, let's welcome—Bobbeeeeee—*Rush*!' I stepped back behind the curtain, stripped them big pants off, already dressed underneath, I didn't wear a mustache then—I snatched my mustache off, I had it stuck on my face—stuck it down in my pocket, and walked out on the stage. I did that for almost five months before the man found out."

"He didn't know it was you?"

"He did not know—the man was payin' me, I think I was gettin' ninety or ninety-five dollars a night. That was money in them days. 'Cause I'm gettin' my money and the MC's, and he don't know that it's the same person. When he found out five months later, he came to me, he said, 'Man, let me tell you somethin'.' And I guess that's first time a man just sat up and called me the name motherfucker right up in my face. He said, 'You a lyin' motherfucker.' He said, 'But you damn good. Don't let no motherfucker know it but me.' And he kept me there for a year! That's where the change of clothes come in—it was did because

I cheated the man, and it started workin'. I'd come out as the Tramp, then I'd come out as Bobby Rush. And the public did not never know. Really, what I was, a MC."

"Really what you were was a great actor."

"Yeah, that's 'bout what it is. And even when I'm on the bandstand, my moves and what I do on the bandstand, it's acting. I'm a actor."

IV

Dangerous—let me tell y'all what dangerous really is
Like a child that won't mind
Like runnin' a stop sign
Bein' in the wrong place, y'all
At the wrong time
That's dangerous—I tell you
That's dangerous
—"Dangerous"

"Someone asked me what's my biggest downfall. I guess my biggest downfall, that I didn't take advantage of the people who loved me, who really loved me for me. That was Albert King, Muddy Waters, Howlin' Wolf, and Little Walter. Let me tell you what these guys used to do, when I was just a teenager. They used to call me and say, 'Hey, Blood, come go with me.' I don't know what kind of person I was for a grown man to want a teenager to follow him.

"I look back on that and I tell you that my daddy, when I was ten years—now, what I'm 'bout to say now—a pair of mules and a wagon was a very important thing to a farmer. But he would trust me with a pair of mules and a wagon at ten years old. And at ten or eleven years old I would take it to town to gin the cotton and bring it back. Now, that's ten or fifteen miles. That's a lot of trust in a kid. I must have been a trustworthy kid. He'd say, 'You take this to town, and here's what you do. You go and ask Mr. Bill what the cotton sellin' for today. If it's high enough, you sell it, if not, decline to sell it, bring it back, we sell it later.' He let me judge the price. And I know the going price—if I'm gettin' fifteen to eighteen dollars, out of—when you gin the seeds, you sell the seeds, you know? But I know if they anytime below twelve dollars, we'll wait till the next week, they might go up. They go up and down, rise and fall. Next week, when they go up, we sell. You sell when the price is up. But my daddy let me judge.

"I remember one time I come back home, and I sold for twelve ninety. My mother said, 'You could have waited.' My daddy said, 'That was his judgment.' I sold because I heard some white guys talkin' about, 'Next week the cotton goin' down.' I'm a little boy. I'm hearin' these grown mens as they politically talkin', and white mens at that, talkin' about the price goin' down. And I sold. And next week, sure enough, went down to like eight dollars. My dad knew that, if I made the decision to sell, there's somethin' behind it, even if it was wrong, I made a good decision for the time. I didn't think about it until it was too late to ask my dad why he did this, but I must have been a pretty trustworthy kid."

In the 1980s Bobby Rush bought a house in Jackson, Mississippi. It made touring Deep South clubs easier, but it required violating a prohibition Bobby Rush had known all his life.

"At a young age, my mother, you couldn't tell whether she was white or black. One day we went to town, a little place called Carquit, Louisiana, about five or six miles from where we lived near Houma. Carquit also is my publishing company name, and my son's name. We didn't have a car at the time, we had to drive a wagon. I came to town with my mother and father. At that time all the kids couldn't come to town to buy shoes, so what my mother and dad would do, is take a string, and medjur the kids' feet with a string. And you put a piece of tape on it and you write their name on it. And you buy shoes accordin' to the length of the string. So I went to town, and I didn't get out the wagon. My daddy got out the wagon, went in the store. He was in the store for ten minutes, maybe, and these two or three white guys come up. They knew my mother. Her name was Mattie. They said, 'Hey, that Mattie?' My mother looked around. She said, 'Yeah.'

"One of them said, 'She with that nigger.' He said, 'Where that nigger that you with?' So my mother looked around, she said, 'He's in the store.' They said, 'Well, what you doin' with this nigger?' She said, 'I'm a nigger, too.' She got out of the wagon, walked back to the back of the wagon, and they went in the store. I couldn't hear every word she said, but my mother bein' a good-lookin' woman, and a smart woman, I know now that she fronted for my daddy. She went and told these white guys who she was and what she was doin'. She had to prove to them that she was black also."

"How did they know her name?"

"Looking back, this guy who was with them who was the third person, knew her name. And I guess he must have told them, 'Mattie got this black man.'"

"But he didn't know she was black?"

"He did not know. He went inside, but he believed this guy in the store. Apparently the store owner assured them that she was also what they call a nigger. Then she came out of the store, and she talked to these guys, and they talked with a smile. So whatever my mother told these gentlemen was soothing. 'Cause my mother was smart enough to cover up for my daddy. Because they was comin' there to do harm, or start somethin'. But my mother took care of it. And I know my mother covered it up, because when my dad came out the store, he didn't know what went on. And my mother never mentioned to my daddy, 'bout nothin'.

"I saw it happen again a year or so later. Two white guys came to bring ice. At that time they had ice men comin' by your house. We lil kids sittin' out in the yard, and the ice men come, and most of the time they would come to the gate, open the gate, and come in. So I'm sittin' by the gate playin', and someone said, 'Hey—it's some niggers in here.' Referrin' to us, my sisters and brothers, the kids. He said, 'I thought some white folks live here. We been bringin' this ice to niggers all this time?' 'Bout this time he says, 'Hey! You want some goddamn ice?' My mother walked to the door, he said, 'Oh, I'm sorry, ma'am, I thought niggers were livin' here.'

"My mother said, 'We don't use that kind of ice. But we use ice.' That's what she said to 'em. And they went on to serve her not knowin' whether she was black or white. But they thought she was white, because when she walked out, they said, 'We thought niggers lived here.' We was kids playin' in the yard, just lil bitty kids, couple of sisters and brothers of mine, the rest of them was in the field workin'. Anyway, they continued to bring ice, I don't what ever come of that, I don't know what she said to my father about it, I was too young to know what happened, but I remember that situation. I wasn't frightened about it, 'cause I'm a kid. He told her, 'I thought niggers lived here.' When she come to the door, because she looked like this blonde-haired white woman. She had blue eyes and blonde hair."

"But this came about because of—I can't remember whether it was your great-grandmother or grandmother."

"What happened was—my great-grandmother and grandfather was from Jackson, Mississippi. We was told as kids not to never come to Jackson, Mississippi. Now, my mother explained to us why. She said, 'Because my grandmother—which is yo' great-grandmother—and grandfather was a slave. Yo' great-grandmother was a slave, and she was the youngest one could walk out of ten children. There was a couple under her that was too small to walk. But the ones who could walk, they were five, six, seven, on up, up, up, these kids, their half-brother, which was a white guy, who was half-brother to my great-grandmother, taken them from Jackson, Mississippi, and fleed with them to Eudora, Arkansas. He stole his sisters and brothers from his daddy.'"

"And he set them up in living quarters in Eudora?"

"Way my mother tell it, he left them with someone he knew there, who had a house. They had used to work some kind of way with his daddy. They was black, workin' for this white man. He set 'em up, so they could farm, and be free. Because they had the same daddy and different mamas."

"This is before the Civil War—when? 1850s?"

"My grandmother, if she were living today she'd be a hundred and eight. We talkin' about her mother's mother. My mother was born 1906. And my grandmother—had to be 1885, or somethin' like that, probably. Fifteen, twenty years old when she had my mama. You can step it back like that. She had 'em very young, she had all the children, ten of 'em, before she was thirty. So you may be talkin' about a hundred and fifty years back, or a hundred seventy-five years back."

"You were telling me that the man had so many children with his wife, and so many—"

"He had a lot of children. He had at least five or six children by his wife. He had five or six children, maybe seven—it could of been eight by this black woman which was my great-grandmother. But there was two children that they never saw anymore. But they stayed back with they mother, which was his concubine, which was my great-grandmother. My great-granddaddy, I don't know what happened to him. I understood that he worked for this white man, and dared to open his mouth about all these children that were none of his. Although they had a couple of children, but I don't know that side of the family. I just know this white man's children, who had a chance to flee from this man. There was a couple more, maybe three more, that they never saw anymore. He willed land to my great-grandmama and the children. I understand it was a great confusion when he died. I don't know what the confusion was, but I know we was dared to come back this way again. And I think out of my family I'm the first one that migrated back. I was told, definitely, to never come back this way. I was told that from the time I was born. My mother always taught, Don't ever go to Mississippi. Don't ever go to Jackson."

"I guess at first you didn't know what she was talking about."

"As a young boy I didn't know, but after I grew up, I knew what she was talkin' about. I knew before I decided I was gonna move there. It's a touchy thing. I haven't talked about this, not in a single interview. I never talked about this, noplace, I never mentioned this to nobody but my family. I didn't mention it while my dad lived."

"You made a decision to go to Jackson. From your childhood, you heard, 'Don't go there.' Like telling a Jew not to go back to Germany or Poland. But you made the choice to do that."

"I wanted to make a difference. Because when you run away from a situation, that don't solve the problem. Why don't you go back and straighten out the mess? Because, see, if I have the ability to straighten it out, then it's my responsibility. Because if you don't have the responsibility to do it, then it ain't your responsibility to even try. See, woe unto the man who knows better and don't do better. He will be whipped with many stripes. I think I'm a perfect example of one who can cross this bridge, come back. Because I'm gonna tell you something, I have no beef with my people, if I ever find them, or whoever they are. It ain't no beef with them about what it is, it's about the whole situation. Whether they black or white. Somethin' need to be done—the truth need to be told. What happened so long, I think we as a race have shut our mouths too long. We get shocked about the black and white issues, the things we know, that we don't wanta tell no one, so what we learned we don't wanta pass it down, and we get caught up in this kind of situation."

V

I wanna get close to you as I can get
Close to you as water is to wet
I wanna get close to you as cold is to ice
Close to you as two is to twice
I wanna get close to you as fun is to a joke
Close to you as fire is to smoke
Close to you as nine to ten
Close to you as air is to wind
—"I Wanna Get Close to Ya"

"All I'm about is music. I'm not lookin' for no woman, I'm not lookin' for nothin', and people see that in me. I'm not lookin' for anything but friendship. I want friendship among black and white. And I'm one of the few guys left who—I mean, honestly—I ain't got no bones to pick with nobody. I mean, no ax to grind. That's why I did that song, 'But I Ain't Got No Ax to Grind with Nobody.' Did that in 1975, I believe it was. And I really don't. And I don't want nobody have no ax to grind with me. I get so sick of the black and white issue. I know it exists, but I'm much stronger than that, better than that, I'm about more than that. I'm not surprised by whatever people do or say about me, because the devil do his job. I'm not surprised that God delivered me to where I am now, because it's in the Word, he said he would. Just be thankful when he do. I'm so thankful that I'm not trapped in that. Because if I was, I don't think I could live on the bandstand, and be as free on the bandstand. You talkin' about a free man? I'm the only free man playin' the blues. I'll keep from callin' names, but I can tell you now there ain't many guys left playin' the blues who are free. Because most of them is playin' what they have to play in order to get the job. They have to play what his audience want him to play or expect them to play."

"The Rolling Stones. It ain't just blues players. Anybody can get trapped."

"That's right."

"But what you're saying is, Bobby Rush can decide what tunes he's gonna do, what his show's gonna be like, and he's free to be what he wants to be and who he wants to be onstage."

"If you a millionaire and can't be free with what you do or say, you're not free. I'm free because I'm not bound or chained to anything. If I play a Muddy Waters song tonight, I know tomorrow I don't have to play it. But if you play it tonight and got to play it tomorrow night, and the next night you don't play it and you get criticized for not playin' it, that's bound. That's bound."

Unlike any other artist in his field—at least, any that I know of—Bobby Rush has maintained, over more than four decades, control of his destiny in regard to booking, recording, and promotion. He and his wife, Bertha Jean, have been married over thirty-five years. He owns a large part of the Jackson neighborhood where he resides—in a house with eight bathrooms. None of this happened by accident. Bobby Rush's life, like his house—and his art—is unconventional but carefully and deliberately constructed.

"I went to Little Milton one time, a long time ago, and I saw Little Milton had this big bus, and the whole bit, and I know he wasn't makin' no great big money. I said, 'Little Milton—how you do this?' He sit and told me a few things, how he go about doin' what he do, and I kind of took as a pattern Little Milton, what he do. If people wouldn't hire him, he would hire himself. He would deal with bookin' the door, and doin' whatever he have to do to keep his name out there. Milton wasn't too selfish to share that with me, and I thank him today, 'cause he put me onto somethin' that—I will never starve because of what I learnt from his situation. There was nobody doin' what he do at that time—Tyrone Davis and them wasn't doin' that kind of thing he do."

"Little Milton was one of the first of the dreamy, sexy, romance-blues singers. He was one of the first guys to go down on his knees."

"Right. He's a great survivor. Course you know I got many friends in this bidness. I regret a lot of things. I regret not respondin' to Albert King's friendship. He used to come sometime four or five hundred miles to see me. And I probably, lookin' back on it, I must have took it a little for granted. But he just liked me that well. So did Muddy Waters. He just loved Bobby Rush and always tried to do things for me and with me. I didn't take advantage of the thing I could have took because I didn't want anybody to give me anything, I wanted to earn it. It wasn't no disrespect, I just wanted to earn it, I didn't want no handout. I wanted to earn my way. Lookin' back on it now, maybe I should have just been in his presence more. Because some of the time I was off, maybe I could have went to him like he came to me. But when you're young, you have things you wanted to do or things you should have been doing, or think you should have been doing, and I was probably someplace I shouldn't have been. I should have been with Muddy every chance I got.

"This what I'm doin' ain't new. It's been did before. You see, I didn't sell out. I could've sold out twenty-five years ago, and went to doin' 'Hoochie Cootchie Man.' But I didn't sell out. Because Muddy Waters and them didn't sell out. Because when Muddy Waters and them was doin' *what they do*, they didn't go in the studio, 'Let's do a record for crossover, so I can get some white audience.' They weren't thinkin' about this. These cats was in there cuttin' what they knew to cut, and hopin' and prayin' that it sold records. When I get to the bandstand, I don't go up tryin' to make people like me. I do what I do hopin' you like me. When they was cuttin', they wasn't even thinkin' about they were gonna play for no white people. When I cut a record I don't wanta think about no white and black audience. I wanta think about a audience. I want to do what I know to do, and hope they like it. And I guess people can see that in me.

"I know I'm a winner. I'm a winner in this sense—I know I'm blessed, to do what I do. And it's a gift that God give me to do what I do. This—what I do—is a gift. I didn't go to school to learn what I learned. I didn't get what I got from a book. I got what I got because I'm born to do what I do. And I haven't always applied my talent like I'm doin' it now. Because for maybe twenty-five years, I neglected the things that I shouldn't have neglected. First thing is, all these years I played harp, for a long, long time I put the harp down. I can remember back in the mid-fifties and sixties, I did not let nobody know I play harp. Because my surroundings—the people that I associated with—said to me—I want you to listen what I'm sayin'—'Man, that's dumb to do. Why you blowin' harp like them old Muddy Waters.' Y'know wha' I'm talkin' about?"

"Hey, man, I was there. You 'member when Stax wouldn't put a harmonica on a record?"

"That's right."

"Because that was low-rent."

"That was the low end of the totem pole."

"We don't want people to think we playin' that old blues stuff, this is soul music."

"That's what I'm talkin' about. But it's our fault—when I say the one who knows—we keep silent. See, if you talk about it, that's a way of teaching. But if you keep silent about it, then the kids just would not know, because—what happens with the blues, in the neighborhoods, they just ain't playin' the blues. And the few that's playin' it, talkin' about it, degradin' it. Like it's a degraded thing to do. They only sayin' that because they've been *told* by a few uppity black folks and a few white folks, that it ain't nice to do."

"You know what W. C. Handy called that attitude? 'Art in the high-brown sense.'"

"That hits the nail on the head. Let me tell you what I get, and I got this no later than last night. I went up to get me a sandwich last night, and a lady 'bout twenty years old, workin' in the sandwich place, she says, 'Aw, that's Bobby Rush?' She says, 'I just—ooh, come here, Bobby Rush. Listen. Give me your autograph—my grandmother just love you!' Now there was some other young ladies there. She won't say *she* love me, because she 'round her peers, you follow me? So I took her in the back, I said, 'Baby, I'm gonna give you a autograph for your grandmother, but you make sure you give it to your grandmother, 'cause your grandmother love me.' She whispered to me, '*I* love you too. And I listen to the blues. My girlfriends think I'm crazy, 'cause I listen to the blues.' Listen what she said to me.

"And I remember me gettin' caught up in that thing as a black man. I remember when wah-wah first was comin' out. See, what happened with wah-wah—wah-wah was designed because people like Albert King—the white guys could not play what he played, so they made wah-wahs. So after the wah-wahs got popular, here come black guys buyin' wah-wahs. I told 'em, 'Let me tell you somethin'.' I said, 'You guys have got to be out your mind, you got to be drunk in the head. Why in the hell would you wanta buy a wah-wah to try to sound like a white boy who's tryin' to sound black? Why you want to sound like somebody who's trying to sound like you?' That's what the wah-wah was designed for. Because they couldn't quite get the—now, soon as the guitarists came in where they could sound like Albert or B. B., now the wah-wah's not popular. Because now you got the white guys who can sound really like 'em. So they don't need the wah-wah. Clapton comes in, says, 'We don't need the wah-wah, we can do this too.' Now the wah-wah's out of style.

"So, I was tellin' them as black men, 'Why you tryin' to duplicate yourself who's tryin' to duplicate you?'"

"Well, we live and learn. You got back to playing the harp."

"I got back to playin' the harp because I grew up. When you learn better you do better. I grew up to find out what I was giving away was a big plan. If you notice, back when the disco day was in, I had my name in most of my records. I'd call Bobbyrush a hundred times in my records. I did that because there was a plan to take the identity from artists. Especially the black artist. Where that come in at, because the radio station would play ten records without callin' who they are, they call it nonstop music. But the first aim was not to have disc jockeys be popular. So you have a number, 'stead of a name, 'stead of E. Rodney Jones there'll be number so-and-so. And he could hire anybody to put a record on. But when you get a personality—like Wolf—you can't hide a Wolf. So that was a way of cuttin' the value down. And it's like the blues of today—I feel the blues is on a uprise, *accidentally*. But it's also been talked down from this standpoint, because I don't think everybody wants the blues to be popular, because when you make the blues popular, you also sayin', I got to pay mo' money. If you can keep the value off of blues, you can get it for less money. If you take the value off of gold, what is it worth?

"But I know personally that you can make mo' money off of blues than any other thing out here for the money that you put in it. Let me tell you what I'm talkin' about. If you want to make a million dollars, take you two hundred thousand dollars, and make a million dollars. If you do country-western, to make a million dollars you got to spend eight hundred thousand. Because the white guys get paid mo' money. It cost mo' money to put it on. You make mo' money but it take mo' money to put it on, so your take-home is less money. But you can do a blues fest and pay the guys little or nothing, because they keep their value down. And they do it among themselves, 'cause it's a unionalized thing. You don't wanta pay Buddy Guy too much money because if you pay him too much money, here come old Albert Collins, gone want this money. Y'know wha' I'm talkin' about? Here come a few other guys, and first thing you know, we have a bunch of guys who want big money. But I just want the world to know that it ain't but one Bobby Rush. And you can't get this noplace else but here. And I want to always be economic enough that I can do favors for people who desire to see or have me in they place. I think the one that's gonna survive is the one who know how to live in a way where you won't overprice yourself, and price you out of bidness. Because who keep you in bidness—'scuse me. *Uph!* I had to sneeze."

"Bless you."

"Thank you. Who keep you in bidness is the people that you work for. Because three into two don't go. If the people you doin' bidness with can't make money, how can they afford to have you? You got some people who will hire you because they like you, but most the time it's a repeat, they hire you because you make money for them. Nevertheless, a lot of time people will hire you because they like what you doin', you satisfy they customers. But even if you satisfy a person's customers, in the long run you gotta make money for him, because satisfyin' is one thing, and makin' money for him another thing. 'Cause what you like is one thing, what you can make a livin' at is another."

"Well, the way you have it now, it's really interesting, because it's like the old time R&B reviews, but it's stripped down."

Over the years Bobby Rush has created a persona rather similar to, if less intimidating than, the late Georgia novelist Raymond Andrews's *Apalachee Red*, another powerful character of mixed breeding. The persona is one of sexual potency but moral integrity and, above all, humor. These days, blues shows consist largely of competent bands featuring mostly guitarists and singers. The Bobby Rush show harkens back to the days of vaudeville, burlesque, and beyond, to the minstrel and doctor shows of yore. With him in Jacksonville, in addition to his rhythm section, were three dancing girls. From the moment the girls hit the stage, we are deep in psychodrama, as Bobby Rush attempts to keep each of them convinced that she is number one in his affections. The power of Bobby Rush's performance is controlled brinksmanship: it threatens to go beyond the bounds of good taste but is unfailingly redeemed by humor. There is something hilarious about Bobby Rush's singing to a dancer's behind while she is using it to dance with. Never offensively sexual, the Bobby Rush stage show is closer to *The Honeymooners* than to *Boogie Nights*. The audience at Jacksonville Beach, from toddlers to geezers, were rapt; Bobby Rush simply didn't allow anyone's attention to wander, and the usually lethargic beach bunch whistled, stomped, and yelled.

Though his recording career didn't take off until he recorded his first hit, "Chicken Heads," for Galaxy in 1971, Bobby Rush has made over a hundred and sixty records, many of them regional successes, and could do many shows without repeating a single number. His songs reveal the man's boldness and command of his idiom, from primitive harp to sophisticated synthesizer. He is, like Bob Dylan, an inspired synthesist. A partial list of his influences would include Percy Mayfield, Sonny Boy Williamson, Solomon Burke, Don Covay, the Beatles, Willie Dixon, Leiber and Stoller, Otis Redding, Robert Johnson, Phil Harris, the Doors, Sammy Davis Jr., and Arthur Godfrey. The first Bobby Rush record I remember hearing was "Wearin' It Out," recorded in 1983. It was my introduction to the persona of which I've spoken—this "Bobby Rush" character, a sort of cross between Dr. Ruth and Jelly Roll Morton's "Winin' Boy." The theme that persists, from *Wearin' It Out* through *Sue, What's Good for the Goose Is Good for the Gander, Handy Man, One Monkey Don't Stop No Show, Hen Pecked*, and *Lovin' a Big Fat Woman* is unselfish love and devotion, which Bobby Rush somehow manages to make deliciously scandalous and exciting.

"If you notice, my show is really a play. It's like a Broadway play. If you see me four or five times, you'll really know my show is a play. 'Cause it seems like, when I'm on the stage, if you saw me the first time, that I'm just havin' fun, it's got no structure. But it's got so much structure. If I open a show, where I got three or four girls with me, I open the show with something that relates to them being related to me. Like 'She's So Fine.' I'm talkin' 'bout 'she's so fine,' I'm relating to the girl that she's so fine, but I'm also feedin' the men's heads, and they lookin' at the ladies, they also can say it to they ladies, or someone they know and have in they mind, or someone they know in their life. She's so fine. And when they look at the girl, they can say, 'Yeah, she's fine, but my old lady's fine, too.' And he put hisself in the shoe of lookin' at a lady so fine to him. If you think money, you think about Rockefeller. But the overall thought is, I wish I had some of it. You think about yourself, havin' some of this money. When I'm talkin' 'bout 'she's so fine,' I let the guy put his own body, own soul, into what I'm talkin' about, so it will relate to him about his situation, his woman. Or to a lady about her man and her situation."

"Songs like 'Sue' and 'Wearin' It Out' are like plays in themselves."

"Yeah, they're plays in themself. I won't ever do a song like 'Wearin' It Out' until I establish what I'm about—establish a situation where I can look in women's face and men's face, and they'll say, 'He's sixty-something years old. I wonder what he's about.' One lady may say, 'Oh, he's sixty-somethin', he can't do nothin',' but someone say, 'Well, chile, I bet he can, too, he looks like he could do something.' Speakin' of me on a sexual standpoint. You follow me? Then I go through this bit, to play the blues and act like I act on the bandstand, with the energy, then I'll come in, do a 'Wearin' It Out.' It all depends on what I see in the person's eyes. What I read. If I read them sayin', 'Oh . . . come on . . . can't be. . . ,' then I'll wear it out. I'll do that—and get the people to say, 'Damn. He sixty-somethin' years old, maybe he will wear it out.' But I do it in a sense that I talk about me and my lady. So I won't be no threat. They know I'm not lookin' to be hookin' for someone else's

woman. It's about me and my woman. This is what I do, I be wearin'
it out. And I talk about me goin' away from home and comin' back, I
don't even speak to my kids, I get home and I ain't got time to do all
this, I got to wear it out. I put the dog out the house. But most the time,
if a man away from home, he have a dog, he gone be kind to the dog.
That's all right to be kind, but I just put the dog out for a minute. After
that then I'll go get the dog. I let 'em know that not for abusin' the dog,
lettin' 'em know I'm puttin' the dog second in my life."

"How did you write that song?"

"What inspired me to write the song, because, I think—deep down
inside? I think I'm a bad man. I think I'm a great lover. I say, I think.
And my wife told me that. And I believe her."

Laughter from interviewer and interviewee.

"Why would she lie to you?"

"But—but you know, earlier in my life, I wasn't always this quiet little
guy. I been around. And God has given me the strength and energy, and
I don't think a man can act no more than what he feel. I think if I, I
just believe if I felt like—I don't know how a sixty- or seventy-year-old
man would feel—but I think if I felt like people tell me they feel when
they sixty or seventy, I couldn't do what I do. But I'll tell you now, I do
the same thing I did when I was twenty. And just as often. So I can say
that, and feel good about it, and smile about it, 'cause it's no joke to me."

"The great thing is, you're really educating somebody. You're talkin'
about the boy in the band, if his old lady wanta be kissed under the neck,
he says, 'I ain't doin' dat.' It's got the humor, but it's got a little serious
message in there."

"Always. Plus, you should always do whatever it take to make a relationship work. Whatever that is, to make it work, and any man would
know what it is, and a woman would know what it is. You might not
agree to do it, but deep down inside, you know it. And my thing is, that
I do almost anything to please my family situation. I say almost anything.
I'm a man, I stand up to be a man, but there ain't much I won't do to
make it pleasin' to my situation at home. And I kind of says that on
the stage. I was doin' a show the other night in Little Rock, I was tellin'
about 'I'm not henpecked,' and sayin' I come home and give my old lady

all my money, and a guy sittin' there said, 'I ain't doin' that shit, man, I ain't givin' no woman all my damn money.' He was sittin' by his self, I said, 'Yeah, that's why yo' ass by yo' self.' The people just fell out. He sittin' there talkin', don't have nobody with him. But that's pretty much the way it is, if you don't wanta give up, if you don't give, you can't get. Because no one lives in this life not giving. One way or another. And that's the truth. You know. I use the words, 'bein' henpecked, but bein' pecked by the right hen.' 'Cause we all henpecked.

"I use the sayin' that—bein' in Chicago for a long time I know guys who call theirselfs the pimps and those ladies who's workin', what have you, but I notice that when a man fall in love, or a woman fall in love, the biggest pimp give some woman his money. You know wha' I'm talkin' about? He got somebody that he give to. The biggest hustler, hustle for someone."

"Like that Bob Dylan song, 'You Gotta Serve Somebody.'"

"Exactly. That's right. You got to. As the old sayin' say, Everybody got a boss. You may be workin' for yourself, but you got a boss. I may be self-employed, but if the people don't come to see me, who is the boss? They the real bosses. Then I don't have a job. So everybody work for someone.

"So, as a young man, I didn't know—just to kind of sum up all this, I really didn't know where I was goin', didn't know what to look for or expect. I just knew I wanted somethin' better than the situation I was in. Didn't know where to go get it, didn't know who gonna supply it, didn't know how to aks for it, I—I didn't know words to put it in. But I just felt like there was somethin' that was better than me standin' on the stage doin' what I do, doin' what I saw as I grew up. To make money. And I just didn't wanta be the guy who stood up . . . just sung . . . and siddown. Now, co'se durin' that time, there was a little mo' entertainin' than it was players, y'know wha' I'm talkin' about? At that time. I always say that good don't make you. What make you is good and different. 'Cause everybody good. You go to hear the players now, all of 'em good. But every time you get good, and you different—that's when you stands out. Course now, everybody that stands out don't always make it. But the one always make it who sets they foot up to make it, or who's cut out to make it. Because everybody that say yes don't mean yes. Everybody who pick up a harp, or pick up a guitar, or who get on the stage, everybody ain't born to do it. Some of them is man-made, some of them is handmade, but the real people, the real guys, sooner or later they'll make it. It may be years, it may be twenty, thirty, forty, fifty, a hundred, whatever, but the real guys, they'll stick out. They'll go down in history."

"The real people don't give up."

"You know, it can get awful tough. But I don't think I would give up. Well, I'll probably give up. Another forty years and I'll give up."

"You've been faithful, you've been a faithful servant over the years."

"It's been rough, though. You know where my head is, and I don't take credit for those things."

"I know—we can't take credit for our next breath, but I don't know anybody else who would have hung in there, and kept his dream, and took care of sick children, and everything you have done."

"I remember I was playin' in Marks, Mississippi. I had a date booked on a Saturday night, and I told the guy, I said, 'Listen, I don't think I can make it because my mother passed.' He said, 'Aw, Bobby—my people gonna be so disappointed,' and I saw in his eyes—I said, 'I'll make it.' I buried my mother at three o'clock in the afternoon. I did a show at six thirty for him. These kinds of things. When I buried my daddy, I worked the night before—I went to the wake, went to work in Camden, Arkansas, come back from Camden, Arkansas, buried my daddy one o'clock the next day, and went to Little Rock, Arkansas, to work that night. Because I didn't want to let people down. That was five months ago."

"What's the hardest thing about being on the road?"

"The hardest thing about bein' on the road is gettin' ready to go on the road. Once you on it, from one point to another point, that's the hardest thing. Say I'm gettin' ready to leave Chicago, goin' to New Jersey. Just the preparation, gettin' ready to go—once you into it it's not hard, but preparin' for it is hard. It's like goin' to the bandstand. Twenty minutes, maybe ten minutes before I get ready to go on the show is the hardest time. But once I'm on the bandstand, that's easy. An hour away from my show is easy, 'cause I got another hour. I got forty-five more minutes. Those are easy times. But ten minutes to, I say, oh God, I don't have but ten minutes till time to do the show. But after you're on the stage, then it's easy again.

"I think the physically hardest thing is that you stay up day and night. I leave someplace, you go in to do a show tonight in St Louis, Missouri—I got to be in El Dorado, Arkansas, tomorrow, I'm just givin' a name. I got to leave out right after the show. I wake my driver up, ten thirty or eleven o'clock, get him out of the hotel, come pick me up in the bus, go to the next town. Got to be there at four o'clock, sound check, you get there at three, do the sound check at four, sometime you have time to go take a shower, sometime you don't. Sometimes you just have to go in the washroom and you wash up, you do what you have to do, you sponge up, and you go onstage smilin' like you been in a hot tub for two hours. Those are the hard times, but after you on the stage for five minutes, you forget about where you've been or what you should have done."

"You actually moved to Jackson to make touring easier."

"So it wouldn't be so hard on me and take so much of my time. I was in the Deep South, and into the country rural area mostly, especially durin' that time—"

"That's where your gigs were?"

"Right, 'cause if I'm in Memphis, then I have to leave Memphis and go far as New Orleans, which is four hundred miles. But if I'm in Jackson, Mississippi, I can go to Atlanta, Georgia, I can go to part of Arkansas, Oklahoma, then go to New Orleans, then I can go back to Memphis, which is nothin' but two hundred miles. 'Cause when you talk about anything beyond Memphis, you talkin' about St Louis and you'll be talkin' 'bout Chicago or what have you, but you don't work them kind of places that often. In the South I have about two thousand clubs I work in about seven states. You don't have that many clubs in the northern part of the country. When you're talking about Illinois, you're really talkin' 'bout Chicago. There may be a few scattered places like Rock Island, Illinois, or maybe Danville, Illinois, or Rockford, Illinois, but that's not an everyday thing you do a show in those places. But pretty much 90 percent of the workhouses in Illinois, in Chicago. When you talk about Michigan, you talkin' about four or five different towns, but mostly you're talkin' about Detroit. Although you have Flint and Saginaw, Kalamazoo, places like that, and Muskegon, which I work, but then you may be talkin' 'bout eight houses I work in Michigan. In Georgia I got fifty-two. I could show you on my map, I got 'em all across Georgia. I have the location and the whole bit. I haven't worked a lot of these places in the last eight or ten years, because I kind of outgrew it, but I always keep 'em there, because these little country towns always welcome me back. This weekend was a prime example. It was the tax thing for me this weekend [April 15], I said I got to work somethin' close and local, so what I did, I put somethin' together in Dumas, Arkansas; Wrightsville, Arkansas, which is like Little Rock; then this place called Prichard, Alabama, a suburb of Mobile. That's what I do when the chips are down. But other than that, I try to go to bigger places to get my name across and elevate me to some other level, so my price can go up. But nevertheless, I don't forget where I come from. I can always go back to do places like, if I went to Iowa, it wouldn't be Des Moines, it would be Waterloo. Cedar Rapids. The outskirts of towns, that's where I can get over, because pretty much you don't need radio most of the time, you just need posters and some handbills. It's just like a one-eyed man is hell in a blind house. I'm the only entertainer there, so there's no competition.

"I have so many things that I want to do, that I haven't had a chance to do, and I'm not angry about the things I haven't had the chance to do, because the time hasn't been right for a lot of things that I wanted to do. I think the time is now for me to do the things that are necessary for me to do. I think even twenty years ago, I couldn't do the things that are open for me now as a bluesman. I think now is the time for me to do something that's gonna open the way up for a lot of people like myself. Not only just for a black entertainer, but for entertainers, period, that have anything to do with the blues."

———————

Still, there are times when Bobby Rush does reminisce and second-guess:

"What happen, you get comfortable because you makin' a good livin'. You stay in Chicago, and you eat up fifteen or twenty years, nobody know you but Chicagoans, and *they* don't know you from a record standpoint, and I missed out on a lot of things."

"But don't you think you were learning all that time, and you're much more together now than you might have been?"

—"Now, when I look back at it, it was the best thing ever could've happened to me. Best thing ever happened to me, I wasn't discovered until I got my thing together. It was a hurting thing because I wanted to be some other place. But at one time, I wanted to be there but I was so secure, I was afraid to leave what I had going, afraid I would lose my regular thing. But if I had taken a chance at that, I think sometime that I would have been more known, but when you think about it, it maybe woulda hurt me. 'Cause I didn't have my craft together. When I look back at this, I'm so happy that God has fixed this the way he fixed it. I cried about it, but you got to be careful what you pray for, you might get it. I asked God to deliver me and give me what I needed. I didn't know that he was givin' it to me. And when I look back at it, I thank him now because he definitely give me what I needed. At that time I could not see it. But now I know that I'm put here for another purpose other than just a blues singer. I know that now. I'm pavin' the way. And I know that somewhere down the line, whether I'll be livin' to see it or not, that I'm history. Because I know, now, when I look back at Muddy and Howlin' Wolf, who's now gone, I look at B. B., and some of the guys, I know when I look in the mirror, I'm lookin' at that same guy now. It's just that I'm one of the guys who talks about it, like Martin Luther King talked about his death before he died. I'm here to talk about, I know I'm history. It's just a matter of time. If I just live long enough, I'm gonna be living history, if I don't, I'm gonna be history. Because when you put this much time into something, somewhere down along the line, you're history."

FOR REAL: MARVIN SEASE

One afternoon I was driving between Jacksonville, Florida, and Brunswick, Georgia, when I saw a van with the name Marvin Sease painted on its side. I don't remember exactly what else it said, but it conveyed the sense that Marvin Sease was a musician, and he was soulful. Little did I know. Several years later, we met. His story is one of the most moving I've ever heard.

Marvin Sease was born half a century ago in the little town (pop. maybe three thousand) of Blackville, in Barnwell County, South Carolina, between and a bit east of Augusta and Savannah, Georgia. "Blackville," Marvin has said, "is strictly a country town. My father was a sharecropper there. He planted and picked cotton, corn, tomatoes, watermelons, cantaloupes, cucumbers, he grew everything. I remember when I used to pick cotton and chop cotton and stuff, we would make two dollars a day, and that was considered, I guess, fair money at the time. And I can't forget about whippin's in the field, my father would whip me, mostly because he was forced to do it because I would sing in the fields, and the guy that we worked for, and lived on his plantation, he always felt like I was annoying and stopping the other hands from working, that's the way he used to put it, and there were times when he'd say, 'Charley, you better talk to that boy, and tell that boy he's not no singin' star.' I remember those words. And he would make my father whip me, and I remember this one time he said, 'Charley, if you don't whip that boy, I will.' And I stood there and my father whipped me and I cried, with tears in my eyes, and I said, one day I'm gonna show this man that I'm gonna be a star. And you know, for many years that haunted me. Many, many years, that haunted me, those words, that this guy said. That was my most inspiration."

Marvin's family attended the Calvary Baptist Church in Blackville. "We would go every Sunday and when they had revivals, because my parents was hard on us for the church, we had to go to church," Marvin remembers. "If religious music or anything religious came on the radio, we was forced to listen to it. Sometimes on the way home from school I would walk a few blocks after school was out and get the bus at another stop, just to stop by what we called the cafe [a jukejoint] on the outside and listen to them records—they had an old Piccolo [jukebox] and the people that lived that way, they would be in there playin' those records—it was way back in the early days of the blues then, people like Jimmy Reed and Howlin' Wolf."

Contrary to the slogan, families that pray together don't always stay together. Marvin: "My mom and dad separated when I was twelve, and my father went to Charleston. I was the fourteenth of my father's twenty children. My mom and daddy had nine, but my father married seven times, and there was children by all the wives except one." (No wonder Marvin has become famous as a performer of sexy, earthy love songs.) Marvin, again: "My father said who wanted to stay with mom could, they didn't separate in anger, it was a very peaceful separation, and I think everyone stayed with mom for a year, and then the brother just older than me left and went to Charleston. My older sister had gotten married and gone up North. My father kept saying come on to those who wanted to come—and my brother kept telling me how nice it was in Charleston, and he didn't have to work in the fields, and so, it wasn't that I had a problem with my mom at this point, but I was just so sick of Blackville, the way I was livin' in Blackville, in poverty. My family was so poor—my younger brothers and sisters, under me, had an opportunity to go as far as they wanted to go in school. Myself and my older brother and my sister was aksed to stop school, to work, to make ends meet. So, one day my father came to visit, and I said to him I wanted to go back with him to try it. I missed my mom dearly when I did it, but it was a key to me, leaving that particular place.

"After moving to Charleston, I didn't have to work, I was able to go to school—but I had done stayed out of school so much, I was like a big boy, and all these little kids were in the grade. I was embarrassed, and—we were still semi-poor, so I didn't have the proper clothing that the other kids had—the mind on school just wasn't there. It was just like somebody offering you a very bad drudge job. All I could think about was singin'. I slept it, ate it, dreamed it. I went to Liberty Hill Elementary and then to Bonds-Wilson High School. I went to the seventh grade in Bonds-Wilson and was promoted to the eighth grade. I went three months into the eighth grade and I just couldn't see past singin' after that. I just—schoolin' didn't interest me, nothin' didn't interest me at that point but singin'. Smokey Robinson—I tried to sound like him. Smokey Robinson couldn't do no wrong in my eyesight. And Aretha Franklin—tell you the truth, I didn't know whether I wanted to sound a hundred percent like Smokey Robinson or try to phrase my voice like Aretha, I was so amazed by the two of them.

"We continued to go to church in Charleston, and I met a guy by the name of Alfonso Lee, he had this gospel group, and one day he heard me singin' in church, at the Reformed House of God. They had a gospel show there, and befo' the gospel show they were singin', the choir led a song, and the gospel group heard me on that song, singing like Smokey Robinson. After the program Al invited me to a rehearsal. I went and they loved the way I sang, and they aksed me to become a member. I joined the Reformed House of God Church and became a member of the Five Gospel Singers, and that's where I would say it basically started for me, singin' gospel there in Charleston. I was fourteen, fifteen.

"I got a job workin' for the sanitation department, and I did that for several years, workin' on a garbage truck—they've modernized it now, call it a sanitation truck—I did that till I was nineteen. Anything to me was better than workin' in the fields. Matter of fact, Al Lee was the one got me that job. He was working for the sanitation department, and I was in his gospel group, and I didn't have a job. He had a pretty good position, like a foreman, and he spoke to his supervisor about hirin' me.

They lied about my age so I could get the job. I worked there till I was eighteen, then I went and got a job with the longshoremen. The pay was very shockingly good there, but it wasn't stationary, it was more like day work. If I didn't get hired today as a longshoreman, I'd try to beat it back to the sanitation department to see if they needed someone to go out on one of the trucks. I kind of split myself between those two jobs until I reached twenty.

"I was real happy singin' gospel in Charleston, but I didn't see me goin' nowhere. Then my sister convinced me that the South wasn't for me as far as music, that I should come to the North. My sister at that point was livin' in Plainfield, New Jersey. I stayed with my sister for a couple of years. I got involved with a gospel group in Plainfield, I think they were called the Gospel Commanders, and I learnt then that my mom had moved to New York, and went to New York and stayed with my mom in Brooklyn. I started singin' gospel again, with the Gospel Knights and the Mighty Gospel Crowns, tryin' to find a group that was goin' somewhere in my opinion. There was a lot of groups, but they wasn't goin' nowhere. They all had good jobs and they only sang on the weekends, and they would only go out of town when their vacations and stuff came up—but it wasn't what I wanted. I wanted to sing all the time for a livin'. It wasn't that there was a problem with these groups why I quit—it's just they wasn't goin' the way I was goin'.

"So then, I said, I'm gone sing the blues. That happened in Blackville, at age twenty-one. I had called a guy there that had a club called the Wagon Wheel, his name was Harry Peacock. I told him that I was singin' blues and could I come down there and sing, that I was from Blackville. He didn't even remember me, but some of the younger kids did, so they kind of enticed Harry to let me come. I remember aksin' Harry for five hundred dollars to come. He says, 'You must be crazy.' He says, 'Listen, I'll let you come, but I'm not gone guarantee you no money. I'll give you 60 percent of whatever we make.' I got some musicians together who did not want to go on a gamble, so I had to guarantee the musicians fifty dollars per man—it was three of them—so I'm like, where am I gonna get a hundred and fifty dollars to pay these guys if the show don't turn out? I went on faith, and after the show was over, my 60 percent gave me two thousand dollars. I even gave the musicians a tip, I paid them all a hundred dollars, left me seventeen hundred. I said to myself, Wow. If singers can make this kind of money, this is the job for me right here. I know it, there's no sense in nobody tellin' me nothin' about no job, no school, no nothin'. This is it for me right here. Seventeen hundred dollars—oh, God, you couldn't tell me I wasn't rich.

"So, when we went back to New York—I knew that the guys I had didn't have it, and neither did I, as a musician—I was playin' guitar and singin' the lead vocal—and I said, I'm gonna lay this guitar down, and find a real guitar player, and get me some real musicians, and I'm gonna sing, and I'm gonna make it in show business. I went to all these clubs that had shows, and somehow or other I drew these musicians from other groups, I went to them on a prayer and a hope. There are those who said man, you're dreamin', and there are those who came. And that's how it started. I took in my two brothers and we became the Sease Brothers. But my brothers just didn't take it serious, so I gave up the Sease Brothers and formed a band called the Soul Keys, but soon I said to myself, Marvin, you might as well stayed in gospel, 'cause these guys ain't serious. Then a strange thing happened. I had a dream one night that I was singin' to a multitude of people, and every time I looked back, I didn't see a band onstage. I had that dream about three or four nights in a row. A little later I got a call from a guy who told me, 'These musicians gone hold you back. You should do tracks.' I said, 'Tracks? What is that?' He said, 'Tracks is where you go record the music, and you just stand up and sing live.' I said, 'Nah, that ain't for me.' Before I knew it, I'd hired some of the same musicians, took them to a little eight-track studio, and I sang my part while they played, just to guide them. I told the engineer not to record my voice, and I created all the tracks for a lot of songs that I wanted to sing. Then I started makin' phone calls to clubs and aksed them would they accept me doin' tracks. And that's when I started workin' at Tar Hill Two. The guy there was the first one to book me doin' tracks. Then his cousin at Tar Hill One booked me, and a lot of other clubs. I would play regular disco music, like any deejay would play, and I would stand up and sing, do two shows a night.

"Then one day I met Reid Avenue Esther. She saw me at Tar Hill Two and she said, 'How often do you play here?' I said, 'When he calls me.' She said, 'I'd like to make you a proposition. I'd like to get you to play in my bar, the Casablanca, Thursday, Friday, Saturday, and Sunday, and I will give you two hundred and fifty dollars per night.' I said to myself, That's a thousand dollars a week.

"I played there for years, until I recorded my first album, *Ghetto Man*. People from everywhere came. It was like the only partyin' joint. I mean there was tons of them but this club had the action. Most of the time you couldn't even get in the bar 'cause it was so packed. Around '82 I started there. I kept on playin' there, and a lot of people started talkin' to me about what am I doin' in this bar—man, you are too good to be sitting here. But I couldn't see past that thousand at that time, so I didn't wanta talk about goin' nowhere. People started sayin', Marvin, you should cut a record. So I saved up a little money and I cut *Ghetto Man*. I released it on my label, Early records, in 1986, and it did maybe forty thousand sales. That was the record I put in Joe Long's record store in Brooklyn, Birdell's. I was my own distributor and everything, I had records in the trunk of my car, and I was goin' from record shop to record shop.

"This one place I went to was a white record shop, the guy's name was Mike. I went to him first 'cause his shop was in Queens, where I lived. I aksed him if I could leave some records. He said, 'Who are you?' I said, 'Marvin Sease.' He says, 'What label are you on?' I say I'm on Early records. He says, 'Never heard of it.' I said, 'Well, you will.' He said, 'Is it playin' on the air?' I said no. He said, 'Young man, look around you. What do you see?' I said, 'I see records.' He said, 'But you don't see no space, do you?' I said no. He said, 'I don't even have space to put records that *are* selling, that *are* being played on the air—here you want me to find a space to put yours? If you're not on a label, and you're not being played on the radio, man, ain't nobody gonna come in here and aks for yo' record.' I felt so empty, so lost. Because I wasn't prepared to answer him. I said, 'But—' He said, 'There ain't no buts. You gotta get a record deal and you gotta get it on the air—and then come back.'

"I started walkin' out with my head hung low, and then I turned around. I said, 'Mister, let me aks you something. I see you don't have no space. Let me aks you this, do you have a garbage can?' He said, 'What? Yeah, it's right over there.' He thought I wanted to throw something in the garbage. I said, 'What about this? I know you don't have no space. Could I put six records behind the garbage can? I'll just lean 'em up behind the garbage can.' He said, 'But ain't nobody gonna—' I said, 'Sir, I got a plan.' He said, 'What's your plan?' I said, 'I'm gonna put flyers all over Brooklyn. Posters advertising there's a new artist, new record, new label. Somebody's gonna come aks for this name, Marvin Sease.' He said, 'You just don't give up, do you?' I said, 'Please, sir, I'm beggin' you, Mike, please let me just put six behind the garbage can.' He said go ahead.

"As he told me to go ahead, here comes four black ladies in the door. I said, 'Mister, could you do me a favor? Could you put my record on, please? Don't tell 'em who it is singin', just put it on to play.' He sucked his teeth for a minute, he said, 'Which one of the damn tracks?' I said the one called 'Ghetto Man.' Befo' they cleared the do' good, one lady say, 'My, who's that?' Another one says, 'Ooh, I like that.' She says, 'Is that a single or is it on an LP?' Mike says it's on an LP. She says, 'Who's that?' Mike says, 'That's somebody new. His name is Marvin Sease.' She says, 'How much is the album?' Mike looks at me 'cause we ain't negotiated on a price or nothin'. He just called out a price, whatever the regular price for an album was then. She said, 'Give me one.' The other one said, 'Give me one too, I like that.' Another one said, 'What else is on there?' So he started skippin' through and playin' little bits of different tracks, and they said, 'Yeah, this is nice.' He sold all six right there. Four ladies bought six records. Then he told me to go ahead and leave six more. And as I was leavin' those six, some more people came in and two more records of those six were sold.

"I went to Joe Long next, Joe had no problem with it, he took it. I kept goin' to record shops tryin' to get them to do the same thing. When I got back home that night, that same guy, Mike, was on the answering machine—Marvin, bring me a case of your records. I brought him thirty and the next day he needed thirty more. See, I was so determined, and I guess when Mike told me to get the hell out of there—I said to myself, God, do people treat you *bad*, do people treat you *cold*—but the man wasn't really treating me cold, he was talkin' to me from a business point of view. He had the smallest shop I've ever seen—but I was determined to leave some records somewhere in that little shop. I said, I'm not gonna be turned off by record shops who says I can't leave none. I had this thing I used to say: 'You don't have to pay me right now, you can have it on consignment.' So, some shops ripped me off, and some paid me cash up front—but that was part of my trials, I guess—but I was sellin' 'em out of the trunk of my car, left and right.

"One day this guy from another record shop called me and aksed me how I would like to make a deal, get a record deal. I said, man, that's like aksin' me would I like to be president of the United States, yes, *yes*. He says I know a guy I think can get you a deal, his name is Bill Spitalsky. Bill was affiliated with Spring records at the time, and he got me the deal with Polygram. I did the *Marvin Sease* album, then *Breakfast*, *The Real Deal*, *Show Me What You Got*, and the Christmas EP, and that was it for Polygram."

The tracks on *The Best of Marvin Sease* are taken from all Marvin's Polygram releases except the Christmas one; they include "Do It Tonight," which previously appeared as the B-side of the single record whose A-side was "Tell Me Why." They reveal his wit, his excellent voice and musicianship, his writing and arranging talents, and his outrageously sexy sense of humor. Now recording on the Jive label, Marvin is working on, as he says, "not changin' the style, but making the sound a little more of today, with today's beat, without losin' the roots and soul in what I do." He also has a host of nonmusical writing projects: "I'm writing a book—in fact I'm writing books—I'm writing a book about show business the way it is, opposed to the way people think it is or say it is—and *The Life and Times of Marvin Sease*, and a book about the Candy Licker. People aks me a million times a week, Do you actually do that in life, Marvin? That is the question of my life. So I'm gonna write all about that. And I'm writing a play about the Housekeeper, and I think I'm gonna be the housekeeper in this play."

Marvin estimates that he works forty-eight weeks of the year, playing mostly Georgia, Alabama, Mississippi, Louisiana, Texas, Oklahoma, on what used to be called the chitlin' circuit. After thirty years of acquiring professionalism, Marvin says, "I'm dying to do a gospel album. If you was to name me blues singers and gospel singers, I love more gospel groups than I do blues."

It seems fitting that Marvin should return albeit temporarily to his roots in gospel music, because he still has strong emotional ties to his origins and to his place of origin in Blackville. "I never will forget the time," he says, "when I—well, I wasn't a professional, but I knew then that I was on the road to stardom—I went back to Blackville to do a show, and I invited the guy, the plantation owner, who had forced my father to whip me in the field to come, 'cause I really wanted to prove to him that I did—in my opinion, at that point I considered I had made it, so to speak—and I was so disappointed when I heard that he'd passed away. I was gonna send a limo and everything. I wanted him to see— with all the whippin's that my father gave me, that I made it in show business after all."

Marvin credits his wife, Alwillie ("She got one of them *country* names"), and their nine children with being a great source of strength and moral support for him in his career. Through his dedication, persistence, and determination, Marvin radiates a kind of good health and good humor too rarely associated with blues or gospel music. *The Best of Marvin Sease* is a tribute to a man who knows the true value of music.

To paraphrase Mike the record man, Marvin just don't give up. He really is the real deal. Long may he wail.

WHERE THE PEOPLE SMILE

Memphis has always hated and feared its history. Now after a hiatus of thirty years I live once again in Memphis. I have a nice house and the best neighbors. My neighborhood was once all Jewish and is now all black. Domino's will not deliver pizzas to us who are so fond of pizza. If you come to live in Memphis you may be certain nobody will tell you any of the things you're about to read.

> Folks, I've just been down
> Down to Memphis town
> That's where the people smile
> Smile on you all the while
> Hospitality—
> They were good to me
> I couldn't spend a dime
> And had the grandest time
> I went out a-dancing
> With a Tennessee dear
> They've got a fellow there named Handy
> With a band you should hear
> While those white folks swayed
> How those band boys played
> Real harmony—I never will forget the tune
> That Handy called "The Memphis Blues."
> —"The Memphis Blues," music by W. C. Handy, lyrics by George
> A. Norton

When I came to Memphis at the end of the fifties, Beale Street was in decline, not much there except a few pawn shops, Lansky's menswear, Robert Henry's pool room, Art Hutkin's Hardware, Reuben Cherry's Home of the Blues record store, and Schwab's. By the end of the sixties, courtesy of the person who shot Martin Luther King Jr., Beale Street was history. They dug up the street, tore the buildings down, and that killed Robert, Art, and Reuben. Now it's crowded with tourists looking to spend money. This is called, in Memphis, progress.

―――――――

Accidents of geography—high ground, easily available water—create great cities. Also places like Memphis. The best book about Memphis, fifty-nine years after its publication, is Gerald M. Capers's *Biography of a River Town*. Capers's account stops in 1900, but the description still fits:

> Upon the flatboat town had been superimposed a stratum of society which suffered little from a superficial comparison with the upper class elsewhere in the South, but beneath that stratum surged the old life in all its pristine viciousness. In the numerous dives, gambling dens, and bawdy houses the scum of the river still congregated, and life there was cheap and murder commonplace.

For most of the years of its existence, Memphis has lacked a clear identity in the minds of outsiders. It was only with the deaths of Martin Luther King and Elvis Presley that the world came to have any sort of focus on what Memphis even partly signifies. Death is a good place to start. Death, and theft, and rape, and pain, and sorrow. The fancy music you hear in the background is an unusually complex dirge.

While living in Memphis, I embarked on a book tour that took me through the British Isles during a period of greater than ordinary tension in Northern Ireland. When I returned, people asked, "How was Belfast?" Having read the morning accounts of routine local homicides in the *Commercial Appeal*, one concerning the use of a third of a quarter in a jukebox, another following the conflict between a wife's desire for pork chops and her husband's hunger for chicken, I replied, truthfully, "Compared to Memphis, it was very quiet."

———————

The first steamboats appeared on the Mississippi in 1811, the year a series of earthquakes began that made the river flow north, swallowed the town of New Madrid, Missouri, and formed Reelfoot Lake. Great events stalked the land. In 1819, Capers says, "Andrew Jackson and James Winchester, generals of the American army in the War of 1812, and John Overton, retired chief justice of the Supreme Court of Tennessee, climaxed a long career of speculation in land by founding the town of Memphis on the lower Chickasaw bluff where they owned five thousand acres." Whatever destiny may have in store for it, Memphis has always been essentially a real estate deal. The access to the river, the country's main artery, dictated the eventual existence of a city there, but nobody said the story would be a pretty one.

In the light of what was to come, it's interesting that the first and second mayors of Memphis had black wives—or black women. That is, Mayor Number Two, Isaac Rawlings, a rough tavern keeper, lived with a black woman in open concubinage. Wisely, it turned out, for Mayor Number One, Marcus Winchester, the gentlemanly son of James, was ruined locally by his marriage to a cultured Creole belle from New Orleans. Rawlings's common-law arrangement was tolerated by his fellow citizens, who refused to accept the Winchesters' more idealistic status.

For its first twenty years, Memphis was rivaled by another river town, Randolph, on the second Chickasaw Bluff at the mouth of the Hatchie River. The more northerly Randolph was considered healthier after dengue fever in 1827 and yellow fever in 1828 struck Memphis. In fact, had Jackson permitted construction of a proposed Hatchie-Tennessee canal, Randolph might be known as the Home of the Blues. But Memphis, in spite of plagues and famines, would persist, and Randolph would be burned by order of General Sherman.

The population of Memphis grew from six-hundred-odd in 1830 to over twenty thousand in 1860. During the Civil War (known in these parts as the War of the Northern Aggression) local sentiment was strongly pro-Southern, but on June 6, 1862, when the Battle of Memphis occurred, the city's troops were stationed at other places, and it fell in twenty minutes. Memphis suffered little from the war—how can you demoralize a place whose morals are so hard to locate?

The single most significant event in the history of Memphis must be the yellow fever epidemic of 1878. There had been relatively minor outbreaks of the disease before, but 1878 did the town in. It lost its city charter and was a taxing district until 1893. The fever was far more deadly to white than to black victims, most of whom recovered. By the end of the 1878 epidemic, the city's population had been reduced from over fifty thousand to under fifteen thousand, and blacks in Memphis outnumbered whites by a ratio of over six to one.

This meant that an existing city in a favorable geographical situation lost its traditions, making a clean slate on which creative individuals were able to write the future. Thomas Edison, oppressed by swarms of cockroaches in his Court Square boarding house, figured out how to send electricity along a wire to kill them. Clarence Saunders developed the Piggly Wiggly, the first supermarket; Fortune's Jungle Garden, a near-downtown restaurant too small to hold the crowds after the opera, began serving people in their carriages, becoming a drive-in before the term existed. Later Kemmons Wilson would come in from Arkansas and change the face of the planet with the Holiday Inns, the first of which was on Summer Avenue in Memphis. They tore it down a few years back, those sentimental Memphians.

But when people hear the name Memphis, the first thing they think of is music. This started with the blues, a musical form domesticated by W. C. Handy, a trained musician from Florence, Alabama, who lived in Memphis from 1905 to 1918. Handy's first blues was written for the campaign of Edward Hull Crump, a reform candidate for mayor in 1909. Hired by Crump's supporters to play for political rallies, Handy dashed off an ironic tune—"Mr Crump don't 'low it, ain't goin' have it here"— with the insouciant response, "we don't care what Mr Crump don't 'low, we gonna bar'l-house anyhow."

Over time, Boss Crump, who grew in piety through the years and died in 1954, was responsible for the closing of many colorful places on Beale. It wouldn't have been destroyed, though, had Martin Luther King not been assassinated near there. After the turmoil surrounding that event—tanks and battle-ready troops in residential streets—the city, in a paroxysm of shame, leveled the entire neighborhood where King's followers had marched. Schwab's department store at 163 Beale alone survived, simply because the Schwab family owned the land and couldn't be put off. The store is still there, and is easily the most authentic spot on Beale. They sell everything from pork and beans to overalls. If you can't find it at Schwab's, the saying goes, you're better off without it.

Beale Street reaches from the Mississippi River eastward for about a mile, passing near its terminus a few yards from Sam Phillips's Sun Records, 706 Union Avenue at Marshall, where Howling Wolf, Carl Perkins, Jackie Brenston, Charlie Rich, Roscoe Gordon, Jerry Lee Lewis, Johnny Cash, Elvis Presley, and other eccentrics recorded. The street—no one knows who Beale was—acquired its association with negritude after General Grant moved into a Beale mansion during the Civil War, when blacks in the area, many of them recently freed slaves, gathered around Union headquarters for protection. They had good reason to fear the local whites, particularly the Irish police, who perpetrated "the Memphis Massacre," an attack on their community in May of 1866 that, while costing the lives of two whites, killed forty-four blacks and burned down ninety-one black houses, four black churches, and twelve black schools. Memphis has a long and colorful tradition of racially motivated disorder.

Such is the fecundity, however, of that alluvial soil—the Mississippi Delta, in the famous dictum of David Cohn, starts in the lobby of the Peabody Hotel—that neither police nor Crump nor anyone else could stop the creativity in Memphis. Sam Phillips had the first recording studio, but others soon followed—Cordell Jackson and Moon, Jim Stewart and Estelle Axton's Stax, Donald Crews and Chips Moman's American, Roland Janes's Sonic, Doc Russell and Quinton Claunch's Goldwax, John Fry's Ardent, and many since then. What makes them all different from most of those in New York, Chicago, Nashville, and Los Angeles is that the ones in Memphis are independent, oh boy.

The story of all this music is something you should think about endowing me to write. But I will tell you this. There's a bookstore in Memphis called Burke's. I didn't know Mr Burke the founder—he was dead—but I knew his son, when the store was still in its original location on Front Street. Bill never, so far as I was able to determine, read a book in his life, and cared mostly for baseball. One day when the store had moved onto Poplar I was in there and met Professor Capers. I have turned into him now, a grey-haired old fart in khakis. At some point he told the story of being a Scoutmaster and having among his charges a boy named Shelby Foote. They had scout camp in Crittenden, Arkansas, and sang around the campfire. "I knew Shelby was a genius," Capers said, "when I heard him create a new verse for 'Casey Jones': 'Casey Jones was a dude you know, he drove his train through the whorehouse door.'"

Years afterward, I told this story to Foote's son Huger. Some months later, he said, "I told my father what you said about 'Casey Jones.'"

"What did he say?" I asked.

Huger quoted: "'He came through the window with his dick in his hand, saying, "Look out, girls, I'm a railroad man."'"

That's the Memphis Sound.

The Memphis Sound—it's a real thing, not just propaganda. Evidence of its reality is the long, long time it took the politicians to claim it. Blues musicians like Furry Lewis, Will Shade, and Gus Cannon; swing and jazz musicians like Jimmy Lunceford, Buster Bailey, and Phineas Newborn have all, like the Sun artists I've mentioned, been ignored in Memphis. The degree of indifference to art of any sort in Memphis would be hard to exaggerate. Just as, to his fellow Memphians, Elvis was a reclusive weirdo, so Al Green is that black fellow with his own church. As music becomes more of a business, this indifference is changing to greed. A Hard Rock franchise opened on Beale Street last November, the month Green's Lounge, Memphis's best blues club, burned down.

If you go to Memphis, be careful. The murder rate is not what it was around the turn of the century, when Memphis was the murder capital of the country, but it's still high, and so is the incidence of rape. Recent years have seen some appalling—and appallingly pointless—murders. I'm sparing you a lot of painful details. A few years back, Huger Foote, driving one night in his father's tan Mercedes, stopped for a red light at the corner of Madison and Evergreen in midtown Memphis. Something about Huger inspired a young black man, stopped alongside and carrying a pistol, to shoot him. He drove himself to the Methodist Hospital and went to the emergency room. In Memphis, it helps to be able to take it.

Bad things—of a racial character—have happened in Memphis, over and over again. Resentments exist in Memphis as in Belfast, as in Jerusalem. It doesn't make life impossible in these places, but it doesn't make it easier. Still, you can come to Memphis, stay at the Peabody, go to Al Green's church or even, if you insist, to Graceland, eat barbecue at the Cozy Corner, hear jazz player Calvin Newborn on Beale Street, and count your blessings. Just keep in mind where you are. Blood has flowed in these streets, and the aroma of magnolias is tinged with the bitter smoke of violence.

HANDS UP!

I would never have written for John Whitehead's house organ, *Gadfly*, had not my friend David Dalton led me astray. Plus I needed the money. Another thing that caused me to write "Hands Up!" was that I had made the acquaintance of Bill Parker, who writes and performs very good songs. When I can I like to go back as far as possible in time and then explore later events with the benefit of context. So that's what happens here.

> There were tears on the mail,
> that she wrote me in jail,
> but I'm free from the chain gang now.
> —"I'm Free from the Chain Gang Now" (Lou Hersher-Saul Klein), one of Jimmie Rodgers's last recordings, May 17, 1933. He died of TB on May 26.

Jimmie Rodgers, born in Pine Springs, Mississippi, on September 8, 1897, is known as the Father of Country Music. The beginning of true country music, in the modern sense, is thought by many to be the recording sessions in Bristol, Tennessee, in August of 1927, when an independent producer for the Victor Talking Machine Company named Ralph Peer recorded, among others, Rodgers and the Carter Family.

I A Historical Vignette

Jesse James, shot from behind in St. Joseph, Missouri, on April 4, 1882, by a false friend, Robert Ford, remains one of the best-known Americans, and most people remember the song about "the dirty little coward who shot Mr. Howard [James's alias], and laid Jesse James in his grave."

Mr. Robert L. Kennedy, writing about the song in the Springfield, Missouri, *Leader* for October 18, 1933, recalled that "an old blind woman used to stand in front of the court house in Springfield and sing it by the hour; mourners would drop coins in her tin can. She went up to Richmond, Missouri, and was singing her sad song with tears in her voice when she found herself slapped and kicked into the middle of the street. Bob Ford's sister happened to be passing that way."

The significance of this anecdote lies in the way it reveals the sheer orneriness in the American character: a poor old blind woman can't eulogize a dead outlaw without getting her face slapped by a partisan of his assassin.

II Outlaw Country

Outlaw Country was a marketing device, a way of packaging and labeling a certain kind of white southern music in the seventies. Willie Nelson and Waylon Jennings are probably its two best-known exponents. However, an outlaw, strictly speaking, is someone who is placed outside the protection of the law; it's not a one-sided affair. Outlawry in the sense of wrongdoing, crime, is so much entangled with the roots of country music (the first country record to sell a million copies was Vernon Dalhart's "The Prisoner's Song," recorded August 13, 1924) that its absence rather than its presence should be surprising.

I have to confess that I resent the use of the term *outlaw* in this context, partly for personal reasons. I spent a number of years writing a book that I called *The True Adventures of the Rolling Stones Outlaw Band*. In the sixties, the Rolling Stones, symbols of drugs, sex, and decadent music, all things decent English folk abhorred, were effectively outlawed. By the time the book came to be published, its editor, who had been in the tenth grade when Jimi Hendrix died, was so repelled by Nashville representations concerning outlaws that he wouldn't hear of using the word *outlaw* in my title. But the Stones really were, during the time I was writing about, outlaws. That's one reason Brian Jones is dead. Maybe it's not the term *outlaw* but callow editorial opinion I resent. And in spite of its use as a sales ploy, the outlaw label, even in Nashville, had some justification. After federal narcs in 1977 invaded the studio where he was recording, Waylon Jennings wrote a song called, "Don't You Think This Outlaw Bit's Done Got Out of Hand?" Having the feds bust your session may not establish your outlaw bona fides, but it does give evidence of some seriousness. Charlie Rich is not usually included among the country outlaws, but if ever a man was, he was a true outlaw in his heart. A defining moment for me was the televised 1975 Country Music Awards show on which Jennings handed Rich the envelope containing the name of the Country Music Entertainer of the year. Rich opened it, read—silently—the name John Denver, took out his cigarette lighter, and set the envelope on fire. "People remember things like that," the Nashville songwriter Paul Craft said, not approvingly.

Nashville is a company town, as far as music goes; the big studios there have been owned by major record labels like RCA Victor. Rich, from Arkansas, started his career at Sun in Memphis, where demonstrative behavior was the norm. Nashville by the middle fifties had come to be defined by the conservative politics of Roy Acuff and the equally conservative demeanor of Chet Atkins, who modestly described himself as "a hunched-over guitar player." He played well above his raising. The outlaws, Willie and Waylon, like Jimmie Rodgers and Hank Williams before them, were not interested in playing above their raising.

The list of country entertainers with some claim to outlaw associations is long. It includes, to various degrees and for various reasons, Dalhart, Rodgers, the Carters, Dock Boggs, Carson Robinson, Cliff Carlisle, Gene Autry, Bob Wills, Milton Brown, Bob Dunn, Spade Cooley, Ernest Tubb, Hank Williams, Merle Travis, Webb Pierce, Lefty Frizzell, Ray Price, Merle Haggard, Johnny Cash, Jerry Lee Lewis, Carl Perkins, Charlie Rich, George Jones, Tammy Wynette, Dolly Parton, Freddy Fender, Huey P. Meaux, Jerry McGill, Gram Parsons, Kris Kristofferson, Townes Van Zandt, Steve Earle, Blaze Foley, Jimmie Dale Gilmore, Billy Joe Shaver, Butch Hancock, Steve Young, Johnny Paycheck, David Allan Coe, Hank Williams Jr., and others. We won't have time or space here, of course, to investigate all of these cases fully, or even in part. During the commercial ascendancy of the Outlaw Country promotion, its central figure was Waylon Jennings.

III Waylon

In 1973 Waylon Jennings released *Honky Tonk Heroes*: a collection of songs by the classic Texas songwriter Billy Joe Shaver, a national treasure, along with one song by Donnie Fritts, who's another treasure, aka the Alabama Leaning Man. Raw, poetic, and moving, it made the whole Outlaw Country stance believable. Still, Jennings recalls the chilly reception his outlaw approach initially received in Nashville:

"I never locked myself down to one thing. In fact, when I started that foot and the snare and big bass on the bottom, they said, 'That's not country, that's rock and roll.' I'd say, 'Yeah, but it shore does sound good.'

"They even tried to get me to quit doin' that by tellin' me, the engineers, that if I did it the record would skip on the turntable. When I first came to Nashville, that was the attitude. There was a way you looked, and a way you sounded, and they had a thing called the Nashville Sound, which was wonderful, and it fit me about like syrup on sugar, or sump'm. It just didn't work.

"When I first came to Nashville, they said, 'We love you, don't worry about anything, you don't need a manager, we'll take care of you.' And they did. It was a good ole boy thing. You'd really believe that they cared about you. They'd come from New York and say, 'This is your year, we love you at this label,' and they were laughing at us, they thought we were hicks. And we were. 'Cause we were sittin' down here, gettin' 4 percent, and they were givin' 10, 12, 15 percent to the other artists, anywhere but Nashville. Nashville was the only thing that made money for them. And they had a good little thing goin' there.

"Then me and Willie come along. They almost destroyed me in Nashville, and were out to do it for a while. The Nashville businesspeople thought I was out to destroy everything they had started. I wanted to record with my own band, and they didn't like that, and I wanted to spend more time on records, and I wanted more control over 'em.

"Chet Atkins produced some good albums on me. He was president of the RCA studio. Chet and I had trouble. Chet didn't understand me, and I didn't understand him either. He put me with Danny Davis, a guy who thought you should write everything down, and I don't know what he was doin' producin' country records anyway. He was awful. I would go and cut tracks, and when I'd come back, I didn't even recognize 'em. He'd put horns and all kinds of stuff on there.

"I went out to L.A. just to try something different and used Sonny Curtis and part of Ricky Nelson's band, and I cut 'Lovin' Her Was Easier.' Kris Kristofferson and I had a great record on it; everybody in the trades, Robert Hilburn, everybody said, 'Release that, that's a smash.' And it was a smash, it was a great record. But because I cut it in L.A., they wouldn't release it as a single."

Jennings-sponsored outlaw provocations went much further than a politically incorrect studio choice. In the mid-seventies, when he was red hot, Waylon played Memphis, and his onetime rhythm guitar player and road manager, Curtis Buck, aka Jerry McGill, came to the show in drag. McGill, who had a Memphis rock and roll band in the fifties and recorded for Sun Records, was eluding prosecution for various federal crimes. He had developed a problem traveling with Waylon when they put the metal detectors in airports. But there had been times when McGill's guns—he normally carried three, counting the one in his girlfriend's purse—had come in handy, like the time the cops had McGill's boss under arrest at the Hyatt House on Sunset Boulevard, and McGill talked him out of it. It's a scene we'll save for the film version. Thrown into this mix, Waylon has admitted to using in the past up to $1,500 worth of cocaine daily.

Then there was Willie. Waylon told me that Willie had been driving in Texas when he got sleepy and pulled onto the shoulder for a nap: "The cops saw the car, stopped to check it out, woke Willie up, searched the car, found some pot, and arrested him. He's the only guy I ever knew to get busted for sleeping under the influence." Willie is today the single most prominent figure to come out of the outlaw movement.

IV Willie

Willie Nelson was born in Abbott, Texas, April 30, 1933. Abandoned by his mother when he was six months old, he and his sister, Bobbie Lee, were raised by their father's parents, who gave Willie his first guitar, a Stella. He was six years old. At ten he played his first paying gig, a dance. He was a disc jockey in high school, then served in the air force, attended Baylor University, and worked as a door-to-door encyclopedia and Bible salesman. In 1956 he made his first record, "No Place for Me," paying for it himself. During this period he married (a full-blood Cherokee girl who stuck a fork in his chest), had two children, and divorced. In 1960 he sold "Night Life" for enough money to buy a Buick convertible and move to Nashville. There he had quick success, with two number-one hits, performed by Patsy Cline and Ray Price, in two years ("Crazy" and "Hello Walls"). Though he recorded for Monument and other labels, he remained principally known as a songwriter until, in 1970, his house burned down and he decided to return to Texas.

Ten years in Nashville had caused Willie to forget how scarce in Texas the market would be for his songs. He was reduced to singing them himself. His recording career began in earnest with Western Swing aficionado Jerry Wexler's signing him to Atlantic Records, where he cut two classic albums, *Shotgun Willie* and *Phases and Stages*. Critical rather than popular successes, they paved the way for the enormous reception given to Willie's first Columbia album, *Red Headed Stranger*. It came out in 1975 and became the first country album to go platinum—to sell, that is, a million units. And that was enough to start the downfall of the entire movement.

V The Death of Outlaw

Waylon's next album, *Wanted! The Outlaws*, featured Willie, Tompall Glaser, and even Waylon's wife, Jessi Colter, as outlaws. Though that wasn't as far-fetched as it might seem. Jessi's real name was Miriam Johnson; her stage name came from her great-great-great-uncle, Jesse Colter, who rode with the James gang. Her first husband was guitarist Duane Eddy. After her sister Sharon married Jack Clement, he and Waylon were brothers-in-law, and Cowboy Jack called Waylon Bubba.

Some of Waylon's best work was done with Jack Clement. Clement started at Sun Records, producing hits like "Whole Lotta Shakin'

Goin' On" for Jerry Lee Lewis. Both Clement and Chips Moman, another producer with whom Waylon had artistic and commercial success, are strongly identified with Memphis.

To digress for a moment—but not really—it's worth noting that the outlaw movement could never have started in Memphis, because in Memphis there would have been no novelty to the concept. The music business itself in Memphis has historically been outlaw, or at the least highly independent. Memphis music is in large part about the point where independence encroaches on disturbing the peace, e.g., "Don't Step on My Blue Suede Shoes" and the aforementioned "Whole Lotta Shakin'."

Memphis studios have been independent, so independent in fact that the characteristic act for a Memphis studio is to change the world and then go out of business, which is what Sun and Stax both did.

As noted, Clement worked at Sun, where he wrote hits like "Ballad of a Teenage Queen" and "Guess Things Happen That Way" for Johnny Cash and "It'll Be Me" for Jerry Lee. He was fired by Sun owner Sam Phillips in 1959 for "insubordination." In 1965 Clement opened a studio in Nashville; he would go on to discover Charlie Pride and Don Williams, among others, and to record his bubba Waylon.

Chips Moman, from LaGrange, Georgia, was the first engineer at Stax. In the sixties, Moman became co-owner of American Studios, also in Memphis, where he is said to have had 117 top-ten records in one year. These include Elvis Presley's "In the Ghetto" and "Suspicious Minds." During his sojourn at American he would record hits on the Box Tops, Elvis, Neil Diamond, Dusty Springfield, and Dionne Warwick, among many others.

In 1985 the city of Memphis gave Moman an abandoned fire station to use as a studio, lending him $720,000 for building improvements and recording equipment, and freezing the property tax. During the five years before the same politicians who had seen him as a potential savior got around to running him out of town, Moman produced one album, *Class of '55*, a reunion of Sun alumni Johnny Cash, Jerry Lee Lewis, Roy Orbison, and Carl Perkins. It went to number eighty-seven in *Billboard*, nowhere near high enough to pay back the multimillion advance costs. Memphis eventually padlocked their firehouse and threw Moman in jail for a few days until he gave back their recording equipment. Time for a reprise of "Don't You Think This Outlaw Bit's Done Got Out of Hand?"

Inevitably, it would seem, it was Moman who wrote (with keyboardist Bobby Emmons) one of Waylon's biggest hits, "Luckenbach, Texas," and produced two of Waylon's best albums, *Ol' Waylon* and *Black on Black*. He also produced *Heroes*, with Johnny and Waylon, and *Highwaymen*, featuring Waylon, Willie, Johnny, and Kris.

A further bit of evidence regarding the affinity between outlaws and Memphis: Willie happened to run into Booker T. Jones of the MGs, the Stax house band, at a swimming pool in a Malibu condominium in 1978; the resultant discussion led to one of the most successful albums either would have, *Stardust*, featuring Willie's vocals and guitar and Booker's piano, organ, and lean, tasteful production. Willie was already moving out of the outlaw mode into mainstream acceptance.

What all this Memphis business has to do with Outlaw Country is this: it demonstrates the almost complete inability of commercially obsessed Nashville to produce anything unique. Two places could hardly be more different than Memphis, the uncontested Home of the Blues, and Nashville, the Home of the Green. Waylon and Willie had to have help from Memphis to do what they wanted.

The Memphis multitalent Jim Dickinson has called the music business "a self-devouring organism that vomits itself back up." Outlaw Country was inevitably, in its turn, devoured, and when it came up again, it was wearing a big hat and singing "Achy Breaky Heart."

VI The Boys

Speaking of outlawry, it's a crime to try to tell this story in such a small space: No room here for sufficient examination of even such a major country-crime character as Spade Cooley, the Western Swing wizard who kicked his wife to death with his cowboy boots while forcing his daughter, Melody, to look on. "You're going to watch me kill her," he said, according to Melody's sworn testimony. There's scarcely room to relate the classic anecdote about the time Tammy Wynette hid the car keys and George Jones rode the lawnmower down to the liquor store. In other words, too much is known about this subject to collect here.

Vernon Dalhart, who took his stage name from two Texas towns, was originally called Marion Try Slaughter. Born in Jefferson, Texas, to a solidly middle-class family, Dalhart worked in New York as an opera singer before recording for Edison and many other labels under a variety of pseudonyms. In 1924, with his popularity waning, Dalhart persuaded the Victor company to let him record the "hillbilly" material that resurrected his career. He recorded over five thousand songs, sold over seventy-five million records, lost all his money, and died of heart failure in 1942, while working as a night clerk in a small Connecticut hotel.

A bit about Merle Haggard would be in order, too. Haggard was born in 1937 in Oildale, California, of Arkansan and Oklahoman roots. He grew up in a converted railroad freight car by the Southern Pacific tracks. "First thing I remember knowin' was a lonesome whistle blowin' and a youngun's dream of growin' up to ride," he wrote in "Mama Tried." He really did, as the song says, "[turn] twenty-one in prison," though not, luckily, as the song continues, "doing life without parole." Haggard credits his three years in San Quentin—part of the time a few doors down from death row inmate Caryl Chessman—with turning him away from crime. He was released in 1960.

Haggard learned to play guitar in the fifties, and in 1953 sat in with Lefty Frizzell, one of his heroes. (Frizzell, playing a Bakersfield club called the Rainbow Garden, asked Haggard to sing a song, and Haggard did Jimmie Rodgers's "My Rough and Rowdy Ways.") In the sixties Haggard started playing bass with the underrated California country singer Wynn Stewart, and soon began recording on his own, first for a small label called Tally, and then, in 1965, for Capitol Records. His first number-one hit, a year later, was "I Am a Lonesome Fugitive," and his tenth (in four years), the notorious right-wing anthem "Okie from Muskogee." Though the song was an unprecedented success it failed to represent Haggard's philosophy realistically. Kris Kristofferson said, "Merle Haggard is neither a redneck nor a racist. He just happens to be known for the only bad song he ever wrote." Haggard was, in fact, more a member of the counterculture than its opponent. When country artists began flocking to an alcohol-and-drug-free environment in Missouri, Haggard said, "Branson and me don't warsh." What does wash with Haggard is classic country music, as evidenced by the three albums he recorded as tributes to Bob Wills and Jimmie Rodgers.

It's also worth pointing out that Johnny Cash scooped the whole outlaw ethos in 1968 with his album, *Johnny Cash at Folsom Prison*. He later cut an album at San Quentin, and both performances are available on one superb Columbia CD. Cash never did any hard time, but his rapport with inmates could hardly have been better.

VII Outlaw Myths

Those who care most about country music believe in it almost like adherents to a religion. Musicians in any culture tend to be introverted, intellectual types, good at counting. But in the world of country music they are truck drivers, railroad brakemen, cowboys, rodeo riders, outlaws. The truth is, some of them really have been all these things, have had these occupations and more. These instances of reality have talismanic significance for country fans, because country music is so often trivial and silly, and evidences of reality, like first-class saints' relics, are all the more precious in times of spiritual drought.

This, along with the indisputable power of his singing, is why George "No-Show" Jones could behave in completely unprofessional ways for years and still be regarded as the greatest voice in country music. He sang "The Poor Chinee" and lived to tell the tale:

> My name Sin-sin, me come from China,
> Biggie-low ship, me come along here
> Wind blow hard, it kicky-up bubble-y,
> Ship make-a China boy feel very queer
> Me like-a bowwow, very good chow chow,
> Me like-a little girl, she like me
> Me come from Hong Kong, white man be come along,
> Takee little gal from-a Po' Chinee
> —"The Poor Chinee," V. Feuerbacher, E. Noack

Any career that survives such a song is immortal. But George is the real thing. His father sent George out to sing and play guitar on the streets of Beaumont while he was still a child. George has survived, has even conquered what Waylon has called "the Hank Williams syndrome." This is basically a synonym for self-destructiveness, which was what Hank had instead of the TB that killed Jimmie Rodgers. It was just as real, and just as fatal. Gram Parsons had it, too. So did Townes Van Zandt.

Someone asked George about alcohol, and George said, "The biggest reason I can see for a person drinkin' is just that the songs are so sad, and so true." Kind of hard to object to such patently valid testimony. As Al Jackson Jr. observed to me in another connection, a few years before he was murdered, "It's a funky world."

> Why did I stray from the righteous path?
> Nobody knows but me.
> There on the outside you all can laugh; I don't need your sympathy.
> For after I pay for the liquor I sold, I'll leave this place worth my weight in gold.
> —"Nobody Knows but Me," Rodgers, McWilliams

This music is about pain, hurt, betrayal, being in love and in jail, and it always has been. If you hear country music that's about anything else, beware, it's not real. "Mad Ireland hurt you into poetry," Auden wrote in his 1939 elegy to Yeats. Our subject is the poetry of mad, blood-soaked, Indian country.

Listening to Townes Van Zandt's recording of "Lonesome Whistle" by Hank Williams and Jimmie Davis (who became governor of Louisiana—think he wasn't an outlaw?), I remembered seeing, nearly thirty years ago, Gram Parsons sitting at a piano in Los Angeles, singing the same song with Keith Richards and Mick Jagger.

> I was riding number nine
> Heading south from Caroline
> I heard that long, lonesome whistle blow

Got in trouble, had to roam
Left my gal and left my home
I heard that long, lonesome whistle blow

I'll never see that gal of mine
Lord, I'm in Georgia doin' time
I heard that long, lonesome whistle blow

The power of that connection, from Williams's Alabama boyhood to Parsons, from Waycross, Georgia, to Jagger and Richards, from Dartford, Kent, and to Van Zandt, from Fort Worth, Texas, is hard to exaggerate. It's a real spiritual connection.

Van Zandt, one of a number of metaphysical offspring of Rodgers, Williams, and the outlaw tradition, was a phenomenal talent and truly tortured soul. "Pancho and Lefty," a sizable hit for Nelson and Haggard, is his best-known song. Some of his work, like "Marie," is so powerful that it's painful to listen to (". . . the songs are so sad, and so true").

Parsons, himself a great songwriter, and Van Zandt are both gone now. Parsons, born in 1947, died September 19, 1973; Van Zandt, born in 1944, died January 1, 1997. As to what killed them, the answer lies in something Louis Armstrong said when someone asked him what killed Bix Beiderbecke: "What he died of specifically I don't know. I think he died of everything."

VIII Outlaw's Future

There are good guys remaining in this genre, like Butch Hancock, Joe Ely, Guy Clark, and Steve Earle; Willie and Waylon are still going strong, though Waylon's stopped touring and is selling off his road guitars. They both have new CDs. Willie's, *Teatro*, features Parsons's onetime singing partner Emmylou Harris.

The most hopeful sign I've come across for Outlaw Country in recent years has been Bill Parker, who was born in Indiana, raised in Texas, and now lives in Seattle. Parker has been described as "the illegitimate offspring of Keith Richards and Gram Parsons."

> Dust storms and diamondbacks,
> Pissants and Cadillacs
> Lost poets and madmen
> Salvation and sin
> And the Texas heat and wind

That's from a song called "I-35 Revisited."

> This old life gets harder every day
> You think you're the only one with troubles
> At least it seems that way
> I'm prob'ly damned if I do
> But the message must get through
> I may not be an angel, but I'm
> Good enough for you

That's part of "I May Not Be an Angel."
　　Listening to Parker for the first time, I was pretty much a goner by the time I heard the lines from "Cruising for the King":

> Who grew the sideburns?
> Who was the lightning rod?
> Who always got the girl, 'cept
> When he lost Mary Tyler Moore to God?
> What'cha gonna do for Elvis
> After all he's done for you?

The off-the-wall tragicomedy of "Me & Angelina" came as *lagniappe*, a Louisiana term meaning a nice unexpected extra:

> Me and Angelina,
> Dancin' slow to Gatemouth Brown
> Me and Angelina,
> Walkin' arm in arm till dawn
> I shoulda never left New Orleans,
> I might have been a saucier

"I can't imagine anything better than being a musician," Parker has said. I can't imagine anybody carrying on the outlaw tradition better than Bill Parker.

One of the songs on *I-35 Revisited* (Parker has done other collections of his songs, among them *Honky Haiku, Just Another White Boy,* and *When Hearts Collide*) is a prayer: "(Grant Me) Wisdom and the Light to See." It's the kind of song everyone should have the chance to hear:

> Don't need diamonds or a mansion
> Got no use for no limousine
> The only riches I would ask for,
> Grant me wisdom and the light to see
>
> Part the waters that I may reach you
> Grant me wisdom and the light to see

It's also evidence that prayers are answered, even the prayers of an outlaw.

DISTANT THOUGHTS

When Jack Johnson was asked why white women loved black men like him, he replied, "We eat cold eels and think distant thoughts."

On August 5, 2014, the poet Diann Blakely died of respiratory failure in a hospital in Georgia. Diann was born June 1, 1957, with a congenital lung disorder, alpha-1 antitrypsin deficiency. This was not properly diagnosed until the year 2000. In 2001, my first two books, *The True Adventures of the Rolling Stones* and *Rythm Oil*, were republished, and Diann reviewed them in the weekly paper the *Nashville Scene*. My friend Nanette Bahlinger was living in Nashville. Nanette and I had met in Brunswick, Georgia, on the coast, where in 2001 I was still living. One day I went out to my mailbox and there was a large manila envelope from Nanette. It contained Diann's review. Writers try not to respond to reviews because it's a chump thing to do. Only once before had I done this, when my friend Walter Dawson of the *Memphis Commercial Appeal* compared me to Jerry Lee Lewis. I had to thank Walter for that. But Diann's review was so well written, insightful, perceptive, that I got in touch with the *Scene*'s editors and said, I don't know who this Diann Blakely is, but I'd like to thank her. Weeks later I received an e-mail from her, and so began a conversation that ended only with Diann's death. These are some excerpts from the beginning of that conversation. Diann and I were married in Brunswick, in a lawyer's office with our parents, a Catholic priest, a stuffed black bear, stuffed turkeys, boars, and other forms of preserved wildlife.

She was never in good health, but she was fiercely determined and an obsessive worker. Her poetry speaks for itself. Life for us was not easy, but its depths were profound. I will never know anyone to whom I can talk as Diann and I talked. We were together for a few good years as well as some bad ones. She was five seven and never weighed a hundred pounds, usually hovering around eighty. She was at her best a great, heroic spirit with a good, sweet heart. After we started talking via e-mail, it took me six months to get up the nerve to call her on the phone. It's hard to believe I will never again hear her unique voice. But reading these sincere, heartfelt messages, I can hear her once more. These exchanges mean everything to me, and I hope they have meaning for others.

18 May 2001
How sweet of you! I adore presents . . .
DB
3037 Woodlawn Drive
Nashville TN 37215

23 May 2001
Of course! I enjoy petits choux though usually in winter. You might like this book; it's a first novel and clunks in places as does the review but it's also genuinely redolent of Memphis.
Rev. of Leah Stewart's *Body of a Girl*
http://www.nashscene.com/cgi-bin/article.cgi?story=This_Week :Arts:Books
My, what big gloves you have! Assuming that it *is* you . . .
You *must* consider using the photo on the jacket of your next book. Speaking of which, do your publishers plan to send you westward for the So. Festival of Books here? The event has become less literary and more "market-driven" since its inception, but it's surely the only one in the country which holds readings in legislative and state supreme court chambers. I mention this, for whatever it's worth, because those who write about music tend to draw good crowds and to sell goodly numbers of books.
And, I hasten to add, it would be lovely to meet you.
I taught for a dozen years and mostly adored it. V. Bell Jr. shines as one of the very best teachers I was lucky enough to encounter, which is why I mentioned him earlier. He's brilliant—no, "brilliant" is the wrong word. Vereen has "a mind so fine no idea [can] penetrate it," to quote Eliot on H. James. (Actually, I think I first heard that

quotation in one of his classes.) Which, in addition to his Heideggerian vocabulary, would probably make him insufferable were he not so violently and uniquely profane. Makes for fascinating verbal juxtapositions . . .

I love the English language like Keith Richards loves his guitar.

Parcel is finally en route. I ain't about to offer a full-scale list of neuromuscular excuses for its delay to someone who has Broken His Back, but I had this rather melodramatic asthma attack on New Year's Eve, ripped some muscles in my neck, have good weeks and bad ones, the latter requiring long and tedious stints with my physical therapist, unamusing drugs that make me too stupid and clumsy to walk downstairs safely, much less drive except to the PT, etc. etc. etc.—

--- Original Message ---
From: <Dblakely@aol.com>
To: <ftmudge@bellsouth.net>
Sent: Thursday, June 07, 2001 2:00 AM
Subject: Re: Nomenclature
In a message dated 6/6/01 12:04:29 AM, ftmudge@bellsouth.net writes:
<< To my students as Sensei. >>
Mine called me a goddess once; however, since the title resulted from my decision to postpone a test or paper, I think I must regard the honor with an Olympian-size grain of salt.
Where do you teach?

SB to DB
Your package arrived. I am greatly honored that you sent me your work. It is wonderful, simply and complicatedly amazing. I'll be a lifetime reading it.

Other people have tried writing blues-influenced, RJ [Robert Johnson]-influenced poetry. Their work never worked, in my opinion; yours does, powerfully, frighteningly, deeply, darkly. (Langston Hughes's does, of course, but he never directly invoked RJ, if indeed he ever heard him.)

I'm more astonished than ever that you wrote about my work, and more than ever grateful. You are the real thing, a genuine treasure. I love the way you write. I love your titles, your images, your lines. You remind me of poets I love such as Creeley and Levertov, Donne and Hopkins. Words are objects in your work, you can walk all the way around them and see the shadows they cast.

I also appreciate very much the way you look in the pictures on the back of *Farewell, My Lovelies*. (I tried to write every sentence in the Stones book in such a way that each one could be spoken aloud by Philip Marlowe.) Most of the people who like my writing and get in touch to say so are wider than they are tall. Which is fine if they like it but seems odd to me. It's a relief to be read for a change by someone with a neck. Flannery used to say that there is nothing that does not require a writer's attention. I see the quality of your attention shining in your eyes and am, all over again, grateful to be noticed by them.

Please, please, please take care of yourself.

Your friend,

John Francis Frater

P.S.

Here's a lil pome of my own devising:

> I'm just a Japanese cowboy
> Longing for old Tennessee
> I'm just a Japanese cowboy
> Wondering if you think of me

> The stars shining over Kyoto
> Make me hanker for old Alabam
> And every time I eat sushi
> I hunger for sugar-cured ham

> Turn me loose where the samurai yodel
> Nashville keeps calling to me
> I'm just a Japanese cowboy
> A Dixieland kamikaze

Let me ramble around the Panhandle
Where the lazy old gators roam free
I'm just a Japanese cowboy
'Neath the shade of the buttermilk tree

Wranglin' cotton out in the moonshine
So my mammy will be proud of me
I'm just a Japanese cowboy
The Suwannee's where I want to be
I'm just a Japanese cowboy
A Dixieland Kamikaze
(Attached please find some South Georgia local culture.)

SB to DB 9/8/01 @9:00 PM
I got a package from you. I like Thom Jones's book but everybody in it has epilepsy.
Do you know Prevert's "Blood Orange"?
Your poem is amazing. So many elements brought together.
Do you know about the dual levitation of St. Teresa and my patron St. John of the Cross? It's a great story and I have an interesting story about it.

<< I like Thom Jones's book but everybody in it has epilepsy.>>
Thank you, once more, for making me laugh.
To be fair, in one particularly grim story, the protagonist doesn't have epilepsy but some terrible and terminal form of cancer. I haven't read many of these, but lots of my guy friends really like Jones so I thought you might too.
<<Do you know Prevert's "Blood Orange"?>>
I don't read books by perverts, even if they're ostensibly about fruit. You just never know . . .
Are lavendar flowers called society garlic because society ladies use them instead to cook, or have their cooks use them instead of the clove kind?
Is it okay for me to give Ron your e-mail and street address? He says he'd love to be in touch with you . . .

<<Do you know about the dual levitation of St. Teresa and my patron St. John of the Cross? It's a great story and I have an interesting story about it.>>

No, I don't know either story but am not rising from this bed until you tell it to me.

September 8, 2001

There's a marvelous book by Blaise Cendrars, one of my favorite people, called *Sky: A Memoir*. It's primarily about levitation though it's about many other things as well. In it he tells the story of—well he quotes from Father Bruno's book on St. John of the Cross:

"One day, on the Feast of the Most Holy Trinity, Father John of the Cross was in the parlor—it was a little parlor, two and a half meters high and five feet long by five feet wide, the floor was paved with red brick, the walls were of grey stone and the ceiling was supported by brown beams. Father John was sitting on a chair and the Reverend Mother, on the other side of the grill, was seated on a bench. He was speaking of the mystery, 'his favorite mystery,' and his soul plunged into this ocean of fire. The ardor of the Spirit carried off the body, and, as Father John clutched his chair, it carried away the chair, too. He rose up to the ceiling. Teresa of Jesus was ravished by this same impulse of love. Doña Beatriz de Cepeda y Ocampo, the future Beatrice of Jesus, opened the door and came in to give her relative a message, and so witnessed this truly transcendental rapture. 'There is no way one can speak of God to my Father John of the Cross, because he immediately goes into ecstasy and causes others to do the same,' said Teresa very charmingly, by way of excuse."

Well, it was a few years ago, 1994, I think, and two of my friends, Ken and Susan O'Neal, were about to marry. I was asked to read that well-known passage from I Corinthians 13 at the ceremony. We'd had a rehearsal and then gone to a rehearsal cocktail party, followed by a rehearsal dinner, followed by drinks at a jazz bar. Nanette was here for the wedding, staying at Susan's apartment. I had come to the rehearsal with Ken, who for some reason didn't join us at the bar. When at last we left the bar, Susan was going to drive me to my house, then she and Nanette would go home. As we hit the causeway from St. Simons, heading back over to the mainland, I thought the wisest course of action was to light a reefer. I was in the middle of telling the story given above, about the dual levitation of Teresa and John. Nanette had just passed the cigaret back to me when a bright display of red and blue lights erupted behind us. Susan, the happy bride, had been in her elated inebriation speeding along, heedless. We'd been pulled over by a Glynn County police officer and a Georgia state trooper. What the trooper was doing on St. Simons I don't know. One of them came up, took Susan's license, and went back to where they were parked. Nanette, also drunk—none of us could have hit the floor with his hat—opened her door, threw her legs out, and yelled to the police. "She's getting married in the mornin'." The trooper, shining his flashlight at her, said, "Ma'am, get back in the car, please." I was in the back, alone, eating, for the first and only time in my life, a partially smoked marijuana cigaret. It's not as tasty as it sounds.

It seemed forever we sat there. Probably it was ten minutes, fifteen at the most. Then the cops came up, the Brunswick officer told Susan to pull her car over on the shoulder well away from the traffic, and the trooper left. "I'm gone give y'all a ride home," the officer said.

And, to my amazement, that's just what he did. Once we'd dropped off the womenfolk, he said, "That trooper was bein' a asshole. I told him don't worry about it, I'd take care of y'all."

I saw him later, and thanked him again, at the video store next to the P.O. where I mail things to you—his wife worked there. That is, until she told him she wanted a divorce and he shot them both dead while sitting out front in a car. It was about a year after the wedding. I think he was too sensitive for police work and probably other things. But I've always believed that he was so sympathetic and forgiving that night, the night before the wedding, because St. Teresa and St. John were in the car with us.

By all means give Ron my e-address.

I do not know why Society Garlic is called that but I'll investigate.

WHY THEY CALL IT THE BLUES

The late comedian Flip Wilson used to say, "The reason why I like the blues, 'cause when the record wears out, it still sounds the same." Would that everyone spoke of the blues with such insight and, as they say in Jamaica, overstanding. Flip was right: the blues is subtle; its appeal lies, like most true pleasures, beneath the surface.

These days the blues is or are everywhere, or damn near; I turned on my computer tonight and was invited by my Internet Explorer home page to "jam with blues man Buddy Guy" on a live broadcast from the House of Blues. This portends, for the blues, serious dangers. Buddy Guy is a real—genuine—great musician, but nothing exists that greed will not attempt to debase.

When musicians talk about playing the blues, they are referring not to an emotional statement about being unlucky in life and love but to a musical form, usually one of twelve bars, though sometimes eight or sixteen. While certain songs with the word *blues* in the title, such as Johnny Mercer and Harold Arlen's "Blues in the Night" and W. C. Handy's "St. Louis Blues," have become classics of popular music repertoire, they are not, in the strict formal sense, blues.

However, Peter Gammond, in *The Oxford Companion to Popular Music*, writes, "The blues, unlike ragtime or jazz, can only be defined as a form in its more superficial aspect. The wider implication of the blues lies in its spirit, a spirit which is the basic ingredient of all true jazz." The longtime *New Yorker* music writer Whitney Balliett has put it more succinctly: "Jazz would be an empty house without the blues." Atlantic Records president

Ahmet Ertegun, who ought to know if anybody does, once observed, "Black music is the most popular music of all time—and has been since it got started good, about 1921." Of course, black music is not all blues, but the blues is basic not only to most black music but to much modern classical as well as popular music. Blue notes, the flatted third, seventh (and sometimes fifth) tones of the Western eight-note scale, are found in the work of Gottschalk, Stravinsky, Gershwin, Bernstein, and a great many other composers. Thus the influence of this twentieth-century music, the blues, has become by the eve of the millenium so pervasive as to be ubiquitous.

But what about the blues in the popular sense, them low-down dirty blues that Memphis audiences have known and loved? As we approach the end of the nineteen-hundreds, how are the blues getting along? Are their vital signs weak or strong? The answer is, yes and no. All the original blues masters of the acoustic period are dead, and the innovators of the second-wave electric era, like John Lee Hooker and B. B. King, are getting old. (The original electric innovators, Eddie Durham, Bob Dunn, Charlie Christian, and T-Bone Walker, are, sad to say, also long departed.) Still, there are more blues festivals than ever, and a number of notable young blues performers, many of whom are white.

Part of the reason for this is that the blues at their most characteristic possess certain qualities of permanent value. The blues speak in exalted language of dramatic situations. This is what Homer, Sophocles, Shakespeare, and Tarantino, among others, also do, in their various ways. Blind Willie McTell's method is to tell his beloved,

> I'm gonna cut yo' head fo' different ways,
> that's long, short, deep, and wide.
> When I get through usin' this rusty, black-handled razor, you
> gonna be booked out for a ambulance ride.

Marlowe or McTell, it's all poetry. I was at Furry Lewis's flat on Mosby one night when Allen Ginsberg stopped by. Ginsberg sat at the foot of Furry's bed in a chrome and leatherette kitchen chair while Furry played. "I'm gonna tell you, baby," Furry sang, "like the Chinaman told the Jew—'You no likee me, I no likee you.'" It was all in fun, and Ginsberg, charmed by the master poet Furry, played a sort of psalm of praise on his harmonium, beginning with the words, "We thank you, oh King." Ginsberg knew royalty when he saw it, even in the ghetto.

Poetry, including—especially—the poetry of the blues, doesn't make much money. B. B. King says he's a millionaire, and I have to believe him, but show me another millionaire bluesman. I believe it was Edward Dahlberg who said, "There is no money in poetry, but then there is no poetry in money either." Gus Cannon to the contrary:

> I wash my teeth in diamond dust
> I don't care if the banks go bust
> Done got to the place
> where my money don't never run out

This is poetry about money, no doubt about it, but its power lies not in its accuracy but its irony. Gus worked as a yardman all his life. Furry swept the streets in Memphis for over forty years and retired without a pension. "I ain't got nothin', I ain't never had nothin', I don't expect to ever get nothin'," I once heard him say. "But I'll tell you this: I'm just as smart as any man in this house." He always was, whatever the house.

Men like Furry and Gus existed on the outer fringes of the recording industry, an industry that no longer has any fringes. You couldn't get away from music these days if you tried. Keith Richards has said rock and roll music killed communism, and there may be truth in that contention, but music has a hard enough time saving itself and can hardly be expected to save the world, especially when you consider the people, Ahmet Ertegun excepted, running record companies these days. The music business is more than ever characterized by our old adversaries greed and avarice. The record company executives are not all equally reprehensible, but the better ones are unable to alter the direction the music business is going, which is toward cannibalism. As Jim Dickinson famously observed, "The music business is a self-devouring organism that vomits itself back up."

The problem is, you don't want yourself or anyone you care about being devoured. All of us who were around at the time saw what happened to Elvis Presley. Some of us watched as Alex Chilton went from having the number-one record in the country at the age of sixteen to washing dishes in New Orleans a couple of decades later. Alex is okay now, but he's had to be a survivor. Keith Richards, another survivor, has talked with me about our seeing our closest friends fall by our sides. He didn't exaggerate.

―――――――

That's why, when a kid with talent comes along, you feel fearful for him and for yourself. If you're like me, you've had your heart broken too many times already.

One of my most valued friends is a wonderful crazy man who is both a judge and a blues lover. A little over a year ago, he told me to meet him at Rafters, a second-story blues club near the beach on St. Simons Island. St. Simons is off the South Georgia coast not far from my home. Eight o'clock found us sitting at the end of the bar, watching Barbara, the attractive barkeep, draw beers. It was an open-mike night, when players could sit in with the house band. Up the stairs came a white boy, not quite twelve years old, carrying a guitar case. Opening it, he strapped on a solid-body electric approximately as big as he was and stepped onstage. His first note brought me to my feet; I stood up on the rung of my barstool. The kid was blond and looked as if he should be wearing a baseball glove, but his attack, his tone, were those of a ferocious professional musician. He played twelve lacerating bars, then leaned into the vocal mike: "Everybody wants to know—why I sing the blues." I was still standing.

"You want to go sit down front?" the judge asked.

"*Yeah.*"

The set was short but most impressive. It included songs associated with B. B. King, Sonny Boy Williamson, Howlin' Wolf, Elmore James, and an amazing version of "Voodoo Child" the kid performed on his knees with the guitar behind his head. When he came off the stage, I asked him how he'd gotten into the blues. "My mama and daddy are divorced," he said. "And my daddy lives in Jacksonville. I go down there sometimes to see him. He has a lot of CDs, and one day I picked up one and played it 'cause I thought the cover looked cool, and it was by Stevie Ray Vaughan." The boogie bug had bitten the boy.

Given a cheap pawn-shop guitar by his father, he took it into his bedroom and for the most part, his mother told me, didn't come out for a couple of years. When he finally emerged he told her he'd figured it out. He had, too. Now if he only knew someone who could figure out what to do about what he figured out. Talent, as every artist learns sooner or later, isn't enough.

Once the legendary Memphis drummer Phineas Newborn Sr. and his wife, Rose, were visiting B. B. King and his wife, Martha. In those days Martha was working at a laundry and trying to convince B. B. to get a real job. Martha had purchased some draperies and the two couples sat and watched the man from the department store take them off the wall and repossess them. Still B. B. stubbornly persisted in wanting a career in show business, and Phineas, ever the clear-eyed optimist, said, "It's money in it—if you can ever get to it."

Getting to it is the hard part. Allman Brother Butch Trucks's prodigious nephew, Derek, whom I first saw when he was twelve, has been from at least that age a remarkable guitarist. He did not, however, sing, write songs, or look at the audience. Now he is grown and has become an Allman Brother himself, and that's fine. The kid I saw at Rafters, though, plays phenomenal guitar, sings, and engages the audience completely. The first time I saw him I happened to sit near a couple of older black men who obviously thought this white boy who sang "If you don't love me, girl, I know your sister will" was the cutest thing since Sammy Davis was a pup.

The kid is now thirteen, has grown quite a bit, is living in California, and has acquired two amateurish-appearing semi-official "managers," which is two more than he needs, but he doesn't know any better, and neither does his family. Atlantic Records paid for some demonstration recordings that, the kid told me, had been judged "not MTV-quality." Which is crazy, because MTV doesn't play blues anyway. The boy is a real talent, but his circumstances are so unprotected that I can't bring myself to give his name. May he prosper.

After we saw Bireli Lagrene, the great Belgian jazz guitarist, when he was eighteen—in London, 1985—my friend asked what was going to happen to him.

"People will rob him," I said. "Women will break his heart. If he's lucky, in eighteen years he'll be thirty-six, and if we're lucky we'll be around to hear what he's doing."

Bereli is still around, still performing and recording, and looks likely to be doing the same in 2010. The kid from Rafters is still around, too, and so are you and I, but as the Bible says, none of us is or are promised tomorrow. We are not, in fact, promised anything. I've said it before, and I'll say it again: that's why they call it the blues.

MR. CRUMP DON'T LIKE IT: IF BEALE STREET COULD TALK

When I look back on my life, one unceasing source of wonder is not only that I have survived over fifty years by writing, but that I have done it while living in an illiterate environment like Memphis. Once I say that, many exceptions leap to mind. None of which has anything to do with what comes next. How this came about I don't remember. Cybill Shepherd, the model and actress from Memphis, hired me to write two television scripts about the history of Memphis music. I must say I took the assignment seriously. My model was William Burroughs's *The Last Words of Dutch Schulz*. That's where I stole the idea of having three things happening all the time.

Part One

1

MEDIUM SHOT. The center of the universe. Vast spaces, distant moving lights, coming to focus on the Milky Way galaxy.

NARRATION:	SOUNDTRACK:
. . . orchestras which set the rhythm of the year, summing up the sadness and suggestiveness of life in new tunes.	Synthesizer beeps and hums (cross between Pac-man and Sneeky Pete w. fuzz-tone): *beep beep beep aww*

2

STILL. LONG SHOT. The earliest photograph of Beale and Main Streets in Memphis, Tennessee. The camera scans the picture, bringing us closer to the corner signpost, which is not yet legible.

NARRATION:

All night the saxophones wailed the hopeless comment of the "Beale Street Blues" . . .

SOUNDTRACK:

Street noise contemporary with photograph: car horns, air brakes, mule harness, human voices

3

CLOSE SHOT. First color shot. Forklift seen from beneath platform. We cannot see what is being lifted on the rising steel slab.

NARRATION:

. . . while a hundred pairs of golden and silver slippers shuffled the shining dust.

SOUNDTRACK:

Gears grinding, banjo tuning, guitar feedback.

4

CLOSE SHOT. Newspaper advertisement for Memphis slave market. Camera moves in to focus on crude caricature of black boy.

NARRATION:

At the gray tea hour there were always rooms that throbbed incessantly with this low, sweet fever . . .

SOUNDTRACK:

Heavy footfalls, the sounds of people marching in chains.

5

LONG SHOT. The local solar system, moving to focus on the Earth. Earth DISSOLVES to become eighteenth-century globe on library table, spinning, in CLOSE SHOT. As globe stops we focus on Africa, particularly the section including the west coast from Gambia to southern Angola and across the continent from Kenya to Mozambique. The Gold and Slave Coasts are clearly marked.

NARRATION:

. . . while fresh faces drifted here and there like rose petals blown by the sad horns around the floor.

SOUNDTRACK:

Synthesizer/siren wail (cross between Jimi Hendrix on STP and police on attack).

6

CLOSE SHOT. Slave poster. Focus on one word: NEGROES.

NARRATION:

The first object which saluted my eyes when I arrived on the coast was the sea and a slave ship . . .

SOUNDTRACK:

Marching in chains. Birdcalls. Whips cracking.

7

CLOSE SHOT. "FLAGELLATION of a Female Samboe Slave" by William Blake. Camera moves in to focus on tied hands.

NARRATION:

. . . which was . . . riding at anchor and waiting for its cargo. This filled me with astonishment, which was soon converted into terror . . .

SOUNDTRACK:

Marching sounds growing louder. Harsh voices shouting commands in African dialect.

8

MEDIUM SHOT. A naked black boy, back to camera, stands by a thorn bush in bright sunlight. As he turns to look at camera we see that he is peeing. A long pole, its end charred and smoking, thrusts onto screen, striking the boy between the shoulder blades, knocking him forward. Camera pulls back to reveal an entire tribe being driven through a sandy region of dry spiny plants, the men chained by their necks to logs they carry on their shoulders. The women and children, unchained, move along crying. White and black men on foot and horseback, armed with guns, poles, clubs, and whips, drive them along.

NARRATION:

. . . when l was carried on board. I was immediately handled and tossed up to see if I were sound by some of the crew and I was now persuaded that I had gotten into a world of bad spirits and that they were going to kill me.

SOUNDTRACK:

Marching sounds. Saxophone squeals. Banjo tuning. Gunshots.

9

CLOSE SHOT. Forklift. Coming down on our heads.

NARRATION:

When I looked round the ship and saw a large furnace or copper boiling . . .

SOUNDTRACK:

Chains, guns, whips, gears, saxophone, banjo.

10

MEDIUM SHOT. STILL. Beale and Main. We approach sign post but fasten on a peripheral point of interest, a woman's ankle or policeman's pistol.

NARRATION:

. . . and a multitude of black people of every description chained together . . .

SOUNDTRACK:

Contemporary street sounds.

11

STILL. (Engraving from daguerreotype) Slaves on the deck of the bark *Wildfire.*

NARRATION:

... every one of their countenances expressing dejection and sorrow ...

SOUNDTRACK:

Sea sounds. Waves against a wooden hull. Wind.

12

STILL. Illustration of slave holds on HMS *Brookes.*

NARRATION:

... I no longer doubted my fate and, quite overpowered with horror, I fell motionless on the deck and fainted.

SOUNDTRACK:

Chains rattling, groans, cries, sound like watermelon struck by baseball bat.

13

MEDIUM SHOT. The enslaved tribe, driven by guns and whips, burst over a rise, thrown by their momentum headlong across a white beach into the surf of an ocean bay where a sailing ship waits in the calm fair day.

NARRATION:

When I recovered, I found some black people about me.

SOUNDTRACK:

Chains, guns, whips, cries, sea.

14

MEDIUM SHOT. Mississippi river steamboat. White, with gingerbread. Pretty brown and yellow girls in colorful 1890's dresses on deck.

NARRATION:

I asked if we were to be eaten by these white men with horrible looks, red faces, and long hair.

SOUNDTRACK:

Gentle birdcalls. The steamboat's whistle.

15

STILL of pawn shop owner holding guitar.

NARRATION:

Voice of Billie Holiday quoting club owner: For vy I should pay you two hundred dollars, you stink my goddamn show up?

SOUNDTRACK:

Banjo tuning, miscellaneous crowd sounds from 1977 Beale Street music festival.

16

STILL. Dead Two-Gun Charley.

NARRATION:	SOUNDTRACK:
Voice of River George: Charley, Charley, where are you? They got me, Charley!	Surf, slaves, guns, cries, banjo, saxes, howls, sirens.

17

CLOSE SHOT. Slaves in surf, sinking in sand, waves breaking in their faces, all screaming, the women holding up children.

NARRATION:	SOUNDTRACK:
(whistling) Zip-a-dee-doo-dah, Zip-a-dee-ay! My, oh my, what a wonderful day!	As in 16, fading.

18

STILL. Oil painting. "The Voyage of the Sable Venus" by Thomas Stothard.

NARRATION:	SOUNDTRACK:
It was the great migration in human history. Historian J. D. Fage estimates that in the eighteenth century alone seven million African slaves came to the New World.	Tenor saxophone *a capella*. Cows lowing softly.

19

MEDIUM SHOT. Slaves in surf. Water covers all but five hundred out of the original seven thousand. Camera pulls back to reveal panyarers starting to corral the now manageable living. This shot is mostly water.

NARRATION:	SOUNDTRACK:
Visitors to Zanzibar were always impressed by the "lovely white shells" covering the bottom of the bay and clearly visible through the gin-clear water. The shells were the bones of slaves.	Surf, wind, tired voices, heavy breathing.

20

LONG SHOT. A lush green field at dawn. Low clouds of mist. CLOSE SHOT of wet leaves of grass and spiderweb heavy with dew. CHANGE FOCUS to reveal a monumental white-bearded black man in white robe, standing among monumental white cattle, Brahman or Charolais, playing a saxophone that, catching the sun, shines through the mist.

NARRATION:	SOUNDTRACK:
Silence.	Tenor, cows.

21

CLOSE SHOT. Forklift lowering an old black man in a wheelchair onto an outdoor stage. SUPER: GUS CANNON.

NARRATION:	SOUNDTRACK:
Voice of Gus Cannon: In playin' a banjo, I named myself Banjo Joe. I started tryin' in here in Memphis when the *Jim Lee*, *Katy Adams*, was runnin' up Mississippi sloppy down there.	Gus begins "Walk Right In."

22

MEDIUM SHOT. Mississippi steamboat with girls on deck as before approaching cobblestone landing. Girls laughing, twirling parasols.

NARRATION:	SOUNDTRACK:
Voice of Will Shades. The *Katy Adams*, they used to call that a woman's boat, a woman's boat on the water. All the women would foller that boat . . . just pay fifty cents for cabin fare . . . and that's the way they made they money—go up and down the river. They used to wear "Nation" sacks in them days—and they used to wear their money twixt their legs, hung on a sack tied round their waists. They didn't tote nothin' but gold dollars in them days—and they had so much money, when they got back to Memphis they be hump-backted, they couldn't straighten up. That's right, I'm tellin' you the truth.	"Walk Right In" continues.

23

STILL of Gus Cannon in box-back suit with banjo, ca. 1925.

NARRATION:	SOUNDTRACK:
Voice of Gus Cannon: I got 'quainted with a fellow here played a banjo, they called Coonjint John and he called me his son, I could beat him playin' a banjo.	"Walk Right In" continues.

24

STILL of Gus Cannon and wife in cotton field posing for *Saturday Evening Post* photographs, 1968.

NARRATION:	SOUNDTRACK:
Voice of Gus Cannon: Later on I come on down, 'Fesser Handy tried to—show me somethin but I couldn't—do it but I still tried to—play my banjo.	"Walk Right In" continues.

25

CLOSE SHOT. Gold record in walnut frame hanging on painted rough wooden interior shack wall. Camera pulls back to reveal white leghorn chicken coming in front door. The record is "Walk Right In" by Gus Cannon.

NARRATION:	SOUNDTRACK:
Voice of Will Shades: Beale Street, Memphis—there used to be a red light district, so forth like that. Used to be wide open houses in them days. You could used to walk down the street in days of 1900 and like that and you could find a man wit' throat cut from y'ear to ear.	"Walk Right In" continues.

26

CLOSE SHOT. Gus Cannon's grave in the rain.

NARRATION:	SOUNDTRACK:
Will Shade continues: Also you could find people lyin' dead wit' not their throat cut, money took and everything in their pockets, took out of their pockets and thrown outside the house. Sometimes you find them with no clothes on and such as that. Sometimes you find them throwed out of winders and so forth, here on Beale Street.	"Walk Right In" ends under sound of rain.

27

LONG SHOT. Black-and-white. A bright-skinned girl wearing a fox cape crosses from Beale Street to Gayoso. By the Gayoso Street sign a gold-toothed young man in a white suit poses beside a mule and wagon.

NARRATION:

Will Shade continues: Sportin' class of
women runnin' up and down the street all
night long . . . git knocked in the head with
bricks and hatchets and hammers. Git cut
with pocket knives and razors, and so forth.

SOUNDTRACK:

Sleepy John Estes's "Goin' to
Brownsville" begins.

28

CLOSE SHOT. Long grass. Brown rabbit crouching.

NARRATION:

Will Shade continues: Run off to the
foot of Beale and some of them run
into the river and drown.

SOUNDTRACK:

"Goin' to Brownsville" continues.

29

LONG SHOT. Sleepy John Estes onstage at 1977 Beale Street music festival. SUPER:
SLEEPY JOHN ESTES.

NARRATION:

Voice of Sleepy: Memphis has always
been the leader of dirty work in the world.

SOUNDTRACK:

"Goin' to Brownsville" ends.

30

MEDIUM SHOT. Sleepy John Estes in his coffin.

NARRATION:

Voice of Furry Lewis: When Beale
Street was sho 'nuf in its bloom, yes,
wahn't nothin' on Beale Street but just
everything wide open, they had four or
five music houses, and P. Wee had like
a—all night gambling house—they called
them crap houses then—this town was
wide open at that time—

SOUNDTRACK:

Furry Lewis: "See That My Grave Is Kept
Clean" begins.

31

STILL. P. Wee's Saloon (exterior)

NARRATION:

Furry continues: . . . and I used to go to
P. Wee's when I first started out—and
that place never closed 'cause they had

SOUNDTRACK:

"See That My Grave Is Kept Clean"

a night bouncer and a day bouncer and the
man get off for the daytime and the night
bouncer come on and keep it open all night.

32

MEDIUM SHOT. Interior P. Wee's Saloon. P. Wee, four feet six inches tall, wearing
a white apron, stands at the bar arm-wrestling a gigantic head-shaved black man.
Gaslights. Sweat pours from their faces.

NARRATION: SOUNDTRACK:

Furry continues: And the reason why they   "See That My Grave Is Kept Clean"
did that because they taken the key one
time and tied it round a jackrabbit's neck
and never could catch the jackrabbit and
never could close up.

33

CLOSE SHOT. P. Wee's as before. Focus on forearms and faces, straining, veins
bulging, as P. Wee slams the bigger man's arm down. Camera pulls back to reveal
laughing customers and two black men, one also wearing a white apron, the other
wearing·a porter's cotton jacket.

NARRATION: SOUNDTRACK:

The black men speak: Apron: "See That My Grave Is Kept Clean" fades.
Mr. P. Wee whupped Jack Johnson!
Porter: (speaking in the manner of Stepan
Fetchit) He undefeated.

34

LONG SHOT. Mississippi River seen from under large oaks on Fourth Chickasaw
Bluff looking across a metal roof. A barge comes into view.

NARRATION: SOUNDTRACK:

The Indians called it Mississippi, Big River.   Barge horn. Mockingbirds and cardinals
They hauled hundred-pound catfish from   singing in trees.
its channels and hunted bear and buffalo
on its shores. The first white men saw the
Mississippi somewhere around here—give
or take a hundred miles—in 1541. Spanish
soldiers led by Hernando de Soto, they were
the last knights in armor—brave, cruel,
obsolescent. They were followed as they
came by a trail of buzzards in the sky.

35

LONG SHOT. Mississippi River from another angle, south of Memphis. From the Delta Refining plant within a grove of trees on President's Island spews thick black smoke.

NARRATION:	SOUNDTRACK:
The Spaniards would punish their captured Indians by feeding them to dogs. Relations hereabouts have always been interesting.	Furry Lewis: "I'll Be Glad When You're Dead, You Rascal You."

36

LONG SHOT. Under oaks on bluff as in 35. Camera PANS from River to Indian mound.

NARRATION:	SOUNDTRACK:
The Indians fought bravely—no good came to De Soto, who was buried in this river. But the white men kept coming: Spanish, French, English, American—and at last the Indians were forced to sell the land here to the United States government for five cents an acre.	"Glad When You're Dead." Dogs barking.

37

STILL. Map of Memphis circa 1820s.

NARRATION:	SOUNDTRACK:
The first white men to make a killing on this ground in a financial sense were the real estate entrepreneurs James Winchester, John Overton, and Andrew Jackson. Later, as president, Jackson sent the Indians on the Trail of Tears to Oklahoma. James Winchester's son, Marcus Winchester, became the first mayor of the town, named Memphis after the ancient river city in Africa.	"Glad When You're Dead" fades. Steamboat whistle, shouts.

38

STILL. The earliest engraving of the riverboat landing at Memphis.

NARRATION:

That was in 1827. Memphis was a frontier town, where there were not many respectable men and fewer such women, especially white women. Like many other Memphis white men— including the second local mayor, Isaac Rawlings—Marcus Winchester lived with a black woman.

SOUNDTRACK:

River sounds and song of roustabouts unloading cargo:
If you don't believe, babe—*hump*!
I'll treat you right—*hump*!
Let down your window—*hump*!
And blow out de light—*hump*!

39

STILL. Notice of lottery in Memphis *Enquirer*, 1836, including "a yellow girl, Matilda, as a prize valued at $1100. Colonel RM. Johnson is said to have purchased a pack of tickets. . . . No doubt Matilda is in his eye."

NARRATION:

Marcus Winchester was called "the most graceful, courtly, elegant gentleman that ever appeared upon the Main Street," and Davy Crockett called him "a friend I never can forget." But the mayor's fellow citizens were outraged when he took his Afro-American lover—she was a Creole from New Orleans—in marriage. Winchester was voted out of office and only his courage kept him and his family from being driven out of town.

SOUNDTRACK:

Military drums. Marching sounds. Distant rifle fire.

40

LONG SHOT. Hunt Phelan house on Beale Street. Exterior.

NARRATION:

Though Memphis's first two mayors were against slavery, most local whites were not. The slave trade flourished in Memphis long after the federal government had declared it illegal. The trade came to an end during the Civil War with the Battle of Memphis, a very brief—twenty-minute—naval engagement in 1862. Headquarters for federal troops

SOUNDTRACK:

Gus Cannon: "Raise a Ruckus Tonight."

were on Beale Street. At this house
General Grant planned the siege of
Vicksburg. Blacks in the area, wanting the
protection of the federals against the local
whites, began to gather around here.

41

STILL. Color lithograph. Mississippi River with steamboats and cotton barges.

NARRATION:	SOUNDTRACK:
In the 1820s Memphis had been a collection of riverfront shacks. The cotton gin and the steam engine created a new era in river trade.	"Ruckus."

42

LONG SHOT. Scale model. The Gayoso House by gaslight on a foggy evening, flanked by great dark trees. DISSOLVE to CLOSE SHOT of magnolia.

NARRATION:	SOUNDTRACK:
By 1846, Memphis had a few mansions and the Gayoso House, the finest hotel in the state, its white columned front facing the river, its other sides surrounded by forest.	"Ruckus."

43

LONG SHOT. Beale and Main, 1866. Night. An unarmed black Union soldier and a white whore, arm in arm, laughing, meet an armed Irish cop at the corner. The cop's hand goes to his pistol; the soldier and the whore stop laughing. Then eight more black soldiers walk out of the shadows. Cop moves on, humming "Wearin' o' the Green."

NARRATION:	SOUNDTRACK:
During the Civil War, Memphis, never a citadel of purity, was corrupted like any conquered city. The human situation after the war was complicated locally by the presence of many freed slaves and many Irish who had fled the 1844 potato famine. The Irish had replaced the city leaders who had been disenfranchised during the war—the mayor, the aldermen,	"Ruckus" fades. Whistling fades.

the firemen, the police were Irish
almost to a man. At the same time,
patrolling the city were about four
thousand black soldiers stationed
at Fort Pickering by the old Indian
burial mound. Neither the Irish nor the
blacks—no ethnic group in Memphis—
suffered from an excess of education or
morals. *Harper's Weekly* for May 5, 1866,
called the city "the worst behaved . . .
in the Union" with "a floating
population made up of the dregs of both
armies."

44

LONG SHOT. Night. Exterior shotgun house. Barefoot teenaged black girl runs
into house, which is surrounded by white men with rifles and torches. The house
is burning, and the girl has rushed into it to warn her neighbor, an old man.
Finally she runs out of the house, is struck by rifle fire, and falls back into the
flames.

NARRATION:

That same week, a fight broke out when
Irish police arrested two black men near
Fort Pickering. A policeman was killed,
and a three-day bloodletting began that
left forty-six blacks dead, four churches
and nearly a hundred houses burned.
Some very ugly things happened to
innocent black people, including women
and children.

SOUNDTRACK:

Reprise of Furry Lewis's "I'll Be Glad
When You're Dead, You Rascal You."
The white men shout: "Kill them all and
burn the cradle!" The black girl shouts:
"Uncle Cyrus!" The white men shout:
"Blow her damn brains out!"

45

LONG-SHOT. Dusk. Street corner piled with wood coffins. Nearby a barrel
of tar is burning, smoking grandly. A mule-drawn wagon loaded with
coffins rolls past. A door opens and two men carry out a purple-faced woman
on a blanket.

NARRATION:

The next year—as if the city needed more
trouble—Memphis suffered its second

SOUNDTRACK:

Furry Lewis's "Saints": "When the moon
has turned to blood."

serious outbreak of yellow fever. Five hundred and fifty died. Six years later the fever killed about two thousand Memphians. In 1878, when the yellow fever came again, more than half the city's fifty-five thousand inhabitants left. Six thousand whites and fourteen thousand blacks stayed. More than ten thousand blacks survived; all but about two thousand whites died. Memphis went bankrupt, lost its charter, and didn't become a city again until 1893.

Wagon-driver calls, "Bring out your dead."

46

STILL. Medicine show with jug band onstage, blacks in blackface.

NARRATION:

In spite of—and partly because of—its misfortunes, Memphis remained a fertile field for speculations. Jefferson Davis, the president of the Confederacy, came to Memphis after the war and went into the insurance business. At the same time . . .

SOUNDTRACK:

"Saints." Furry w. jug.

47

MEDIUM SHOT. NIGHT. Interior. Bedroom in rooming house. Large young man in blue suit down on hands and knees stretching copper wire from bed leg to leg of bedside table. Then he sits at table beside a key apparatus and tosses with his left hand a shoe to the far side of the bed. CLOSE SHOT. Roaches. CLOSE SHOT. Hand hitting key. CLOSE SHOT. Roach hitting wire, sizzling.

NARRATION:

. . . a young man named Thomas Edison was working at a telegraph office just off Main Street and living next door at a boarding house where the roaches were so bad that he developed a means of transmitting electric current to electrocute them.

SOUNDTRACK:

Raspy cylinder transcription of brass marching band. Sound of laughter when roach hits wire.

48

LONG SHOT. STILL. Piggly Wiggly store.

NARRATION:

Purged by the yellow fever of what had
passed for gentry, stripped of the few
traditions it had known, Memphis had
become a blank page on which innovative
men drew the plans for a new century.
You didn't need family in Memphis as you
did in Boston or Charleston—you didn't
even need money if you had the right
idea—like Clarence Saunders with the first
supermarket, the Piggly Wiggly—

SOUNDTRACK:

Brass band FADES into sound of
trumpet and slide guitar playing twelve-
bar blues. Distant. Tentative but strongly
rhythmic.

49

STILL. W. C. Handy in full marching regalia.

NARRATION:

. . . or if you knew when other people had
the right ideas—like W. C. Handy, who
wrote down the blues he heard on Beale
Street—

SOUNDTRACK:

As in 48.

50

Ed Crump circa 1909.

NARRATION:

. . . or if you just knew when to tell other
people what to do, like this carrot-topped
hayseed from Holly Springs, Mississippi,
the Red Snapper, Ed Crump.

SOUNDTRACK:

"Mr. Crump" by Little Laura Dukes and
the Beale Street Originals, 1977 Beale
Street Festival.

51

CLOSE SHOT. Memphis City Directory 1909. Gayoso Street. Camera scans names of
whores.

NARRATION:

In 1909, when Mr. Crump ran for
mayor, Memphis society didn't reach the
greatest heights, but it had depths that
went all the way to Hell.

SOUNDTRACK:

As in 50.

52

STILL. Corner Main and Madison in Memphis, 1909.

NARRATION:

Voice of W. C. Handy: Mr. Crump was running on a cleanup ticket. He was going to drive out gambling and drive out other things with which gambling was associated . . .

SOUNDTRACK:

As in 50.

53

CLOSE SHOT. Memphis *Commercial Appeal*, January 1983. "Mayor Declares War on Sleazy Activity."

NARRATION:

Handy continues: . . . and there were those among us who didn't believe he was going to do what he said he was going to do—you know how things are today—

SOUNDTRACK:

As in 50.

54

MEDIUM SHOT. Interior. Night. Hammitt Ashford's gaslit saloon, December 1908. Black men and women drinking and gambling. The door bursts open and a handsome young Italian, Bill Latura, strides in, makes an announcement, shoots six men apparently at random, and walks out. The bartender ducks behind bar when Latura comes in. After door closes, bartender peeps over bar.

NARRATION:

Roosevelt Sykes talking about Beale Street from 1977 festivals: "cut my buddy in two."

SOUNDTRACK:

Roosevelt Sykes same festival "Can't Be Lucky All the Time." Latura says: "I'm turnin' this joint into a nigger funeral parlor."

55

LONG SHOT: Roosevelt Sykes at 1977 Beale Street Festival.

NARRATION:

Roosevelt continues.

SOUNDTRACK:

Roosevelt continues. "Dirty Mother."

56

LONG SHOT: Ma Rainey at 1977 Beale Street Festival.

NARRATION:	SOUNDTRACK:
Ma. Rainey talking: "Never had enough of nothing, and it's too damn late now."	Ma Rainey with Prince Gabe and Millionaires from 1977 Beale Street Festival, "Got My Mojo Workin'."

57

CLOSE SHOT. Mojo products on sale at A. Schwab's, 163 Beale Street.

NARRATION:	SOUNDTRACK:
A world war and a depression happened, but Memphis didn't rush into the twentieth century.	Johnny Woods: "Blue Moon" from 1977 Beale Street Festival.

58

MEDIUM SHOT. Camera PANS the lobby of the Peabody on a Saturday night in the near future. Lights, drinks, rednecks.

NARRATION:	SOUNDTRACK:
It was still the capital of a rural world. But Edison's electricity . . .	As in 57.

59

LONG SHOT. The moon. CLOSE SHOT. Johnny Woods on tractor playing harp or drinking or looking profound as a wise old monkey.

NARRATION:	SOUNDTRACK:
. . . had entered the music.	As in 57.

60

LONG SHOT. Sun Records. 706 Union.

NARRATION:	SOUNDTRACK:
After World War II, a young man from W. C. Handy's hometown came to Memphis and started the Memphis Recording Service. It wasn't much when it started, but Sam Phillips's studio would produce music that, like W. C. Handy's, would change the world.	Rufus Thomas from 1977 Beale Street Festival: "Stormy Monday."

61

STILL. Elvis Presley and B. B. King together.
STILL. Elvis Presley and Rufus Thomas at Goodwill Revue, Rufus in Indian headdress.

NARRATION:	SOUNDTRACK:
Mr. Crump died in 1954, the year Elvis Presley's first records were released. Crump had told white people and black people in Memphis how to vote, how to think, how to live. And all the time this music was going on, making the sound of freedom.	As in 60.

62

LONG SHOT: B. B. King at the 1977 Beale Street Festival.

NARRATION:	SOUNDTRACK:
B. B. talking: "Hard times been all over."	B. B. King from 1977 Beale Street Festival: "I Like to Live the Love I Sing About."

63

CLOSE SHOT: Furry Lewis's grave.

NARRATION:	SOUNDTRACK:
Silence	Reprise Furry Lewis's "See That My Grave Is Kept Clean."

PART ONE ENDS

Part Two

1

CLOSE SHOT. Burning Bible. The book is open to the passage in Isaiah (6:10) that reads, *Make the heart of this people fat, and make their ears heavy, and shut their eyes; lest they see their eyes, and hear with their ears, and understand with their heart, and convert, and be healed.* The pages curl and blacken and burst into flame.

NARRATION:

Voice of W. C. Handy: I am thankful for the gift of song that had its beginning in family prayer around the hearth of an Alabama cabin. I'm thankful for the memories of a mother who in her prayers always said . . .

SOUNDTRACK:

Furry Lewis: "When I Lay My Burden Down" ("What you gone do when the world's on fire?")
Sounds of dry wood burning.

2

CLOSE SHOT. Ext. Night. Burning church. The church should be old, wooden, draped with honeysuckle, and deserted.

NARRATION:

Handy continues: " . . . I thank thee Lord that we live in a Christian land and a Bible country." I'm thankful for being a part of an oppressed race . . .

SOUNDTRACK:

Furry Lewis continues. Burning wood, wind.

3

LONG SHOT. Earth in space. Blue green, spinning. Zoom in through cloud cover toward North America.

NARRATION:

Handy continues: . . . that I didn't follow the golden calf of music but through adversity was thrown down among the lowly . . .

SOUNDTRACK:

F. Lewis continues.

4

LONG SHOT. Storefront church, Memphis.

NARRATION:

Handy continues: . . . and took out of their hearts a song . . .

SOUNDTRACK:

F. Lewis continues.

5

LONG SHOT. Mississippi River from above, moving mudcolored slit in the earth's green banks.

NARRATION:

... that caught the wings of the morning and fell onto the world's weary ear and then ...

SOUNDTRACK:

F. Lewis ends.

6

Series of shots. Beale Street, Memphis, Tennessee, today. The camera eye seeks relief and finds none. The effect should be that experienced by a typical lover of music and adventure from the Netherlands or Nepal who comes to see Beale Street and finds that it no longer exists.

NARRATION:

Handy continues: ... found a place to cheer and comfort the heart of humanity. God of our fathers ...

SOUNDTRACK:

Musical shards from Beale Street, phrases from whorehouse pianos, theater bands, sidewalk jugs, and harmonicas, lost in the wind. A woman's laughter.

7

LONG SHOT. Darkness, distant fires. Houses? Trees? Stars?

NARRATION:

Handy: ... in thy loving kindness, Thou hast brought us dry shod through the stormy sea. Thy truth shall free us, thy light remove our blindness. Ethiopia stretches forth ...

SOUNDTRACK:

Space sounds on church organ.

8

CLOSE SHOT. Explosion. Reverse zoom to LONG SHOT of mushroom cloud.

NARRATION:

Handy continues: ... her hands unto Thee.

SOUNDTRACK:

Jimmy Lunceford: "I'm Nuts About Screwy Music."

9

LONG SHOT. Horizon. Dawn.

NARRATION:

Silence.

SOUNDTRACK:

Bird calls, mockingbirds and cardinals early morning chat. Church bells.

10

LONG SHOT. Camera follows boy with ducktail down street in Memphis. Black neighborhood. Chinaberry trees, sparrows on broken sidewalks. The boy walks to the redbrick East Trigg Avenue Baptist Church. He looks like someone who would come to burn a cross in front of it, but he goes up the steps and into the service, where a black woman is singing in a mighty voice.

NARRATION: (LATE IN SHOT)	SOUNDTRACK:
Voice of preacher from 1977 Beale Street Festival: Jubal Cain and Tubal Cain . . .	Bells fade. Queen C. Anderson (as nearly as possible) singing "Steal Away." We hear her before we see her.

11

MEDIUM SHOT. Preacher in red shirt at 1977 Beale Street Festival.

NARRATION:	SOUNDTRACK:
Preacher continues: . . . and the whole damn family is going to hell.	Festival background sounds.

12

LONG SHOT. Interior. Beale Street Baptist Church, 1944. A. Philip Randolph is speaking.

NARRATION:	SOUNDTRACK:
Randolph calls Crump "the Memphis political boss who out-Hitlers Hitler" and gets Amens.	Carla Thomas, 1977 Beale Street Festival: "Lord Send Us the Power."

13

Series of shots. Cells in Criminal Justice Center, Memphis Tennessee.

NARRATION:	SOUNDTRACK:
When Mr. Crump became mayor, Memphis was the murder capital of the country. By the time he died, Memphis was the nation's cleanest and quietest city. The murder rate was still high.	Carla Thomas continues.

14

Lithograph depicting the Underground Railroad.
STILL. Mat Reynolds and his army band, in uniform, carrying instruments.
STILL. Watercolor. "The Old Plantation."
STILL. Sam Thomas and the Young Man's Brass Band, civilian dress with instruments.

NARRATION:

The first band of any prominence on Beale Street was organized just after the Civil War by Sam Thomas and was known as the Young Man's Brass Band. Thomas, who learned to read and play music during the war when he was in contact with the bands of the northern army stationed at Ft. Pickering, became one of the finest cornet players in America. He was the first of a great line of musicians that sprang up on Beale Street, and his early activities did much to lay the foundation of one of the world's music centers. In view of this contribution, of his ability, and of the fact that a great deal of money was made by others on music he arranged and composed it seems cruel that he finally . . .

SOUNDTRACK:

Early brass band in concert.

15

CLOSE SHOT. Report of Sam Thomas's death from asylum records.

NARRATION:

. . . died, broken and disheartened, in the Shelby County Insane Asylum.

SOUNDTRACK:

Chickenyard fiddles.

16

MEDIUM SHOT. Sonny Criss at the 1977 Beale Street Festival. INTERCUT STILLS of early bands—James Harris, Robert Baker, the Letter Carrier's Band, Buster Bailey with Duke Ellington, Johnny Dunn with Lew Leslie's Blackbirds, including early (high school annual) photos of Criss and a picture (video) of his grave. Also notice of his suicide in *Down Beat*.

NARRATION:

Following Sam Thomas came the Bluff City Band, organized by Professor James L. Harris, a former barber. The next band was organized in 1880 by Robert Baker. Out of this band came John R. Love, who was a teacher and bandleader for over fifty years. Love developed the Young Men's

SOUNDTRACK:

Criss at 1977 Beale Street Festival: "St. Louis Blues."

Band, the Chickasaw Band, the Letter
Carrier's Band, and directed the Royal
Circle Band. Another great music teacher
was G. P. Hamilton, whose pupils went on
to play with such men as Duke Ellington
and Fletcher Henderson.

Speaking of dance music, the first
prominent orchestra leader of Beale Street
was West Dukes, who came to Memphis
just after the Civil War. Before the war his
master had taught him to play the violin
so that he would be able to furnish music
for the dances in the community. Dukes
learned to read music before he could
read or write his name. Following West
Dukes came Jim Turner, greatest of the
early orchestra leaders and the discoverer
of W. C. Handy.

Voice of W. C. Handy: I couldn't tell
the story of "The St. Louis Blues" and
leave out one about a morning when my
old teacher down in Florence, Alabama,
called our class together and instead of
hearing our lessons began to question
us as to what we intended to do and
be in life. Some wanted to be doctors,
lawyers, teachers, merchants, and so
forth, and when he came to me, I said I
wanted to be a musician. He read me a
lecture. Said music would bring me to the
gutter. Musicians were idlers, dissipated
characters. He wrote my father a note
which when he read, he said, "Sonny, I'd
rather follow you to your grave than see
you be a musician." I was determined,
and I found out a lot about music without
their knowing it. Then I got away from
home and worked a year to get enough
money to go to Wilberforce University

to study theology. And we had the
Cleveland depression, found ourselves
broke and hungry. I organized a quartet
in Birmingham, Alabama, to go to the
World's Fair in Chicago. We sang our
way to Chicago, but the fair had been
postponed. Our quartet sang its way to St.
Louis, looking for work which we couldn't
get, and we disbanded. And I found that
my teacher's prophecy was true, because
music did bring me to the gutter. It
brought me to sleep on the levee of the
Mississippi River, on the cobblestones,
broke and hungry. I could have returned
to my hometown, Florence, but I decided
on that levee to fight it out with two
Handys. One that says Go back home and
get ready and go to Wilberforce, and the
other saying Fight it out and stick to your
music. Which I did. Twenty-one years
later all of this hardship went into one
song one night. And if you've ever slept
on cobblestones or had nowhere to sleep,
you can understand why I began this song
with "I hate to see the evenin' sun go
down."

17

CLOSE SHOT. B. B. King backstage at the 1977 Beale Street Festival.

NARRATION:	SOUNDTRACK:
On soundtrack.	B. B. talking about how blues is the grammar school level of music, and how people like Phineas and Fred Ford have taken music to the grad school level.

18

CLOSE SHOT. Catfish. Great big one swimming in deep water.
LONG SHOT. Wolf River. Dragging for body.
MEDIUM SHOT. Beale Street Festival Band from 1977 Beale Street Festival.

NARRATION:

Beale Street's music has passed in succession from W. C. Handy and Charlie Bynum through Jimmy Lunceford, Al Jackson Sr., Phineas Newborn Sr., Bill Harvey, Onzie Horne, to Phineas Newborn Jr., Calvin Newborn, Oscar Dennard, Al Jackson Jr., George Coleman, Fred Ford, Booker Little, Harold Mabern, James Williams, and many, many others, some of them young musicians whose names we don't know yet. This music will not die until life does.

SOUNDTRACK:

Festival Band.

19

NEWSREEL FOOTAGE. Martin Luther King leading marchers.
SERIES OF SHOTS. Neighborhoods in Memphis today. Contrasts.

NARRATION:

Tuff Green, Charles Lloyd, Frank Strozier, Nathan Woodard, too many to name, Ben Branch, who was standing with Dr. King on the Lorraine motel balcony when the bullets hit him . . .

SOUNDTRACK:

1977 Beale Street Festival Big Band.

20

LONG SHOT. Festival Big Band.
INTERCUT STILLS from high school annuals, promotional photographs the older the better, contemporary with late forties and early fifties.

NARRATION:

. . . the great Doughbelly, a little short fellow, tenor player who could blow people off the bandstand, never recorded . . .

SOUNDTRACK:

Big band.

21

NEWSREEL FOOTAGE. Memphis mayor Henry Loeb refusing sanitation workers' demands, 1968.
INTERCUT VIDEO of rooming house bathrooms, approaching window.

NARRATION:	SOUNDTRACK:
From Blind Tom to Art Tatum, scary piano players are a tradition in American music . . . and there was never a scarier one than Phineas Newborn Jr. (Story of Phineas replacing W. C. Handy 1957)	Phineas Newborn Jr. at 1977 Beale Street Festival.

22

VIDEO. Phineas Newborn Jr. at 1977 Festival.
INTERCUT STILLS early photos, etc.

NARRATION:	SOUNDTRACK:
Did you ever hear of Dishrag and the Four Cup Towels?	PN Jr '77.

23

VIDEO. Calvin Newborn at 1977 Festival.

NARRATION:	SOUNDTRACK:
Church's Auditorium, the Palace Theater, the Grand, the Old Daisy, the New Daisy, the Club Handy . . .	Calvin Newborn '77.

24

VIDEO. 1977 Festival All Star Band.
INTERCUT STILLS, memorabilia, and VIDEO of Martin Luther King saying "I have been to the mountaintop."

NARRATION:	SOUNDTRACK:
	All Star Band

25

VIDEO. 1977 Festival Final Jam.
INTERCUT VIDEO of small boys saying, "I don't know exactly why Martin Luther King's birthday should be a holiday, but I know it should."
INTERCUT STILLS. Black deck hands on the Mississippi singing patriotic songs after the Civil War. Slave poster. Saturday Evening Dance at Buena Vista Plantation, Clarke County, Alabama, 1867. A minstrel troupe in Knoxville, Tennessee, 1897. W. C. Handy at age nineteen. Elvis Presley, same age. Shots of closed historic studios in Memphis. Black soldiers. A lynching. Signs, White only. STILLS from Joe Low of Martin Luther King's assassination.

NARRATION:

Voice of W. C. Handy: I see, though my
eyes are closed./I see, though my eyes are
closed./I see so much good in all mankind,/
Much more than I e'er supposed.//

SOUNDTRACK:

Final jam '77.

26

VIDEO. Beale Street today.

NARRATION:

Handy: My thoughts are the/eyes of my
heart./My thoughts are the eyes . . .

SOUNDTRACK:

Final jam '77.

27

VIDEO. The Mississippi River.

NARRATION:

Handy: . . . of my heart/They bypass the evil
for the good,/and keep them far apart.//

SOUNDTRACK:

Final jam '77.

28

LONG SHOT. E. H. Crump Boulevard and Mississippi Street. A white-bearded black
man wearing a white suit and carrying a tenor saxophone is standing on the yellow
line. As he begins to play, the secretaries in the high-rise office buildings in b.g. get up
from their desks—redheads, Chinese girls, black girls, blonds, in miniskirts, bikinis,
baby doll pajamas, get up and begin to dance. From a cloud-bank a staircase descends,
and on it descends Furry Lewis, wearing a white top hat and tails, carrying a glowing
white guitar. Partway down the stairs Furry stops and waves his hat for applause.

NARRATION:

Handy: O Lord, who has made me see,/
Continue to strengthen me//Tho' darkness
o'er me impose/

SOUNDTRACK:

Festival jam. Schmaltzy "Stairway to
Paradise" cuts in.

29

VIDEO. Beale Street today. Should end with shot of grass-covered empty block.

NARRATION:

Handy: Tho'darkness o'er me impose/I
count my blessings every one/I see though
my eyes are closed.

SOUNDTRACK:

Choir, jagged trumpet.

PART TWO ENDS

RED HOT AND BLUE

Many years ago I was struggling to find a grab-hold to the book business. I knew a man, John Fergus Ryan, a strange and wonderful person and one of the funniest people ever. John was never a skilled stylist, but he was so funny that it didn't matter. He did a number of things for *Esquire* and then *Esquire* asked him to profile Elvis Presley. John was very smart, but this time he went off in the wrong direction. He wrote to Elvis's manager, "Colonel" Tom Parker, saying that Elvis was loved by everyone except intellectuals, and if he could write a piece about Elvis in *Esquire*, the intellectuals would love Elvis. Parker was smart enough to know there are only twelve intellectuals in the world and went back to rolling dice. So it happened that one day I asked John whether he would mind if I tried to do the Elvis piece. He gave it to me. At the time my family physician was Elvis's family physician. My mother and Priscilla went to the same beauty parlor. I knew people who knew Dewey Phillips, the genius disc jockey who played Elvis's first record eleven times in a row and changed the world. I told my friend Milton Pond at Poplar Tunes Records that I was looking for Dewey, who was living in silent disgrace in Millington, just north of Memphis but across the tracks. I don't remember whether I got Dewey's number or he called me, but then there we were on the phone. Dewey said he was at a furniture store on Easley Street in Millington. I thought he'd said Easy Street, and I said, I find that hard to believe. The next afternoon, with my friend Charlie Clarke, I drove to Millington. Charlie's father was the family physician I spoke of above. He had been on Dewey's TV show and knew Dewey. Dewey was alone in an empty room—empty except for a chair, a desk, and a telephone, God knows what happened there. Charlie said, Hi, Dewey, and Dewey said, Hello, Claude. We talked a bit about record labels and then he said the thing about Elvis and Natalie Wood that launched my career. This book is dedicated to Dewey. He may have been crazy but was a genius and very like a saint.

A railroad engineer's watch, held by an old man with a slight tremor, shows the time to be half past the hour, then snaps shut. The old man, the preacher in this small country church, dressed in institutional black suit, tie, and shoes, says to the undertaker, another somber dresser, "Where are the pallbearers? Where's the *body*? I got to preach a wedding at three o'clock."

In a nearby pew, Dewey's mother, a plain woman in her sixties, whispers to his widow, Dot, with a sad smile: "Might know Dewey'd be late."

Outside a Stuckey's tourist center between Memphis and Adamsville, Tennessee, a black hearse is parked by a matching limousine among pickup trucks, vans, motorcycles, Winnebagos with comic bumper stickers. A black-sleeved arm reaches out the hearse driver's open window (Paul Harvey's voice on hearse radio saying "Paul Harvey—page *one*"), the hand drumming nervously against the door. The driver, who looks too young to be driving a hearse, consults his watch, gives a yip, and races inside.

At the soda fountain, three young men dressed as pallbearers are telling a very fat young pallbearer to hurry. Unperturbed, he proceeds noisily and ruminatively to demolish a large chocolate soda. Around the room, on the walls and display shelves, are "souvenir items"—polyurethane horse-turd ashtrays, ceramic praying hands, much Elvis junk, including a plastic doll dressed in red and black.

Going out, the pallbearers cross the parking lot toward the big black cars, passing a long-haired, multiracial band just getting out of a Volkswagen van with a license plate frame that says ROCK AND ROLL WILL NEVER DIE. The hippie musicians stare at the pallbearers as they leave, while a farmer and his wife, arriving in an old pickup, stare at the band.

Out on the highway, going ninety miles an hour, the hearse and limousine pass a man on a tractor. At the church, the pallbearers are greeted without much ceremony by the undertaker and carry Dewey's body inside. The undertaker is just about to open the coffin when all heads turn to look at Elvis Presley, coming in dressed like the Stuckey's Elvis doll—red shirt, black suit and cape. His wife, Priscilla, with her black beehive hairdo, white patent leather boots, and miniskirt, is a living doll beside him.

A few minutes later, Elvis and Priscilla are sitting between pallbearers Claude Cockrell (the fat one) and Dickie Lee. "Only forty-two years old," the preacher is saying, "struck down in middle age, but still a man who had spiritually *matured*, who had left behind the world of show bizness, rock and roll—"

"Remember the time Dewey was on the air and thought the TV station was on fire?" Dickie Lee says.

"I ought to. It was my smoke bomb," Claude says.

"—and the firemen came on the set—" Dickie says.

"—with their hoses. And their axes." Claude says.

Elvis starts to laugh, and so do the pallbearers. People turn to look toward the offending laughter as (on the soundtrack) a rocking country blues guitar begins to play and a rough voice sings, "I boogied for the doctor—boogied for the nurse—gonna keep on boogiein', till they throw me in the hearse. I got the boogie disease . . ."

Our perspective sweeps across the church to the coffin, closing to Dewey Phillips's face, smiling.

Dewey, ten years old, smiling, dances barefoot around a blind one-man band as "Boogie Disease" continues. Also dancing barefoot are two black children, younger than Dewey, and the crowd increases as Dewey calls to people and pulls them over to hear the music and maybe throw a coin in the old man's hat, which is upside down before him. Two other white boys, Dewey's friends, and an old man wearing a denim jumper and smoking a pipe stop to listen, everyone smiling until a well-dressed man and woman have trouble getting in the door (now somewhat blocked by the street revelry) of F. Wilson's Sundries, where, outside, stacked near two gas pumps that sit on the dirt, are field corn, watermelons, cantaloupes, bushels of potatoes, and field peas. F. Wilson himself is in the store window, dusting the pushplows, singletrees, post hole diggers, kerosene lamps, straw hats, work shirts, bandanas, and so on. An NRA sign is in the window, posters—a tent revival, Rabbit's Foot Minstrels— adorn the brick walls of the exterior. Once inside, the man and woman can be seen through the window speaking unsmiling to F. Wilson, who comes down from his step stool and rushes out with his feather duster to chase away the blues player and his crowd.

"Stop that! Get that noise out of here! This is a business!" Wilson comes toward the blind man, shaking the feather duster, threatening. Dewey, thinking Wilson is about to strike the old man, trips him, and Wilson falls so as to sit down too hard on the watermelons.

"Oh, my," the blues player says. "Run, Dewey!"

Wilson chases Dewey—the old man takes the coins from his hat, puts on the hat, takes off his dark glasses, folds them and tucks them away in his shirt pocket, picks up his drum, and strolls away in a dignified manner, while Wilson pursues Dewey: "I don't want that nigger music around my store, and I don't want you around, either!"

That night Dewey lies awake in bed near an open window, hearing the sounds outside. Night birds cry, train whistles moan, a black church service can be heard in the distance, a lead voice singing over other voices, guitar, drums, clapping and shouting, "Holy Spirit don't you leave me—don't leave me in the hands of this wicked world."

The sounds are a kind of solace, and Dewey goes to sleep still listening, as the faroff train whistle rises above the church chorus.

———————

Six years later, on an autumn day in 1942, a Trailways bus pulls to a stop outside F. Wilson's faded facade to take on gas and passengers. Dewey, one of his friends from the previous scene at Wilson's, and a younger boy are having their picture taken under a banner that says B.Y.P.U. CHOIR. They are herded aboard the bus—"Dewey, you boys take care of little Arvil"—and three hours later arrive at the Trailways station in Memphis, where they are met by an officious Baptist lady.

"Don't go out of the hotel without letting me or Reverend Bradford know," the woman says. "And don't order anything from room service, you'll get your meals at the church."

She leads the boys, who are carrying small suitcases and paper bags, toward the curb, where her DeSoto is parked. As she speaks, a smiling black man in a yellow suit and two pretty black girls, both laughing, walk past, heading toward distant raucous music. Seeing the boys look at the girls, the woman adds, "And whatever you do, *don't* go to Beale Street."

At the Gayoso Hotel, a little later, the boys are talking. "Naw, Dewey, we can't go to Beale Street," Buford says. "They pacifically told us not to. We spozed to go to choir practice."

"We *got* to go to Beale Street," Dewey says, looking out the open window, where the music continues, somewhat louder now, only a block away. "I been waitin' years for this."

The three boys sneak out of their room and, using the stairs, peering out at each floor (seeing radio station WHBQ on the third floor and the dance band ballroom on the second), reach the lobby, where Dewey and Arvil, the youngest boy, hold up as Buford is waylaid by the choir director, a florid-faced man who leads Buford into the elevator.

Dewey and Arvil arrive at the corner of Beale and Main just as the lights come on for the evening. They walk past Beale Street's pawnshops and dives until they reach A. Schwab's, its windows filled with clothing, hardware, and voodoo items, among the latter incense, candles, money drawing potions, devil's shoestring, mojo hands. A smiling, red-haired man standing in the doorway says, "Boys, if Schwab's don't have it, you better off without it."

When Dewey and Arvil turn to leave Schwab's, they see a black man run up to a neighboring pawn shop, waving a pistol, shouting backdoor accusations. His intended victim, the shop's puller (who pulls in customers), falls out of his cane-bottom chair, runs in, then out a side door, as the pistol-waver follows, both running in and out, just managing to miss each other. Dewey and Arvil, thinking they are about to see a murder, stop and watch, and so do other people on the street, until the two men, one coming around from the side door, the other coming out the front, face each other, and the armed man points the pistol as a hush falls on the street and the pistol clicks—no bullets. "They do that ten times a week," an old black man says.

Drawing nearer to the music, which is not so raucous now—lighter and more complex, but still swinging—Dewey and Arvil wind up in front of the Palace Theatre. When Dewey tries to buy tickets, he is told that by law whites are allowed in only on Thursdays. Dewey is disappointed, Arvil is relieved. They start back up Beale Street, but as they pass the alley beside the Palace a door opens with a burst of light and sound. Dewey runs down the alley to peer in the door while Arvil stands on the sidewalk yelling for Dewey to come back. Dewey stands mesmerized by the black musicians and dancers onstage with the Phineas Newborn band. A boy younger than Dewey, Phineas Newborn Jr., is playing the piano. As the show progresses, Dewey is as fascinated by the master of ceremonies (Rufus "Snow White" Thomas, who dances with his partner, "Bones," and spouts colorful dialogue—"We gonna ball an' squall an' climb the wall") as by the other performers.

Rufus and Bones step into the alley for a breath of air, see Dewey, but learning that he just wants to watch the show, let him stay.

Dewey, back in Adamsville in his mother's kitchen, bounces a basketball with one hand while with the other he twists a radio dial as at the same time he relates his Beale Street discoveries to Willie, his family's black maid. Dewey stops talking as his mother and two sisters come in the back door. When the rest of the family leave the kitchen, Willie turns off the radio and tells Dewey that the kinds of things he saw on Beale Street are not important. There's a war on, and he'll be going to the army soon. He must grow up and think about earning a living. Dewey's response is to snitch a taste of the cake icing Willie is making, and she slaps his hand, a love pat.

When we next see Dewey he is doing the cooking, on a camp stove not far behind Allied lines invading Germany. Battle sounds echo nearby. A black sergeant turns his back for a moment on his squawking shortwave radio, and Dewey tunes in an armed forces broadcast: "Clyde McCoy and his Orchestra, coming to you transcribed from the Skyway Ballroom high atop the Hotel Peabody in downtown Memphis, Tennessee."

"Get away from that radio, man, I got to locate our position," the sergeant says.

"Just a minute, Sarge," Dewey says, as "Sugar Blues" fights through the static.

"Nice," the sergeant says.

Dewey shrugs. "Now back to the war."

———————

Two years later, Dewey, twenty-one years old, stands before a large conveyor oven at the Taystee Bread Bakery on Madison Avenue in Memphis, wearing a baker's hat at an angle. (Taystee is not a neighborhood bakery but a large bread factory producing many loaves daily for Mid-South chain groceries like Piggly Wiggly.) Behind Dewey stand other men and women in baking garb, all watching the oven, as the conveyor belt brings forth bread loaves shaped like gingerbread men. The bakers whistle and cheer.

"What is this?" the manager, dressed in more civilian-like clothing, says as he comes in, followed by men in truck drivers' uniforms. "Where's the bread? The men have deliveries to make. Who's responsible for this?"

Dewey salutes and says, "Would this be a bad time to ask for a raise?"

———————

Dewey, fired from the bakery, finds work as a stock boy at Grant's dime store on Main Street in Memphis, a block away from Beale, and spends his spare time around the store's record counter. The two record salespeople, a man and woman, are constantly at odds with each other, the man playing records like Arthur Godfrey's "Too Fat Polka," the woman countering with Kate Smith's "God Bless America." When in mutual disgust the two resign, Dewey asks for the job, and Grant's manager agrees to give him a try.

Playing records that appeal to black and white, old and young, keeping the customers' attention between songs with a kind of free-associative hillbilly-hipster monologue delivered over a microphone he has plugged into the store's record player and public-address system, Dewey becomes a local sensation. When he literally stops traffic on Main Street with Frankie Laine's "Mule Train," he is written up in the columns of the evening newspaper, the *Press-Scimitar*, and Sam Phillips (no relation), who engineers big-band broadcasts from the Hotel Peabody and has ambitions to enter the record business, comes down to introduce himself to Dewey. Dot, Dewey's future wife, who works across the street from Grant's, comes in to buy a record and meets Dewey.

Less than a year later, Dewey and Dot, now married and expecting a child, are lying in bed listening to *Red Hot and Blue*, a fifteen-minute WHBQ radio program of popular music. "I ought to do that show," Dewey says. "I'd do it for nothing, if they'd let me."

"Why don't you go over to the station and ask them?" Dot says. "Maybe Grant's would sponsor it. They could sell more records if you were on the radio."

Gordon Lawhead, the station's overworked program director, who has been doing *Red Hot and Blue*, gives Dewey a chance to try broadcasting. The radio station personnel think his first show is a disaster until the people of Memphis begin to call in to say how much they like the new, unconventional announcer. Before this time, radio announcers have been formal, stiff, coldly professional. Dewey is unschooled, makes mistakes on the air, laughs at himself, and has a good time, as do his listeners. "I'm just as nervous as a frog on the freeway with his hopper busted," he says, laughing, and the world within the sound of his voice laughs with him.

A series of short scenes depict how Dewey's early shows are received in the homes of various characters, including Elvis Presley, seen at age thirteen in his parents' housing-project apartment, holding a guitar, listening to Arthur Crudup's "That's All Right, Mama" on Dewey's show, sadly watching his mother, who is drinking and taking diet pills. When the song ends, Dewey tells his listeners about a contest to name his first son—all of Dewey's three sons were named in radio contests.

In Dewey's first year on the air, *Red Hot and Blue* expands by popular demand from fifteen minutes to three hours daily. Dewey becomes a local celebrity, and enthusiastic teenagers flock around him at the radio station, among them Claude Cockrell, Dickie Lee, Stella Stevens, and George Klein, who is hired by the station to look after things and keep Dewey from accidentally burning the place down.

Dewey's show is never interrupted—he does the news, the commercials, plays records. He is, as Dickie Lee has said, "the *worst* reader." He plays records he likes many times in a row without interruption, and he makes people he knows, like Sam Phillips, Dickie Lee, and Claude Cockrell, local legends, talking to them on the radio as if he is using the telephone: "Dickie Lee—better get that Lincoln back up here now, show's nearly over." Dickie, buried in the bushes behind Fortune's Jungle Garden, lying down with a local honey in the front seat of Dewey's Lincoln, borrowed for the date, raises up and stares at the yellow-glowing dial.

Dewey does commercials for people who haven't bought commercial time, and nonsense sayings he uses one night are heard all over Memphis the next day, especially in the high schools. He is "Daddy-O Dewey," and Memphis loves him as he loves Memphis. This sequence ends with his doing a remote broadcast from a Memphis nightclub called the Eagle's Nest, where Doug Poindexter and the Starlight Wranglers (with Scotty Moore and Bill Black) are performing, and a very young Elvis Presley sings a country song with them, but he doesn't sing it very well, being too shy for effective performing, and he and Dewey do not meet.

That night, as Dewey leaves the Eagle's Nest, a young woman (seen before at WHBQ) asks him for a ride home. On the way they have a collision with another car, causing several fatalities. Dewey is badly hurt, receiving a leg injury that will lead to osteomyelitis and cause him serious pain all his life.

Dewey, at the Veteran's Hospital in Memphis, is still on the air, broadcasting from his bed. Sam Phillips, Dot, and Claude Cockrell are with him, Claude engineering the broadcast. A reporter and photographer from the *Commercial Appeal*, Memphis's morning newspaper, are there doing a story on the phenomenal local DJ.

Next, Dewey and Sam are at the Rev. Herbert Brewster's East Trigg Avenue Baptist Church, where Brewster's classic songs, such as "Move On Up a Little Higher," are sung by the lead singer of the choir, Queen C. Anderson. As Anderson sings, Elvis Presley, the only other white person at the church, comes in.

In the following scene, Dewey and Sam are at Sam's newly formed Memphis Recording Service Studio at the corner of Union and Marshall, where the epoch-making Sun Records were cut. A car parks outside and a man wearing a prison guard's uniform gets out, opening the door for three black men in handcuffs. Dewey tells the men that he's been playing the record Sam cut on them in the Nashville penitentiary, and they say, "Yes sir, we been hearin' you play it."

"You can go on," Sam tells the prison guard. "They got real good coffee next door. Just leave me the keys. These boys will be fine here with us."

Sometime later, the guard comes back in, to hear Johnny Bragg's celestial falsetto on "Just Walkin' in the Rain."

Dewey, on the air at WHBQ, wonders aloud how many listeners he has. He asks listeners to blow their car horns, so he can judge the size of his audience by the amount of noise they make. (Memphis has an antinoise ordinance and has for several years been awarded the title of the nation's quietest city.) The horn-blowing brings Dewey a call from police chief McDonald, who reminds Dewey that in Memphis, blowing a car horn except in an emergency is against the law. Dewey tells the audience what the chief has said, adding, "So I can't tell you to blow your horns at 11:30." On cue, Dewey's faithful listeners, some of them getting out of bed, cause the Mississippi Delta to echo with horn blasts.

Elvis Presley, just graduated from high school, parks a Crown Electric Company truck and goes into Sun Studio (Memphis Recording Service).

A few months later, Dewey and Sam are playing eight ball in Robert Henry's poolroom on Beale Street. Dewey asks Sam what he's been doing lately, and Sam says he has a potential artist, a white teenager—"who could be that mother lode I've been lookin' for, a white boy who sounds black"—but he hasn't come up with anything to record. If he does, Sam says, I'll let you hear it, see what you think. Dewey asks the boy's name, and Sam says, "Elvis Presley." Dewey shoots, sending the cue ball bouncing off the table.

———————

Elvis, guitarist Scotty Moore, and bassist Bill Black are at Sun, just finishing a song. Sam, chin in hands, tells them to take a break, and Bill, playing around, begins a rocking version of "That's All Right, Mama." Elvis joins in, and Sam tells them to start the song again. This time he records it—we see the needle biting into the acetate. When the song ends, Sam says that they'll have to get it to Dewey Phillips, and Elvis, excited, says, "I can't believe it, a record I made on *Red Hot and Blue*."

———————

We see Dewey broadcasting at WHBQ, followed by shots of the audience showing what the world looked like before rock and roll. Then Dewey says that he has a new recording by a young man from Memphis named Elvis Presley, and the needle drops.

———————

Elvis, too nervous to stay home and listen to his record on the air, is at Suzore's No. 2 movie theatre, hiding in the dark. Gladys, his mother, comes down the aisle looking for him—Dewey wants to interview him. Dewey continues playing "That's All Right, Mama" while waiting for Elvis to arrive at the radio station. We see a boy, ten years old, who has been keeping count, telling his sister, who is seven, that Dewey has played the record eleven times, and the little girl says that Dewey is really a great man.

———————

The next day, at the Poplar Tunes Record Store, Joe Cuoghi, the owner, calls Sam Phillips: "What you and Dewey up to? I got seven thousand orders for Elvis Presley's record, and it's not even pressed up yet, there's only one copy. But what is it? Country? Rhythm and blues? I wouldn't even know where to put it if I had it." The little girl we saw last night listening to *Red Hot and Blue* with her brother is at the store, trying to buy the record.

Dewey and Elvis, on Beale Street, go upstairs to the Flamingo Club, a black nightspot where the Phineas Newborn Sr. band is playing. When they come in, everyone at the club welcomes Dewey—he, not Elvis, is the celebrity. Dewey introduces Elvis, and Elvis does a song, "Mystery Train," with the band. The audience get up and dance.

Dewey, Sam, and Jack Clement (a record producer hired by Sam) are playing football in Overton Park, Memphis's central park, but Dewey is playing from inside a Lincoln convertible. In the distance, Elvis can be heard, singing a country ballad. Then we see him from backstage at the Overton Park Shell, an outdoor concert arena, as he finishes the first show with a song that leaves the (all-white) audience less than overwhelmed. Elvis asks Dewey what he's doing wrong, and Dewey tells him not to sing any more hillbilly songs on the second show, to start with "Good Rockin' Tonight" and do what he did at the Flamingo. At the second show, Elvis slays the audience.

Dewey at WHBQ console, Bill Haley's "Rock Around the Clock" playing. Copy of *Commercial Appeal* nearby—we see a story headed "Memphis Censor Board Bans Teen Movie—Churches Oppose Rock and Roll." The record ends and Dewey says, "That goes out to Lloyd Binford—" (censor board chairman) "How you doin', Lloyd? Better call Sam."

Elvis Presley, Scotty Moore, and Bill Black are leaving Sun Studio. Young hopefuls Carl Perkins, Jerry Lee Lewis, and Johnny Cash are there, just sitting, looking as if they may have been sitting for days. "See y'all later, we got to go to the Hayride," Scotty says.

We see the trio performing at the Louisiana Hayride, a man with a straw hat and cigar, "Colonel" Tom Parker, watching from the side of the stage.

Dewey and Elvis are at Dewey's house, talking. "I told you I don't know nothin' about bein' a manager, son," Dewey says.

"This Colonel Parker came out to the house and talked to Mama," Elvis says. "But he wants me to leave Mr. Sam and sign with RCA Victor, and I don't want to let Mr. Sam down."

Dewey tells Elvis that Sam has other artists, and the important thing is for Elvis to stay true to his raising, to the music he has grown up on.

Dewey, on the air at WHBQ, plays Carl Perkins's "Blue Suede Shoes" and says that tomorrow the television show *Pop Shop* will begin. Then we see the first day of *Pop Shop*. Harry Fritzias, the (gay and crazy) floor manager and de facto director, tells the cameramen to keep rolling, no matter what happens. Harry tells Dewey that there is one minute till airtime, then puts on a trench coat and an ape mask.

We see the show on a later day when Dewey announces that Jerry Lee Lewis is present. Jerry tries to lip-sync "Whole Lotta Shakin'" while Dewey scratches the record, starts it over, and finally breaks it, driving Jerry crazy, after which he interviews Jerry, who is at the same time attacked by Fritzias, a madman in an ape mask who keeps reaching over Jerry's head from behind, mussing the Killer's hair. This is followed by Harry rolling a bowling ball into Dewey's console, demolishing it— and then Harry opens boxes containing gifts from viewers, softening up the gifts first by throwing the boxes down on the studio floor and jumping on them. The last box we see him open contains, as it happens, a hornet's nest. They all—Harry, Dewey, the cameramen—run out of the broadcasting room, and the television viewer is left with an unmanned camera showing a record playing. The record ends, Dewey races in—the TV screen shows his hand starting the record over—races out. These events are seen through the eyes of teenagers coming home from school.

———————

Next we see Elvis on the Steve Allen television shows wearing a tuxedo, singing to a hound dog. It is a dismal performance, and we see Dewey and Dot watching it at their house. A few minutes later, the phone rings, and it's Elvis. Dewey tells him to come home.

———————

Elvis comes home, to Russwood Park, the baseball stadium in the heart of Memphis. He is a giant star and the favorite son of the town. He sings his new release, "Hound Dog," while Col. Parker sells photos in the audience. The response is tremendous.

———————

At the Memphian Theatre, Dewey, Elvis, and others watch a private screening of Elvis Presley's new movie, with Elvis and an actress named Anne Neyland. The other people watching are serious, even solemn, while Dewey laughs and throws popcorn, to their discomfiture.

———————

We next see Dewey in the company of Anne Neyland in the flesh—she is a guest on *Pop Shop* for a week, during which she is placed in a chair behind Dewey and virtually ignored until her last day on the show, when she attempts to splatter Harry with a pie and gets it in the face, as they say in Memphis, her own self. Harry winds up wrestling Anne and her manager to the floor, to the amusement and edification of Memphis high school kids.

———————

We then see Elvis, to his eternal credit, bringing Dewey another Hollywood actress, Natalie Wood. The three go to the Fairgrounds together, ride the rides, act silly, have fun, and Natalie invites Dewey to Hollywood: "I know everybody out there would like you," she says.

———————

Dewey and Elvis are in an office at Universal Studios. Elvis plays an acetate copy of his new recording, "Teddy Bear," and tells Dewey that he can't let Dewey have the record because the Colonel and RCA have a big promotion planned. They are joined by Claude Cockrell, the Colonel, assorted hangers-on, and other actors, including Nick Adams and Yul Brynner.

"You a lil short feller, ain't you?" Dewey says to Brynner, who stalks away, insulted.

Elvis is embarrassed, and Col. Parker pulls him aside to say that he has to get rid of Dewey, because Dewey doesn't fit in—Elvis needs Hollywood, and the records are nothing compared to Elvis's acting career. Elvis says that he wouldn't have a career if it weren't for Dewey, but the Colonel is adamant.

———————————

The next day, Dewey, Elvis, Nick Adams, and Claude Cockrell are in the war room at Universal's special effects department. Elvis gives Adams forty thousand dollars for Adams's house mortgage, and Adams leaves. "Hell, Elvis," Dewey says, "You give all these strangers cars and money, why don't you give *me* something?"

Elvis turns away and starts playing with the model battleships, exploding them with remote control devices. A technician comes in, looks around, and says, "You just destroyed twelve thousand dollars worth of models."

"Hell," Dewey says. "Why don't you give *me* twelve thousand dollars?"

"What for?" Elvis says.

"You *owe* me," Dewey says.

Elvis, offended, walks out.

———————————

Dewey and Claude are flying back to Memphis, Claude saying, "You got off on the wrong foot with Yul Brynner, but telling Elvis he owed you—it was the truth, but it turned him off, that was the last straw."

"Naw," Dewey says, opening a briefcase and taking out an acetate—"Teddy Bear." "*This*," Dewey says, "is the last straw."

———————————

Dewey, on WHBQ, plays "Teddy Bear." Delivery trucks arrive at Graceland, bringing teddy bears by the hundreds. We see Elvis there, surrounded by fluff, looking glum.

Then, back at WHBQ, *Pop Shop*. Harry, in costume, on camera, performs simulated sex on a lifesize pasteboard Jayne Mansfield, giving the studio executives an excuse for taking Dewey off the air. *Pop Shop* ends with this show. In a meeting a few months later, the executives, talking about the revenues they are missing by having Dewey on WHBQ radio instead of network programming, decide to kill *Red Hot and Blue*. Dewey is seen playing his last record on WHBQ—the song is Chuck Willis's "I Don't Want to Hang Up My Rock and Roll Shoes."

At Sun Studio, the cowboy actor Lash LaRue, Dewey, Scotty Moore, Bill Black, and Jack Clement are talking—Lash talks about his recent sewing machine bust (he was arrested at the Memphis Fair Grounds with stolen sewing machines and typewriters), mentioning that Elvis offered to help him but he didn't want Elvis to get mixed up in it. All of the group at Sun are depressed—Scotty says that he and Bill have had to leave Elvis because they were paid so little they couldn't afford to stay.

Jerry Lee Lewis comes in and they ask him about his recent fiasco in England—having been forced to abort his tour because of bad publicity about marrying his thirteen-year-old cousin.

When they are feeling gloomiest, Sam Phillips walks in and tells them he's just learned he's a millionaire. Dewey, without hesitation, says that he has a job in Little Rock, which is true, and that the people he's working for there are building a 100,000 watt station for him, which is false.

Next we see Dewey, fired again, leaving the Little Rock station, being driven back to Memphis by Dickie Lee, taking pills. Dickie tells him not to worry, things will get better, and Dewey says that he's right, what else could go wrong?

What goes wrong is that Elvis, drafted into the army, is shattered by his mother's death. We see him with Sam and Dewey at Graceland, all of them despondent. Gladys's body lies in state on the pool table. Sam convinces Elvis, who has refused to allow the undertakers to bury his mother, to let her go.

Dewey, back on the radio at WHHM in Millington, a Memphis suburb, is playing "That'll Be the Day" by "the late great Buddy Holly." He announces Elvis's return appearance in Memphis—on the occasion of his release from the army—at Russwood Park. Talking to some girls at the station, Dewey asks them if they want to go to Graceland and see Elvis.

Dewey and the girls, at Graceland, climb over the stone fence. "Are you sure he's expecting us?"

"Aw yeah," Dewey says. "I always get in this way." Dewey spills his pills, gropes in the grass trying to recover them.

Early on another evening, Dewey is walking up the driveway to Graceland. Elvis's Uncle Vester, guarding the gate, calls Elvis, asking what to do with Dewey. "Keep him away," Elvis says. Vester, with a good grace, asks Dewey to stay with him and talk, and Dewey does. Toward the early morning hours a police car stops by, and Dewey, Vester, and the cops get into a crap game (there is something about Memphis that makes you want to get down on your knees and shoot dice).

While the crap game is going on, Dickie Lee drives by, sees Dewey, and stops. "Dickie," Dewey says, getting to his feet, "take me to the hospital, man, I'm in pain."

Dickie drives Dewey not to the hospital but to his house, where Dewey tells Dot, "I got osteomyelitis, I hurt, I need drugs."

Dot holds Dewey, seeing over his shoulder their sons, who have been awakened, watching.

Later she tells Dewey, "I can't stay here. You're out of work, you can't hold a job, it's no good. I've got to go for the kids' sake."

"I'll get straightened out," Dewey says. "I'll be responsible." Dot, almost convinced, says, "Dewey, if you really mean it—if you're serious, I'll know, I'll come back, it'll be all right. You know I love you, I'll always love you."

Dewey walks into Oakley Ford, on Union Avenue in Memphis, and announces that Elvis (who is always giving people cars) has told him to pick out a Thunderbird. Two days later—after the people at Oakley's have learned that Elvis did no such thing—Dewey and the car are found parked by the interstate near Memphis, Dewey asleep in the backseat, his feet sticking out the back window.

Dewey on a Memphis city street, hitchhiking, playing with the cars, swinging at them as if they are baseballs and he is Willie Mays. A car filled with teenagers picks him up, and Dewey says, "Y'all want to meet Elvis?"

"Who needs Elvis?" a girl says. "We have the Beatles."

Dewey is outside the Memphis Mid-South Coliseum, where the Beatles are appearing, trying to get in, trying to get a message to George Klein, his protegé, who replaced him on WHBQ. Some people inside recognize him, and one says, "Man, Dewey looks bad."

Dewey stands by the roadside on a lonely stretch of highway outside Memphis. A young man drives up, sees that it is Dewey standing there, and tries to give him a ride. "No thanks," Dewey says. "I'm waitin' for Elvis."

The young man shakes his head and drives away. Then Elvis arrives in a limousine driven by his factotum Sonny West. Dewey gets in, sweating, ranting. "I'm goin' back on the radio, Elvis, I just need some money till I get started."

"Do the Clam," the ultimate Elvis Presley junk song, comes on the radio. Elvis drops Dewey on the street in Memphis, and he and Sonny watch Dewey walk away. "I hope I don't end up like that," Elvis says. "Man, I'm goin' back to work."

"What?" Sonny says.

"I'm goin' back to singin' for real people. When we get back to the house, I'm gonna give you some money. See that Dot gets it, okay?"

———

North Memphis, Macon Road, December 1967. Dewey approaches some men who, like everyone else in Memphis, were his friends when he was successful, and tries to borrow some money. "I need to buy some Christmas presents for my kids," Dewey says.

The men laugh. "Get some money from your friend Elvis," one of them says.

Randy, Dewey's oldest son, comes up, and Dewey walks away with him, silently, tears in his eyes. They go to Dewey's mother's house. Dot is there. She has prepared dinner and welcomes him sweetly.

———

Dewey is at the Memphis City Auditorium with Ray Brown (old-time WHBQ announcer, now concert promoter) and Ray Charles, April 4, 1968, eight thirty PM. This afternoon Martin Luther King has been killed in Memphis, and no one comes to the concert.

———

Elvis is with Scotty Moore and other musicians in Los Angeles for the "boxing ring" comeback show, June 1968. "Remember when Dewey broke Jerry Lee's record while Jerry was trying to lip-sync?" Scotty says.

"Yeah," Elvis says, laughing. "I got to call old Dewey."

———

A recording session at Sam Phillips's new studio on Madison Avenue in Memphis. Sam the Sham—Sam Samudio, whose "Wooly Bully" was the top selling single in 1965—is singing a silly nursery rhyme song with obvious disdain. During a pause, Dewey, in the control room with the producer, engineer, and a couple of people who do not appear to have any real function, hits the talkback switch and says, "This song don't get it. You sing great blues, do some blues."

"That's my song, man," one of the extra people says. "We're trying to cut a hit record here, we don't need your help."

A few minutes later, Dewey, his feelings hurt, is standing outside the studio. A light rain is falling. A man walks past Dewey, goes in the studio, and says to the three or four men sitting in the lobby, "I always did think Dewey didn't have sense enough to come in out of the rain."

"You know," an older man says, "Dewey never really got over that wreck, when that girl got killed."

A squeal of tires on wet pavement sends Dewey's mind back to that night at the Eagle's Nest—but he thinks not of the wreck but the show. In his imagination he sees the band and the awkward teenager singing with them and realizes for the first time that it was Elvis. Standing in the rain, he shivers and laughs aloud. "That was Elvis," he says.

A boy comes out of the studio, leaving, and asks Dewey if he wants a ride. "Yeah, thanks," Dewey says, adding to himself, "I got to tell Scotty Moore."

On the soundtrack, as Dewey rides home through the rain, the Prisonaires sing, "Just walkin' in the rain, getting' soakin' wet—knowing things have changed—somehow I can't forget."

At his mother's house, Dewey goes into his room, turns on the radio to the basketball game. Memphis State is losing. He turns the dial to WHBQ and lies down on the bed. George Klein says, "Here's a golden oldie from the man who started it all—" and, uncharacteristically for him (but not for Dewey), scratches the record, as it begins: "That's All Right, Mama."

Dewey, drifting into a sleep from which he will not awaken, smiles.

INDEX